OLD ENGLISH POETRY

A BROWN UNIVERSITY
BICENTENNIAL PUBLICATION

Carving on the west face of the north cross at Castledermot, county Kilkenny, showing a harpist playing his instrument. This carving, probably made in the tenth century, served as a model for the reconstruction of the Sutton Hoo harp. (Photograph by David H. Greene.)

OLD ENGLISH POETRY

FIFTEEN ESSAYS

❧❀❧

EDITED BY

Robert P. Creed

BROWN UNIVERSITY PRESS

PROVIDENCE, RHODE ISLAND

1967

The essay by Burton Raffel, "On Translating *Beowulf*,"
is reprinted by permission from *The Yale Review*,
LIV (Summer 1965), copyright 1965 by Yale University.

Designed by David Ford

Printed in the United States of America

PREFACE

❦❦❦

This book celebrates two institutions: Brown University on the occasion of its two hundredth birthday and Old English poetry.

By a happy coincidence, as Brown University approached its two hundredth anniversary, it was able to assemble half a dozen Old English scholars who were working or had recently worked within its walls. A number of other scholars agreed, on somewhat short notice, to join this nucleus in making this birthday gift.

The gift is composed of fifteen essays that tend to group themselves into three divisions. The first group consists of "The Sutton Hoo Harp Replica and Old English Musical Verse" by Jess B. Bessinger, Jr., and "Metrical Uses of the Harp in *Beowulf*" by John Nist. Both deal with the problems of the performance of Old English poetry to the accompaniment of the harp. Yet these two essays with their differing approaches and differing tones mark almost the extremes of this book.

This last point is important. In one respect—the most important of all—there is a deep-lying unity in this volume. Adrien Bonjour speaks for every contributor when he says, "it is the poetry that counts." Every contributor, no matter the approach he takes, assumes that the poem or poems he writes about are worthy of loving and even lavish study.

Yet—and this is the point I began to make a moment ago—this deep belief in the goodness or excellence of the poetry has not produced total agreement about the sources of that goodness or excellence. There are differences of emphasis, even open disagreements, among the essays of this volume, as the reader will soon discover. This is as it should be. Old English poetry is both sturdy and various enough to foster strong and exciting disagreements.

vii

The second part of this volume deals with poetry other than *Beowulf*: *Genesis* (both *B* and *A*), *The Dream of the Rood*, *The Phoenix*, the great elegies, and the *Leiden Riddle*. Toward the end of his essay on the Tempter in *Genesis B*, Alain Renoir writes what I shall use as a comment on the exciting and unusual approaches to Old English poetry in these pages:

My purpose has been to analyze the poem from the point of view of my own time; if Old English poetry cannot be appreciated from the point of view of our own time, teachers of English literature ought to abandon it with all dispatch and turn it over to the linguists and antiquarians. Nor must we forget that a work of art may legitimately mean to a later period something that it never meant to its original audience; in fact, it almost necessarily does, and it is perhaps the mark of a great poet that he is able to produce something that will adapt itself to the understanding of subsequent ages.

Louis H. Leiter and Edward B. Irving, Jr., appear to second Renoir's plea, since they examine their poems, *The Rood* and the elegies, partly through a criticism that is very much a matter of our times, the still so-called new criticism. New criticism colors my own essay on *Genesis A*, but this essay, like Isaacs', Taylor's, and Greenfield's in the third part, owes even more to another new approach, that pioneered by Francis P. Magoun, Jr., in his paper "Oral-Formulaic Character of Anglo-Saxon Narrative Verse" in *Speculum*, XVIII (1953).

On the other hand, J. E. Cross follows a very old approach —the medieval fourfold method—in the next essay. What he discovers is, however, a new understanding of the design of *The Phoenix*. George K. Anderson also follows an older path and seeks in his study of the *Leiden Riddle* to unravel the complex relationship of a poem to its own cultural milieu.

The third group of essays deals with *Beowulf*. Adrien Bonjour's "Jottings on *Beowulf* and the Aesthetic Approach" appropriately heads this section with a defense both of the unity of the poem and of "the pre-eminence of the poetic perception" that makes *Beowulf* "great poetry."

Larry D. Benson studies the background of the poem, what he calls its "Pagan Coloring," in order to demonstrate "artistry where we thought we detected blunders." His approach is largely through a familiar form of historical scholarship, yet his conclusion—"Christianity is part of the very fabric of *Beowulf*; the pagan elements are not"—is calculated to generate heat as well as light.

Neil D. Isaacs, Paul B. Taylor, and Stanley B. Greenfield, on the other hand, explore from newer perspectives, though each from a different angle, the complex art of the poem. Isaacs examines the poem by means of a little-tried method, the convention of personification, and achieves new readings as well as much new understanding. Taylor employs the approach worked out by Magoun, Albert B. Lord, and other students of traditional verse narrative, but Taylor gives a new dimension to this recently developed procedure. Greenfield works through a method that is the offspring of Linguistics and Criticism and is at most only a few years old.

R. E. Kaske's approach is, like Benson's, not so new. Philology and History have been the handmaidens of Scholarship as long as Scholarship has existed. Yet this is, I believe, the first time that these venerable ladies have been made to join forces in a vigorous attempt to eradicate the "Jutes" from *Beowulf*.

In the final essay Burton Raffel takes the reader into the problems of the poet in the act of creating—the old poet dead for perhaps twelve hundred years and also the new poet who struggles in our time to create anew the vision of the great Geatish hero.

The essayists are not the only contributors to this birthday gift. The circulation and reference librarians of Brown University and of Harvard University's Widener Library have extended many courtesies and displayed much patience. Mr. Dwight Scott contributed many hours helping me check quotations and references in many of the essays. Mr. David A. Jonah, librarian of Brown University and chairman of the Bicentennial Publications Committee, listened to all phases of planning and assembling and gave his wise advice and kind consent. Mr. Grant Dugdale, director of the Brown University Press, has also given his time and advice to the planning and making of the book.

Mary Louise Creed, my wife, has contributed the time, the patience, and the love in which this gift could best grow, to the honor, it is hoped, of the two institutions it celebrates.

Robert P. Creed

CONTENTS

❧❧❧

xi

CONTENTS

PART ONE

THE HARP AND
OLD ENGLISH POETRY

THE SUTTON HOO HARP REPLICA
AND OLD ENGLISH MUSICAL VERSE

Jess B. Bessinger, Jr.

Of two dissimilar, but in some respects equally baffling, musical instruments of the seventh and tenth centuries—a diminutive harp and a four-hundred-pipe organ, which together suggest the remarkable gamut of early English musical art—only the smaller and earlier is available for experimentation.[1] There are no physical remains of the organ installed at Winchester in 963, the grandiose descendant of more modest Byzantine, Frankish, and (probably) English models, which was designed to be played by two men on separate manuals of twenty notes each with air supplied by twenty-six bellows worked by seventy men, so that, as a contemporary put it, "every one stops with his hand his gaping ears, being unable to bear from nearby the din which the various voices produce. The music of the pipes is heard throughout the town . . ."[2] Centuries earlier, during Caedmon's lifetime, there had been buried in the ship-cenotaph at Sutton Hoo, Suffolk, a delicate harp standing a trifle over fifteen inches high.[3] The recovery of its damaged fragments in 1939 led to the reconstruction in 1946–47 of a playable replica and more recently to renewed work upon the seventh-century Taplow Barrow harp fragments from a grave in Buckinghamshire, which indicate a slightly smaller companion instrument to the Sutton Hoo harp.[4] Since very little is ever likely to be learned from documents—that is, musical scores—about the kinds of music played by harp or organ in the pre-Norman period,[5] our ignorance is provoked by other evidence, meager and scattered, which does survive, and by the certainty that some Old English verse was sung or chanted or in some fashion recited to the accompaniment of a harplike instrument.[6]

The harp and organ are not, of course, the only early instruments of which we have some bare knowledge. The string, wind, and percussion instruments of F. M. Padelford's extensive catalogue evoke indeed a sort of ghostly Sutton Hoo Philharmonic;[7] but only the harp type exists today for practical study, and a harp of the Sutton Hoo type or another is the only instrument associated with vocal performances in contemporary documents. What the harp sounded like; how it was tuned and played; what, in general, it signified in Anglo-Saxon musical culture are issues to be examined (certainly not to be settled) here. This is a provisional report upon one amateur's acquaintance with a working model that is itself currently undergoing revision in the British Museum workshops.[8] The questions to be asked even of a revised construction can perhaps be properly framed only by some ideal future congress of harpists, musicologists, archaeologists, and literary scholars.

Let us begin by returning briefly to the Winchester organ in which a few structural details afford information about Old English music which may be usefully applied to the harp we know. What kind of music was the organ intended to play? As long ago as 1776 Sir John Hawkins asked about the organ whether some kind of "consonance," some form of polyphony, would not necessarily have resulted from the existence of a relatively sophisticated organ keyboard; and Apel has lately called Hawkins' conjecture "a distinct possibility."[9] Needless to say, one could not have performed a toccata and fugue on the Winchester organ, whose "keys" were apparently sliding stops or knobs that had to be pushed and pulled for each tone. The two organists at Winchester, therefore, could theoretically produce at least four sustained tones at once and could change these tones to produce unison chords or combinations of linear and chordal movement in as many as four parts. The organ is evidence that a polyphony was known, or in Apel's words, "a kind of true polyphony," which is sometimes today called heterophony and which was "known in Greece as early as

4

Plato's times."[10] Thus the lack of written musical scores for this kind of music in Anglo-Saxon England does not argue against the possibility of such music;[11] the instruments were at hand to produce, one might almost say to elicit, plurilinear or chordal music. The Winchester organ argues that the Sutton Hoo harp (on which, because the strings are so closely placed, it is almost impossible not to produce chords) may not be unique in its harmonic possibilities. Possibly the four-handed playing of the organ suggests a kind of analogue to the basic chording possible on the six-stringed harp—one thinks of an easy arrangement of a pentatonic scale falling into two tetrachords—but I do not know how far it would be logically permissible to argue from the structure of one instrument toward the various physically possible levels of style and sophistication with which it and other instruments might be played. We should not, in any case, rush in where Apel hesitates to tread. It is clear only that the Winchester organ shows how the mechanics of musical instruments may affect, if not govern, the structure of their music. In the case of Anglo-Saxon harps, "remembering that their mechanics may influence the structure of tunes and therefore the verse of songs,"[12] we may someday hope for an authoritative study of the varieties of early verse against the live background of its sometime accompanying instrument with all its plain limitations and surprising acoustic potential. If we can never recover lost songs, the harp that accompanied them may yield a few hints about the possible shapes and general effects of lost performances; we have at least a real harp and some damaged libretti to go by.

We know something, too, about the musical world in which the harp was played. For the musical and poetic theorist no part of early English history is more crucial than the second half of the seventh century—a confluence of new learning, new Boethian and Gregorian musical doctrine, new religion, and new literary forms with the mixture of Germanic, Celtic, and Mediterranean aesthetics already to be found in barbarian England. Caedmon was singing in the north some time before

680, in which year Pope Agatho sent Master John, the pre-centor of St. Peter's, to sing and teach Gregorian music at Wearmouth;[13] a decade earlier, Roman musical theory, at first restricted to Kent, had begun to spread to churches in other parts of England.[14] The Synod of Whitby had made inevitable a rapid spread to the north of Gregorian (that is, Benedictine) musical teaching, which had flourished in East Anglia since the founding of Felix' school at Dunwich in 631 and before that at Canterbury.[15] The Sutton Hoo ship-cenotaph is dated at about the time of the council at Whitby, probably toward the close of the period 650–70. Since the cenotaph contains or implies so many strikingly pagan and Christian features together, the harp deposited there may have been used in real life as in iconography and literature for both secular and religious music and singing; further, it belonged to a period in which Germanic song and Gregorian song co-existed and may therefore have influenced each other.[16] Finally, narrative songs treating among other continental heroes Beowulf and Ingeld were evidently sung in England during this period: the shaping of the poem *Beowulf* as we know it some time after about 700 would require songs about the heroes of the poem to be current before that date, whatever the relations may have been between early songs and unique text. If those songs and others like them were typical heroic lays, they must have been performed repeatedly with a harp of some kind; we should expect to find reflexes of oral song in surviving written verse, frequently in earlier poems, less frequently in later ones. We might hope, then, to discover in the Sutton Hoo instrument some facts or theories about inter-related aspects of a seminal period of English civilization: especially about the chronology of poetry; about the assimila-tion of Germanic, Roman, and Celtic elements in Old English musical and literary culture; about the structure and even the acoustic features of Old English musical verse; and something about the nature of its compositional techniques. What follows here is a modest prolegomenon to a comprehensive survey of this kind.

As a physical object the harp is a reminder of the unparalleled richness in British archaeology of the Sutton Hoo treasure, which shows Anglian, Swedish, Celtic, and Lombard influences mastered and absorbed by native Anglian artists in brilliantly original forms, surrounded by imported Egyptian and Irish, Merovingian and Byzantine pieces.[17] The harp was a treasure among treasures, although the existence of the Taplow Barrow harp proves that the Sutton Hoo instrument was not a luxurious accident. We do not, on the other hand, know just how typical the harp was; certainly there were also harps of different, larger, triangular design (a well-known example is shown in the Junius Manuscript[18]) in the latter part of the Old English period, supplementing harps of the Sutton Hoo type, which are themselves represented into the twelfth century. While the Sutton Hoo type is confirmed for the eighth and ninth centuries by carvings on Irish stone crosses, other types occur on these crosses also. Its dimensions and the details of its reconstruction have been described fully by R. L. S. Bruce-Mitford.[19]

The timbre or characteristic tone of the harp is harder to describe. Perhaps, as in the case of the classical guitar, acoustic variety is one of its characteristics. When lightly touched, it seems naturally to produce almost the soft resonance of a Japanese koto, and this charming softness is increased as the strings are less tightly wound on their pegs; today's casual player or a hypothetical accompanist of quiet lyric verse in former times might well use the harp for a long time without discovering or thinking to search for any other kind of tone. Nevertheless, other qualities of tone exist in the harp. Fast steady finger work in imitation of exercises for the clavichord or classical guitar or of the prescription in the Exeter Book's *The Gifts of Men* ("One man can touch the harp with his hands; he has the cunning of quick movements upon the joyful instrument"[20]) produces a sharper, more reverberant, middle-frequency brilliance. But plucking with the fingers or with a plectrum must have been the original, if not the standard, Germanic harpist's technique, as it is still when the modern clairschach or the full-sized orchestral harp is played in conservatories or on the concert platform. Plucking, as opposed to light finger-stroking, produces on the harp replica a variety of hard, glassy, brittle sounds like those of the banjo or ukulele. Other but minor changes of tone can be brought from the harp by touching or striking the strings at different vertical levels, low and close to the resonator or high and toward the peg-arm. Given its apparently modest character, the harp's acoustic possibilities are somewhat surprising even without the use of a plectrum to differentiate further its basic timbre and ordinary volume.

Before treating further the harp's timbre and volume with their implications for the harp's social context and utility as a verse-accompanying instrument, we might notice that modern discussion of the harp has concentrated so far less upon its sounds than upon its striking size and shape. Its smallness sometimes provokes a conjecture that it may have been a sort of toy instrument or a sort of "after-dinner" harp[21] or perhaps a symbolic funeral gift.[22] In the course of its first reconstruction its size and shape were quite naturally puzzling. It was "the first instrument of its kind . . . to be discovered, a type not hitherto recognized by musicologists, and the earliest reconstructable instrument of post-Roman Europe."[23] The earliest known harps, dating from about 3000 B.C., were Sumerian, developed probably from the hunter's bow and so bow-shaped with no frontal pillar to absorb tension from the strings. This crucial pillar first appears in Syrian harps of the ninth century B.C. and is a feature of Western European harps afterwards, usually producing a triangular instrument like the Homeric *kitharis* or *kithara*, the Irish clairschach, or the familiar modern symphonic harp.[24] A quadrangular harp like the one found at Sutton Hoo thus posed musicologically a contradiction in terms. To be sure, a small quadrangular framed instrument with a feature resembling a frontal pillar and in general clearly adapted for plucking and strumming like a standard primitive harp had been noticed in some early drawings and carvings, notably on stone crosses in county Kilkenny and county Kildare. These usually had been described as badly rubbed or eroded and hard to interpret.[25] New photographs of these impressive stone monuments kindly furnished to me by David H. Greene nevertheless show some important sculptural details with gratifying clarity. A critical example, one of two harp carvings at Castledermot, Kilkenny, that on the west face of the north cross, is reproduced as the frontispiece of this volume. There was at first, in any case, little unanimity about the significance of the Irish carvings. Nicholas Bessaraboff, for example, insisted that the carving on the cross at Ullard, Kilkenny, was not a harp at all but a *cruit*, a relation of the Celtic chrotta, Welsh *crwth*, and Middle English rote or crowd, with strings parallel to the resonator rather than perpendicular to it as in a true harp.[26] It will be recalled that the Sutton Hoo harp fragments were discovered in 1939 but not definitively assembled for several years because of the war; meanwhile, without knowing of the Sutton Hoo discovery, Sachs had indicated that the Irish cross figures were true harps, quadrangular in form and asymmetrical as to the peg-arm, on the grounds that they resembled a harp with perpendicular stringing shown in a twelfth-century manuscript at Cambridge University.[27] The Sutton Hoo harp was reconstructed, not from the fragments, but from fresh materials, with guidance from the Irish crosses, the Cambridge manuscript, and related evidence. This was a period of converging coincidence and mutually stimulating scholarship, a time during which musical, historical, archaeological, and literary research made the Sutton Hoo instrument a prominent exhibit in the culture of medieval England and Ireland. In 1942, also without knowledge of the Sutton Hoo harp, John Collins Pope published *The Rhythm of Beowulf*, which posits a harp for the rhythmic organization of Old English poetry; and after the war Francis P. Magoun, Jr., was the first to make the application of Greek and Serbian oral-formulaic theory to Old English poetics, a major common factor to the three bodies of heroic narrative verse being the use of a traditional string instrument to accompany and indeed to help formulate the singer's musical performance.[28]

The harp at the center of these developments repays close

and repeated examination. It is no toy but a working instrument with the relatively soft, slight tone of many early string instruments, whose potential for fullness of tone should not, however, be underestimated. In strength of tone as in portability the harp compares with a modern orchestral harp as a clavichord compares with a concert grand piano; but a clavichord is neither the symbol of a piano nor yet a miniature piano. The harp answers to practical expectations in a number of ways, being a handy size to pass about at a group entertainment like that described by Bede in the Caedmon episode, or to cradle in a seated player's lap in a position like that implied by some Old English poetic references or like that shown on the Irish crosses and in later English miniatures.[29] Within a large hall or a noisy room it might provide a traditional rhythmic base, at least, for the performing singer, comforting and useful to him even if all but inaudible to his audience. Its volume is amplified when it is placed on a plank or table, although in my experience this renders the sound thick and overresonant.[30] If the harp as now provisionally reconstructed was used to accompany poetry, then the oral component of such performances must have been more typically verse for the chamber than for the hall. It is true that the harp can be smitten or thrashed like a jazz guitar, or like the Norse harp in the Eddic *Völuspa*,[31] or for that matter like the Homeric instrument in Kipling's *Barrack-Room Ballads*. "When 'Omer smote 'is bloomin' lyre"—the unconscious assumption of some such rugged technique may explain the objection sometimes made that the Sutton Hoo harp looks too fragile to stand up under truly heroic abuse. It is not fragile; but in any case few today think of early English poetic gatherings as invariably composed of roisterers in a barnlike hall. There were, of course, halls, large and small, in Anglo-Saxon England: those at Yeavering, Northumbria, King Edwin's seventh-century manor, were heroically spacious, while the one discovered recently in Whitehall, described as large in early reports, is really not much larger than a sizable living room.[32] One could fill it easily with a quiet and thoughtful touch upon the small harp's strings. With the harp in hand one feels that the musical poetry appropriate to its design and size must have often been performed in a setting of some privacy as well as of a signal refinement.

Yet it is true that a plectrum brings a louder, more public tone from the harp and, in fact, radically changes its timbre.[33] Old English references to performances with or without the use of a plectrum probably imply quite different kinds of harp tone. These references indicate that the plectrum was not always used and, further, that its use was both especially praised, as in the Exeter Book's *The Fortunes of Men*, and pointedly ignored, as by the West Saxon translator of Gregory's *Liber regulae pastoralis*, who took pains to delete a simile about the plectrum from the original Latin and to substitute a new sentence: "How then shall we consider the thoughts of men if not as the stretched strings of a harp, which the harpist tightens and touches [i.e., strings up, tunes?] quite differently [*swiðe ungelice tihð and styreð*], and thus prevents their producing a tone that he does not desire? He touches them all with one hand in order to make them produce one sound [*ðy þe he wile ðæt hie anne són* (or *song*) *singen*; Henry Sweet: 'to make them sound harmoniously'], but he touches them diversely."[34] If this passage is what it appears to be, the first reference in English to chorded music, then chordal music for an Old English harp is confirmed for the ninth century at least, in addition to the linear music we may take for granted. We have seen that the Winchester organ provides strong collateral evidence for some kind of heterophony (i.e., something more complicated than merely linear music) in the tenth century.

The actual tuning of the Sutton Hoo harp and, needless to say, the melodies played on it are beyond reconstruction, though perhaps, like the songs the sirens sang, not beyond conjecture. The six pegs of the harp carried six strings for which a normal gamut at this period would be some pentatonic scale—a major scale with its third or fourth and seventh notes omitted, the octave to be reached on the sixth note. Other tunings are, of course, possible; the hexachord is one, the basis of our familiar do re mi, developed (not necessarily invented) by the Benedictine Guido d'Arezzo in the eleventh century.[35] Extreme differences of pitch, much larger than the span of an octave, are unlikely to have been drawn from this harp, because great differences of tension would be hard to obtain and maintain upon its strings; yet even this difficulty, if it be real, could be met with strings of different sizes. A narrower tuning than octave or hexachord is, of course, easy to obtain; six strings of the same or similar thickness can be tuned to a kind of chromatic blur or, avoiding tonal identity, tuned closely together in pairs, giving three pairs of close-interval chords, an arrangement perhaps well suited to a less than elaborately melodic kind of recitative. This is an area of theory calling for many practical experiments by specialists.

As to manual techniques, which would partly govern the kinds of music produced, illustrations of the eighth to twelfth centuries commonly show two-handed playing for harps both of the smaller quadrangular and of the larger triangular shape. The Cambridge University manuscript already mentioned shows a second person holding or steadying an instrument of the Sutton Hoo type on the harpist's knees. Possibly such a position helps illustrate the *wit Scilling* reference in *Widsith* (103–8), if *Scilling* is the name of another singer and not the name of the singer's harp, 'The Bright-Toned One,' which seems possible on general grounds. Widsith, it will be recalled, says, "Scilling and I together sang with clear voice; loud to the harp the song rang out." This possibly joint or antiphonal performance has an analogue in the practice of the Finnish Kalevala singers who sang in pairs, each man with his harp or kantele.[36] If it is indeed an analogue, the *Widsith* reference describes two singers working with one harp, as in the Cambridge manuscript. Although most of the literary and iconographical exempla seem to imply or stipulate individual harpists playing with both hands, modern harpists tell me that one-handed playing would be extremely natural upon an instrument of this size: first, because the six strings, placed close together, lie naturally within the compass of one hand as

the other holds the instrument; and second, because the plectrum is most easily used, of course, for a linear attack with one
hand. I have not seen a Celtic quadrangular harp on a cross at
Iona which is said to show the harpist kneeling, thrashing the
strings with his right hand.[37] One-handed chording has already
been noticed in the Alfredian translation from Gregory.

To summarize, then: The evidence of the monuments, the
documents, and the harp replica allows of techniques for one
and two hands with and without plectrum in linear and
chordal styles; the instrument itself gives us six tones arranged,
no doubt, in different ways by individual players in various
times and places but conceivably and practically, for this
instrument at least, in a pentatonic scale, five tones plus the
octave.

If we may turn now from relative certainties to hypotheses
in order to suggest some possible varieties of harp-and-voice
performance, we may do so without lingering over the fact
that many Old English poems, including some that one might
like to use as living texts for the demonstration of musical
verse, are unlikely ever to have been sung at all in their surviving manuscript forms. It is as hard to imagine the bookish
author of *Brunanburh* singing his entry into the annal as it is
easy to believe that lost oral panegyrics of Athelstan were
composed in 937; Cynewulf cannot have intoned runic sig-
natures into his very formulaic poems. But the earlier poetry
or late poetry manifesting an early style, having more regularly end-stopped, linear, preclassical verse units, lends itself
conveniently to musical accompaniment.[38] There is no reason
in logic or nature why even late-classical run-on verse should
not sometimes have been sung in Anglo-Saxon times, if only
as a tour de force by some musical antiquarian: the partly
run-on decasyllabic Serbo-Croatian heroic line permits oral
musical performance, and evidently the Greek hexameter did.
Unhappily for sound theory, we know too little about Old
English music to dogmatize pro or con about its application
to the Old English verse we possess. I would venture to argue
only that amateurs of the Old English harp should be able to

hypothesize inoffensively about the possibilities of such an application, and to do this one must perforce cite and on occasion indulge in the recitation of an existing written text. We need not take up arms here, therefore, about the orality or bookishness of *Beowulf*, for example, which must have been musical in some early stages of its premonumental formation and is undeniably bookish in the unique surviving manuscript. In what follows I use the verb *sing* not in its strict oral-formular sense but simply to mean an oral presentation to musical accompaniment, whether singing in the ordinary sense, or some style of formal chanting, or the use of some sort of mannered recitative style, a kind of *Sprechstimme*, which in public recital of Old English verse today is as far as most of us will dare to go.

First, then, Old English poetry could have been sung to an undifferentiated background of harp music with no regular relation between verse and instrumental melody or metrical ictus—a heterophonic style, if I understand that term correctly. Early Irish poetry was apparently sometimes recited in this fashion from the sixth century onwards.[39] Supposing that this free rhapsodic style were known in England, perhaps spreading to or from Anglo-Celtic areas along with the small harp, it would have been as adaptable to later run-on verse as to early end-stopped verse, which fact would theoretically make available to would-be singers a musical accompaniment to the oral production of poems like *Beowulf*, now sometimes considered purely literary.

Or a harp could provide a rhythmic base without systematic melody, which would be likely enough if the strings on a small harp, already nearly equal in length because of the slight curvature of the peg-arm, were also nearly equal in tension and thus in tone. Volume would be irrelevant; the rhythmic beat would be nonlinear and percussive, conceivably with occasional rapped tambour effects on the resonator or perhaps with a mixture of thrashing and chording. Improvisations of this kind run the risk of sounding like some amalgam of the flamenco guitar, Jamaican calypso, and *musique concrète* but

can serve at least as a reminder of the harp's unexplored possibilities—as a reminder also that certain designs in the Sutton
Hoo plaques have been linked by Norman Davis to Maori
carvings in New Zealand.[40]

A less disturbing technique, not necessarily simpler to produce, requires a running melodic accompaniment to the verse
like that given in modern Yugoslavia by the gusla. We have
noted that such a correlation of verse and instrument is hard
to imagine with the run-on style of late-classical Old English
poetry, but the Serbo-Croatian linear accompaniment as transcribed (in its astonishing complexity) by the late Béla Bartók
for Milman Parry and Albert B. Lord is nevertheless used for
run-on epic verses as well as for the larger number of verses
that are end-stopped.[41] A continuous musical accompaniment,
progressive or repetitive, cannot therefore be ruled out for Old
English musical verse.

Finally, the harp might have given some intermittent or ves-
tigial melodic and rhythmic aid to the singer, whether in early
verse or in later stages of the run-on style. That is, it might
have provided decorations now and then at pleasure along
with a functional ictus whenever initial rests occurred in
measured recitation and possibly whenever some special
rhetorical effect was desired. This is substantially Pope's
theory in *The Rhythm of Beowulf*,[42] which may be compared
with G. S. Kirk's analogous suggestion about Homeric
musicology and prosody: "Rarely a Homeric verse will begin
with a word whose first syllable is by nature short, like the
preposition διά: . . . its explanation . . . is almost certainly that
the missing weight was supplied by a strong musical chord
accompanying the first syllable. The same kind of explanation
seems to apply to comparable phenomena in *Beowulf*."[43] Kirk
does not provide an example; we select one from the *Iliad*:

$$\overset{\shortmid}{\underset{\smile\smile}{\delta\iota\grave{\alpha}}} \overset{\smile}{\mu\grave{\epsilon}\nu} \mid \overset{\rule{1.5em}{0.4pt}}{\overset{\smile\smile}{\grave{\alpha}\sigma\pi\acute{\iota}\delta os}} \mid \overset{\rule{1.5em}{0.4pt}}{\grave{\eta}\lambda\theta\epsilon} \overset{\smile}{\phi\alpha} \mid \overset{\rule{1.5em}{0.4pt}}{\epsilon\iota\nu\hat{\eta}s} \mid \overset{\rule{1.5em}{0.4pt}}{\overset{\smile\smile}{\overset{\smile}{o}\beta\rho\iota\mu o\nu}} \mid \overset{\rule{1.5em}{0.4pt}}{\overset{\smile}{\epsilon\gamma\chi os}} \text{ (III.357). We}$$

may borrow Richmond Lattimore's translation (Chicago,
1951) and add emphasis to it to parallel the lengthening of an
iota by the Homeric *kitharis*: '*All* the way through the

glittering shield went the heavy spearhead.' So the Old
English scops, we may believe, like the Homeric *aiodes*, used
harp techniques that left traces or rather gaps in the composition of later traditional poetry. These can be filled with good
effect by a modern performer, harp in hand.

Leaving prosody and oral theory to turn to lexicography,
one discovers that the harp's physical characteristics explicate
the Old English musical vocabulary and perhaps help refine a
definition or two. The vocabulary of musical criticism in Old
English is limited, but for our needs, critical. It does not, of
course, really tell us how the music or musical poetry sounded:
How much of twentieth-century musical culture could be
reconstructed from even the most brilliant and reliable of
reviews, say, those of a George Bernard Shaw or an Ernest
Newman? In Old English the critical vocabulary, if we may
call it that, consists mainly of adjectives expressing traditional
respect for a clear, distinct utterance from the singer, words
like *scír* 'bright' in *Widsith*, *sweotol* 'clear' and *hador* 'clear-
voiced' in *Beowulf*. Alongside these are to be arranged
adjectives and verbs applied to tone production in the harp,
and these words are commonly translated rather loosely as
commendatory also; it may be that their definitions can be
sharpened with the help of the harp replica.

In the Exeter Book's *The Riming Poem* and *The Fortunes of
Men*, for example, a loud tone and a marked resonance in the
harp are noticed by the poets but in specific rather than
general terms and possibly not in terms of undiluted admiration. The *Fortunes* passage is a brief realistic description,
crammed with detail, of a virtuoso harp soloist at work—a
piece of musical criticism written by a poet, it is important to
observe, not about a scop, but about a harpist:

> Sum sceal mid hearpan   æt his hlafordes
> fotum sittan,   feoh þicgan,
> and a snellice   snere wræstan,
> lætan scralletan   sceacol, se þe hleapeð,
> nægl neomegende;   biþ him neod micel.   (80–84)

One man must sit with a harp at his lord's feet, receive his payment, and ever rapidly wrest the strings, allowing the leaping plectrum, the noisy nail, to make its loud sounds; he is very earnest [*or* he is much in demand].

The text is bad here, but the emendations *sceacol* 'plectrum' for MS *gearo* and *neomegende* 'sounding' for MS *neome cende* are reasonable. The latter is a *hapax*, however, and with only this context and the snarling, piercing sound of a plectrum briskly applied to the Sutton Hoo replica to judge by, there seems little reason to follow either Clark Hall and make *néomian* mean 'to sound sweetly' (queried, to be sure) or Joseph Bosworth and T. Northcote Toller and make it mean 'to produce harmonious sounds'; better to leave it neutral (simply 'to sound') or to allow it to take part dramatically in its context, as above. Elsewhere the lines imply a considerable volume, while a plectrum leaping along the strings in the execution of rapid scale passages produces a rather unpleasantly sharp, rasping tone. Thus one detects almost a faint Shavian note in an accurate and even penetrating vignette that stresses such words as *wræstan* 'to wrest, bend, apply pressure to' (which is precisely what a plectrum strongly applied does to the strings) and *scralletan* 'to sound loud and piercing' and ends with such an ambiguous remark.[44] Since this violence of tone, contrasting with the harp's soft resonance under other techniques, can be reproduced by obvious, if somewhat demanding, techniques on a simple but adaptable instrument, we should certainly not imagine that all references to the harp's sound in Old English need refer to the same sound.

Another harp solo is described, this time without mention of a plectrum, in *The Riming Poem*, which pictures a lively feasting scene in former happy days, a setting not very congenial, however, either for a quiet harp solo or for a sensitive household musician:

> Gomen sibbe ne ofoll,
> ac wæs gefest gear,   gellende sner,
> wuniendo wær   wilbec bescær.

Scealcas wæron scearpe,   scyl wæs hearpe,
hlude hlynede,   hleoþor dynede,
sweglrad swinsade,   swiþe ne minsade.
Burgsele beofode,   beorht hlifade . . .   (24b–30)

The joy of peace did not decline; on the contrary there was a prosperous season, a twanging harp string, [until] a stream of miseries ended an enduring compact. Servants were active, the harp was shrill, it sounded loudly, shouting made a din, the music rang out, was not overcome [*lit.*: did not greatly diminish, i.e., rose up strongly]. The hall of the fortress shook [as] it towered splendidly . . .

The passage as a whole appears to have been put down, as in some modern instances, by a music critic who enjoyed writing intricate commentary more than he enjoyed music. The words here translated 'twanging' and 'shrill' are usually rendered more blandly as 'sonorous,' 'resounding,' or the like. The first of these, *gellende*, cannot have denoted mere resonance in a performance that helped shake the building. The word is used of a harp or harp string in this place only but is used elsewhere in Old English within contexts of distress, loneliness, death, or alcoholic excess to describe the cries, croaks, shrieks, yells, and howls of predatory birds, beasts, monsters, and drunken tyrants. It is used also in technological contexts for grating, creaking, or crashing sounds and in contexts of danger and death in battle to describe clanging armor and the whining whistle of spears in flight. It is with these last lethal vibrations that the musical vibrations of the poetic reference have most in common, physically and aurally.[45] The adjective *scyl* is another *hapax* that again may be rendered neutrally, unless one prefers to translate with an ear to harp acoustics in a roomy, noisy place, in which case he will translate *scyl* 'shrill, high-pitched' and its partner *gellende* 'noisily vibrating, twanging.'[46]

With the paradox of a delicate instrument equally suited to modest accompaniments in a private chamber and to bombast in the hall, we may return finally to the seventh century and the Anglo-Saxon organ: in two poems by Aldhelm that contrast the harp and organ are observations that confirm the extremes of acoustic effect noted here in the Sutton Hoo replica and implied in Old English poetic references. In *De Virginitate* Aldhelm contrasts a placid scoplike performance of cultivated verse (to chorded string accompaniment) with the bombast of the organ: "But if someone turns from the songs of the strings, and desires something more powerful than the plucking of chords [*quam pulset pectine chordas*], . . . refusing to be content with graceful song [*cantu gracili*], he may delight his ear by listening to the mighty organ, with its thousand-fold blasts from bellows filled with wind."[47] His Riddle 13 (*Barbita*), on the other hand, treats the harp (and horns and trumpets) as clamorous rivals to the sound of the great organ itself:

> Buglers may blow curved horns of hollow brass
> And harps twang loud, and noisy trumpets blare,
> But from my vitals burst a hundred strains;
> My mighty voice makes mute the sounding strings.[48]

It would seem that the Sutton Hoo harp replica and early English (and Anglo-Latin) literature are mutually illuminating, not just for general authentication but also in some concrete details.[49] The harp responds positively to the literary tests we can impose on it, in the sense that the references can effectually be tried out on the harp, while the harp in turn is a lively commentator on the references. It deserves continuing attention as a veritable instrument such as was used for solo performance and to accompany poetry in Anglo-Saxon England and doubtless in early Ireland also, even though we are most unlikely ever to recover the music of an instrument unstrung for thirteen hundred years. It is a remarkably competent instrument, unassuming and opulent at once, which rested with other treasures in the cenotaph chamber alongside a goose-down pillow and several pairs of leather slippers; it would have been as much at home in a popular tune as in a panegyric. In any case it belonged to someone, perhaps King Æthelhere of East Anglia, who composed or patronized the composition of seventh-century music and musical poetry with

tunings and techniques about which one can make at least a
few tentative statements and a few guesses.

NOTES

1. Versions of this paper read in demonstration of my working model
of the harp replica in Washington at the Modern Language Association
English 1 Discussion Group (December 28, 1962); in Chicago before the
Philological Club (May 1, 1963); in New York before the Medieval Club
(November 29, 1963); and in Toronto, New Haven, and Bryn Mawr
before academic groups during 1963 and 1964 have had the advantage
of much stimulating and corrective discussion. I am grateful also to
R. L. S. Bruce-Mitford, keeper of British and mediaeval antiquities in
the British Museum; Peter H. T. Shorer, senior museum assistant; and
Peter Crossley-Holland of the British Broadcasting Corporation for wise
counsel and generous practical assistance, and to Raymond P. Tripp,
Jr., who made the body of my replica from British Museum specifications. This copy, which may be heard as an accompanying instrument on
a recording, *Beowulf, Caedmon's Hymn and Other Old English Poems*
(Caedmon TC 1161; New York, 1962), was strung by Donald Warnock
and subjected to practical comments by Miss Carla Emerson, harpist,
and Mrs. Betsy DuVally Bessinger, guitarist, among others. Of the musical scholars who have examined the replica, I am most in debt for
criticism and guidance to Harvey Olnick, Edward E. Lowensky, and
Martin L. Bernstein.

2. Willi Apel, "Early History of the Organ," *Speculum*, XXIII (1948),
191–216; quotation, p. 206.

3. R. L. S. Bruce-Mitford, "The Sutton Hoo Ship-Burial," *Proceedings of the Royal Institution of Great Britain*, XXXIV, Part III, No. 156
(1950), 440–49; for a description of the harp see especially pp. 446–48
and Plate II. On p. 447 the height of the instrument is given as "some 18
inches," but later specifications furnished me by Peter H. T. Shorer
reduce this figure.

4. C. L. Wrenn, "Sutton Hoo and *Beowulf*," in *Mélanges de Linguis-
tique et de Philologie: Fernand Mossé in Memoriam* (Paris, 1959), pp.
495–507, especially p. 501; see also Wrenn's "Two Anglo-Saxon Harps,"
Comparative Literature, XIV (1962), 118–28.

5. See n. 16.

6. Familiar references to harp-and-voice performances and useful, but
sometimes contradictory, discussions are to be found in L. F. Anderson,
The Anglo-Saxon Scop (Toronto, 1903); Andreas Heusler, *Die altger-
manische Dichtung* (Berlin, 1923), pp. 36–39; H. M. and N. K. Chadwick,

The Growth of Literature (Cambridge, Eng., 1932), I, 572–76, 588 ff.; John Collins Pope, *The Rhythm of Beowulf* (New Haven, 1942), pp. 88–95; Winfred P. Lehmann, *The Development of Germanic Verse Form* (Austin, Tex., 1956), pp. 128–31; Jess B. Bessinger, Jr., "*Beowulf* and the Harp at Sutton Hoo," *University of Toronto Quarterly*, XXVII (1958), 148–68; and Wrenn, "Two Anglo-Saxon Harps." To the English and continental references in these texts may now be added one to harp-accompanied Old Frisian alliterative heroic verse in the *Vita Liudgeri*, ed. G. H. Pertz, *et al.*, *Monumenta Germaniae Historica, Scriptores* (Hanover, 1876), II, 412; compare an appendix to the *Lex Frisionum* of *ca.* 802 (Karl A. Eckhardt, *Die Gesetze des Karolingerreiches* [Weimar, 1934], p. 126). See P. Sipma, *Fon Alra Fresena Fridome: In Ynlieding yn it Aldfrysk* (Sneek, 1947), especially chap. xxiv, "It Foarliteraire Tiidrek [*sic*]," and the references there cited. Compare also n. 33.

7. "Old English Musical Terms," *Bonner Beiträge zur Anglistik*, IV (1899).

8. R. L. S. Bruce-Mitford kindly informs me in a letter of March 11, 1964, that "a large number of minute fragments of the missing resonator, and other pieces belonging to the harp, have been identified since the reconstruction was made," but that he is not yet certain "that they make any substantial difference." It is hoped that the revised version can be completed shortly. My copy of the Museum's replica differs from it chiefly in the necessary absence of the original's handsome silver-gilt and cloissonné escutcheons, whose design matches that of other native objects in the boat-grave, and in the placing of the pegs on alternate sides of the tone-arm so as to dispense with the need for the tuning key provided for the awkwardly small and closely placed pegs of the Museum model. A concession to practical convenience in my copy that may possibly have some slight acoustic significance in what follows is the substitution of nylon strings for the original's strings of horsehair or gut; the original strings, at any rate, were organic, not wire, and the tone-producing qualities of nylon and gut are sufficiently close.

9. "Early History of the Organ," pp. 207–8.

10. *Ibid.*, p. 207.

11. See Cecil Gray, *The History of Music* (London, 1928), p. 28: "The history of music, indeed, consists largely in the progressive and gradual reduction to writing of elements in the musical *ensemble* which had previously been improvised, and it is only in modern times that notation has come to represent for us the whole of a musical work. To take for granted, then, that the notation of the ancients was as comprehensive and precise as our own, and to suppose that because only a bare voice part was committed to writing they must therefore necessarily have been entirely ignorant of harmony, is a quite indefensible position to take up. The *reductio ad absurdum* of such an argument would be to maintain that

the Egyptians could not have had any music whatsoever, because, so far as we know, they do not seem to have employed any system of notation at all."

12. W. L. Renwick and Harold Orton, *The Beginnings of English Literature to Skelton* (2d ed.; London, 1952), p. 439.

13. Bede, *Historia Ecclesiastica Gentis Anglorum*, ed. C. Plummer (Oxford, 1896), IV, xviii.

14. *Ibid.*, IV, ii.

15. *Ibid.*, II, xx.

16. The influence is demonstrable on the Continent during the Old English period and in England at the end of the period and later. The vernacular songs of Godric, a centenarian who died in 1170, are the first recorded examples of English melody outside the Church; the tunes are an elaboration of a Kyrie eleison formula that precedes and follows them in the MS. See Gustave Reese, *Music in the Middle Ages* (New York, 1940), pp. 241–42, who contradicts the opinion of J. W. Rankin in "The Hymns of St. Godric," *PMLA*, XXXVIII (1923), 699–711, that the tunes were an outgrowth of earlier English secular song. Willi Apel, *The Notation of Polyphonic Music, 900–1600* (4th ed.; Cambridge, Mass., 1949), traces the rise of polyphony in religious and secular music. For the pre-Norman period see Peter Wagner, *Einführung in die gregorianische Melodien* (3d ed.; Leipzig, 1911), I: Gregory's reforms of liturgy and church music alike reached England in his own lifetime from the date of the decree of 595 and reached the Frankish area under Pepin and Charles (pp. 197–99); between Rome and the vernacular areas there was a lively exchange of liturgical developments, so that, for example, Frankish treatment (*ca.* 840–1140) of a certain response supplanted the Roman treatment even in Rome—"Kräftig lebte auch ausserhalb Roms die liturgische Schaffenskraft" (p. 137); the bold and imposing melodic sequences of Notker and his school at St. Gall (*ca.* 840–912) were a development of native Germanic style (influenced by the Byzantine)—"wie eine Reaktion des Volkgesanges gegen der hohe Kunst der Kirche" (pp. 264–65). I know of no evidence for the interrelation of English pentatonic melody with Gregorian modes in the Old English period contemporary with the Sutton Hoo harp, but I suppose that Caedmon's song at the beginning of the literary period may in this regard have resembled Godric's at the end. Supposition is free, if sterile, since Caedmon's melodies left no trace. It will be noted that Bede (*Historia Ecclesiastica Gentis Anglorum*, IV, xxiv) takes Caedmon's melodies for granted in his discussion of the poet's English songs, either because they were unremarkable as native melodies applied freshly to Christian song or unremarkable as church melodies adapted to native oral musical poetry.

17. British Museum, Department of British and Mediaeval Antiquities,

THE SUTTON HOO HARP

The Sutton Hoo Ship-Burial: A Provisional Guide (London, 1947, 1956); compare the Appendix by R. L. S. Bruce-Mitford, "The Sutton Hoo Ship-Burial," in R. H. Hodgkin, *A History of the Anglo-Saxons* (3d ed.; Oxford, 1952), II.

18. See the facsimile in *The Caedmon Manuscript of Anglo-Saxon Biblical Poetry*, introduction Sir Israel Gollancz (Oxford, 1927); or the illustration in Henry Ellis, "Account of Caedmon's Metrical Paraphrase," *Archaeologia*, XXIV (1832), 329–40, Plate LXXIX; or in *The Cædmon Poems*, trans. Charles W. Kennedy (New York, 1916), p. 223. References to MS illustrations of harps are collected in Padelford's "Old English Musical Terms," p. 30. J. D. A. Ogilvy has kindly pointed out to me the great interest of the harp pictures in MS Cotton Tiberius C.vi (*ca.* 1050); see Francis Wormald, *English Drawings of the Tenth and Eleventh Centuries* (London, 1952), No. 32, pp. 68–69, and the references there cited. For the large triangular harp see also Plates XX, XXXIX.

19. "The Sutton Hoo Ship-Burial," *Proceedings of the Royal Institution of Great Britain*, Plate II.

20. Ll. 49–50. Poetic texts are translated or quoted in this essay from *The Anglo-Saxon Poetic Records*, ed. G. P. Krapp and E. van K. Dobbie (New York, 1931–53), I–VI. Francis P. Magoun, Jr., trans., *The Kalevala* (Cambridge, Mass., 1963), reminds me that Väinämöinen's dextrous finger work is similarly noted in his harp-playing: "He lowered some ten fingernails, stretched five fingers / to fly about on the strings, to skip about on the resounding strings" (44: 245–48). This detail may be added to Magoun's "Conceptions and Images Common to Anglo-Saxon Poetry and the *Kalevala*," in *Britannica: Festschrift für Hermann M. Flasdieck* (Heidelberg, 1960), p. 181.

21. Francis P. Magoun, Jr., in a review in *Speculum*, XXIX (1954), 126.

22. The general problem of symbolism in the Sutton Hoo ship burial is difficult. The arguments against symbolism in J. M. Wallace-Hadrill, "The Graves of Kings," *Studi Medievali*, Ser. 3, I (1960), 177–94, would also exclude the harp as a symbolic object. On royal and Wodenistic symbolism at Sutton Hoo see Wrenn, "Sutton Hoo and *Beowulf*," p. 495, and the literature there cited. On phallic symbolism at Sutton Hoo see Magoun, in *Speculum*, XXIX (1954), 126. Wrenn suggests but does not press a symbolic value for the harp in "Sutton Hoo and *Beowulf*," p. 503, and in his "Supplement" to R. W. Chambers, *Beowulf: An Introduction* (3d ed.; Cambridge, Eng., 1959), p. 522.

23. R. L. S. Bruce-Mitford, "The Sutton Hoo Ship-Burial," *Nature*, CLXV (1950), 339.

24. *Grove's Dictionary of Music and Musicians*, ed. Eric Blom (5th ed.; London, 1955), IV, s.v. "Harp"; Roslyn Rensch, *The Harp* (New York, 1950); H. J. Zingel and Hans Hickmann, "Harfe," *Die Musik in Geschichte*

und Gegenwart, ed. Friedrich Blume (Kassel, 1956), V, 1507–63; David H. Paetkau, *The Growth of Instruments and Instrumental Music* (New York, 1962).

25. Hortense Panum, "Harfe und Lyra in alten Nordeuropa," *Sammelbande der internationalen Musik-Gesellschaft*, VII (1905–6), 1–40; Curt Sachs, *The History of Musical Instruments* (New York, 1940), pp. 260–64.

26. *Ancient European Musical Instruments* (Boston, 1941), pp. 214–16.

27. *The History of Musical Instruments*, p. 262. The illustration was reproduced from St. John's College MS 40, known as the Psalterium Triplex, by Bruce-Mitford, "The Sutton Hoo Ship-Burial," *Proceedings of the Royal Institution of Great Britain*, Plate II.

28. "Oral-Formulaic Character of Anglo-Saxon Narrative Poetry," *Speculum*, XXVIII (1953), 446–67.

29. On the physical and the social position of the harpist and/or harpist singer see Norman E. Eliason, "The Þyle and Scop in *Beowulf*," *Speculum*, XXXVIII (1963), 267–84, especially n. 14, p. 269; compare J. D. A. Ogilvy, "*Mimi, Scurrae, Histriones:* Entertainers of the Early Middle Ages," *Speculum*, XXXVIII (1963), 603–19, especially pp. 606–7, 609, 613.

30. Raymond P. Tripp, Jr., in a letter of March 19, 1964, writes in discussion of the harp replica's sounding box or resonator that some internal member, which may have been lost among the harp fragments, must have acted as a bridge between the upper and lower surfaces: "The sound waves emanating from the upper and lower sounding boards tend to neutralize one another. For this reason, the harp (along with some of its modern Scandinavian counterparts) sounds much louder when placed on something like a table, which operation has the effect of directing the sound waves in a uniform pattern."

31. Ed. Gustav Neckel (Heidelberg, 1914, 1927), p. 10, stanza 42.

32. Full reports on Yeavering and Whitehall are not yet available. On the former see Rosemary J. Cramp, "*Beowulf* and Archaeology," *Medieval Archaeology*, I (1957), 57–77, especially pp. 68–77; also compare the short report in the same journal, pp. 148–49, and that by Brian Hope-Taylor in *Listener* (October 25, 1956), pp. 649–50. An early report by H. J. M. Green on the Whitehall excavations will be found in *Illustrated London News* (June 29, 1963), pp. 1004–1007.

33. (a) Plectra of various shapes, kinds (including the fingernail), and (probably) musical functions are to be noted in Joseph Bosworth, *An Anglo-Saxon Dictionary*, ed. T. Northcote Toller (Oxford, 1882–98), and Toller's *Supplement* (Oxford, 1921); in C. W. M. Grein, *Sprachschatz der angelsächsischen Dichter*, ed. F. Holthausen and J. J. Köhler (Heidelberg, 1912); and in Padelford's "Old English Musical Terms," s.v. *nægel, hearpe-nægel, slege(l), hearp-slege*, and *sceacel*. Very broadly,

THE SUTTON HOO HARP

these names for a very common, but not indispensable, device (used today by some guitar and banjo players under the name "pick" and made in many shapes of materials ranging from wood through ivory and plastics to steel) suggest respectively two, possibly three, forms and functions: a fingernail or slightly curved fingernail-shaped sliver for light strumming and plucking with clawlike action toward the player; a stouter wedge-shaped instrument (not much larger, however, than a thumbnail) for striking or "whipping" the strings with a fanning action away from the player; a finger ring with projecting nail for a strong plucking or striking attack on the strings.

(b) In ninth-century Frisia the wergild paid for a wound to the hand of a harpist *qui cum circulo harpare potest* 'who can play the harp with a ring-plectrum,' a goldsmith, and a female weaver was a fourth part greater than that for the same offense to other persons of the same class: Sipma, *Fon Alra Fresena Fridome*, p. 111, quoting Eckhardt.

(c) See below the discussion of the plectrum in *The Fortunes of Men*, pp. 16–17.

34. Ll. 80–84. *King Alfred's West-Saxon Version of Gregory's Pastoral Care*, ed. Henry Sweet (London, 1871), pp. 174–75 (Cotton and Hatton MSS). This passage is discussed at slightly greater length in Bessinger, "*Beowulf* and the Harp at Sutton Hoo," pp. 159–60. It is an open question why skill with the plectrum was particularly valued in Frisian society in the ninth century but apparently thought of less reverentially in Alfred's England. See n. 33b.

35. Percy A. Scholes, *The Oxford Companion to Music* (London, 1950), p. 387, and the references there cited.

36. Tauno F. Mustanoja, "The Presentation of Ancient Germanic Poetry—Looking for Parallels: A Note on the Presentation of Finnish Runos," *Neuphilologische Mitteilungen*, LX (1959), 1–11.

37. Romilly Allen, *Early Christian Monuments of Scotland* (Edinburgh, 1903), cited by Panum, "Harfe und Lyra in alten Nordeuropa," p. 19.

38. Kemp Malone, "The Old Tradition: Poetic Form," in *A Literary History of England*, ed. Albert C. Baugh, *et al.* (New York, 1948), pp. 20–31; see especially pp. 26–28.

39. Pádraig Ó Broin, "The Early Lyric in Gaelic," *American Scholar*, XXXI (Winter, 1961–62), 73. Compare Gerard Murphy, *Early Irish Metrics* (Dublin, 1961), p. 1, describing "rimeless non-stanzaic alliterative verse, without syllabic equality in the lines" as the earliest Irish poetic form, but without reference to the harp or to Germanic similarities.

40. "Man and Monsters at Sutton Hoo," in *English and Medieval Studies*, ed. Norman Davis and C. L. Wrenn (London, 1962), pp. 321–29, with plates.

41. Albert B. Lord, *The Singer of Tales* (Cambridge, Mass., 1960), p. 54.

25

42. Pp. 88–95.

43. *The Songs of Homer* (Cambridge, Eng., 1962), pp. 89–90.

44. *Biþ him neod micel:* See Bosworth, *An Anglo-Saxon Dictionary*, ed. Toller, and Toller's *Supplement*; and Grein, *Sprachschatz der angelsächsischen Dichter*, ed. Holthausen and Köhler, s.v. *néod*, for this formulaic verse. In context here it seems with equal plausibility to mean 'he tries hard,' or 'he is greatly in demand,' or 'his technique is a strain on him.' The modern performer who attempts to illustrate the passage on the harp replica—an attack on the strings that "bends" them but is nevertheless rapid and with a high-arching plectrum action—will sympathize with the last translation.

45. Compare Homer *Odyssey* xxi.404–11, with lethal bow-stringing, a simile of harp- or lyre-tuning, and with a likening of the plucked strings of the *phorminx* to a swallow's cry ($\chi\epsilon\lambda\iota\delta\acute{o}\nu\iota$ $\epsilon\emph{ἰ}\kappa\acute{\epsilon}\lambda\eta$ $\alpha\upsilon\delta\acute{\eta}\nu$), as Odysseus prepares to slaughter the suitors.

46. The acoustics of an Old English string instrument figure in L. K. Shook, "Old-English Riddle 28—Testudo (Tortoise-Lyre)," *Mediaeval Studies*, XX (1958), 93–97, in which an interpretation using, among other things, musical onomatopoeia is well argued. It seems to me that the critical verses 7b–12 of the riddle, about which I shall reserve discussion, possibly refer both to the surprising resonance and volume of the instrument mentioned (which is harplike, if not a harp in fact) and to its variety of tonal effects; if so, the passage is an analogue to those in the other two Exeter Book poems just cited.

47. Aldhelm, *Opera*, ed. Rudolph Ehwald, *Monumenta Germaniae Historica, Auctorum Antiquissimorum* (Berlin, 1919), XV, 355–56, 11. 66–70.

48. *The Riddles of Aldhelm*, trans. J. H. Pitman (New Haven, 1925), p. 10, l. 2: *Et citharæ crepitent strepituque tubæ modulentur.*

49. Wallace-Hadrill, "The Graves of Kings," p. 179, writing somewhat skeptically about the evidence of kingship at Sutton Hoo, suggests that it is not enough for archaeology to illuminate literature; ideally, he says, poetry should cast light on archaeological finds as well.

METRICAL USES OF THE
HARP IN *BEOWULF*

☙❦❧

John Nist

Although *Genesis, Exodus,* and *Judith* are interesting excep-
tions, in general the Anglo-Saxon alliterative line has evolved
from fewer syllables to more syllables. Indeed, the constant
growth in average number of syllables per line from *Beowulf*
through *Piers Plowman*, the medieval metrical analogue to
the heroic verse of Old English, may be quickly seen in the
following brief chart:

Poem	Date	Mean of Syllables Per Line
Beowulf	*ca.* 725	10.217
Andreas	*ca.* 850	10.38
Maldon	*ca.* 1000	10.98
Gawain	*ca.* 1375	13.7
Piers Plowman	1387	14.4

With the lengthening of the line the bardic harp probably
ceased to be a percussional instrument of functional metrical
accompaniment and became a melodic instrument of musical
decoration. During its evolution the alliterative line probably
also lost several important features of the earlier tradition: the
principle of overstress in a language that gives functional
precedence to morphology rather than to syntactical positioning; the dramatic sense of heavy juncturing induced by the
high occurrence of contiguity of major stresses within the line;
and the primitive delight in syncopation as developed and per-
fected under the conditions of oral chant with the harp filling
in the juncture rests of truncated measures.[1]

Modern scholars of *Beowulf* seem to have very poor ears for
the rhythm of the poem. They have been corrupted, as it were,

by an anemic tradition of silent reading, classical foot scansion, Sievers' Five Types of verses, and emotional timidity in the presence of tremendous gut energy. Many of these same scholars call for *Beowulf* to have a "dignity" in performance that, if ever executed by the scops of the eighth-century mead halls, would have put whole bands of hard-drinking warriors into a coma. One may argue, and indeed must insist, that details in this heroic-elegaic monodrama[2] are scarcely dignified: man-eating, shoulder-wrenching, head-lopping, carcass-dragging, serpent-slaying, home-burning, dragon-dumping— all add up to a passionate hyperbole that hits with an enormous wallop. In fact, a retainer cannot even banquet in the expectation of a peaceful digestion: if fear that he may be devoured before dawn does not upset his stomach, then Grendel's severed head, trailing blood across the floor, is guaranteed to make him cry for the bicarbonate. It would be very strange, to say the least, if the cadences[3] of *Beowulf* did not mirror the immense excitement in the subject matter of the poem. That they do mirror such excitement is, of course, what makes them true metrical progenitors of the sprung rhythm of Gerard Manley Hopkins and the jazz rhythm of Vachel Lindsay.

Perhaps the closest modern equivalent to the rhythm of *Beowulf* is that of Lindsay's syncopated poem *The Congo*. It is certainly true that "Fat black bucks in a wine-barrel room" is a metrical analogue to and a slight variation on the same dipodic structure that governs and controls *Oft Scyld Scēfing sceaþena þrēatum* and all the other 3,181 lines in *Beowulf*.[4] Lindsay's basic line, unless halved as in "And all of the other / Gods of the Congo," is the same line as that of the Old English heroic tradition. In other words, both lines support two dipodic measures of approximate isochroneity, close junctured with a central caesura, in which a total of four primary (maximum and major) stresses operate together with varying collocations of secondary (minor) and tertiary (minimum) stresses and/or open junctures.[5] One may indeed create several variant examples of the basic rhythm of both lines by using such words as *honeysuckle, typewriter, blackbird,* and *black*:

(1) honeysuckle typewriter blackbird black
(2) honeysuckle honeysuckle honeysuckle black
(3) typewriter typewriter typewriter black
(4) blackbird blackbird blackbird black
(5) blackbird honeysuckle typewriter black.

Each of these synthetic and nonsensical lines has the same metrical weight—that is to say, even though the longest line has thirteen syllables and the shortest only seven, all the lines take about the same amount of time to pronounce. The reason for this enforced isochroneity, felt by William Ellery Leonard[6] as early as 1918 but never explained by him, is simple: open junctures between contiguous stresses, neither of which is tertiary (as in *blackbird* [blǽk + bɨrd], for example), take up the time slack created by missing syllables. For the sake of typographical convenience primary stress (whether maximum [′] or major [ʌ]) may be symbolized by S (strong), secondary stress (the conventional minor [∖]) by L (light), tertiary stress (also known as minimum [◡]) by O (zero), and open juncture (usually [+]) by P (pause). Without indicating either optional internal close juncture (/), which is never punctuated, or obligatory internal close juncture (//) and terminal close juncture (#), which are always punctuated,[7] one may metrically analyze the above variants of dipodic rhythm as follows:

(1) SOLO SPLO SPLP S
(2) SOLO SOLO SOLO S
(3) SPLO SPLO SPLO S
(4) SPLP SPLP SPLP S
(5) SPLP SOLO SPLO S.

All five lines are members of the same metrical family, that of dipodic rhythm. Line four is perfectly matched in Lindsay's "Boomlay, boomlay, boomlay, BOOM."

So typical are the dipodic cadences of the five lines analyzed above in the rhythm of *Beowulf* and *The Congo* that one can create the following mongrel poem in Old English and modern English without any sense of metrical contradiction:

Honeysuckle typewriter blackbird black
And a blackbird blackbird honeysuckle black
While a good old negro in the slums of the town
With oft Scyld Scēfing sceaþena þrēatum
Preached at a sister for her velvet gown.
Howled at a brother for his low-down ways,
His prowling, guzzling, sneak-thief days,
As he monegum mǣgþum meodosetla oftēah;
egsode Eorl, syþþan ǣrest wearþ
fēasceaft funden, with a typewriter black
And a boomlay, boomlay, boomlay, BOOM!

The demonstration above offers proof that *Beowulf* and *The Congo* are alike in that they both are written in dipodic rhythm. The great similarity of Hopkins' rhythm to that of *Beowulf* and to Lindsay's poem becomes evident if one adds to the mongrel poem a few lines from Hopkins' sonnet *Carrion Comfort*, which I deliberately rearrange from a six-stress line to a four-stress line for the sake of illustration:

Not, I'll not, carrion comfort, Despair,
Not feast on thee; not un-[H]twist—
Slack they may be—these last [H] strands
Of man in me . . .

As may be gathered from this latest edition to the mongrel poem, the cadences of Hopkins' sprung rhythm are the same as those of the jazz rhythm of Lindsay and the dipodic rhythm of *Beowulf*; the big difference is that Hopkins' lines are longer —as seen in the fact, for example, that his sonnet holds a 19 to 14 edge in the total number of syllables and a 3 to 2 advantage in the full amount of major junctures over a linearly more conventional sonnet such as John Donne's *Batter My Heart*. This edge and advantage may be seen in the following juxtaposition of alternating lines, first from Donne and second from Hopkins, third from Donne and fourth from Hopkins:

Divorce mee,'untie, or breake that knot againe,
*Nay in all that toil, that coil, since (seems) I kissed
the rod,*

Take mee to you, imprison me, for I
Hand rather, my heart lo! lapped strength, stole joy,
    would laugh, chéer.

But even though Hopkins does lengthen the traditional line, he nevertheless maintains the principle of piling up stresses; such piling up, of course, is responsible for what he calls "springing the line" to produce sprung (i.e., abrupt) rhythm.[8] The contiguity of stresses, in turn, permits the syncopation indicated by the marking of H above, a symbol that signifies possible harp juncturing in the bardic performance of Old English. Modern criticism knows from recorded readings that Lindsay fills out weak measures by prolongation, but Lindsay does not have the harp for functional percussive accompaniment. The scops who recited *Beowulf* did have such an instrument, and it therefore is the primary key to their metrics.[9]

It is perhaps no exaggeration to state that any genuine theory of the rhythm of *Beowulf* must account for the use of an accompanying harp. Indeed John Collins Pope has made this metrical demand quite clear.[10] Pope's own theory, however, suffers from several major flaws: by using five degrees of stress, Pope makes a distinction that the human ear will scarcely permit; by combining these five degrees of stress with a tempo analysis drawn from music, he greatly complicates the simple bases of dipodic rhythm; by making much of musical-time patterns in *Beowulf*, he disorganizes the results of his analysis; in direct contradiction of the fact that anacruses are merely completion of time between the lines, Pope forces them inside the line units of the poem; by disregarding the fact that alliteration reinforces syllables by overstressing them, he relegates primary stresses to the position of secondary stresses; rather drastically, Pope is willing to call any measure introduced by anacrusis a weak measure; in direct contradiction of his own belief in harp substitution he distorts primary-stressed syllables into prolongation rather than keep them at normal length and fill up the remainder of the measure with a harp beat. The result of these several flaws, of course, is a reading that does considerable violence to the metrics of *Beowulf*. Just how much violence may be determined by the fact that Pope finds 268 varying cadences in the poem—a number bordering on the fantastic. With so much variation a basic rhythm simply ceases to exist.

If Andreas Heusler has taught Anglo-Saxon scholars about the principle of anacrusis,[11] then Gerard Manley Hopkins has taught them that some anacruses may be extracadential or what the great Jesuit poet calls "outrides."[12] Since the cadences of the Old English line begin with the first primary stress (S) in each half-line, initial and medial anacruses must either be incorporated into the metrical patterns of preceding measures or be classified as outrides. Thus the *Oft* of *Oft Scyld Scēfing* is an initial outride; in like manner the *þæt wæs* of *þæt wæs gōd cyning* is a medial outride. Both kinds of outrides, of course, are not a part of the cádences proper of the poem, for these cadences begin with the first primary stress in each half-line. The first primary stress, in turn, is usually dictated by the alliteration within the line.

Alliteration itself is the key to the general overemphasis of stress so well defended by Leonard—an overemphasis unmistakably to be inferred when one considers that *Beowulf* was probably neither sung nor merely read aloud but chanted. In chanting, the normal prose stress of any syllable would be increased one degree of intensity: primary-stressed syllables become overstressed; secondary-stressed syllables become primary-stressed; tertiary-stressed syllables become secondary-stressed. A recitative chanting of *Beowulf* would strengthen the principle of alliterative overemphasis, thus permitting secondary accents to fall on syllables that modern readers tend to slur and weaken. This introduction of secondary accents into the measures of *Beowulf* is automatically accompanied by open junctures, which substitute for missing tertiary stresses. Hence syncopation is employed far more often in the cadences of *Beowulf* than in those of its Middle English metrical analogue *Piers Plowman*.

The syncopation of cadences must have been greatly emphasized by the percussional use of the harp. Although in many instances a primary-stressed syllable is called upon to fill one measure of a half-line when it is not preceded by anacrusis, there are almost equally numerous cases where a primary-stressed syllable must fill one measure of a half-line that is preceded by anacrusis. Thus contiguous primary-stressed syllables are as marked a feature in the dipodics of *Beowulf* as in the sprung rhythm of Hopkins. In recitation the reader is obliged either to distort the first of these primary-stressed syllables by undue prolongation in order to fill the measure or to retain normal syllabic length and fill the remainder of the measure with the musical-rest value of a harp chord. Pope, like Leonard and Heusler before him, would distort by prolongation. It is the contention here that such prolongation is unnecessary, since the harp can be most reasonably employed to fill the remainder of the measure. Thus a harp chord (H) substitutes for the missing secondary stress (L) in the same manner in which open juncture (P) substitutes for missing tertiary stress (O). When H substitutes for L, the same cadential features are in operation: hence SPLP is equivalent to SH, and SPLO is equivalent to SHO. Indeed, this theory of percussional harp substitution immensely simplifies the picture of dipodic rhythm in *Beowulf* and allows a new kind of descriptive analysis of its patterns and features.

The most obvious position for harp substitution is between two contiguous primary-stressed syllables. That harp chords may have occupied precisely such a position in earlier Old English poetry seems to be borne out by the following passage from Caedmon's *Hymn* with its notable lack of initial or medial anacruses of more than a single syllable:

Hē ǣrest gescēop [H]   eorðan bearnum
heofon tō hrōfe,   hālig Scyppend;
þā middangeard [H]   moncynnes Weard, [H]
ēce Drihten,   æfter tēode
fīrum foldan,   Frēa [H] ælmihtig.   (5–9)

The metrics of this passage calls for harp substitution after

33

gescēop, -geard, Weard, and *Frēa.* Such percussional rests draw attention to the internal rhyme between *-geard* and *Weard* and give peculiar emphasis to *gescēop, Frēa,* and the first word immediately following each syncopation dramatized by the harp. There can be little doubt that such a metrical use of the harp is functional.

Beowulf, together with most of Old English poetry, abounds in such elementary metrical patterns as those found in Caedmon's *Hymn.* Indeed, the opening three-line exordium of this great heroic poem proves the point:

> Hwæt! wē Gār-[H]Dena in gēar-[H]dagum,
> þēod-[H]cyninga þrym [H] gefrūnon,
> hū ðā æþelingas ellen fremedon! [13]

It proves something else—namely, that since a harp chord substitutes for missing secondary stress, such a chord may occur between a primary and a tertiary stress, as in *þrym* [H] *gefrūnon,* to produce the following half-line cadence: SHO SPL//. Thus harp syncopation always follows immediately after a primary stress to take the place of a missing secondary. This type of syncopation, in turn, is responsible for establishing sixteen basic cadences, which account for an overwhelming majority of the lines in *Beowulf.* As understood here, a cadence is a quantitative metrical unit extending from the first primary stress (S) of a half-line to the last syllable of its second measure. Keeping in mind the fact that harp substitution in *Beowulf* may be actual or optional, depending on whether there is a following cadential anacrusis that can be admitted instead, and that outrides are never admitted into the measures proper of the poem, one may list the sixteen basic cadences of the poem in the order of their frequentative importance, with five examples of each, as follows:

(1) SPLP SPL(P,/,//,#,O):   *(9) SH SPLO:
   gomban gyldan (11a)   *bāt bān-locan* (742a)
   ylda bearnum (150a)   *Wulf Wonrēding* (2965a)

lȳt-hwōn lōgon (203a)
fold-weg mǣton (1633b)
þrēo hund wintra (2278b)

fēond man-cynnes (164b)
bearn Ecgþēowes (957b)
wīs-hycgende (2716b)

(2) SPLO SPL(P,/,//,#,O):

wǣpnum geweorðad (250a)
geōmrode giddum (1118a)
weorðode weorcum (2096a)
sunnan ond mōnan (94b)
niht ofer ealle (649b)

(10) SOLP SPL(P,/,//,#,O):

mago-driht micel (67a)
swutol sang scopes (90a)
mago-þegn mōdig (2757a)
æþeling manig (1112b)
gamelum rince (1677b)

*(3) SH SPL(P,/,//,#,O):

of feor-wegum (37a)
þæt heal-reced (68a)
in bīor-sele (2635a)
in gēar-dagum (1b)
ond lof-geornost (3182b)

(11) SPLP SOL(P,/,//,#,O):

feohtan fremedon (959a)
feorran feredon (3113a)
ellen fremedon (3b)
dryhten Higelāc (2000b)
hlǣw oft ymbehwearf
  (2296b)

*(4) SPLP SH:

Ðā se ellen-gǣst (86a)
wæs se grimma gǣst (102a)
þonne edwīt-līf (2891b)
Nū ys lēodum wēn (2910b)
þā his brōðor læg (2978b)

**(12) SHO SH:

þæt fram hām gefrægn
  (194a)
hū hē frōd ond gōd (279a)
Him on mōd be-arn (67b)
oð ðæt ān ongan (100b)
þē þā dēað fornam (488b)

*(5) SPLO SH:

sinc-fāge sel (167a)
sorh-fullne sīð (512a)
ēhtende wæs (159b)
Ēadgilse wearð (2392b)
Ēanmundes lāf (2611b)

*(13) SOLO SH:

wlite-beorhtne wang (93a)
here-sceafta hēap (335a)
meotod-sceaft bemearn
  (1077a)
heaðo-wylma bād (82b)
heaþo-rǣs fornam (557b)

*(6) SHO SPL(P,/,//,#,O):

geong in geardum (13a)
fen ond fæsten (104a)
forð onsendon (45b)
Men ne cunnon (50b)
helm ond byrnan (1022b)

(14) SPLO SOL(P,/,//,#,O):

fæhðe ond fyrene (137a)
cempan gecorone (206a)
flōd æfter faroðe (580a)
samod ætgædere (329b)
helpe gefremede (551b)

(7) SPLP SPLO:

rondas regn-hearde (326a)
aldor Ēast-Dena (392a)
sunu Ecglāfes (1808a)
Bēowulf Scyldinga (53b)
dohtor Hrōðgāres (2020b)

*(15) SH SOL(P,/,//,#,O):

wēold wīde-ferhð (702a)
bād bolgen-mōd (709a)
blǣd wīde sprang (18b)
blōd ēdrum dranc (742b)
swāt ǣdrum sprong (2966b)

(8) SOLO SPL(P,/,//,#,O):

Hwīlum hīe gehēton (175a)
beran ofer bolcan (231a)
mægen-wudu mundum
(236a)
ealle ofercōmon (699b)
Yrre wǣron bēgen (769b)

(16) SPLP SOLO:

swylcra searo-nīða (582a)
eorlum ealu-scerwen (769a)
eallum æþellingum (906a)
hȳran heaþo-sīocum
(2754a)
healdeð hige-mǣðum
(2909a).

Those cadences marked with one asterisk (numbers 3, 4, 5, 6, 9, 13, and 15) have one harp chord built into their metrical texture; the one cadence marked with two asterisks (number 12) incorporates two such harp chords. Thus half of the sixteen basic cadences in *Beowulf* are the product of harp substitution for missing secondary stress.

To establish the relative frequency of the sixteen basic cadences, one must reinterpret Pope's statistics.[14] From such a new examination of dipodic rhythm in *Beowulf* the following chart emerges:

BASIC CADENCES OF HALF-LINES OF *BEOWULF*: RELATIVE FREQUENCY

Cadence	Without Anacrusis		With Anacrusis		Total
	a	b	a	b	
(1) SPLP SPL	473	518	118	169	1,278
(2) SPLO SPL	475	272	29	11	787
*(3) SH SPL	2	1	358	417	778
*(4) SPLP SH	0	0	162	385	547
*(5) SPLO SH	77	197	59	157	490
*(6) SHO SPL	167	134	7	8	316
(7) SPLP SPLO	153	126	8	1	288
(8) SOLO SPL	204	37	28	0	269
*(9) SH SPLO	82	142	11	20	255
(10) SOLP SPL	103	82	2	3	190
(11) SPLP SOL	103	52	9	6	170
**(12) SHO SH	0	0	34	122	156
*(13) SOLO SH	29	74	11	11	125
(14) SPLO SOL	63	31	6	0	100
*(15) SH SOL	28	50	5	1	84
(16) SPLP SOLO	53	6	8	0	67
TOTALS	2,012	1,722	855	1,311	5,900

Total number of half-lines considered	6,324
Half-lines not catalogued: "hypermetric"	22
missing or conjectural	18
Percentage of half-lines catalogued	93.3

From these statistics it is evident that the sixteen basic cadences combined account for an overwhelming majority of the half-lines in *Beowulf*: for 5,900 out of the 6,324 actually considered. In brief, more than 93 per cent of the half-lines have a rhythmic signature based upon one or another of these cadences, which thus classify accurately more than nine of every ten lines. There can be little doubt that the system of scansion developed here—even though hypothetical at best— brings the dipodic rhythm of *Beowulf* into sharp focus and accentuates the presence in the poem of the uniformity in diversity and diversity in uniformity that is at the core of great literature. The harp is a major factor in the maintenance of that rhythm.

In addition to the metrical functions of the harp in maintaining the rhythm of *Beowulf*, there are certain aesthetic uses for that percussional instrument. These aesthetic uses have to do with formulaic expressions as governed by alliteration and internal rhyme with cases of special emphasis and with heavily syncopated passages of emotional heightening. Formulaic expressions, though of greater originality and wider variety than in other Old English poetry, abound in *Beowulf*. The harp helps call the attention of the audience (and one should never forget that this heroic monodrama was designed primarily for oral performance) to such expressions by means of dramatic musical junctures. Thus a tame and rather halting line like 197 takes on a touch of excitement when the harp supports the formula: *on þæm* [H] *dæge þysses lifes*. Here harp substitution for missing secondary stress reinforces the alliteration to heighten the general accentual pattern of a line that has few syllables. Similarly, in line 144 this type of percussive syncopation permits a sharp focus to fall upon the alliteration on *r: Swā* [H] *rīxode ond wið rihte wan* [H]. So ubiquitous, in fact, is the harp in the formulaic expressions of the poem that its hero can seldom speak without being properly identified by a syncopational chord in the appositional second half-line: *Bēowulf maþelode, bearn* [H] *Ecgþēowes*. The same harp formula applies to the speeches of the old Danish king whom the mighty Geat has come to help: *Hrōðgar maþelode, helm* [H] *Scyldinga*. Indeed, this type of harp formula introduces one character after another into the texture of *Beowulf*:

Oft Scyld [H] Scēfing (4a)
secg [H] on searwum (249a)
wæs his eald-[H]fæder (373a)
cwēn [H] Hrōþgāres (613a)
betst [H] beado-rinca (1109a)
frēan [H] Ingwina (1319a)
bearn [H] ond brȳde (2956a)

fēond [H] man-cynnes (164b)
cniht-[H]wesende (372b)
Ār-[H]Scyldinga (464b)
mæg [H] Higelāces (737a)
Fin [H] Hengeste (1096b)
bēod-[H]genēatas (343a)
nē mægþ [H] scȳne (3016b)

These fourteen examples, therefore, are only a minute portion of the harp formulas in the poem.

Internal rhyme is not very frequent in the lines of *Beowulf*, but when such rhyme is employed, it produces stress reinforcement. This kind of stress reinforcement, in turn, is usually accompanied by harp juncturing. In line 9, for instance, *him* and *ymb* constitute a nearly perfect consonantal rhyme. The reinforcement of this internal rhyme coupled with the metrical evidence of both the preceding and the following line shows that line 9 fits into the scansional system of its immediate environment as follows:

$$
\begin{array}{l}
\overset{\text{s}\quad\text{p}\quad\text{l}\quad\text{o}\quad\quad\text{s}}{\text{weorð-myndum þāh}} \\[4pt]
\overset{\text{o}\quad\text{l}\ \text{p}\ \text{s}\qquad\text{s}\ \text{p}\qquad\text{l}}{\text{oðþæt }him\text{ [H] æghwylc}} \qquad \overset{\text{o}\ \text{o}\ \text{s}\qquad\text{s}\ \text{o}\qquad\text{(l)}}{\text{þāra }ymb\text{-[H]sittendra}} \\[4pt]
\overset{\text{l}\ \text{o}\qquad\text{s}\qquad\text{s p l p}}{\text{ofer hron-[H]rāde . . .}} \qquad\qquad\qquad\qquad\qquad \text{(8b–10a)}
\end{array}
$$

Thus the primary stressing of *him* and the immediately following harp chord draw closer attention to *Scyld Scēfing*, who is the recipient in the following lines of obedience and tribute, and to the fact that everyone paid tribute; they also help to heighten the vowel alliteration of the line by permitting an emphasized juncture to precede the primary stressing of *æg* in *æghwylc*. Similar clues to primary stress are also supplied by means of internal rhyme in lines 88, 100, and 279:

$$
\text{þæt hē dōgora ge}\overset{\text{s}}{hwā}m\text{ [H]} \qquad \overset{\text{s}}{dr\bar{e}am}\text{ [H] gehȳrde . . .}
$$
$$
\text{ēadiglīce,} \qquad \text{oðð}\overset{\text{s}}{æt\ \bar{a}n}\text{ [H] }\overset{\text{s}}{ongan}\text{ [H] . . .}
$$
$$
\text{hū hē }\overset{\text{s}}{fr\bar{o}d}\text{ [H] ond }\overset{\text{s}}{g\bar{o}d}\text{ [H]} \qquad \text{fēond oferswȳðeþ . . .}
$$

The accompanying use of the harp, of course, draws attention to the rhymes themselves.

In the metrical texture of *Beowulf* there are a few individual cases in which one primary stress seems to be missing in a half-line where neither alliteration nor internal rhyme are present to furnish a clue as to where harp substitution should take place. In such instances one must rely upon his sense of rhythm (admittedly subjective and fallible) to indicate the exact placing of the juncture of a harp chord. The reader may call instances of this kind those of special emphasis, for example, line 96: *ond gefrætwade foldan scēatas.* Here *ond* introduces a half-line that has only one syllable of primary stress (*fræt*). Since *ond* normally would receive tertiary stress (O), what is the reader to do? He can do one of two things: he can introduce the line with a harp chord and raise *ond* to secondary stress, yielding a cadence pattern of HLO SPLO for the first half-line; or he can raise *ond* to primary stress and follow it with a harp juncture, yielding a cadence pattern of SHO SPLO. Regardless of the method that the individual performer chooses to employ, the basic dipodic rhythm of the line remains unchanged. Moreover, since such cases of special emphasis are rare indeed (less than 1 per cent), one need not argue over the exact placing of harp substitution. But for the mere sake of metrical consistency, it seems slightly more desirable to heighten the introductory word to primary stress, as Hopkins does with "AND" in line 10 of his sonnet *The Windhover*, and then to follow it with a harp chord—especially since internal harp substitution is an overwhelmingly preponderant feature in the rhythm of *Beowulf*.

One last special aesthetic use of the harp is that of emotional heightening. Emotional heightening means that metrical excitement evidenced in dramatically important passages that call for a strong syncopation marked with harp junctures. Such strong syncopation draws the attention of the audience more closely to the vivid, serious business at hand and produces an artistic effect comparable to A. E. Housman's famous "shiver down the spine." The passage that describes Grendel's slaughtering and eating of the Gēat warrior Hondsciō provides an excellent example of this emotional heightening engendered by the percussional use of the harp:

> Þā his mōd [H] āhlōg; [H]
> mynte þæt hē gedælde,   ær þon dæg [H] cwōme,
> atol āglæca,   ānra gehwylces

līf [H] wið līce,   þā him ālumpen wæs [H]
wist-fylle wēn.   Ne wæs þæt wyrd [H] þā gēn,
þæt hē mā [H] mōste   manna cynnes
ðicgean ofer þā niht.   Þrȳð-swȳð behēold [H]
mæg [H] Higelāces,   hu se mān-[H]scaða
under fær-[H]gripum   gefaran wolde.
Nē þæt se āglæca   yldan þōhte,
ac hē gefēng [H] hraðe   forman sīðe
slæpendne rinc, [H]   slāt [H] unwearnum
bāt [H] bān-locan,   blōd [H] ēdrum dranc,
synsnædum swealh; [H]   sōna hæfde
un-[H]lyfigendes   eal [H] gefeormod,
fēt [H] ond folma. . . .   (730–45)

The use of harp substitution (H) in these intensely dramatic lines serves to hei͵ͷhten tʰɛ emotional tone of the entire passage. The recurrent ᵥ mployment of the measures SH and SHO immeasurably strengthens the aural impact and reveals how effective an aesthetic device such percussional harp accompaniment can be. There is little in later literature to rival this syncopated power.

Similar emotional heightening may be found frequently in the metrical texture of *Beowulf.* Another example of this aesthetic device is encountered in the passage where the poet says that the Danes lived riotously happily until one (Grendel) began to perform his deeds of sin—that hellish fiend! The audience immediately notices the emotional heightening when the scop mentions the "one":

Swā ðā driht-[H]guman   drēamum lifdon,
ēadiglīce,   oð ðæt ān [H] ongan [H]
fyrene fremman   fēond [H] on helle.   (99–101)

The double harp substitution in line 100 (after *ān* and *-gan*) shows that something important is to follow and that the audience had better pay strict attention (indeed the poet repeats this formula when he speaks about the dragon in line 2210). The harp juncturing after *fēond* places the terrifying phrase *on helle* in a position of dramatic emphasis. The artistry of the *Beowulf* poet is indeed superb.

Thus the percussional harp, even while executing its basic metrical function of strengthening weak measures, may serve to heighten the emotional tone of intensely dramatic lines by means of heavily emphasizing the syncopation. So important is the harp for the rhythm of *Beowulf* in all its metrical and aesthetic features that the poem itself cries for a future edition that will indicate the exact placing of every musical chord of the scop. Such an edition would be of incalculable value for bardic performance and critical commentary, for it would be a modern equivalent of Vitellius A.xv—a manuscript that perpetuates rather than replaces the oral tradition of *Beowulf*.[15] And that tradition continues to demand the metrical accompaniment of a functional, not decorative, harp.

NOTES

1. See John A. Nist, *A Structural History of English* (New York, 1966), pp. 200–201.

2. For a discussion of this terminology in connection with the structure of *Beowulf* see John A. Nist, "The Structure of *Beowulf*," *Papers of the Michigan Academy of Science, Arts, and Letters*, XLIII (1958), 307–14. Adrien Bonjour agrees; see his *Twelve "Beowulf" Papers, 1940–1960, with Additional Comments* (Geneva, 1962), pp. 49–50.

3. For a definition of the term "cadence" see Nist, *A Structural History of English*, p. 60; for an extended discussion on this rhythmical unit and concept see John A. Nist, "The Word-Group Cadence: Basis of English Metrics," *Linguistics* (The Hague), No. 6 (June, 1964), pp. 73–82.

4. For a pioneer study in dipodic rhythm see George R. Stewart, Jr., "A Method towards the Study of Dipodic Verse," *PMLA*, XXXIX (1924), 979–89.

5. From an understanding of the Germanic tradition of stress on the root syllable and from the fact that inflections remain undamaged for a relatively long period of time, one can say that Old English supports four degrees of stress. Thanks to the alliterative tradition of oral poetry and its built-in principle of overstress and to the lack of a reliance upon the grapheme and the visual morpheme and the habit of silent reading, the stress patterns of Old English, like those of modern German, tend to discriminate morphemic boundaries rather than those of syntactical

units. The result of such discrimination is that Old English achieves more maximum (′) and major (∧) stress than does modern English. Syllables that present-day readers of the language slur and weaken to minimum stress (◡) their Anglo-Saxon forefathers would probably maintain at minor stress (`). For a discussion of the four degrees of present-day English stress see George L. Trager and Henry Lee Smith, Jr., *An Outline of English Structure* (Washington, D.C., 1962), pp. 35–39.

6. See "*Beowulf* and the Niebelungen Couplet," *University of Wisconsin Studies in Language and Literature*, No. 2 (1918), pp. 99–152, and "Four Footnotes to Papers on Germanic Metrics," in *Studies in English Philology: A Miscellany in Honor of Frederick Klaeber* (Minneapolis, 1929), pp. 1–13.

7. The four kinds of modern English juncture also obtain in Old English. Briefly defined and illustrated, these four kinds of Old English juncture are as follows:

(a) Open juncture (+) defines morphemic and word boundaries on stressed elements—*Gār* + *Dena.*

(b) Optional internal close juncture (/) defines word-group boundaries without the need for written punctuation—*Đā cōm* / *of mōre* / *under misthleoþum* /.

(c) Obligatory internal close juncture (//) defines phrasal and clausal boundaries with the need for written punctuation—*Grendel gongan* // *Godes yrre bær* //.

(d) Obligatory terminal close juncture (#) defines sentence boundaries with the need for written punctuation—*Reced hlynsode* (#).

For a discussion of the four kinds of present-day English juncture see Trager and Smith, *An Outline of English Structure*, pp. 46–49.

8. See Harold Whitehall, "Sprung Rhythm," *Kenyon Review*, VI (1944), 333–54.

9. See John Collins Pope, *The Rhythm of Beowulf* (New Haven, 1942).

10. *Ibid.*

11. See *Deutsche Versgeschichte mit Einschluss des altenglischen und altnordischen Stabreimverses* ("H. Paul's Grundriss der Germanischen Philologie," Vol. VIII [Berlin, 1925–29]), I.

12. See "Poetic Theory," in *A Hopkins Reader*, ed. John Pick (New York, 1953), pp. 71–124.

13. All quotations from *Beowulf* are from R. W. Chambers' edition as re-edited by A. J. Wyatt (Cambridge, Eng., 1914).

14. See *The Rhythm of Beowulf*, pp. 231–386.

15. For a discussion of the oral-tradition aspects of Vitellius A.xv see John A. Nist, "Textual Elements in the *Beowulf* Manuscript," *Papers of the Michigan Academy of Science, Arts, and Letters*, XLII (1957), 331–38.

PART TWO

GENESIS AND SHORTER OLD ENGLISH POETRY

THE SELF-DECEPTION OF
TEMPTATION: BOETHIAN
PSYCHOLOGY IN *GENESIS B*

❦

Alain Renoir

Rosemary Woolf has written that the author of the Old English poem *Genesis B* "approaches his subject from the psychological rather than from the dogmatic point of view," and the contention is amply borne out by her penetrating analysis of the behavior of Adam and Eve in comparison with relevant aspects of the lapsarian tradition.[1] This psychological element is, I believe, largely responsible for the powerful impact of the poem upon modern readers who may not necessarily believe in the historical veracity of the events therein: instead of merely being told what happens, we are made to share in the emotional experience of the protagonists. Charles W. Kennedy points out, in reference to the poem, that "the imagination of the Anglo-Saxon religious poets, when stirred, is often intense, conjuring up visions grim or lovely with a vividness that has power to startle."[2] But startling vividness may be psychological as well as visual or auditory, and so it is with *Genesis B*. While Miss Woolf confines her analysis of the poet's psychological approach to the behavior of Adam and Eve, I suggest that her observations can be applied to the Tempter as well as to the tempted. This extension of a psychological reading, which can include Satan and all his followers as well, affords us additional insight into the artistry of the poet's treatment of the temptation of man.

The view expressed by Kennedy that "the Satan of *Genesis B* may in a real sense be called the hero of that poem"[3] is at the same time correct and misleading, depending upon whether we consider the statement within the context of the poem as it has come down to us or in relation to the lost document of which the present text is a 616-line fragment. Although no one can tell what the lost document was like, it is generally assumed to have followed the outline of some unknown apocryphal version of the Book of Genesis;[4] Satan plays no part in the biblical Genesis and is certainly not the hero of any of the known apocryphal versions. Within the fragment, however, Satan is, if not the hero in the usual sense of the word, at least the prime mover of the action: the extant text relates the revolt of the angels and the temptation of man, both of which are presented as the direct result of Satan's manipulations. Thus Satan's motivation may be regarded as the key to the action and to its underlying psychology.

At the risk of stating the obvious, I wish to insist that Satan's motivation for the Temptation is revenge for the sake of revenge. Since Satan is chained at the bottom of hell, his desperate situation is immutable, and his words indicate that he entertains no illusion about his predicament:

> Wa la, ahte ic minra handa geweald
> and moste ane tid   ute weorðan,
> wesan ane winterstunde,   þonne ic mid þys werode—
> Ac licgað me ymbe   irenbenda,
> rideð racentan sal.   Ic eom rices leas;
> habbað me swa hearde   helle clommas
> fæste befangen.   Her is fyr micel,
> ufan and neoðone.   Ic a ne geseah
> laðran landscipe.   Lig ne aswamað,
> hat ofer helle.   Me habbað hringa gespong,
> sliðhearda sal   siðes amyrred,
> afyrred me min feðe;   fet synt gebundene,
> handa gehæfte.   Synt þissa heldora
> wegas forworhte,   swa ic mid wihte ne mæg
> of þissum lioðobendum.   Licgað me ymbe
> heardes irenes   hate geslægene
> grindlas greate.[5]   (368b–84a)

Alas, if [only] I had control of my hands and could escape for a single hour, be it only a winter hour, then I with this band—! But iron bonds lie about me, and a rope of chain rides [athwart]; the hardest of hell fetters have seized me fast. Here is great fire from above and from below. Never have I seen a more hateful country. The blaze, hot over hell, never subsides. A clasp of rings, a cruelly hard rope, has hindered my movement, taken from me my power to walk; [my] feet are bound, my hands captive. The ways are closed to these doors of hell, so that I can by no means [escape] from these limb fetters. Great bars of hard iron forged in heat lie upon me.

Satan makes it clear to his followers that they too are doomed to share his eternal torment, for he informs them that he and they must henceforth *þis wite þolien, / hearm on þisse helle* 'endure this punishment, harm in this hell' (367b–68a). Nor does he permit them to doubt for an instant the futility of revenge: *Ne magon we þæs wrace gefremman, / geleanian him mid laðes wihte* 'nor can we perform vengeance for this, pay Him back with any hatefulness' (393b–94a). Thus the revenge planned by the fallen angels seems to be undertaken for its own sake, since absolutely no physical betterment may come to them as a result. That this is the way the poet wants us to understand the motivation behind the temptation of man is obvious from Satan's words to his followers in respect to Adam and Eve: *Siððan ic me sefte mæg / restan on þyssum racentum, gif him þæt rice losað* 'afterwards I can rest more easily in these chains, if that kingdom is lost to them' (433b–34). The remainder of this essay will, hopefully, suggest that this evil but desperate sentiment (which, incidentally, is psychologically effective because its pathos is essentially human) is in keeping with the conventions of the tradition to which the poem belongs.

As revenge is the motivation for the Temptation, so there must be a motivation for revenge. From the statistical point of view Satan has no grounds for revenge, for God had allowed him *swa micles wealdan* 'so much power' (253b) that he *sceolde his drihtne þancian | þæs leanes þe he him on þam leohte gescerede* 'should thank his Lord for the gift which He gave him in that kingdom' (257b–58a). From the psychological point of view, however, he has perhaps the strongest of all motivations. The defeat that God inflicted upon him and his followers when they rose in revolt has been total and therefore humiliating; and humiliation—however thoroughly deserved —is one experience that no one can forgive, especially an *engyl . . . ofermod* 'proud angel' (262) who has just succumbed to the temptation *ofermede micel | ahebban wið his hearran* 'to stir up great pride against his Lord' (293b–94a). This is the same sentiment that urges Milton's Satan to wage war against heaven rather than submit to the obligations of "The debt immense of endless gratitude, / So burdensom, still paying, still to ow." [6]

The motivation for revenge becomes even more obvious if we place the action against its social background and consider the formulaic nature of early Germanic poetry. *Genesis B* is usually dated somewhere in the tenth century [7] and has been proved to be an Old English rendering of an earlier Old Saxon poem presumably composed by the author of the *Heliand*. [8] The importance of these facts is that we know that the Germanic people of that period considered revenge a binding duty even when the injured party had fully deserved the injury. For example, readers of the Old Icelandic *Brennu-Njáls Saga*, which related events of the late tenth and early eleventh centuries, will recall how the slaying of Svart at Hallgerd's command brings about the long series of mutually cancelling revenges that eventually culminate in the death of the innocent Gunnar. Although the initial killing was perpetrated without valid reason by a member of Gunnar's own household, Hallgerd makes it brutally plain that Gunnar's failure to avenge the well-deserved revenge killing of one of his disreputable kinsmen would be considered utterly shameful; if he were faced by the fact, *myndi hann þá hefna frænda síns eða sitja fyrir hvers manns ámæli* 'he would then avenge his kinsman or endure every man's scorn.' [9]

To appreciate the full significance of the foregoing observation, we must take into account the theory, brilliantly advanced by Francis P. Magoun, Jr., in 1953 and since accepted by an ever-growing number of scholars, that Old English poetry was of fundamentally oral-formulaic character.[10] Two subsequent investigations by followers of Magoun have implications of special importance for the present argument: one is by Robert P. Creed who has pointed out that the oral-formulaic poet may occasionally have to reckon with an audience ready to correct him when his performance falls short of its expectations;[11] the other is by David K. Crowne who has demonstrated that the same formulaic theme may turn up in both religious and heroic poetry and adapt itself to either with equal ease.[12] In the present context the implication of these investigations is that the author of *Genesis B* or that of the Saxon original—it matters little which—would normally have had to treat his subject matter according to the expectations of his audience; and his audience would have expected a humiliatingly defeated rebel to seek revenge for his humiliation, however fully deserved it may have been. Thus, when the poet has Satan engineer the Temptation, he is being faithful to his source; but when he goes on to emphasize that Satan undertook his revenge for its own sake, he transcends the religious narrative in order to develop a familiar theme and make his protagonist's emotions immediately meaningful to the intended audience of the poem.

Another and more obvious implication of the theory of formulaic composition must be considered before we may analyze the psychological aspect of the Temptation. Although a formulaic theme may be adapted to a situation that it antedates by hundreds of years,[13] the process is two-sided, and some aspects of the situation must be adapted to the theme. In Old English religious poetry the most obvious result of this mutual adaptation is that the heavenly hierarchies take on an external resemblance to the Germanic comitatus: in *Genesis B* God reminds us somewhat of a powerful chieftain (*drihten* 'ruler' [299a], *hearra* 'lord' [358b], *drihtna drihten* 'ruler of rulers' [638a], *waldend* 'leader' [673a]), surrounded by a comitatus of angels. As J. M. Evans has recently shown,[14] Satan's position is that of a high-ranking member of this group, who *ahof hine wið his hearran* 'set himself against his Lord' (263a) in order to erect for himself a *godlecran stol* 'better [more divine?] throne' (281b) where, as *ofermoda cyning* 'proud king' (338a), he may rule over such *rofe rincas* 'brave warriors' (286a) as have betrayed their *þegnscipe* 'service' (326b) to their rightful Lord. Similarly, Adam and Eve remind us of minor retainers to a powerful *hearra* 'lord' (542a); and after their transgression has earned them their *herran hete* 'Lord's hate' (819a), Adam's words clearly suggest the nature of both their former and their present relationship to God:

> Nis me on worulde niod
> æniges þegnscipes,   nu ic mines þeodnes hafa
> hyldo forworhte,   þæt ic hie habban ne mæg.
>
> (835b–37)

For me there is no pleasure [left] in any kind of service in the world now that through my own doing I have lost my Lord's good will so that I can no [longer] have it.

Adam's account of himself is that of a retainer who has foolishly lost the favor of his Lord, and the nostalgic tone of the utterance puts us in mind of another lordless retainer who speaks his sorrow in *The Wanderer*:

> Forþon wat se þe sceal   his winedryhtnes
> leofes larcwidum   longe forþolian,
> ðonne sorg ond slæp   somod ætgædre
> earmne anhogan   oft gebindað.[15]   (37–40)

Indeed he knows, he who must go for a long time without the wise counsel of his beloved lord, when sorrow and sleep together closely bind the solitary man.

It is a commonplace that separation from his lord and comitatus was perhaps the worst tragedy that could befall a member of the Germanic comitatus.

In a way Adam's tragedy is like that of the fallen angels, for

52

they too have become hopelessly separated from their rightful Lord and comitatus. The Anglo-Saxons, we must recall, did not usually take to the notion that one might shift allegiance from one lord to another for the sake of convenience or personal advancement. In the Parker MS of the Anglo-Saxon Chronicle, for example, the entry for the year 757 records that after Cyneheard had killed Cynewulf at Merton the latter's retainers rejected his generous offer of mercy and fought to the last beside their dead lord: *Ọnd hiera se æþeling* [i.e., Cyneheard] *gehwelcum feoh ond feorh gebēad, ọnd hiera nænig hit geþicgean nolde; ac hīe simle feohtende wǣran, oþ hīe alle lǣgon* 'and their prince [Cyneheard] offered each of them money and life, and none of them would accept it; but they continued to fight, until they all lay dead.' When on the next day Cynewulf's alderman in turn attacked and killed Cyneheard, the followers of Cyneheard refused to accept mercy and to enter the service of the man who had just felled their lord: *Ọnd þā gebēad hē him hiera āgenne dōm fēos ọnd londes, gif hīe him þæs rices uþon. . . . Ọnd þā cuǣdon hīe þæt him nænig mǣg lēofra nǣre þonne hiera hlāford, ọnd hie nǣfre his banan folgian noldon* 'and then he offered them whatever they wanted of money and land, if they would grant him that kingdom. . . . And they said that no kinsman was dearer to them than their lord, and [that] they would never follow his murderer.'[16]

This is the behavior that Germanic society expected from an honorable retainer; and the behavior of the rebel members of the heavenly comitatus in *Genesis B*—as the author and audience of the poem must have known full well—has been exactly the opposite. But their having formed a dissenting band and taken to themselves a new lord does not alter the fact that they have, through their own fault, lost their rightful Lord and comitatus. In addition, their illegitimate lord's failure to establish them *hean on heofonrice* 'high in the kingdom of heaven' (358a) despite their having democratically [*hine*] *to hearran gecorene* 'chosen [him] as lord' (285b) is not designed to assuage their sorrow at having traded the love of the *allwalda* 'Ruler of all' (292a) and the bliss of existence *on þam*

leohte 'in that country [light?]' (258a) for eternal torment in a
place of *þystro and hæto* 'darkness and heat' (389b). Because
they have aspired to rule over their Lord they have been para-
doxically dealt the fate of the lordless retainer who has no one
to succor him in his greatest need, and they know that they
have brought it upon themselves.

If we accept the validity of my arguments, we must also
accept my corollary contention that the rebel kingdom is, if
not a fool's paradise, certainly a fool's hell. The comitatus of
Satan has been intentionally patterned after that of God, but
our realization of the glaring contrast between infernal darkness and despair, on the one hand, turns it into a grotesque
and pathetic parody of its model. Thus, when God sits Lucifer
hehstne to him on heofona rice 'nearest [highest] to him in the
kingdom of heaven' (254a), he elevates him to the highest
possible bliss in the radiance of heaven; but when Satan
promises the highest reward at his disposal to the prospective
tempter of mankind, he merely offers him a share of the
deepest despair in the darkness of hell: *Sittan læte ic hine wið
me sylfne* 'I shall let him sit by me' (438a). This is no tempting
reward, except, of course, to such as have not yet realized that
the scale of infernal values is an inversion of that of heaven,
so that here the highest are the lowest. Satan is deceiving his
comitatus, and this deception is one of a series that consti-
tutes a bitter paradox: just as the rebel angels have been
deceived into trading joy for sorrow, so man will be deceived
into trading joy for sorrow, and the Tempter himself is
deceived into trading sorrow for greater sorrow. Indeed, the
words with which Satan prefaces his offer are designed to lure
his followers into thinking in terms of heavenly rather than
infernal values:

> Gif ic ænegum þægne   þeodenmadmas
> geara forgeafe,   þenden we on þan godan rice
> gesælige sæton . . .   (409–11a)

If I in the past have given lordly treasures to any retainer,
while we sat blessed in that good kingdom . . .

To the paradox of the deceived deceiving someone else, we must add another: the rebel angels are deceived because they want to be. Satan, the archdeceiver, is as much a victim of his own deception as are his followers and mankind. He makes such utterances as the following:

> Næfð he [i.e., God] þeah riht gedon
> þæt he us hæfð befælled   fyre to botme,
> helle þære hatan,   heofonrice benumen ...
>
> (360b–62)

He [God] has not however done rightly [in] that he has thrust us down to the bottom of the fire, of this hot hell, deprived us of the kingdom of heaven ...

When he further reveals that *Ne gelyfe ic me nu þæs leohtes furðor þæs þe he* [i.e., God] *him þenceð ... niotan, | þæs eades mid his engla cræfte* 'I do not believe that country [is] any longer for myself, which he [God] intends to enjoy, that blessedness with the power of his angels' (401–2a), he has made it painfully clear to himself and his followers that their common lot will never be improved; and yet he and they keep on striving for the rewards of hell just as angels may be expected to strive for the rewards of heaven. This is self-deception of the most obvious kind, and the poet surely means it to be understood as such, for he tells us that they brought their undoing upon themselves *þurh hygeleaste* 'through folly' (331b), and he accounts for their behavior with the statement that *Hie hyra gal beswac* 'their foolishness led them astray' (327b). *Beswican*, incidentally, is precisely the verb that the poet also uses to describe the Tempter's intentions toward man (451b) and the actual Temptation (601b). Thus, we may say that within the context of *Genesis B* the temptation of man is actually an act of self-deception on the part of the Tempter and his infernal colleagues.

Considered in this light, the Temptation scene reveals a pathos that might otherwise go unnoticed. When Satan's emissary addresses Adam and Eve *mid ligenum* (496a), his words are indeed lies (*ligenum*) insofar as they hide his criminal intention; but from another point of view they are rather a pathetic expression of the self-deception that urges him on, for they depict him as he desperately wishes he could see himself. Our first cue occurs with his initial question to Adam: *Langað þe awuht,* / *Adam, up to gode?* 'do you yearn at all after God, Adam?' (496b–97a). Because the question assumes a craving for God, it anticipates a positive answer. Yet there is no reason why Adam should crave for anything, since he lives in the bliss of the earthly paradise, where God pays him regular visits. The Tempter, on the other hand, no longer enjoys such a relationship with his rightful Lord, since he shared the fate of Satan when God *Acwæð hine . . . fram his hyldo* 'banished him from his favor' (304a). Thus, far from applying to Adam, the initial question suggests the despair of one who *Wæs ær godes engel* 'was once the angel of God' (349b) and who craves for the God whom he has rejected. The impression becomes more concrete when the fiend fondly proceeds to describe the majesty of the world at God's disposal:

Brade synd on worulde
grene geardas,   and god siteð
on þam hehstan   heofna rice,
ufan alwalda.   (510b–13a)

Green fields are broad in the world, and God sits on the heights of the kingdom of heaven, the ruler of all above.

The significant concepts and images here are spaciousness (*brade*), greenness (*grene*), and loftiness (*on þam hehstan . . . ufan*). The speaker's eternal abode, on the other hand, is an *ænga styde* 'narrow place' (356a) at the bottom of *þa deopan dala* 'the deep valleys' (305a) that lie *on þa sweartan helle* 'in . . . dark hell' (312b): the significant concepts and images are narrowness, depth, and darkness. By having the Tempter unwittingly call our attention to the radical contrast between what was his home and what now is, the poet impresses upon us the extent of the inner tragedy suggested by the opening question.

This longing of the fallen angel for his lost happiness grows more defined as he turns toward Eve after he has failed to foist the forbidden fruit upon Adam. He speaks, as he had to Adam, about the light and spaciousness of the world of God, but the important thing for us is that he especially emphasizes the joy one experiences in approaching the throne of one's Lord and feeling secure in his friendship:

> Æt þisses ofetes!   Þonne wurðað þin eagan swa leoht
> þæt þu meaht swa wide   ofer woruld ealle
> geseon siððan,   and selfes stol
> herran þines,   and habban his hyldo forð.   (564–67)

Eat of this fruit! Then your eyes shall become so bright that you might afterwards see far and wide over all the world, [even to] the throne of thy Lord himself, and have his favor henceforth.

The emphasis upon the value of actually beholding the throne and enjoying the favor of one's Lord again puts us in mind of the nostalgic musing of the lordless retainer in *The Wanderer*:

> Gemon he . . .
> hu hine on geoguðe   his goldwine
> wenede to wiste.   Wyn eal gedreas!
>
> . . . .
> Þinceð him on mode   þæt he his mondryhten
> clyppe ond cysse,   ond on cneo lecge
> honda ond heafod,   swa he hwilum ær
> in geardagum   giefstolas breac.   (34–44)

He remembers . . . how his gold-giving lord entertained him at a feast in his youth. All happiness has vanished! It seems to him in his mind that he embraces and kisses his lord and on his knee lays his hands and his head, as he in times past enjoyed the throne of gifts.

Just as the lonesome speaker of *The Wanderer* summons memories of *selesecgas ond sincþege* 'hall retainers and the taking of treasure' (34) in a vain effort to drive away an unbearable reality, so the Tempter recalls the various hierarchies

of heaven in an effort to deny the unbearable reality of his own
state of degradation:

> [Adam] Tyhð me untryowða,   cwyð þæt ic seo teonum
>   georn,
> gramum ambyhtsecg,   nales godes engel.
> Ac ic cann ealle swa geare   engla gebyrdo,
> heah heofona gehlidu;   wæs seo hwil þæs lang
> þæt ic geornlice   gode þegnode
> þurh holdne hyge,   herran minum,
> drihtne selfum;   ne eom ic deofle gelic.   (581–87)

> [Adam] accuses me of lies, says that I am a cruel messen-
> ger, bent on injuries, not at all God's angel. But I know
> so well all the orders of angels, the high slopes of heaven;
> it was a long time that I served God eagerly with a loyal
> spirit, my Lord, the Lord himself. I am not like a devil.

The first thing one notices about the passage is that the
speaker is protesting far too much. Since Eve has presumably
not heard his conversation with Adam, there is no reason for
broaching the dangerous topic of the latter's accusations when
much more might be accomplished with the mere statement
that Adam bluntly refused to obey an order supposedly issued
by God himself. Had not God conveniently *wacran hige* / . . .
gemearcod 'destined a weaker mind' (590b–91a) for Eve, we
may assume that the needless protestations would arouse her
suspicions concerning the Tempter's intentions. His insistence
upon piling up unnecessary evidence of his angelic nature puts
us in mind of *The Pardoner's Tale*, where Chaucer unequivocally reveals the inner turmoil that upsets his young murderer by having him give an apothecary a string of needless
explanations why he needs the poison intended for his own
associates:

> [He] preyde hym that he hym wolde selle
> Som poyson, that he myghte his rattes quelle;
> And eek ther was a polcat in his hawe,

> That, as he seyde, his capouns hadde yslawe,
> And fayn he wolde wreke hym, if he myghte,
> On vermyn that destroyed hym by nyghte.[17] (853–58)

Unlike Eve in *Genesis B*, however, the apothecary in *The Pardoner's Tale* has not been created with a 'weaker mind.' The answer he gives his customer assures the latter that the particular poison he gets is of a kind intended for a much larger animal than a rat, a polecat, or any other vermin. It is so powerful that there is no one who, having eaten or drunk, as he says:

> Nought but the montance of a corn of whete,
> That he ne shal his lif anon forlete;
> Ye, sterve he shal, and that in lasse while
> Than thou wolt goon a paas nat but a mile,
> This poysoun is so strong and violent.   (863–67)

In effect, the lies have saved the novice murderer nothing but the necessity of acknowledging his criminal intentions aloud "under the trone / Of God" (842–43). Emotionally, it is one thing to plan a murder, but quite another to admit to oneself that one is a murderer.

Self-admission is precisely what the Tempter of *Genesis B* pathetically strives to avoid. In this respect the structure of his self-defense before Eve is revealing, for it is that of a syllogistic argument. The first premise is that Adam denies the Tempter's angelic nature (581–82); the second premise, forcefully introduced by the denial 'but on the contrary' (*Ac*), is that the Tempter is thoroughly acquainted with celestial geography and has served God a long time (583–87a); and the conclusion is that he has therefore nothing in common with the infernal powers (587b). The premises are factually correct, but the argument is logically invalid: the fact that one has a knowledge of celestial geography and has faithfully served God for a long time does not necessarily imply that one thereby comes straight from heaven and is still a faithful servant. It is important to note that the Tempter mentions his time in the service of God in the past tense (*wæs*), so that the facts he presents are as scrupulously correct as the conclusion is illogical. We may accordingly say that he has gone out of his way to list accurate but unnecessary facts in order to formulate an illogical argument.

The facts listed are unnecessary—and even potentially detrimental—to the Tempter's formal purpose of bringing about the fall of man, but they are very necessary to the satisfaction of his uncontrollable craving for the world he has foolishly and irremediably rejected. There is a tone of frustrated anger in his assertion that Adam has accused him of being what he actually is: *teonum georn, | gramum ambyhtsecg, nales godes engel* 'bent on injuries, a cruel messenger, not at all God's angel' (581b–82). Nor can the reader or listener fail to note that Adam has made no such accusations; he has merely expressed his doubts as to the validity of the message and remarked that the bearer does not look like the other angels. In other words, the Tempter's irrational anger leads him to describe on his own a shoe that fits only too well and may never be taken off once it has been worn. We must likewise note the nostalgia of his account when he dwells on his experience in the bliss of heaven. He knows, in the present, all the angelic hierarchies *swa geare* 'so well,' as well as the 'high slopes of heaven'; and he served his Lord, in the past, *geornlice . . . | þurh holdne hyge* 'eagerly, with a loyal spirit.' We sense a sorrowful possessiveness in his reference to God as *herran minum, | drihtne selfum* 'my Lord, the Lord himself,' as well as the expression of intensely gnawing jealousy in the usurpation of the term *min hearra* (542a), which Adam has correctly used earlier to express his own relationship with his Lord. Coming hard upon these remembrances of things past, the Tempter's conclusion that he is not like a devil takes on the pathetic tone of a cry from the soul: *ne eom ic deofle gelic.* He does not actually deny that he is a devil, he only refuses to admit that he looks like one. Nor can we fail to observe that his assertion to Eve is in reality an answer to Adam's earlier remark on his physical appearance: *þu gelic ne bist | ænegum*

60

his engla þe ic ær geseah 'you are not like any of His angels that I have seen before' (538b–39). He had no opportunity to answer Adam's observation to his face, but failing to answer it now would in effect constitute an admission that his degradation from angel to devil is so real that it is apparent even to such a contemptible observer as a man whom Satan has scornfully described as *of eorðan geworht* 'made of earth' (365b). Just as the young man of *The Pardoner's Tale* plans murder without admitting to himself that he is a murderer, so the Tempter of *Genesis B* hopelessly strives to bring about the fall of man without admitting to himself that he is no longer one of the blessed angels. On one level the Temptation thus becomes an act of unequivocal self-deception.

The Tempter's insistence upon drawing illogical conclusions from correct statements is noteworthy in yet another respect. Just as God, who is all spirit, can produce only correct reasoning, so the devils, who are the contrary of God, are unable to produce anything but illogical arguments. Satan argues for the Temptation, although it will prove no help to him and his followers, and the Tempter deceives himself through crooked logic into denying his own infernal nature.

As always when trying to analyze psychological motivation, we may return again to Chaucer for revealing comparisons. Just as the Tempter has fallen from the service of God to that of Satan, so Chaucer's Criseyde in *Troilus and Criseyde* falls from the bed of "oon the gentileste / That evere was, and oon the worthieste" (V, 1056–57) into that of a repulsively shrewd and selfish military man "of tonge large" (V, 804) with "sterne vois and myghty lymes square" (V, 801). Just as the Tempter suffers emotionally from his degradation and refuses to recognize it, so we are told of Criseyde that "Ther made nevere woman moore wo / Than she, whan that she falsed Troilus" (V, 1052–53), and she makes a pitiful attempt at hiding from herself the significance of her action: "I mene wel, by God that sit above" (V, 1004). We recall how, in her confusion and despair, she then goes on to transfer to her new lover the allegiance that the code of courtly love would

61

have her reserve for the better man whom she has betrayed:

> But syn I se ther is no bettre way,
> And that to late is now for me to rewe,
> To Diomede algate I wol be trewe. (V, 1069–71)

But of course there is a point beyond which self-deception no longer works, and the next thing Chaucer tells us is that "she brast anon to wepe" (V, 1078).

If we return for a moment to the earlier analogy between the social structure in *Genesis B* and that of the Germanic comitatus, the foregoing comparison with Troilus and Criseyde affords us an additional insight into the action of the Temptation. Just as Criseyde attempts to cover up her degradation by behaving toward her new lover as the code of courtly love would expect her to behave toward the lover she has betrayed, so the Tempter attempts to cover up his degradation by behaving toward his new lord as the code of the comitatus would expect him to behave toward the Lord he has betrayed. He accordingly serves Satan by volunteering for the Temptation and carrying it out faithfully, and his outwardly delighted reaction upon witnessing the final success of the enterprise emulates the reaction we should expect of a faithful retainer who has done his rightful lord's bidding. But acting in conformity to the mere letter of the law is no substitute for the real thing; and just as Criseyde's behavior is off key when she has no sooner promised to love her new suitor than she begins "to sike" (V, 1006), so there is something wrong with the overdone exuberance with which the Tempter celebrates his victory. The speaker of *The Wanderer* is emphatic in asserting that custom expects a freeman to keep his emotions to himself:

> Ic to soþe wat
> þæt biþ in eorle   indryhten þeaw,
> þæt he his ferðlocan   fæste binde,
> healde his hordcofan,   hycge swa he wille.
>
> (11b–14)

I know indeed that for a noble man there is a very lordly
custom that he must bind fast his thoughts, keep [fast]
his innermost thoughts, let him think what he will.

Yet, the Tempter indulges in a ludicrous display of emotions
as he childishly skips and laughs at the thought of his having
at last earned Satan's approval:

> hloh þa and plegode
> boda bitre gehugod, sægde begra þanc
> hearran sinum: "Nu hæbbe ic þine hyldo me
> witode geworhte, and þinne willan gelæst
> to ful monegum dæge." (724b–28a)

then the messenger with bitter thoughts laughed and
played, said thanks to his lord for both: "Now I have
gained your destined favor, and have performed your will
for many a day."

Just as Adam noticed earlier that the Tempter did not really
look like an angel of God, so the audience of the poem may
now notice that he is not acting like a member in good
standing of the Germanic comitatus. In this respect it is significant that in the passage quoted above the words *hearran
sinum* 'his lord' are spoken by the poet rather than by the
devil, who even this late in the game reserves the lordly title
for God himself. In relation to man he rejoices that *hit is nu
Adame eall forgolden / mid hearran hete* 'it is now all paid
back to Adam by the hate of the Lord' (756–57a).

But this momentary exultation is short-lived, for even the
most energetic self-deception must eventually come to terms
with reality. Criseyde must face the fact that, despite her
rationalizations, no good word about her "unto the worldes
ende / Shal neyther ben ywriten nor ysonge" (V, 1058–59);
and the Tempter must face the fact that the only reward
awaiting his action is the obligation to rejoin his impotent
master amidst the eternal flames of hell:

> Nu wille ic eft þam lige near,
> Satan ic þær secan wille; he is on þære sweartan helle
> hæft mid hringa gesponne. (760b–62a)

Now I wish [to go] nearer the flame again, I want to seek
Satan there; he is captive, bound with chains in dark hell.

Within the context of *The Battle of Maldon* a similar willingness to do what has to be done for the sake of a hopeless cause
is a magnificent illustration of the indomitable spirit of the
ideal comitatus: *Hige sceal þe heardra, heorte þe cenre, | mod
sceal þe mare, þe ure mægen lytlað* 'our minds must be the
firmer, our hearts the braver, our courage the greater, as our
strength lessens' (312–13).[18] The Tempter's words suggest a
pathetic awakening to a painful reality; although he has lived
up to the right code, he has done so for the sake of the wrong
comitatus and must therefore share his master's inglorious
fate.

Considered thus, the Temptation reads like the conclusion
to a medieval tragedy as defined by Chaucer's Monk in the
Prologue to his *Tale*:

> a certeyn storie,
>
> .   .   .   .
>
> Of hym that stood in greet prosperitee
> And is yfallen out of heigh degree
> Into myserie, and endeth wrecchedly. (1973–77)

The Tempter has fallen from the glory of heaven into the
ignominy of hell, and he must now come to a wretched end in
the seat Satan promised him at the very bottom of the infernal
regions. We need not wonder, then, that the poet—either the
English adapter or the author of the original Old Saxon poem—
should wish to emphasize the element of self-deception. By
doing so, he has produced a narrative whose lesson in Christian
morality is worth all the sermons in the world.

The foregoing analysis is the product of a twentieth-century
reading of *Genesis B*, and one may object that the internal
motivation that I have tried to isolate could not possibly have
been intended and developed by an Old English or Saxon poet.
The objection deserves two answers. The first is that it is
irrelevant: my purpose has been to analyze the poem from the

point of view of my own time; if Old English poetry cannot be appreciated from the point of view of our own time, teachers of English literature ought to abandon it with all dispatch and turn it over to the linguists and antiquarians. Nor must we forget that a work of art may legitimately mean to a later period something that it never meant to its original audience; in fact, it almost necessarily does, and it is perhaps the mark of a great poet that he is able to produce something that will adapt itself to the understanding of subsequent ages. The second answer is that I believe the poet could have meant his work to convey the lesson that I have discussed above. Even if he and his intended audience had never read Boethius' assertion in *The Consolation of Philosophy* that the evildoer merely *Nectit . . . catenam* 'fastens the chain' [19] to himself—just as Satan's evil must be held ultimately responsible for the *racentan sal* 'rope of chains' (372a) that bind him—both must have known something of the Boethian view that evil is its own punishment. In fact, because they were medieval Christians, the interpretation that I have proposed may well have been much more obvious to them than to us, since they would probably have seen in the poem an illustration of the internal hell that awaits those who revolt against God. Be this as it may, an awareness of what might be called the Boethian psychology of evil is at least helpful—though not necessary—to our understanding of what I have proposed as the poet's intention and achievement. Thus analyzed, *Genesis B* remains the story of the temptation of man, but it also becomes a powerfully effective object lesson on the tragedy of self-deception.

NOTES

1. "The Fall of Man in *Genesis B* and the *Mystère d'Adam*," in *Studies in Old English Literature in Honor of Arthur G. Brodeur*, ed. Stanley B. Greenfield (Eugene, Ore., 1963); see especially p. 187.
2. *The Cædmon Poems*, trans. Charles W. Kennedy (New York, 1916), p. xxvi.

3. *Ibid.*, p. xxxvii.

4. See Woolf, "The Fall of Man in *Genesis B* and the *Mystère d'Adam*," p. 188 and n. 3, for the possible source in Avitus' *De originali peccato*. *The Cædmon Poems*, trans. Kennedy, p. xxvi, accepts the poem as a paraphrase from the Old Testament without discussing the possibility of an apocryphal source; and S. H. Gurteen, *The Epic of the Fall of Man* (New York, 1896), p. 93, points out Eastern influence. The most impressive student of the problem, J. M. Evans, points out in "*Genesis B* and Its Background," *Review of English Studies*, N.S. XIV (1963), 16, that if the poem "was indebted to any tradition at all, it was to the literary and not the theological."

5. All quotations from *Genesis B* are from *The Junius Manuscript*, ed. G. P. Krapp ("The Anglo-Saxon Poetic Records," Vol. I [New York, 1931]); the edition follows the manuscript in printing the text along with *Genesis A*, of which it is an interpolation between line 235a and line 851b, inclusive.

6. *Paradise Lost*, ed. H. Darbishire (London, 1960), IV, 52–53.

7. See for instance *The Cædmon Poems*, trans. Kennedy, p. xxv.

8. This theory, first developed by Edward Sievers in *Der Heliand und die angelsächsische Genesis* (Halle, 1875), was corroborated by the discovery in the Vatican Library of a fragment of the Old Saxon text, subsequently edited and discussed in comparison with the Old English text by K. F. W. Zangemeister and W. Braune, in *Bruchstücke der altsächsischen Bibeldichtung* (Heidelberg, 1894).

9. *Brennu-Njáls Saga*, ed. E. O. Sveinsson (Reykjavik, 1954), chap. xlv, p. 117.

10. "Oral-Formulaic Character of Anglo-Saxon Narrative Poetry," *Speculum*, XXVIII (1953), 446–67. Magoun has further developed and illustrated his theory in subsequent essays: e.g., "Bede's Story of Caedman: The Case History of an Anglo-Saxon Oral Singer," *Speculum*, XXX (1955), 49–63; and "The Theme of the Beasts of Battle in Anglo-Saxon Poetry," *Neuphilologische Mitteilungen*, LVI (1955), 81–90. See also Stanley B. Greenfield, "The Formulaic Expression of the Theme of 'Exile' in Anglo-Saxon Poetry," *Speculum*, XXX (1955), 200–206; Adrien Bonjour, "*Beowulf* and the Beasts of Battle," *PMLA*, LXXII (1957), 563–73; and especially the masterful essay by Robert P. Creed, "The Making of an Anglo-Saxon Poem," *ELH: A Journal of English Literary History*, XXVI (1959), 445–54. Arthur G. Brodeur accepts the theory with reservations in his monumental *The Art of Beowulf* (Berkeley, Calif., 1959), p. 3, and the publication of Albert B. Lord's impressive study *The Singer of Tales* (Cambridge, Mass., 1960) has since made it very difficult to disprove the validity of Magoun's theory.

11. "The Singer Looks at His Sources," in *Studies in Old English Literature in Honor of Arthur G. Brodeur*, pp. 44–52. The influence of the

audience upon the oral-formulaic poet is studied at length in Lord's *The Singer of Tales* and has been discussed by Tauno F. Mustanoja, "The Presentation of Ancient Germanic Poetry—Looking for Parallels: A Note on the Presentation of Finnish Runos," *Neuphilologische Mitteilungen*, LX (1959), 1–11; and by Alain Renoir, "*Judith* and the Limits of Poetry," *English Studies*, XLIII (1962), 1–11, and "Point of View and Design for Terror in *Beowulf*," *Neuphilologische Mitteilungen*, LXIII (1962), 154–67.

12. "The Hero on the Beach: An Example of Composition by Theme in Anglo-Saxon Poetry," *Neuphilologische Mitteilungen*, LXI (1960), 362–72.

13. In "Oral-Formulaic Theme Survival: A Possible Instance in the *Nibelungenlied*," *Neuphilologische Mitteilungen*, LXV (1964), 70–75, I have argued that the oral-formulaic theme isolated by Crowne, "The Hero on the Beach," turns up several hundred years later in the *Nibelungenlied* and must therefore have existed in the Germanic repertory before the Saxon invasion of England. In a paper delivered before the General Literature Section at the 1963 annual meeting of the Philological Association of the Pacific Coast, Michael Nagler likewise demonstrated that several identical oral-formulaic themes appear in both *Beowulf* and the Homeric poems, thus suggesting the pervasiveness of a given theme within widely different branches of the same linguistic family.

14. "*Genesis B* and Its Background," p. 119.

15. All quotations from *The Wanderer* are from *The Exeter Book*, ed. G. P. Krapp and E. van K. Dobbie ("The Anglo-Saxon Poetic Records," Vol. III [New York, 1936]), pp. 134–37.

16. "Cynewulf and Cyneheard," in *Bright's Anglo-Saxon Reader*, ed. J. W. Bright, rev. J. R. Hulbert (New York, 1957), p. 15.

17. All quotations from Chaucer are from his *Complete Works*, ed. F. N. Robinson (2d ed.; Boston, 1957).

18. In *The Anglo-Saxon Minor Poems*, ed. E. van K. Dobbie ("The Anglo-Saxon Poetic Records," Vol. VI [New York, 1942]), p. 15.

19. *The Consolation of Philosophy* I.iv.18, in *The Theological Tractates and The Consolation of Philosophy*, ed. and trans. H. F. Stewart and E. K. Rand (London, 1957), p. 142.

THE ART OF THE SINGER:
THREE OLD ENGLISH TELLINGS OF
THE OFFERING OF ISAAC

Robert P. Creed

I

Three tellings of the offering of Isaac survive in Old English, one in prose and two in verse.[1] The prose version comprises the first nineteen verses of the twenty-second chapter of the Book of Genesis and rather closely follows, as it should, the Vulgate text it renders.[2] This version is the least interesting, except for the translator's somewhat anxious insertion of the phrase *on ða ealdan wisan* 'according to the old custom' into verses 9 and 10, the verses in which Abraham first builds the altar and then prepares to sacrifice his son upon it. These insertions might pass unnoticed had not the Old English translator earlier called attention to his civilized ways by twice ignoring the phrase *in holocaustum* 'in burnt offering' repeated in the Vulgate with either flat literalness or perhaps with some relish of these barbaric doings. In any case the prose translator only briefly steps out of the tracks of his Latin guide.

Not so the two Old English poets. The poet of the *Exodus* tells in fifty lines (397–446) the story of the *ferhþ-bana* 'murderer' Abraham who silently sets to work to sacrifice his *lást-weard* 'heir,' *bearna sælest* 'best of children,' *his swǽsne sunu* 'his own son,' his *ángan . . . ierfe-láfe, féores frófre* 'own heir, life's consolation,' his *langsumne hyht* 'long hope.'[3] Through the piling up of these epithets we are made to sense the very horror the prose translator underplayed. Abraham becomes a single-minded and grimly determined human being.

69

The poet of the *Genesis* devotes even more lines to this terrible mission. This poet, whether by design or accident, gives even greater prominence to the strange tale by ending his more than two-thousand-line poem (*Genesis A*) with it. Again, his version, like that of the *Exodus* poet, leafs out the bare limbs of the biblical account.

II

We have in these two poetic tellings of Abraham's mission, as Francis P. Magoun, Jr., appears to suggest by printing the two accounts together in his normalized reader,[4] an opportunity to observe and compare the ways of two traditional poets or singers at work on the same story.[5] Taking up Magoun's suggestion, I have analyzed the verses dealing with the offering in the poetic *Genesis* and a portion of those in the *Exodus* account and located a significant percentage of formulas repeated elsewhere in the surviving corpus of Old English poetry.

The results of this investigation can be briefly summarized: 55 verses in the 91 lines (182 verses) of the passage from *Genesis A* are demonstrable whole-verse formulas; 78 more verses contain significant formulas of smaller dimensions, that is, whole-measure formulas (like *sóna ongann* 'at once began' [2860b]) or whole verses containing a single significant variable (like *swá him Fréa tǽhte* 'as the Lord showed him' [2874b], with which compare *þe him Meotod tǽhte* [2886b]).[6] Seven of the 20 verses (10 lines) analyzed from the *Exodus* passage are demonstrable whole-verse formulas. Eight more verses contain significant formulas of smaller dimensions.[7] The last 91 lines of *Genesis A* are thus 73 per cent demonstrably formulaic. The 10 lines analyzed from *Exodus* are 75 per cent formulaic.

A certain number—not very many, to be sure—of the formulas and formulaic systems in the two poetic versions are shared by the two singers.[8] The whole verse formula *þín ágen bearn* 'thine own child,' for example, appears as the first verse of *Genesis* (2852) and as the second verse of *Exodus* (419). The whole verse substitution system *his* [*x*] *sunu* 'his [x] son' appears as *and his ágen sunu* 'and his own son' in *Genesis* (2885b) and as *his swǽsne sunu* 'his own son' in *Exodus* (402a). But perhaps the most interesting repetition occurs in *Genesis*, *ord arǽmde* 'the beginning rose up' (2877a), and *Exodus*, *upp arǽmde* '[it] rose up' (411a). According to Grein-Köhler-Holthausen, the word *arǽmde* 'rose up' occurs only twice in the corpus of Old English poetry—at these two points. But even if each poet or singer had heard the word in the context of this particular story, an assumption that we cannot make on the basis of so few survivals from a once great tradition, each nevertheless associates the word with a different point in that story. It is the point (or beginning) of the third day that *arǽmde* in *Genesis* and Abraham who *arǽmde* in *Exodus*.

III

A great deal more might be said about the filiations between these two passages and the great poetic tradition that fostered them. As I have argued elsewhere, we cannot begin to appreciate traditional poetry until we have traced all such filiations as far as the limited survivals will permit.[9] But neither can we fully appreciate any poetry until we have felt its peculiar rhythms and have focused upon the flow of images it excites as we hear it. It is with this second kind of experience that I wish to concern myself now.

The singer of the *Exodus* introduces Abraham rather abruptly into his comparison of the crossing of the Red Sea to Noah's Flood. But once he has introduced Abraham he uses the story of the patriarch's obedience, in the words of Edward B. Irving, Jr., "to reinforce the central significance of [the] action" of his poem.[10] The significance of *Exodus*, of this largely heroic tale of flight and encampment, of preparations for battle and martial advances onto the sea floor, may well be, as Irving says, "the need for (and difficulty of) obeying God . . ."[11] In any case obedience is the lesson usually enforced by references to and tellings of the offering of Isaac. It is Abraham's *gehyrsumnyss* 'obedience' that God *wolde . . . fandian* 'wanted . . . to try' in the prose translation. It is this single-minded obedience that is displayed in Abraham's silent preparation of the pyre. Then the *Exodus* singer makes the point clear:

> Hé þæt ȝecýþde,   þá hé þone cniht ȝenam
> fæste mid folmum,   folc-cúþ ȝetéah
> ealde láfe   —ecg grymettode—
> þæt hé him líf-dagas   léofran ne wisse
> þanne hé híerde   Heofon-cyninge.   (406–10)

He manifested that, when he took the boy fast with his hands, [and] known among the people drew the ancient heirloom [sword]—the blade rang—that he did not think [know] his [Isaac's] life-days dearer than [that] he should obey the Heaven-King.

Just as Abraham would obediently redden his ancient sword with the blood of his young heir, the poet tells us that the *beorht Fæder* 'bright Father' did not wish to take away the child as a holy sacrifice. Instead, He seizes Abraham's sword with his heavenly hands and then speaks with the voice of glory from heaven. His words illustrate Irving's second point concerning the significance of this smaller action and the larger action of the poem: "the reward which comes to those who trust and obey" God.[12]

Yet after we have given full credit to this singer for his significant emblem of Abraham and his painting of this action, we must, I think, register some reservations. First of all, the singer is rather overfond of piling up epithets. The humanizing and, somewhat paradoxically, purposeful dehumanizing of Abraham through the series of epithets for Isaac I have already quoted is partly vitiated by the series of epithets applied to Solomon (*se wísesta / on weorold-ríċe* 'the wisest in the world-kingdom') and to his temple (*héahst and háligost, / hæleðum ȝefrǽgost, / mǽst and mǽrost* 'highest and holiest, fairest to men, greatest and most famous'), which precedes those signifying Isaac by just five lines. Secondly, the singer is given to puzzling or even embarrassing parentheses: *fyrst ferhþ-bana* 'chief murderer'—a terrible epithet for the patriarch—is followed by *ná þý fǽʒra [fágra?] wæs* '[it (he?)] was never the fairer[?], more doomed[?], more stained[?].' The epithet *ealde láfe* 'old heirloom' is followed by *ecg grymettode* 'the blade rang,' and I am not sure that this verse does not really distract from the seriousness of the scene. Finally, this singer appears to be unable to resist reminding us that God will intervene in the nick of time. Before he tells us that God seizes Abraham's sword, he reminds us that Abraham will become a murderer only *ʒief hine Meotod léte* 'if God should let him.' But even before this, the singer has rhymed (in line 402) *swǽsne sunu* 'own son' with *siʒe-tifre* 'victory-offering.' There is indeed to be a victory, but that will be a little later and after Abraham has suffered the agony of slaying his 'own, beloved son, his only heir on earth, consolation of [his] life, . . . [his] long[-awaited] hope.'

IV

Several generations of scholars have argued that the poem *Genesis A* is merely or largely a paraphrase of the first twenty-two chapters of the Bible, a paraphrase that came to an unaccountably abrupt end. There has been a countertendency recently to argue that *Genesis A* is a reasonably complete poem that ends where it does effectively. In the course of my comments on the final ninety-one lines of this poem I hope to make clear some of my reasons for adhering to the latter critical view.

Even if we dismiss as mere paraphrase much of the middle of *Genesis A*—the frequent genealogies and the brief or perfunctory accounts of the wanderings of Abraham, for example—it would still be difficult to similarly dismiss this final tale. The singer has made the story of Abraham's sacrifice his own. He has done so exactly as we would expect an excellent singer to do. He has kept to the main outlines of the story he has read or heard, but he has done more: he has seen and felt—and he makes us see and feel—all that happens. He is like the illiterate Yugoslavian singer whom Albert B. Lord tells of who listened to the bare twenty-two-hundred-line songbook version of *The Wedding of Smailagić Meho* and later sang a finer version of the song in twelve thousand lines.[13]

The *Genesis* singer's hero is a warrior and a faithful retainer of his Lord: his *Cyning* 'King' will test his *ellen*—his courage, his battle prowess—not his obedience. It would indeed take enormous courage to undertake the perilous quest so horribly laid upon him. In the prose translation God says to Abraham: *Nym ðinne ancennedan sunu Isaac, þe ðu lufast, 7 far to þam lande Visionis hraðe, 7 geofra hyne þær uppan anre dune* 'take thine only-begotten son Isaac, whom thou lovest, and go quickly to the land Visio, and sacrifice him upon a mountain' (verse 2). In the poetry of *Genesis A* God speaks thus to Abraham:[14]

> ȝewít þú ofostlíce, Ábraham, fœ́ran,
> lástas lecgan and þé lǽde mid
> þín ágen bearn. Þú scealt Ísaac mé
> onsecgan, sunu þínne, self to tífre.
> Siþþan þú ȝestíȝest stéapa dúne,
> hrycg þæs héan landes þe ić þé hinan ȝetǽće,
> upp þínum ágnum fótum, þǽr þú scealt ád ȝeȝierwan,
> bǽl-fýr bearne þínum, and blótan self
> sunu mid sweordes ecge and þanne sweartan líeȝe
> léofes líć forbærnan and mé lác bebéodan.
>
> (2850–59)

Depart quickly, Abraham, lay tracks and lead with thee thine own child. Thou thyself shalt sacrifice Isaac, thy son, as an offering. After thou climbest steep mountains, the ridge of this high land, whither I shall direct thee, upon thine own feet, there thou shalt build a pyre, a bale-fire for thy son, and thyself sacrifice [thy] son with the sword's edge and then with dark flame burn the body of [thy] beloved and offer me a gift.

There is considerable expansion here. The prose translator uses twenty-two English words to translate the twenty-one of the Vulgate text. The singer uses sixty-eight words—more than three times the number of the Latin or the English prose. But what is far more significant is the *kind* of expansion. God tells Abraham in good formulas and with some spirit to depart quickly, to lay tracks, and to lead his own son with him. Then He makes vivid the climb up the steep hills, 'the ridge of this high land,' which Abraham must accomplish 'on [his] own feet.' This phrase *þínum ágnum fótum* repeats in another context the word *ágen* 'own' in the formula *þín ágen bearn* and drives home the terrible fact thrust at Abraham with the repetition of *self: onsecgan . . . / self to tífre . . . and blótan self / sunu mid sweordes ecge* 'thyself sacrifice [him] as an offering . . . and thyself sacrifice thy son with the edge of a sword.' With cruel delight this harsh God then conjures the image of the 'dark flame' that will 'burn the body of [Abraham's] beloved.'

I am sometimes almost tempted to believe that the Anglo-Saxon singer had been listening to a reading of Søren Kierkegaard's *Fear and Trembling* just before he dictated or wrote these verses. For his Abraham, the *rinc* 'warrior' whose *ellen* is tested by his *Cyning*, is surely that deeply moved "knight of the faith" the Danish philosopher imagines. Surely his soul shrinks at the first demand for the sacrifice, *þú scealt Ísaac mé / onsecgan . . .*; listens numbly to the detailed description of the climb; and dies in the final *sweartan líeȝe* of the *bæl-fýr*.

The Abraham who listens to this terrible speech moves swiftly as it ends: *sóna ongann / fýsan to fóre.*[15] He has only one thing left to do: 'to show that the terror of the Guardian of Spirits lived in his breast.' For two days and nights (the parallel with Christ's descent into hell would have leapt into the minds of the earliest audiences) he journeys over the waste land (*wegas ofer wǽsten* 'paths over the waste') until, at the dawn of the third, he sees the high hills towering to which the Prince of Heaven has directed him. Then at last he speaks to his two servants:

Þá Ábraham spræc   to his ambihtum:
"Rincas míne,   restaþ incit
hér on þissum wícum.   Wit eft cumaþ
siþþan wit ǽrende   uncer twœ́ʒa
Gást-cyninge   aʒiefen habbaþ."   (2880–84)

Then Abraham spoke to his servants: "My warriors, you
two remain here in this camp. We two shall come again
after we have given our message to the Spirit-King."

Abraham speaks with care. He uses the precise dual *wit* 'we
two,' not the vague plural form *wé*; and he repeats it: 'after
we two have given our message [*uncer* is also a dual form] to
the King of Spirits.' Abraham believes the exact opposite of
what he says: not "we two" but "I alone" shall return. But
we, of course, respond to the greater irony that encloses this
lesser one. *Wit* shall indeed return from this *ǽrend*; but not
before we have suffered symbolic death.

I do not think I am exaggerating the response of a reasonably sensitive listener to the lines that follow. These lines begin
with the lonely final climb of the father and son and their brief
and poignant dialogue:

ʒewát him þá se æðeling   and his ágen sunu
tó þæs ʒemearces   þe him Meotod tǽhte,
wadan ofer wealdas.   Wudu bær sunu,
fæder fýr and sweord.   Þá þæs fricgan ongann
wer wintrum ʒeong   wordum Ábraham:
"Wit hér fýr and sweord,   fréa mín, habbaþ;
hwǽr is þæt tífer   þæt þú torht Gode
to þǽm byrne-ʒielde   bringan þenćest?"
Ábraham maðelode   —hæfde on án ʒehogod
þæt hé ʒedǽde   swá hine Dryhten hét—:
"Him þæt Sóþ-cyning   Selfa findeþ,
mann-cynnes Weard,   swá Him ʒemet þynćeþ."
                            (2885–96)

The prince and his own son departed to that land which
the Lord showed [them], going through forests. The son

bore the wood, the father fire and sword. Then the
man young in years began to ask Abraham: "We two,
my lord, have here fire and sword; where is that offering
that thou thinkest to bring bright as a burnt offering to
God?" Abraham spoke—he had thought on one thing,
that he should do as the Lord commanded—"The True
King himself, Guard of Mankind, shall find that for himself, as seems to him fitting."

This dialogue only slightly expands the Latin of the Vulgate.
But at this point in the Latin text there is nothing to suggest
the three verses between *Ábraham maðelode* and his reply: 'he
had thought on one thing, that he should do as the Lord
commanded.' Abraham's utter loneliness speaks in these lines.
Then he hardens his heart to the very rocks he climbs: *ʒestág
þá stíþ-hyʒdiʒ / stéape dúne* 'brave-minded he then ascended
the steep mountains.'

The action accelerates. Abraham piles up the altar, kindles
the fire, suddenly fetters young Isaac's feet and hands, and
then raises him onto the altar, and then—I am translating, only
substituting the present tense for the preterit—quickly seizes
his sword by the hilt, is about to kill his son with his hands, to
quench the fire with the blood of his child. But this is how the
Anglo-Saxon singer tells it:

> Ongann þá ád hladan,   æled weććan,
> and ʒefeterode   fœt and handa
> bearne sínum   and þá on bæl ahóf
> Ísaac ʒeongne,   and þá ædre ʒegráp
> sweord be ʒehiltum,   wolde his sunu cwellan
> folmum sínum,   fýre scenćan
> mæʒes dréore.
>
>   [/]
>
>   þá Meotodes þeʒn,
> ufan enʒla sum   Ábraham hlúde
> stefne ćieʒde.   Hé stille ʒebád
> áres spræće   and þæm enʒle oncwæþ.   (2902–11)

I have purposely quoted beyond the point where I stopped translating. Only in that way could I hope to demonstrate the drama of the angel's intervention. Before that dramatic harp stroke in the middle of line 2908 the singer has moved swiftly to each stage of the action with the adverb *þá* 'then': *ongann þá, and þá, and þá*. After the harp stroke the single *þá* stands alone. Before that final *þá* the singer has pounded out an overpowering number of simple A verses, verses with no initial, internal, or final rest. In six and one-half lines he uses eight such verses, bearing down at the end with three in succession. There is no relief for Abraham. He is driven forward to the terrible deed by the very beat of the verse.

Then as Abraham raises his sword comes the blessed sound of the harp (/) and then the loud cry of the angel. Abraham, stilled, waits. The angel speaks:

Ábraham léofa, ne sleah þín ágen bearn
ac þú cwićne abreȝd cniht of áde,
eaforan þínne. Him ann wuldres God.
Magu Ebréa, þú médum scealt
þurh þæs Hálgan hand, Heofon-cyninges,
sóðum sigor-léanum selfa onfôn,
ȝinn-fæstum ȝiefum. Þý wile gásta Weard
lissum ȝieldan þæt þé wæs léofra His
sibb and hyldu þanne þín selfes bearn.

(2914–22)

Beloved Abraham, do not slay thine own child, but take thy son alive from the pyre. God grants him glory. Chief of Hebrews, thou shalt thyself receive rewards, true rewards of victory, broad gifts, from the hand of the Holy One, the Heaven-King. For this the Guardian of Spirits wishes to repay [you] happily, that his peace and loyalty were dearer to you than thine own son.

Abraham has won a victory, and with the *sigor-léan* of line 2919 the heroic ethos of the *rinc* and his *ellen* is transformed into a heavenly state. The *þín ágen bearn* of line 2914b echoes and transmutes into joyful relief the pain of *þín ágen bearn* of

God's harsh command at line 2852a. And the *selfa* of line 2919b would restore the human self to Abraham harshly denied in God's earlier repetition of the word.

Ád stód onǽled 'the pyre remained burning.' With these words we suddenly remember that life goes on. Abraham turns from the drama he has just enacted back to human concerns:

> Hæfde Ábrahame
> Meotod mann-cynnes, mǽȝe Lóthes,
> bréost ȝeblissod þá Hé him his bearn forȝeaf,
> Ísaac cwićne. (2923b–26a)

The Lord of Mankind had made happy Abraham's breast —kinsman of Lot—when He gave back to him his child Isaac alive.

The breast that had been filled with nothing but the awe of the Guardian of Spirits is now rejoiced with the return of his child. Abraham turns and sees the ram caught in the brambles. With a different haste he acts now, reddening his sword with the blood not of his son but of the ram. Joyfully he says thanks for all the rewards, those gifts that this *Cyning* pays his *rinc* in return for his *ellen*. The poem thus ends with a thanksgiving that is also a prayer.

IV

Earlier I suggested that I would make clear some of my reasons for agreeing with Bernard F. Huppé that the long poem *Genesis A* is properly completed with this passage. I think my commentary has already revealed my feeling that this drama is the high point and fine climax to a sometimes desultory poem. This drama itself curves upward to the altar and then downward to the final prayer of thanks.

Huppé argues that the Anglo-Saxon audience might have seen in the sacrifice of Isaac what Christian exegetes had seen and were indeed to make explicit, a prefiguring of the crucifixion of Christ.[16] I am led to agree with Huppé by a number of considerations and by one in particular. The second verse of line 2887 reads *wudu bær sunu*. *Wudu*, placed first for purposes of alliteration, is generally and correctly translated as an accusative. But it can also be translated—or rather, *heard* momentarily in Old English—as a nominative. The case of *sunu* is similarly ambiguous. The verse, then, can be caught both ways: 'son bore wood' and 'wood bore son'; or 'the Son bore the Cross,' and 'the Cross bore the Son.' In this remarkable punning line the offering of Isaac not only prefigures the crucifixion of Christ, it sharply figures—images—the later drama of Christianity. Isaac becomes the Son sacrificed in order to mediate between man and God.

The long narrative poem ends with a drama that is both time-bound in the past and timeless, at once the climactic event in the life of the patriarch and a pre-enactment of the central act and ritual of Christianity.

APPENDIX

This appendix is designed to serve two purposes: to provide, as a kind of experiment in practical criticism, a text of the final ninety-one lines of *Genesis A* marked for performance and to provide some indication of the formulas in the singer's repertory.

In his essay "Metrical Uses of the Harp in *Beowulf*" (see pp. 27–43 above) John Nist states, "So important is the harp for the rhythm of *Beowulf*"—and, one might add, the rhythm of almost all surviving Old English poetry—"that the poem itself cries for a future edition that will indicate the exact placing of every musical chord of the scop. Such an edition would be of incalculable value for bardic performance and critical commentary." I agree wholeheartedly, though I disagree at certain points with Nist's actual placing of the "harp chords." But the approach for which Nist so vigorously argues and for which Jess B. Bessinger, Jr., provides further evidence (see pp. 3–26 above) is one of the most exciting new paths to the study of Old English poetry.

In an effort to implement this approach for one particular text, I have marked that text in the following way. A vertical bar (|) before a syllable or a harp stroke indicates that that syllable or harp stroke begins a new isochronous measure. (Measure boundaries generally follow those analyzed by John Collins Pope in

THE OFFERING OF ISAAC

The Rhythm of Beowulf [New Haven, 1942], though my scansion of Old English poetry differs at points from that of Pope, on which, of course, it is ultimately based.) An acute accent (/) placed over a vowel indicates that the syllable that contains the vowel is long and receives primary stress. An acute accent placed over a consonant flanked by two vowels or by a vowel and a diphthong linked by a curved horizontal bracket indicates that the first of the two syllables thus bracketed is short but that the two syllables that flank the consonant must together be given primary stress (i.e., the stress is resolved over two syllables). A grave accent (\) placed over a syllable (or a consonant) indicates that that syllable (or resolved pair of syllables) receives secondary stress. No accent mark over a syllable indicates that that syllable, whether long or short, receives minimal stress. An acute accent or an x placed in parentheses over an empty space indicates either a vigorous harp stroke (/) or a lighter one (x).

In addition to these metrical notations I have employed Francis P. Magoun's indications of formulas (verses or measures repeated with little or no variation) and formulaic systems. Formulas are underlined with a continuous line; the variable element in a formulaic system is underlined with a dashed line, the nonvariables with a continuous line. I have also employed an indicator of my own, underdotting, to connect two elements of a formula separated by an insignificant intrusion. (For the principles and practice of this notation see Francis P. Magoun, Jr., "Oral-Formulaic Character of Anglo-Saxon Narrative Poetry," *Speculum*, XXVIII [July, 1953], 446–67.)

The text of the passage is that normalized by Magoun in *Anglo-Saxon Poems* (Cambridge, Mass., 1956), pp. 7–9.

GENESIS, LINES 2846–2936

|⁽ⁱ⁾ Þá þæs | rínces |⁽ⁱ⁾ se | ríca ongánn

| Cýning ⁽ˣ⁾| cóstian, | cúnnode | ʒéorne

|⁽ⁱ⁾ hwelć þæs | æðelínges | éllen | wǽre,

| stíðum | wórdum |⁽ⁱ⁾ spræc him | stéfne tó:

|⁽¹⁾ "ʒewít þú | ofostlíće, | Ábraham, | féran,   2850

| lástas | lécgan |⁽¹⁾ and þé | lǽde mid

|⁽¹⁾ þín | ágen bearn. |⁽¹⁾ þú scealt | Ísaac mé

on-|secgan, | sunu þínne, | self to | tífre.

| Siþþan þú ʒe-|stíʒest | stéapa | dúne,

| hrýcg þæs | héan landes |⁽¹⁾ þe ić þé | hínan ʒetǽće,   2855

| upp þínum | ágnum fótum, |⁽¹⁾ þǽr þú scealt | ád ʒeʒierwan,

| bǽl-fýr | bearne þínum, |⁽¹⁾ and | blótan self

| sunu mid | sweordes ecge |⁽¹⁾ and þanne | sweartan líeʒe

| léofes | líć forbǽrnan |⁽¹⁾ and mé | lác bebéodan."

Ne for|sæt hé þý | síðe |⁽¹⁾ ac | sóna ongann   2860

| fýsan to | fóre. |⁽¹⁾ Him wæs | Fréan engla

| word on-|drýsne |⁽¹⁾ and his | Wealdend léof.

|⁽¹⁾ Þá se | éadiga | Ábraham | síne

| niht-ræste of-|ʒeaf. ⁽ˣ⁾ |⁽¹⁾ Nealles | Neriendes

| hǽse wiþ-|hogode |⁽¹⁾ ac hine se | hálga wer   2865

| gyrde | grǽgan sweorde, |⁽¹⁾ cýþde þæt him | gásta Weardes

| eʒesa on | bréostum wunode. |⁽¹⁾ Ongann þá his | esolas bǽtan

| gamol-ferhþ | goldes brytta, |⁽¹⁾ hét hine | ʒeonge twǽʒen

| menn ⁽ˣ⁾ | mid síðian. | Mǽʒ wæs his | ágen þridda

|⁽¹⁾ and hé | feorða self. |⁽¹⁾ Þá hé | fús ʒewát   2870

|⁽¹⁾ fram his | ágnum hofe | Ísaac | lǽdan,

| bearn ^(X)| unweaxen, |^(I) swá him be-|béad Meotod.

| Œfste þá | swíþe |^(I) and | ónette

| forþ ^(X)| fóld-weʒe, |^(I) swá him | Fréa tǽhte

| wegas ofer | wǽstan, |^(I) oþ-þæt | wuldor-torht   2875

| dæʒes þriddan | upp ^(X) |^(I) ofer | déop wæter

| ord a-|rǽmde. |^(I) þá se | éadiga wer

|^(I) ʒeseah | hlífian | héa | dúna

|^(I) swá him | sæʒde ǽr | sweʒeles | Éaldor.

|^(I) þá | Ábraham sprǽc |^(I) to his | ambihtum: 2880

| "Rincas | míne, | restaþ |'incit

| hér on þissum | wícum. | Wit ^(X)| eft cumaþ

|^(I) siþþan wit | ǽrende | uncer | twœʒa

| Gást-^(X)| cyninge |^(I) a-|ʒiefen habbaþ."

ʒe|wát him þá se | æðeling |^(I) and his | ágen sunu   2885

|^(I) tó þæs ʒe|méarces |^(I) þe him | Meotod tǽhte,

| wadan ofer | wéaldas. | Wudu bær | sunu, ^(X)

| fæder ^(X)| fýr and swéord. |^(I) þá þæs | fricgan ongann

| wer ^(X)| wintrum ʒeong | wordum | Ábraham:

|^(I) "Wit hér | fýr and swéord, | fréa mín, | habbaþ;   2890

|^(I) hwǽr is þæt | tífer |^(I) þæt þú | torht Góde

|^(I) to þæm | byrne-ʒielde | bringan | þénćest?"

| Ábraham | maðelode |⁽ⁱ⁾—hæfde on | án ʒehógod

|⁽ⁱ⁾þæt hé ʒe-|dǽde |⁽ⁱ⁾swá hine | Dryhten hét —:

|⁽ⁱ⁾"Him þæt | Sóþ-cyning | Selfa | findeþ,   2895

|mann-cynnes | Weard,⁽ˣ⁾ |⁽ⁱ⁾swá Him ʒe-|mét þynćeþ."

|⁽ⁱ⁾Ʒestág þá | stíþ-hyʒdiʒ | stéape | dúne

| upp mid his | eaforan, |⁽ⁱ⁾swá him se | Œća bebéad,

|⁽ⁱ⁾þæt hé on | hrófe ʒestód | héan | landes

|⁽ⁱ⁾on þǽre | stówe |⁽ⁱ⁾þe him se | Stranga tó,   2900

| wǽr-fæst | Meotod,⁽ˣ⁾ | wordum | tǽhte.

|⁽ⁱ⁾Ongann þá | ád hladan, | ǽled | weććan,

|⁽ⁱ⁾and ʒe-|feterode | fét and | handa

| bearne | sínum |⁽ⁱ⁾and þá on | bǽl ahóf

| Isaac | ʒeongne, |⁽ⁱ⁾and þá | ǽdre ʒegráp   2905

| sweord be ʒe-|hiltum, |⁽ⁱ⁾wolde his | sunu cwellan

| folmum | sínum, | fýre | scenćan

| mǽʒes | dréore.

|⁽ⁱ⁾þá | Meotodes þeʒn,

| ufan⁽ˣ⁾| engla sum | Ábraham | hlúde

| stefne | ćieʒde. |⁽ⁱ⁾Hé | stille ʒebád   2910

| áres | sprǽće |⁽ⁱ⁾and þǽm | engle oncwæþ.

|⁽ⁱ⁾Him þá | ofostum tó | ufan of | rodorum

| wuldor-gást | Godes $^{(X)}$ | wordum | mǽlde:

| "Ábraham | léofa, |$^{(l)}$ ne sleah þín | ágen bearn

|$^{(l)}$ ac þú | cwićne abreȝd | cniht of | áde,   2915

| eaforan | þínne. |$^{(l)}$ Him ann | wuldres Gód.

| Magu $^{(X)}$ | Ebréa, |$^{(l)}$ þú | médum scealt

|$^{(l)}$ þurh þæs | Hálgan hand, | Heofon- $^{(X)}$ | cyninges,

| sóðum | sigor-léanum | selfa on-|fón, $^{(X)}$

| ȝinn-fæstum | ȝiefum. $^{(X)}$ |$^{(l)}$ Þý wile | gásta Weard   2920

| lissum | ȝieldan |$^{(l)}$ þæt þé wæs | léofra His

| sibb and | hýldu |$^{(l)}$ þanne þín | selfes bearn."

| Ád stód on-|ǽled. |$^{(l)}$ Hæfde | Ábrahame

| Meotod $^{(X)}$ | mann-cynnes, | mǽȝe | Lóthes,

| bréost ȝe-|blissod | þá Hé him his | bearn forȝeaf,   2925

| Ísaac | cwićne. |$^{(l)}$ Þá se | éadiga bewlát,

| rinc ofer | eaxle |$^{(l)}$ and him þǽr | ramm ȝeseah

| unfeorr | þanan $^{(X)}$ | ǽnne | standan,

| bróðor | Háranes, | brembrum | fæstne.

|$^{(l)}$ Þone | Ábraham ȝenam |$^{(l)}$ and hine on | ád ahóf   2930

| ofostum | mićelum |$^{(l)}$ for his | ágen bearn.

A-|brǽȝd þá mid þý | bille, | býrne-ȝield on-|hréad, $^{(X)}$

| réocendne | wíoh $^{(X)}$ | rammes | blóde,

|⁽ⁱ⁾ onbléot þæt | lác Góde, |⁽ⁱ⁾ sæȝde | léana þanc

and | eallra þára | sǽlða |⁽ⁱ⁾ þe Hé him | siþ and ǽr,   2935

| ȝiefena | Drýhten |⁽ⁱ⁾ for-|ȝiefen hæfde.

SUPPORTING EVIDENCE

2846a: cf. GEN 2153 *nylle ić þá rincas*; MXM I 177 *á scyle þá rincas.*
2846b: cf. GEN 1228 *þæt se eorl ongann*; AND 1126 *þá se ȝeonga ongann*; AND 1607 *þá se hálga ongann.* **2847b:** cf. DAN 218 *hogodon ȝeorne.* **2848a:** cf. AND 649 *swá ić þæs æðelinges*; JLN 37 *þe on þæs æðelinges*; BWF 1596 *þæt híe þæs æðelinges.* **2849a:** cf. EXO 438, EXO 522 *sóðum wordum*; CHR 342 *prístum wordum*; BWF 1172 *mildum wordum.* **2849b:** cf. GEN 684 *hío spræc him þicce tó*; PPs 98.7 *spræc him wordum to.* **2850ab:** cf. GEN 1746 *ȝewít þú nú fǽran.* **2850a:** cf. GLC 1327 *ȝewát þá ofostlíće*; cf. GEN 1746 *ȝewít þú nú fǽran*; GEN 2294 *ȝewít þú þinne eft*; GEN 2511 *ȝewít þú nerian þín*; cf. GEN 1316 *ongann ofostlíće*, etc., for *ofostlíće* as WMF. **2850b:** cf. GEN 1899 *Ábraham sprecan*; GEN 1945 *Ábraham wunode*; GEN 2020 *Ábraham sǽćan*; GEN 2069 *Ábraham sealde*; GEN 2370, GEN 2736 *Ábraham fremede*; GEN 2407 (Hypermetric) *árfæst wiþ Ábraham sprecan*; GEN 2729 *Ábraham settan*; GEN 2773 *Ábraham hæfde.*

2851a: GEN 2402 *lástas leȝdon*; GEN 2538 *lástas leȝde.* **2852a:** GEN 2398, EXO 419; GEN 2189 *ac þín ágen bearn*; GEN 2914 *ne sleah þín ágen bearn*; GEN 2614 *hire ágen bearn*; GEN 2789 *wiþ mín ágen bearn*; GEN 2806 *and his ágen bearn*; GEN 2931 *for his ágen bearn*; cf. ELE 1076 *Godes ágen bearn*; cf. GEN 2885 *and his ágen sunu.* **2853a:** cf. JLN 255 *onsecge sigor-tífre*; JLN 362 *onsæȝde synna fruman*; cf. GEN 1300, GEN 1599 *mid sunum þínum / sínum*; BWF 1226 *bío þú suna mínum*; BWF 2160 *ná þý ǽr suna sínum*; BWF 2729 *nú ić suna mínum.* **2854a:** cf. GEN 2883 *siþþan wit ǽrende*; EXO 155 *siþþan híe ȝesáwon*; EXO 384 *siþþan hé ȝelǽdde*; AND 1381 *siþþan þú forhogodes*; AND 1674 *siþþan þú mid mildse.* **2854b:** GEN 2897 *stéape dúne*; cf. GEN 2596 *héare dúne*; AZA 117 *hêa dúna.* **2855a:** GEN 2899 *hêan landes.*

2856b: cf. BWF 38 *ćéol ȝeȝierwan.* **2857a:** GEN 2904 *bearne sínum*;

THE OFFERING OF ISAAC

AND 1328 *bearnum mínum.* **2858a:** BRB 4 *sweorda ecgum*; cf. BWF 2961 *ecgum sweorda*; cf. BWF 1812 *méćes ecge.* **2858b:** GEN 1926, GEN 2507 *sweartan líeȝe.* **2860b:** cf. GEN 862 *þá sóna ongann*; AND 849 *hé sóna ongann.*

2861a: DHL 33 *fýsde hine þá to fóre*; cf. JUD 189 *fýsan to ȝefeohte.* **2861b:** cf. GEN 2837 *him Fréa engla*; cf. ELE 1307 *móton engla Fréan.* **2862b:** cf. GEN 339 *and his Hearran léof*; RUN 59 *his mágan léof.* **2863a:** JLN 105 *him þá sío éadiga*; cf. GEN 2834 *siþþan wæs se éadiga.* **2863b:** GEN 2677 *Ábraham, þíne.* **2864b:** cf. ELE 1064 *þe þæs Neriendes*; CHR 398 *ússum Neriende*; CHR 1498 *þínum Neriende*; GLC 658 *fore Neriende*; JUD 73 *þá wæs Neriendes*; cf. GEN 1285 *Neriende léof,* etc., for *Neriend(__)* as WMF. **2865a:** cf. JLN 42 *fæste wiþhogode.* **2865b:** DAN 333, AZA 49 *swá se hálga wer*; AND 168 *þær se hálga wer*; AND 1171, ELE 784 *þone hálgan wer*; AND 1395 *wæs se hálga wer*; GLC 108 *þæt se hálga wer.*

2866b: GEN 12 *gásta Weardum*; GEN 41 *gásta Weardas.* **2867a:** cf. GEN 191 *bám on bréostum,* etc., for *on bréostum* as F. **2867b:** cf. GEN 2219 *ongann þá ferhþ-ćeariȝ,* etc., for *ongann þá* as F. **2868a:** GEN 1997 *goldes bryttan.* **2868b:** cf. GEN 2425 *strange twǽȝen,* etc. for [*x*] *twǽȝen* as WVFS. **2869a:** cf. GEN 1734 *mid síðodon.* **2870a:** cf. AND 665 *hé wæs twelfta self*; ELE 854 *and hé wæs þridda self*; cf. DAN 354 *se þær feorða wæs.* **2870b:** cf. BWF 1263 *hé þá fáh ȝewát*; cf. GEN 1210 *ac hé cwić ȝewát.*

2871a: cf. GEN 2768 *mid his ágene hand.* **2871b:** cf. GEN 1357 *eaforan lǽdan,* etc., for [*x*] *lǽdan* as WVFS. **2872a:** cf. AND 1627 *eaforan unweaxne*; MLD 152 *hyse unweaxen*; DEG 11 *ćild unweaxen.* **2872b:** AND 789, VGL 38 *þe him bebéad Meotod*; cf. GEN 125 *swá Se Wyrhta bebéad,* etc., for a more common variation of this formulaic system. **2873b:** cf. GEN 2535 *þá ónette*; cf. GEN 1985 *hæleþ ónetton,* etc. **2874a:** cf. GEN 2050 *forþ framlíće / on fold-weȝe*; cf. GEN 2512 *feorh fold-weȝe*; ELE 215 *fǽran fold-weȝe*; PNT 51 *faraþ fold-wegum*; BWF 866 *þær him fold-wegas*; cf. GEN 2050 *on fold-weȝe,* etc., for *fold-weȝe* as WMF. **2874b:** cf. GEN 2886 *þe him Meotod tǽhte.* **2875a:** cf. AND 198 *wegas ofer wídland.* **2875b:** cf. GEN 119 *þá wæs wuldor-torht.*

2876b: BRB 55; cf. GEN 1331 *ȝeond déop wæter*; BWF 1904 *drǽfan déop wæter.* **2877a:** cf. EXO 411 *upp arǽmde.* **2877b:** GEN 2234, GLC 1224; GEN 1476 *þá-ȝíet se éadiga wer*; GEN 1562 *þæt se éadiga wer*; GLC 590 *him se éadiga wer*; GLC 1105 *swá se éadiga wer.* **2878a:** cf. GEN 1820 *ȝeseah Egypta*; cf. GEN 1321 *ȝearu hlífian,* etc., for *hlífian* as WMF; cf. GEN 2405 *ʒesáwon ofer since | salu hlífian*. **2878b:** GEN 2596 *héarra dúne*; AZA 117 *hêa dúna*; cf. GEN 2854 *stéapa dúne*. **2879a:** GEN 2648 *mé sæʒde ǽr*; MBO 25.54 *iċ þé sæʒde ǽr*. **2879b:** GEN 862, GEN 2542, GEN 2808; JUD 88 (Hypermetric) *forʒief mé, sweʒeles Ealdor*; cf. XST 123 *sweʒeles bryttan*; CHR 543 *sweʒeles ágend*. **2880a:** cf. GEN 1744 *þá se hálga spræc*; BWF 1698 *þá se wísa spræc*. **2880b:** cf. GEN 518 *his ambihtu*, where *ambihtu* means 'message, bidding'; cf. CHR 370 *ára nú ambihtum*; MBO 11.9 *þe þæs ambihtes*.

2881a: AND 1343. **2882a:** cf. GEN 1890 *wunodon on þæm wícum*; GEN 2572 *on þæm wícum*; PHX 470 *swá nú on þæm wícum*; PHX 611 *ne biþ him on þæm wícum*; RDL 49.4 *hwílum on þæm wícum*; BWF 1612 *ne nam hé on þæm wícum*; cf. GEN 2061 *hlynn wearþ on wícum*; cf. GEN 1738 *on þæm wícum his*. **2882b:** cf. AND 400 *hwænne þú eft cyme*; cf. BWF 281 *bót eft cuman*; BWF 1869 *snúde eft cuman*; cf. JUD 146 *wæs þá eft cumen*; MBO 20.13 *ʒe eft cumaþ*; MBO 29.83 *hǽtt eft cuman*. **2883a:** cf. GEN 557 *ne mæʒ his ǽrende*, etc., for *ǽrende* as WMF. **2883b:** GEN 1835. **2884a:** cf. BWF 2 *þéod-cyninga*, etc., for [*x*]-*cyning*( ) as WVF. **2884b:** AND 296; GEN 1506 *aʒiefen hæfde*; cf. GEN 2936 *forʒiefen hæfde*. **2885a:** cf. GEN 2162 *ʒewát him þá se healdend*; AND 225 *ʒewát him þá se hálga*; BWF 1963 *ʒewát him þá se hearda*; cf. GEN 1730 *ʒewát him þá mid cnósle*; cf. AND 990 *hæfde þá se æðeling*; JLN 164 *híe þá se æðeling*. **2885b:** cf. GEN 2806 *and his ágen bearn*; GEN 2189 *ac þín ágen bearn*; GEN 2852 *þín ágen bearn*.

2886b: cf. GEN 2874 *swá him Fréa tǽhte*. **2887a:** cf. ORW 61 *wadan ofer wegas*. **2888a:** cf. GEN 2890 *wit hér fýr and sweord*. **2888b:** ELE 157; cf. ELE 570 *þæt hío friʒnan ongann*, etc. **2889a:** cf. MLD 210 *wiga wintrum ʒeong*. **2889b:** cf. GEN 2625 *Ábraham wordum*. **2890a:** cf. GEN 2888 *fæder fýr and sweord*. **2890b:** cf. DAN 585 *ʒehyʒe þú, fréa mín*; GLC 1222 *ǽr þú mé, fréa mín*.

2891a: cf. PPS 113.10 *hwǽr is hira ágen god*; MBO 10.44 *hwǽr is nú se ríca*. **2892a:** cf. PPS 105.17 *him to God-ʒielde*. **2892b:** cf. EXO 51 *wiernan þóhton*, etc., for [*x*] *þenċan* as WVFS. **2893a:** GEN 1820; cf. BWF 286 *weard maðelode*, etc., for [*x*] *maðelode* as WVFS. **2893b:** cf. CHR 1549 *and on án cweðan*; JLN 69 *hío mé on án sagaþ*; cf. CHR 969 *þrío eall on án*; PPS 82.9 *ealle þá on án*; PPS 132.1 *þætte bróðor on án*. **2894b:** GLC 703 *se meċ Dryhten hét*; cf. AND 5 *swá him Dryhten self*. **2895a:** cf. GEN 2636 *ongann þá sóþ-cyning*; JLN 224, MBO 20.246 *þæt is sóþ-cyning*; MXM I 134 *self sóþ-cyning*;

PPs 120.7 *sáwla sóþ-cyning*. **2895b:** cf. GEN 514 *selfa habban*, etc., for *selfa* plus verb as WVFS. **2896ab:** cf. MBO 29.41 *mann-cynnes fruma / swá him ȝemet þynćeþ*. **2896a:** GEN 2758; CÆD 7. **2896b:** BWF 687 *swá Him ȝemet þynće*; BWF 3057 *swá Him ȝemet þúhte*; MBO 29.41 *swá him ȝemet þynćeþ*. **2897a:** cf. ELE 121 *stópon stíþ-hyȝdiȝe*. **2897b:** See GEN 2854. **2898b:** GEN 2370; cf. HOM I 39 *swá him God bebéad*. **2899a:** See BWF 404 *þæt hé on heo[r]ðe ȝestód*, etc., for this WVFS. **2899b:** GEN 2855. **2900a:** DHL 100, DHL 104 *hú þú on þǽre stówe*; cf. GEN 2524 *on þǽre stówe wé*; cf. GEN 1912 *téon of þisse stówe*; ELE 716 *stópon þá to þǽre stówe*; ELE 802 *þá of þǽre stówe*; JLN 636 *and to þǽre stówe*. **2901a:** GEN 1320; GEN 1549 *wǽr-fæst Meotode*; cf. GEN 1740 *wǽr-fæst hǽle*; GEN 2026 *wǽr-fæst hæleþ*. **2901b:** cf. GEN 1823 *wordum lǽran*; cf. EXO 528 *módum tǽćan*. **2902a:** See GEN 2867. **2902b:** cf. BWF 2046 *wíȝ-bealu weććan*. **2903a:** GEN 168 *and ȝefetero* . . . **2903b:** cf. BWF 745 *fǽt and folma*. **2904a:** GEN 2857 (Hypermetric) *bǽl-fýr bearne þínum*. **2904b:** cf. GEN 2930 *and hine on ád ahóf*. **2905a:** cf. GEN 2926 *Ísaac cwićne*. **2905b:** cf. GEN 2296 *Hío þá ǽdre ȝewat*.

2906a: cf. BWF 1574 *heard be hiltum*. **2907a:** GEN 1010 *folmum þínum*; GEN 2172 *folmum mínum*; GEN 2814, AND 522, RDL 61.3 *folmum sínum*. **2908b:** cf. GLC 708 *ić eom Meotodes þeȝn*; GLC 1243 *meahtiȝ meotodes þeȝn*; cf. GEN 1574 *siþþan wuldres þeȝn*, etc., for [*x*]'*s þeȝn* as WMFS. **2909a:** cf. GEN 1034 *weorðeþ wráðra sum*, etc., for [*x*] (in gen. pl.) *sum* as WMFS. **2910a:** cf. GEN 1807 *torhtum ćieȝde*. **2910b:** cf. EXO 300 *mere stille bád*; EXO 551 *here stille bád*; BWF 301 *flota stille bád*.

2911a: cf. GLC 1220 *gǽstes sprǽće*. **2911b:** cf. GEN 2347 *hé þá Meotode oncwæþ*. **2912b:** DAN 508, SLB I 27; cf. GEN 306 (Hypermetric) *féollon þá ufan of heofonum*. **2913a:** cf. GEN 2298 *Godes ǽrend-gǽst*. **2913b:** AND 300, JLN 351; cf. GEN 707 *wordum sæȝde*, etc., for *wordum* [*x*] as WVFS. **2914ab:** cf. GEN 2398 *þín ágen bearn, / Ábraham léofa*. **2914a:** GEN 2254, GEN 2398. **2914b:** GEN 2852 *þín ágen bearn*. **2915b:** cf. GEN 2801 *cniht of cýþþe*.

2916a: GEN 2185 *eaforan síne*; GEN 2212 *eaforan þíne*; GEN 2224 *eaforum þínum*; GEN 2363 *eaforan þínum*; EXO 412 *eaforan sínne*. **2916b:** cf. AND 1661 *þá him wuldres God*; cf. DAN 277 *þæt wæs wuldres God*; AND 758 *weorðan wuldres God*; AND 1510 *wrát, wuldres God*; GLC 1081 *þæt ić wuldres God*; JLN 180 *and wuldres*

GENESIS AND SHORTER POETRY

God; PPs 68.6 *þú wást, wuldres God*; MBo 20.57 *hwæt, þú wuldres God*. **2917a:** GEN 2205, GEN 2413, GEN 2675. **2918a:** cf. ELE 86 *þurh þæs Hálgan hǽs*. **2918b:** GEN 237 (dat.), GEN 628, GEN 659, GEN 712, EXO 410 (dat.), CHR 1086, GLC 617; see GEN 2884 *Gástcyninge*. **2919a:** cf. JLN 174 *sópum ȝieldum*; cf. CHR 1589 *to sigorléanum*. **2920a:** JLN 168 *ȝinn-fæste ȝiefe*; BWF 1271 *ȝinn-fæste ȝiefe*; BWF 2182 *ȝinn-fæstan ȝiefe*; MBo 20.227 *ȝinn-fæsta ȝiefa*. **2920b:** cf. ELE 1021 *swá hire gásta Weard*. **2921a:** cf. EXO 150 *fácne ȝieldan*. **2922a:** cf. BWF 2922 *sibbe oþþe tréowe*. **2922b:** cf. GEN 1593 *ongann þá his selfes bearn*. **2923a:** cf. GLC 668 *ád onǽled*; JLN 580 *ád onǽlan*. **2923b:** cf. GEN 1729 *Sarra Ábrahame*, etc., for *Ábrahame* as WMF. **2924a:** GEN 459, GEN 1947, XST 64, XST 457, XST 513, AND 69, AND 172, AND 357, AND 446, CHR 244. **2925a:** cf. AND 351, ELE 989 *mód ȝeblissod*; AND 468, GLC 722 *gǽst ȝeblissod*; JLN 287 *ferhþ ȝeblissod*. **2925b:** cf. GEN 2718 *and him his wíf aȝeaf*. **2926a:** cf. GEN 2905 *Ísaac ȝeongne*. **2926b:** cf. JLN 627 *þá sío éadiȝe beseah*. **2928a:** cf. BWF 1805 (C verse) *wolde feorr þanan*; cf. GEN 2083 *unfeorr wǽron*. **2928b:** RDL 49.1 *ánne standan*; cf. AND 882 *íowić standan*; AND 1448 *ðearwas standan*; AND 1494 *stapolas standan*; BWF 2271 *opene standan*. **2929a:** GEN 2621. **2929b:** cf. AND 130 *clammum fæste*; AND 184, AND 1357 *bendum fæstne*; AND 962, AND 1038 *bennum fæstne*; ELE 252, CHR 863 *ancrum fæst(n)e*; DAN 516 *eorðan fæstne*; PHX 172 *wrytum fæstne*; RDL 52.7 *bendum fæstra*; BWF 2718 *stapolum fæste*. **2930b:** cf. GEN 2904 *and þá on bǽl ahóf*.

2931a: GEN 2504, GEN 2673, XST 627, ELE 44, ELE 102, ELE 999; JUD 10 (Hypermetric) *híe þæt ofostum mićelum*; JUD 70. **2931b:** see GEN 2852. **2933a:** cf. JUD 313 *réocendu hrǽw*. **2933b:** cf. MBo 9.59 *eorla blóde*. **2934b:** BWF 1809 *sæȝde him þæs lǽnes þanc*; cf. GEN 238 *and sæȝdon ealles þanc*; GEN 725 *sæȝde bǽȝra þanc*. **2935a:** cf. GLC 606 *eallra þára ȝiefena*. **2935b:** CHR 602 *þe ús síþ and ǽr*; cf. BWF 2500 *þæt mec̀ ǽr and síþ*; cf. ELE 240 *ne hierde ić síþ ne ǽr*; ELE 572 *ne ǽr ne síþ*; JLN 548 *þæt ić ǽr ne síþ*; cf. ELE 975, CHR 1067, MNL 200 *þára þe síþ oþþe ǽr*; ELE 74 *þonne hé ǽr oþþe síþ*; CHR 893 *þára þe ǽr oþþe síþ*; CHR 1052 *þæt híe ǽr oþþe síþ*; GLC 369 . . . *ǽr oþþe síþ*.

2936a: cf. ELE 346 *sigora Dryhten*. **2936b:** CHR 1399, GLC 1133; cf. GEN 2884 *aȝiefen habbaþ*.

THE OFFERING OF ISAAC

NOTES

1. A version of this paper was read before the Medieval Section of the Foreign Language Conference of the University of Kentucky at its April, 1962, meeting. I am indebted to Sarita Gattis Schotta (Mrs. Charles Schotta, Jr.) for her assistance in locating the formulas and formulaic systems of the final forty-one lines of *Genesis A*.

2. The prose version has been edited by S. J. Crawford for the Early English Text Society (Original Series, Vol. CLX) under the title *The Old English Version of the Heptateuch, Aelfric's Treatise on the Old and New Testament and His Preface to Genesis* (London, 1922). Chap. xxii of the Old English translation of Genesis, along with the Vulgate text, appears on pp. 141–43. A drawing in the MS illustrating the offering of Isaac is reproduced as the frontispiece opposite the title page of the volume.

3. Quotations from Old English poetry in the text, footnotes, and appendix are cited in the normalized spelling of *Anglo-Saxon Poems Represented in Bright's Anglo-Saxon Reader*, ed. Francis P. Magoun, Jr. (Cambridge, Mass., 1956). Magoun's excerpt from *Exodus* appears on pp. 9–10 and generally follows the text prepared by Edward B. Irving, Jr., *The Old English Exodus* ("Yale Studies in English," Vol. CXXII [New Haven, 1953]).

4. *Anglo-Saxon Poems Represented in Bright's Anglo-Saxon Reader*, ed. Magoun, pp. 7–10. I should like to note here that the idea of comparing these texts came to me from seeing them printed side by side in Magoun's valuable classroom text. It is a great pleasure to express again my deep indebtedness to my master and friend.

5. I use the word singer as Magoun uses it in his important essay "Oral-Formulaic Character of Anglo-Saxon Narrative Poetry," *Speculum*, XXVIII (1953), 446–67. It is quite possible that the *Genesis* and *Exodus* poets were also literate, though we are unlikely to be able to prove this point. We can, however, prove that each was trained in the traditional and originally oral art of song-making.

6. A detailed tabulation of these results for the *Genesis* passage appears in the accompanying appendix.

7. The supporting evidence for the passage analyzed from *Exodus* (verses 397a–406b) is as follows: **397a** *To þæm mæðel-stede*: AND 658; cf. EXO 543, DAN 145, BWF 1082, MLD 199 *on þæm mæðel-stede*; cf. AND 697 *fram þæm mæðel-stede*; cf. ELE 554 *on mæðel-stede*. **397b** *magan ȝelædde*: cf. GEN 1357 *eaforan lædan*, etc., for [x] *lædan* as a WVFS (Whole Verse Formulaic System). **398a** *Ábraham Ísaac*: AND 793 *Ábraham and Ísaac*. **398b** *ád-fýr onbearn*: cf. PPs 79.15 *fýr onbærneþ*. **399a** *fyrst ferhþ-bana*: cf. GEN 2088 *freora feorh-banan*; cf. GEN 1033 *mé to ealdor-banan*. **400b** *líeȝe ȝesellan*: cf. GEN 2508 *fýre ȝesellan*. **401a** *on bæl-blýse*: DAN 231; cf. GLC 676 *ne on bæl-blæsan*. **401b** *bearna sælest*: PRA 68. **402a** *his swæsne sunu*: cf. CHR 1148 *hira swæsne wlite*; GLC 984

9 1

hira swǽsum were. **402b** *to siʒe-tífre*: cf. JLN 255 *onsecge sigor-tífre.* **403a** *ángan ofer eorðan*: RDL 88.18 *ánga ofer eorðan.* **403b** *ierfe-láfe*: BWF 1053, BWF 1903, PPs 77.70. **404a** *féores frófre*: cf. BWF 628 *firena frófre.* **405a** *léodum to láfe*: cf. EXO 509 *ǽniʒ to láfe*: AND 1081 *ǽniʒne to láfe.* **405b** *langsumne hyht*: cf. GEN 1757 *langsumne niþ*, etc., for *langsum(n)e* as WMF (Whole Measure Formula). **406** *hé þæt ʒecýþde | þá hé þone cniht ʒenam*: cf. DHL 79 *þæt þú ʒecýþdest | þá þú þone cniht to ús.* **406a:** XST 199 *hé þæt ʒecýþde*; DHL 79a. **406b:** cf. DHL 79b (above).

8. Perhaps I should say, more cautiously, by the two songs. Yet this essay attempts to provide some of the evidence for my belief that *Genesis A* and *Exodus* are the work of two different singers.

9. "On the Possibility of Criticizing Old English Poetry," *Texas Studies in Literature and Language*, III (Spring, 1961), 97–106.

10. *The Old English Exodus*, ed. Irving, Introduction, p. 29.

11. *Ibid.*

12. *Ibid.*

13. *The Singer of Tales* (Cambridge, Mass., 1960), p. 79.

14. The passage of ninety-one lines from *Genesis A* is read in Old English on band 10, side II, of *Lyrics from the Old English*, read by Burton Raffel and Robert P. Creed (Folkways Record No. FL 9858; New York, 1964). In the appendix to the present essay I have marked harp strokes (/ or x over empty spaces) at places where in the recording I take carefully timed pauses (in the absence of a harp). In the passages quoted in the body of this essay I have marked the harp stroke at only one powerfully significant point: between the two verses of line 2908. Perhaps this is the place to note that, in recording this powerful telling of the sacrifice of Isaac, I attempted to distinguish only three voices: the voice of the reverent narrator, the puzzled but dutiful voice of Isaac, and the voice of Abraham—a harsh, commanding voice as he tells himself in his dream to sacrifice his own son; a sharply excited and later proudly happy voice as he speaks to himself as the angel; and a flat, almost hypnotized voice as he speaks first to his retainers and then to the son he must sacrifice. That all three voices are indeed Abraham's is, of course, a matter of interpretation.

15. Indeed, as the dissyllabic anacrusis in verse 2860a seems to indicate, Abraham is in motion even before God ends his speech.

16. See "The Caedmonian *Genesis*," in *Doctrine and Poetry: Augustine's Influence on Old English Poetry* (Albany, N.Y., 1959), pp. 131–210, especially pp. 204–6.

THE DREAM OF THE ROOD:

PATTERNS OF TRANSFORMATION

Louis H. Leiter

In a dream, in a vision of the night,
When deep sleep falleth upon men,
In slumberings upon the bed;
Then he openeth the ears of men,
And sealeth their instruction,
That he may withdraw man from his purpose,
And hide pride from man.
He keepeth back his soul from the pit,
And his life from perishing by the sword.

(Job 33:15–18)

The Dream of the Rood[1] is concerned with a process of salvation by means of radical transformation that involves three actors in a universal spiritual crisis. Metamorphosis informs the structure of the poem and gives life and significance to its aesthetic materials.

In presenting these transformations, the poet has recourse to Christian tradition—to the Passion of Christ, the story of the Cross, and the hoped-for conversion of fallen mankind. For poetic reasons the poet casts the Passion, the drama of the Cross, and the salvation of the Dreamer into a series of three almost identical dramatic metaphors that reinforce each other contrapuntally. By this means he achieves amplification, progression, and cohesion among his metaphors. But the metaphors, being dramatic, are also dynamic: they are incremental, varied, and transmuted; they progress through a series of dramatic climaxes. In their final resolution they project a new life, a new state of being, for the three performers—Christ, Cross, and Dreamer.

The drama of the first two performers, Christ and Cross, must be regarded in a special light, that is, not as exclusive historical happenings, but as what might be called rehearsals—actions that demonstrate a method, a way of achieving spiritual rejuvenation. But it is the Dreamer who, through identification of his fate with the radically contrasted experiences—mundane and yet eschatological—of Christ and Cross, validates and enlarges their common fate.

The poem, then, is concerned with the religious experience, but not in the form of belief, or of conversion, or of revelation, or of the nature of any of these, but religion in the sense of change—human transformation. Hence metamorphosis is used quite deliberately and literally for two reasons: the transformations of the performers and, congruent with their change, the transformation of the structure, imagery, and thematic materials of the poem.

For these dramas the poet chose materials close at hand, experience from a daily life that was animated by memories of a pagan past and incidents from his encounter with biblical story. Then, taking the vocabulary of warfare of which he had intimate knowledge,[2] he constructed the three identical dramas that form the poem: the defeat and paradoxical victory of Christ, the hewing down and raising up of the Cross, and the sleep and awakening of the stained and sinful Dreamer.

CHRIST

In the first of these dramatic metaphors the young hero, *frea . . . mancynnes* (33b), who is either king, prince, or lord, has been defeated in battle. This defeat the Cross points up by saying *heton me heora wergas hebban* 'they ordered me to lift up their criminals' (31b). The defeated hero proves he still has the hero's *ellen*, however, since he *efstan elne mycle* 'hastened with great boldness' (34a) and *Gestah he on gealgan heanne* 'ascended the high gallows' (40b). He is tortured, pierced with *deorcan næglum* 'dark nails' (46a), which leave *opene inwid-hlemmas* 'open malicious wounds' (47a), treated ignominiously, while *Bysmeredon hie unc butu ætgædere* 'they mocked us both together' (48a). The prince, *weruda god* 'god of hosts' (51b), is then further tortured and executed, his death being *pearle penian* 'violently extended[?]' (52a). *Weop eal gesceaft,* / *cwiðdon cyninges fyll* 'all creation wept, mourned the fall of the king' (55b–56a). Reinforcements come: *Hwæðere þær fuse feorran cwoman* / *to þam æðelinge* 'still eager ones came from afar to that prince' (57–58a), but these *hilderincas* 'warriors' (61b) find that they cannot save their lord. He is dead: *beheoldon hie ðær heofenes dryhten, ond he hine ðær hwile reste,* / *meðe æfter ðam miclan gewinne* 'there they beheld the lord of heaven, and he rested there for a time, tired after the great struggle [battle, or war]' (64–65a).

They bury him:

> Ongunnon him þa moldern wyrcan
> beornas on banan gesyhðe . . .
> gesetton hie ðæron sigora wealdend.   (65b–67a)

Then men began to make him a tomb in the sight of the murderers . . . in it they then put the lord of victories.

In this act can be seen a paradoxical foreshadowing of his return to life and eventual victory. Like the comitatus around a fallen prince—those around the burned Beowulf, for instance—the warriors, eager but mournful reinforcements, gather to sing funeral songs: *Ongunnon him þa sorhleoð galan* 'they then began to sing a dirge' (67b). The grief-stricken *mæte weorode* 'little band' (69b) remain with their lord: *syððan stefn up gewat* / *hilderinca* 'the cry of warriors went up' (71b–72a), until *Hræw colode,* / *fæger feorgbold* 'the body grew cold, the lovely abode of the soul' (72b–73a).

The poet continues to amplify the battle metaphor: now physically defeated by the enemy, *strange feondas* (30b), but spiritually victorious, the warrior-hero-prince rises phoenix-like from the flames of death: *hwæðere eft dryhten aras* / *mid his miclan mihte mannum to helpe* 'yet again the lord arose with his great strength as a help to men' (101b–2). Consequently, *Hiht wæs geniwad | mid bledum ond mid blisse þam þe þær bryne þolodan* 'hope was renewed with blessedness and with joy to those who had earlier suffered from fire' (148b–49a). Like a warrior-prince, he returns from exile in the foreign country of his captors and executioners: the prince *cwom | . . . þær his eðel wæs* 'came . . . where his native land was' (155b–56b), where he will join his people *to symle* 'at the feast' (141a) of victory.

There are rather complex emotional overtones generated here for which this bare rehearsal of the cohesive metaphor of battle does not completely account. Doubtless the metaphor would serve to capture the emotions of a people to whom warfare was as familiar as their daily bread and catch them up in the excitement of its drama. Their memories and fears would be stirred, but the effect here goes deeper. By identifying with the protagonist of the clearly wrought struggle, the listeners would unconsciously submit to the mimetic powers of the metaphor, supported, to be sure, by the rhythm of the verse, for the poet has at his command means other than that of dramatic metaphor. For example, he achieves emotional heightening by repetition of half-lines, often beginning with the same word, as in the insistent *ongunnon . . . ongunnon* in the two lines *Ongunnon him þa moldern wyrcan* (65b) and *Ongunnon him þa sorhleoð galan* (67b). These two heavily emphasized and paralleled beginnings, echoing an earlier line in which the tree *ongan þa word sprecan* 'began to speak words' (27a), are supported and emphasized with two statements beginning similarly with very strongly dramatic verbs: *curfon hie ðæt of beorhtan stane* (66b) and *gesetton hie ðæron sigora wealdend* (67a).

Repetition, parallelism, shifting of the verb of action to the semantically (though not rhythmically) important initial position, and hints that the message of the Cross is the Word of Christ (*ongan þa word sprecan*) are all deliberate devices for underscoring the significance of the drama enacted in the cohesive metaphor of battle. At the same time they are fairly simple devices of a stylization that achieves emotional heightening precisely at the necessary moment in the battle metaphor. The warrior-hero is dead; his men have had the spirit knocked out of them. Then comes the cluster of sounds *on, un, mo, an, no, or, en, am* in the following lines:

Ongunnon him þa *mo*ldern wyr*can*
beor*nas on b*a*nan* gesyh*ð*e;   curf*on* hie *ð*æt of beorht*an* st*ane*,
gesett*on* hie *ð*æ*ron* sigo*ra* weald*end*.   *Ongunnon* him þa
sorhleo*ð* gal*an*
earme *on* þa æf*en*tide,   þa hie wold*on* eft si*ð*i*an*,
me*ð*e fr*am* þ*am* mær*an* þeod*ne*.   (65b–69a)

In their profound resonance they mime the importance of the climactic change. Thus dramatic ending and equally dramatic beginning demand and receive in various ways the proper aesthetic emphasis.

Not the least of the devices at the poet's command is that which he employs to emphasize the transformation from the paralysis accompanying grief to the activity accompanying release from grief. After using three images of stasis within the space of two lines—*limwerigne* (63a), *gestodon* (63b), and *reste* (64b)—to characterize the astonishment and moral perplexity of the witnesses of the dramatic execution, the poet immediately calls in verbs of action—*ongunnon, curfon, gesetton, ongunnon*—to signal a rebirth, a new beginning, of the spirit in the emotionally depleted men at the exact moment they entomb their warrior-hero-Christ. The transformation is mimed here rather than overtly presented; it is like an echo or the passing of a dark shadow that cannot but emotionally move the reader or listener.

The poet and the warriors of Christ seem to catch their breaths for one shocked moment; then, releasing them, they move into action. Through this action they inspire their defeated neighbors, much as the Cross does the Dreamer, with those breaths of hope without which they cannot rebuild their exhausted moral lives and achieve victory over death. The poet dramatizes this inspiration when he sings of the raising and adorning by the prince's comitatus of the felled and buried Cross. Spiritually changed by participation in the drama of hero-Christ, the men symbolically spiritualize the Cross by adorning it with jewels, thus making it worthy of its future office. In turn, the spiritualized Cross repeats their action when it appears to the Dreamer and ministers to him, admonishing him to minister to other men by carrying its sign in his breast, much as the poet now sings to his rapt audience.

When in the battle metaphor the poet uses *fyll* 'fall,' 'destruction,' or 'death,' in *Weop eal gesceaft,* | *cwiðdon cyninges fyll* 'all creation wept, mourned the fall of the king' (55b–56a), the word is precisely the one that enriches his battle metaphor with the necessary spiritual overtones. Literally, *fyll* refers to the disobedience and fall of Adam, the connotation needed at this juncture to link the death of warrior-Christ in the present drama with the fall of Adam in that old chaos of the Garden, the effect of which is still evident in the felled tree and prostrate speaker. The metaphorical *fyll, aheawen, licgende,* and *þa us man fyllan ongan* | *ealle to eorðan* (73b–74a) of the singer fuse Adam, Cross, tree, and Dreamer in one perpetually repeated drama of loss and redemption, much like the three detailed repetitions of the battle metaphor. The *Rood* poet could depend on his listeners' acquaintance with the doctrine that all mankind rebelled with Adam when he forfeited supernatural life by his transgression in tasting the forbidden fruit. Adam, the first Christ, was "the figure of him that was to come" (Rom. 5:14); "For since by man came death, by man came also the resurrection of the dead. For as in Adam all die, even so in Christ shall all be made alive" (I Cor. 15:21–22); "The first man Adam was made a living soul; the last Adam was made a quickening spirit" (I Cor. 15:45). Singing of the *cyninges fyll*, the poet could quite naturally depend on his audience's hearing 'fall,' automatically recalling Adam, remembering the Dreamer—and making the proper identifications.

The poet constantly expands the battle metaphor through his use of fairly commonplace religious material until it links events in the distant past, Adam's fall, for instance, to events in the more recent past, the felling of the tree and the fall of Christ to the sleeping Dreamer, now lying stained with sins and forgetful of those old tragedies.

What is perfectly clear is the identification of the fall of Adam with the execution of Christ and of the drama of the tree bearing the forbidden fruit with the drama of the Cross bearing the redemptive body—the "firstfruits" of I Cor. 15:20–23: "But now is Christ risen from the dead, and become the firstfruits of them that slept. For since by man came death, by man came also the resurrection of the dead. For as in Adam all die, even so in Christ shall all be made alive. But every man in his own order: Christ the firstfruits; afterward they that are Christ's at his coming."

>   þæt . . . is wuldres beam,
> se ðe ælmihtig god   on þrowode
> for mancynnes   manegum synnum
> ond Adomes   ealdgewyrhtum.   (97b–100)

that . . . is the tree of glory on which God Almighty suffered for the many sins of mankind and Adam's deed of old.

Because Adam sinned in the past, Christ must suffer now; because Adam-man still sins, Christ must re-enact and reverse that drama of the Fall by waging war (thus the central metaphor of battle) against man's Adamic self still enthralled by His old foe Satan. It was in this manner that legend and dogma saw in Adam an antitype to Christ and maintained that the tree whose fruit was forbidden Adam and Eve was the one that served as the Cross of the Crucifixion. The concept that Christ "in his own self bare our sins in his own body on the tree, that we, being dead to sins, should live unto righteousness: by whose stripes ye were healed" (I Pet. 2:24) lies behind the poet's use of the word *fyll* to dramatize Christ's death on the Cross, the evocation of Adam's name in line 100a, and the fallen Dreamer lying as though in death.

The Adam-Christ tradition persisted well into the seventeenth century with notable examples in Donne's *Hymne to God My God, in My Sicknesse*: "We thinke that Paradise and Calvarie, / Christs Crosse, and Adams tree, stood in one place." Or a somewhat more complex version in Crashaw's *Vexilla Regis, The Hymn of the Holy Crosse*:

> Hail, our alone hope! Let thy fair head shoot
> Aloft; and fill the nations with thy noble fruit.
> The while our hearts and we
> Thus graft our selves to thee;
> Grow thou and they. And be thy fair increase
> The sinner's pardon and the just man's peace.

Crashaw clearly fuses tree (crucifix), noble fruit (Christ), sinful man (Adam), with the Prince of Peace; and to that he grafts the just man so that all participate in one grand drama of salvation.

The subtle chemistry of *The Dream of the Rood* strengthens the contrasted identification of Adam and Christ by evoking the legend that saw a connection between Adam's forfeit of mankind to Satan and his ransom by Christ: *Gestah he on gealgan heanne, / modig on manigra gesyhðe, þa he wolde mancyn lysan* 'he ascended the high gallows bold in the sight of many, when he wished to redeem mankind' (40b–41).

Amplifying and reinforcing his basic battle metaphor by choosing the dramatic *lysan* 'redeem' or 'ransom,' the poet directs our attention to the reward demanded for captured warriors. Because it is biblical, 'redeem' also refers to Christ's incarnation in order to purchase forfeited man from that Satan whom the poet characterizes as the enemy: "Even as the Son of man came not to be ministered unto, but to minister, and to give his life a ransom for many" (Matt. 20:28).

An even more apt identification might be made in this manner among Dreamer, Cross-messenger, and Job, who, like the Dreamer, lies sorely wounded (though unlike Job, the

Dreamer admits he is stained with sins): "Yea, his soul draweth near unto the grave, and his life to the destroyers. If there be a messenger with him, an interpreter, one among a thousand, to shew unto man his uprightness: Then he is gracious unto him, and saith, Deliver him from going down to the pit: I have found a ransom" (Job 33:22–24). The *Rood* poet will return to this idea at the end of the poem: *He us onlysde ond us lif forgeaf, / heofonlicne ham* 'He redeemed us [or released us] and gave us life, a heavenly home' (147–48a). That the Lord is a 'ransom' deepens our immediate experience with the familiar Christian materials by pointing to the dramatic metaphor of war and the reward that must be paid the enemy for worthy captives.

But in religious poetry literal fact usually points to spiritual significance. 'Ransom' encompasses sacrifice and redemption, the fundamental ritual of the poem—a ritual that we celebrate through the stained and fallen Dreamer, Cross, and Christ and conversely through the purified Christ, Cross, and Dreamer. Man like Christ and Cross must lose his life to save it: "He that findeth his life shall lose it: and he that loseth his life for my sake shall find it" (Matt. 10:39). In the Mass for the celebration of the finding of the Holy Cross the congregation repeats the prayer after the Gloria: "O God, we were reminded again of the mystery of your passion by the miraculous discovery of the cross of salvation. May we attain eternal happiness through the ransom price you paid for us on that tree of life; who lives and rules with God the Father." In this manner the Church Fathers identified Adam's eating of the forbidden fruit and the consequent forfeiture of man with the ransom paid by Christ on the Cross, seen metaphorically as "the tree of life."

The *Rood* poet strengthens his Adam-Christ identification by recourse to the legend that Adam or his skull or both were buried on Mt. Calvary. He alludes to it when he uses *beorg* in *hie me on beorg asetton* (32b). The word primarily denotes a mountain or hill, yet by its secondary meaning, 'barrow' or 'burial place,' it may direct our attention to the iconographical image of Adam's skull at the foot of the Cross. Because of Adam's fault the world has become a cemetery very much like Ezekiel's valley of dry bones: "The hand of the Lord was upon me, and carried me out in the spirit of the Lord, and set me down in the midst of the valley which was full of bones, And caused me to pass by them round about. . . . Prophesy upon those bones, and say unto them, O ye dry bones, hear the word of the Lord. Thus saith the Lord God unto these bones; Behold, I will cause breath to enter into you, and ye shall live: . . ." (37:1–5). Because of Christ's supreme compassion, Golgotha, that place of the skull and hill of bones, along with the fallen world, the sinful Adam, and the Dreamer lying beneath the towering Cross, shall be redeemed.

The poet gives even greater coherence to the Adam-Christ and tree-Cross identification by employing the imagery of food and eating. Speaking of the execution of the captured warrior-Christ in the battle metaphor, he says *Deað he þær byrigde* 'he tasted death there' (101a) for *Adomes ealdgewyrhtum* 'Adam's deed of old' (100). Adam tasted the fruit; Christ tasted death; now man must perform the same bitter act:

> hwær se man sie,
> se ðe for dryhtnes naman deaðes wolde
> biteres onbyrigan, swa he ær on ðam beame dyde.
> (112b–14)

where is the man who is willing to taste bitter death for the Lord's name as he himself did earlier on the Cross.

But only from this willing act comes salvation: "For if we have been planted together in the likeness of his death, we shall be also in the likeness of his resurrection: Knowing this, that our old man is crucified with him, that the body of sin might be destroyed, that henceforth we should not serve sin. For he that is dead is freed from sin" (Rom. 6:5–7). To purchase salvation and the forfeited paradise, with its eschatological banquet like that at the end of *The Dream of the Rood*, man must taste bitter death as Christ tasted bitter death because

Adam tasted the fruit that exiled us from a blissful kingdom. Christ above all men chose to taste the death that would open the way for exiled man. "But we see Jesus . . . by the grace of God should taste death for every man" (Heb. 2:9).

This ritualistic metaphor of spiritual transformation is amplified further when the Dreamer describes where the Cross will take him:

> þær is blis mycel,
> dream on heofonum, þær is dryhtnes folc
> geseted to symle . . . (139b–41a)

where there is great joy, happiness in heaven, where the Lord's people are placed at the feast . . .

Here at the end of the poem he emphasizes the emotionally charged transformation by contrasting his fallen world with that restored paradise through the simple device of repeating powerful parallelisms: *þær is blis mycel* (139b), *þær is dryhtnes folc* (140b), *þær is singal blis* (141b), *þær ic syþþan mot* (142b), and *þær his eðel wæs* (156b). To summarize the fusions and identifications thus far: As Adam tasted the fruit and brought death, so warrior-Christ tasted the fruit of death; and the Dreamer must taste death with and for his Lord (his present dark night of sleep) in order to taste an eternal feast of life after death.

Thus the fallen Dreamer, representing all sinful men, lying now stained with mortal sins, has been fused with the fallen Adam. Then the poet identifies the Dreamer with the man willing to accept that death for Christ that the Cross endured earlier. Finally, the Dreamer undergoes another transformation identifying him with Christ, who will return to heaven with *þam þe þær bryne þolodan* 'those who earlier suffered from fire' (149b) after the Harrowing of Hell, much as the Dreamer hopes to return to man's lost paradise where he will join the messianic banquet.

Ideas much like these are stated more didactically in *The Phoenix*:

Swa þæt ece lif   eadigra gehwylc
æfter sarwræce   sylf geceoseð
þurh deorcne deað,   þæt he dryhtnes mot
æfter geardagum   geofona neotan
on sindreamum,   ond siþþan a
wunian in wuldre   weorca to leane.
Þisses fugles gecynd   fela gelices
bi þam gecornum   Cristes þegnum
beacnað in burgum,   hu hi beorhtne gefean
þurh fæder fultum   on þas frecnan tid
healdaþ under heofonum,   ond him heanne blæd
in þam uplican   eðle gestrynaþ.   (381–92b)

So is it
With each of the blessed, bearing misery
And choosing the darkness of death for themselves
In order to find eternal life
And the protection of God, repaying pain
On earth with endless glory and endless
Joy. For the Phoenix is very like
The chosen servants of Christ, who show
The world and its towns what comfort and pleasure
Descends from our Father's solace, and how,
In this dangerous time, they can take His grace
As a certain sign of lofty glory
To be lived in that celestial land above.[3]

More obviously in *The Phoenix* than in *The Dream of the Rood* not only Christ but the people suffering in the flames are identified with the immortal bird. We also observe that both Phoenix and Cross come to the chosen and both are seen as ministering agents of grace.

The poem employs a final image to present the dramatic transformation from a lower to a higher spiritual level: stripping, a simple symbolic gesture, reveals the true man. Traditionally the stained garment that is put aside symbolizes the false man, the old Adam, the heavy burden of sinful flesh.

When Christ's foes captured him and brought him to the gallows for execution *Ongyrede hine þa geong hæleð, (þæt wæs god ælmihtig), / strang ond stiðmod* 'the young hero—that was God Almighty—stripped himself strong and resolute' (39–40a). The allusion is to the biblical text: "ye have put off the old man with his deeds; And have put on the new man, which is renewed in knowledge after the image of him that created him" (Col. 3:9–10). To disobey as the old Adam did is to put on the garments of sinfulness; the new Adam, Jesus Christ, must be stripped of those garments before crucifixion. Put off the old Adam and put on the new Christ, as in Shakespeare's "old Adam new-apparelled" (*Comedy of Errors*, IV, iii) and as in his *King Lear*, where the sinful old man is freshly clothed before he rises from what he thinks is the grave. In *Everyman* the hero, varying the symbolism of the ritual action, strips off the old garments, scourges himself, and puts on the robe of contrition:

Knowlege:	It is a garment of sorrowe;
	Fro payne it wyll you borrowe:
	Contrycyon it is
	That getteth forgyenes;
	He pleaseth God passyinge well.
Good Dedes:	Eueryman, wyll you were it for your hele?
Eueryman:	Now blessyd be Iesu, Maryes sone,
	For now haue I on true contrycyon . . .

Ritualistic stripping transformed the tree, ravished from the woods, stripped of the fruit of Christ's body, and *steame bedrifenne* 'covered over with blood' (62a) into the vehicle of redemption. It becomes the guide to the heavenly banquet, after the little band around Jesus had found it and *gyredon me golde and seolfre* 'adorned me with gold and silver' (77), suggestive, perhaps of the prophet Malachi: "Behold, I will send my messenger, and he shall prepare the way before me: and the Lord, whom ye seek, shall suddenly come to his temple, even the messenger of the covenant, whom ye delight in: behold, he shall come, saith the Lord of Hosts. But who may abide the day of his coming? and who shall stand when he appeareth? . . . And he shall sit as a refiner and a purifier of silver: and he shall purify the sons of Levi, and purge them as gold and silver . . ." (3:1–3). The once stripped but now adorned Cross *leohte bewunden* 'surrounded with light' (5b) and bearing gems *swylce þær fife wæron / uppe on þam eaxlege-spanne* 'there were five up on the shoulder-beam' (8b–9a) symbolizes, by contrasting the five bloody wounds with the five shining gems,[4] the dynamic process of physical and spiritual transformation lying at the heart of the poem. Having been stripped, mocked, slain, buried, and resurrected, the Cross and Christ became one. The Cross, the first Adam's tree, served as a bloody gallows, but through consciously sharing warrior-Christ's fearful experience, it changed, like Ezekiel's valley of bones, into a quickening spirit, into a guiding sign:

> syllicre treow
> on lyft lædan,   leohte bewunden,
> beame beorhtost.   (4b–6a)

a marvelous tree, stretching [leading] aloft, surrounded with light, the brightest of beams.

This sign *ærþan . . . him lifes weg / rihtne gerymde, reord-berendum* 'opened the true way of life to the people' (88b–89). So neatly does the *Rood* poet's language enrich and amplify his basic metaphor that if we are not careful we might miss the significance of 'stretching' in the expression *on lyft lædan*: extension, expansion, or stretching in space, as the poet well knew, symbolizes at once both God's suffering on the Cross and his dominion over the universe. John Donne also knew this when in "A Valediction: Forbidding Mourning" he identified his lovers with the beatified and then declared that, although separated, their two souls:

> endure not yet
> A breach, but an expansion,
> Like gold to ayery thinnesse beate.

Now all of this points directly to the central drama of the Dreamer who, as he lies *mid sorgum gedrefed, | forht . . . wæs for þære fægran gesyhðe* 'stained with sins, sorely wounded with evil deeds' (20b–21a), shares the stripping-adornment imagery with the Cross and Christ, but he does this only by extension of previous resemblances, by, as we might say, final association. No specific image pictures the Dreamer's being stripped and adorned; nevertheless, he does rise from his defeat, no longer stained with wounds, but carrying in his breast the 'best of signs.' He is changed, transformed, into a man:

> blíðe mode,
> elne mycle, þær ic ana wæs
> mæte werede. (122b–24a)

with great zeal, happy in mind, there where I was alone with little company.

In this, one of the many parallels linking the three major actors in the redemptive drama, the Dreamer thus reminds us that, like the Cross and warrior-Christ on Calvary, he has only a *mæte werede* 'a little company' with him.

The significant act of stripping and adorning functions ritualistically as a *metanoia* for the dreamer because it renders mimetically the biblical text that avows that it is necessary to strip off the old man Adam and ritualistically to adorn oneself with the Cross in order to release the new man Jesus Christ from his enthrallment in the dark prison of the human heart. To bear the Cross on the human body or to carry 'in one's breast,' as the Dreamer declares, 'the best of signs,' is dynamically and dramatically to suffer death on the Cross with Christ, while purging, by means of ritual lustration, the old enemy of mankind.

The poem thus seems to contain a vivid metaphor of war, capture, execution, and apparent death that leads para-doxically to a purgation and transformation of the protagonist of the metaphorical drama. The metaphor contains a redemp-tive truth stated as a perennial paradox: man may save his life by losing it; though the spirit be incarnate in the flesh, that flesh may undergo purification through suffering until such time as flesh and spirit become one in God. Furthermore, the mimetic action contained in this metaphor will, as though to reinforce its communal and ritual aspects, be repeated twice in the exfoliating design of the poem, with the Cross and Dreamer as protagonists.

From another point of view the metaphorical battle would dramatize a timeless transformation going on inside man always, a continuous inward process of defeat and victory, much as the dream or vision is internal, personal, yet universal, a ritual of spiritual conversion. Creating that drama of salvation, like a profound and insistent glow, the imagery illuminates, with its literal meanings and subtle connotations, the significance to all men of the Dreamer's transformational experience.

THE CROSS

Defeated and captured as though in battle, the Cross *wæs aheawen holtes on ende, | astyred of stefne minum* 'was cut down at the edge of the wood, taken from my stem' (29–30a). *Genaman me ðær strange feondas* 'strong foes seized me there' (30b) and exiled it: *Bæron me ðær beornas on eaxlum, oððæt hie me on beorg asetton, | gefæstnodon me þær feondas genoge* 'men carried me on their shoulders, until they placed me on a hill, enemies enough fastened me there' (32–33a). Enslaved and ordered to perform their tasks, the Cross declares that they *geworhton him þær to wæfersyne, heton me heora wergas hebban* 'they made me into a spectacle for them, ordered me to lift up their criminals' (31). Commanded not to counterattack by its lord, the Cross says *Ealle ic mihte | feondas gefyllan, hwæðre ic fæste stod* 'I could have killed all foes, yet I stood fast' (37b–38a). Now the warrior-Cross is *þurhdrifan ... mid deorcan næglum* 'pierced with dark nails' (46a) and wounded: *On me syndon þa dolg gesiene, | opene inwidhlemmas* 'the wounds are visible on me, the open malicious wounds' (46b–47a); *eall ic wæs mid strælum forwundod* 'I was all wounded with darts' (62b). Ignominiously mocked, *Bysmeredon hie unc butu ætgædere* 'they mocked us both together' (48a), the Cross is tortured: *Feala ic on þam beorge gebiden hæbbe / wraðra wyrda* 'I endured on that hill many cruel experiences' (50–51a). Then the Cross is killed, *þa us man fyllan ongan / ealle to eorðan* 'people began to cut us down completely to the earth' (73b–74a), and buried, *Bedealf us man on deopan seaþe* 'they buried us in a deep hole' (75a).

Like the warrior-Christ, the Cross is raised and adorned with symbolic riches:

> Hwæðre me þær dryhtnes þegnas,
> freondas gefrunon,
> ond gyredon me   golde ond seolfre.   (75b–77)

Still the disciples of the Lord heard of me and adorned me with gold and silver.

Though defeated, the Cross paradoxically becomes a *sigebeam* 'cross of victory' (127a) and returns to its native land, the kingdom of the spirit:

> ac ðurh ða rode sceal   rice gesecan
> of eorðwege   æghwylc sawl,
> seo þe mid wealdende   wunian þenceð.   (119–21)

every soul who proposes to dwell with the Lord must seek the kingdom away from earth through the Cross.

Through a felicitous use of imagery the poet deepens our dramatic involvement with the fate of the Cross much as he did with the fate of Christ. The Cross refers to itself as a vehicle, a means of passage from this earth to the heavenly kingdom in the lines just quoted, while the Dreamer declares that the Cross *on þysson lænan life gefetige / ond me þonne gebringe þær is blis mycel* 'will fetch me from this transitory life and bring me where there is great joy' (138–39). The poet's language here would surely have evoked images of rituals and their emotional meanings, for it sounds very much like the Preface to the Holy Cross from the Mass that is read from

Passion Sunday through Wednesday of Holy Week: "It is truly right and just, proper and helpful toward salvation, that we always and everywhere give thanks to you, O Lord, holy Father, almighty and eternal God; for you ordained that the salvation of mankind should be accomplished upon the tree of the cross, in order that life might be restored through the very instrument which brought death, and that Satan, who conquered us through the tree, might also be overcome by it."

If the instrument that brought death becomes the vessel of salvation, perhaps it will not be amiss to see that the secondary meaning of the words used for 'cross' express through a most familiar image its function as a vehicle of redemption. *Beam* (6a), *wudu* (27b), and *beam* (97b) can all mean 'ship' as well as 'cross,' and *sigebeam* (127a) could connote 'ship of victory' as well as 'cross of victory.' This conjecture would then be strengthened by reading *on lyft lædan* (5a) as 'leading aloft.' Without pressing the poetic idea too far, however, we might recall that St. Hippolytus in the third century wrote: "The world is a sea, in which the Church, like a ship, is beaten by the waves but not submerged." And we are all acquainted with the architectural nave (ship), the main body of the church in which the congregation gathers. In the sixteenth century Donne could still write *A Hymne to Christ* in which he evokes much the same idea:

> In what torne ship soever I embarke,
> That ship shall be my embleme of thy Arke,
> Whence sea soever swallow mee, that flood
> Shall be to mee an embleme of thy blood . . .

Donne's subtle poetic sensibilities complicate what is in *The Dream of the Rood* a simple idea by identifying the church with Noah's ark or the ark of the covenant, the sea with the Flood (sea-whale with poet-Jonah), and the universal lustration of the Flood with the purgation-regeneration of Christ's blood. *Gestigan* (34b) means 'to mount,' yet it also strengthens the connotations suggested here through its secondary meaning, 'to go on board,' as does *holmwudu* (91a) by suggesting an ocean ship. And all these link back to *on lyft lædan* (5a).

Much of what I have been calling attention to here—the Cross as vehicle—is part of the hymn *Crux Fidelis* sung in the Reproaches of the Good Friday Mass, and it seems to confirm what at first may appear to be pure conjecture: the tree-Cross, the adorned Cross, the food-tasting imagery, the wounds of sinfulness, the Flood as an antitype of the world's lustration through Christ's sacrifice. The hymn goes:

> See His side is open now,
> Whence to cleanse the whole creation
> Streams of blood and water flow.

Then all of this is united in the verse that reads:

> Tree which solely was found worthy
> Earth's great victim to sustain,
> Harbor from the raging tempest,
> Ark, that saved the world again,
> Tree with sacred blood anointed
> Of the lamb for sinners slain.

Here we have a marvelous series of transformations of tree to Cross, to harbor, to ark, to Cross, to doorposts anointed with the blood of the sacred passover lamb, and none of it causes the slightest confusion. Nor apparently did it in *The Phoenix*, where we must follow the rapid metamorphosis of the old phoenix to a corpse, to an apple, to a worm hatched as though from an egg (apparently referring to the brazen serpent lifted up in the wilderness, Jesus rather than Satan), to an eaglet, to an eagle, and finally, to a rejuvenated phoenix that is not only Jesus Christ but all mankind:

>   Þonne fyr þigeð
> lænne lichoman;   lif bið on siðe,
> fæges feorhhord,   þonne flæsc ond ban
> adleg æleð.   Hwæþre him eft cymeð
> æfter fyrstmearce   feorh edniwe,

siþþan þa yslan   eft onginnað
æfter ligþræce   lucan togædre,
geclungne to cleowenne.   Þonne clæne bið
beorhtast nesta,   bæle forgrunden
heaþorofes hof;   hra bið acolad,
banfæt gebrocen,   ond se bryne sweþrað.
Þonne of þam ade   æples gelicnes
on þære ascan bið   eft gemeted,
of þam weaxeð wyrm,   wundrum fæger,
swylce he of ægerum   ut alæde,
scir of scylle.   Þonne on sceade weaxeð,
þæt he ærest bið   swylce earnes brid,
fæger fugeltimber;   ðonne furþor gin
wridað on wynnum,   þæt he bið wæstmum gelic
ealdum earne,   and æfter þon
feþrum gefrætwad,   swylc he æt frymðe wæs,
beorht geblowen. . . .

             Swa se fugel weorþeð
gomel æhter gearum,   geong edniwe,
flæsce bifongen.   (219b–59a)

           And then it's gone,
Flesh and bone burned in the flames
Of a funeral pyre. Yet, in time
He returns, his life re-born after
The flames drop lower, and his ashes begin
To fuse together in a shrivelled ball,
After that brightest nest is burned
To powder and that broken body, that valiant
Corpse, slowly starts to cool.
The fire flickers out. The funeral
Pyre sprouts a rounded apple
Out of a bed of ashes, and that pellet
Sprouts a wonderful worm, as splendid
As though hatched from a lustrous, pale-shelled egg.
He grows, flourishing in the holy shade
And soon the size of an eaglet, soon,

Fattening on pleasure, as large in form
As any proud-winged eagle. Then
His feathers return and he is as he was
At the beginning, blossomed brightly to life
And eternal beauty. . . .
So the Phoenix grows, dropping a thousand
Years and taking on youth.

Here the image of ashes reminds the listeners of Adam's original clay and hell's fire; the apple reminds them of the Fall and the fruit of the tree of life; the worm recalls Satan and the brazen serpent, Nehushtan-Christ. Yet these complexities enrich rather than confuse: Cross is both tree and vessel, Christ is both serpent and savior, phoenix is both God and man. Only these paradoxes are capable of suggesting the full nature of the spiritual experience. For the experience is not only profound and complex; it goes beyond the visible and the mundane, and this relating of images is an attempt to express what is hidden, inward, and miraculous.

In the *Crux Fidelis* and *The Phoenix* the very rapid transformations through which the poet carries the Cross and the bird become a device through which he forces individual images to bear a massive burden of meaning. In *The Dream of the Rood* the rapid transformations in such a passage as the following accomplish much the same thing, while at the same time serving as a graphic demonstration of the central transformational process dramatized in the battle metaphor:

> Eall ic wæs mid sorgum gedrefed,
> forht ic wæs for þære fægran gesyhðe.   Geseah ic þæt fuse
> beacen
> wendan wædum ond bleom;   hwilum hit wæs mid wætan
> bestemed,
> beswyled mid swates gange,   hwilum mid since gegyrwed.
> (20b–23)

> I was all completely troubled with sorrows;
> I was afraid because of the beautiful vision. I saw the
> hastening sign

Vary in hanging and colors; at times it was wet with
    moisture,
Stained with the flow of blood, and at times adorned with
    treasures.

After the transfigured tree has become a cross, it is then
imbued with the numinous. Miming possible future trans-
figuration for the similarly stained Dreamer, it also symbolizes
the dramatic means by which man attains wholeness and salvation. By suffering with the Cross and Christ in a similar
transformational experience, the Dreamer undergoes an identical metamorphosis and elevation of spirit.

This passage has vividly dramatized for the benefit of the
Dreamer a visual presentation of the process of transformation, ranging from a depleted spiritual state ('stained with
blood') to an exalted one (symbolized by 'adorned with
treasure'). Similarly, transformation is also dramatized in the
parallel phraseology of *hwilum hit wæs mid wætan bestemed*
(22b) and *hwilum mid since gegyrwed* (23b), which strongly
contrast the beginning and the end of the spiritual change. The
Rood poet reinformed this illumination of the Dreamer's inner
vision by making him observe the changing light surrounding
the Cross and by the gradual metamorphosis of his own
insight through a series of 'I saw' phrases that dynamically
pass from the Dreamer's 'I thought that I saw' to tree, to sign,
to master, to God, in this manner: *þuhte me þæt ic gesawe
syllicre treow* (4); *Geseah ic wuldres treow* (14b); *Geseah ic þæt
fuse beacen* (21b). But when the phrase is next repeated, it
incorporates the image of God, and it is the Cross that speaks,
because, having shared Christ's pain, it can truly say *Geseah
ic þa frean mancynnes* (33b); *Geseah ic weruda god* (51b).
"Seeing" in the rhythm of the transformation drama has
become a metaphorical way of expressing involvement in
suffering, death, burial, and resurrection. The next change
occurs at the end of the drama of the Cross when the phrase
undergoes a transformation itself and becomes *Ic þæt all
beheold* 'I beheld all that' (58b)—"to behold" has taken on the

additional meaning "to be involved in the painful experience itself." Because of all this the Cross plays the role of a *beacna* (118b) and towers in the heavens above the Dreamer who miraculously beholds, not at the end, but at the beginning of his own transformational experience, all the heavenly hosts gazing at the Cross: *Beheoldon þær engel dryhtnes ealle, / fægere þurh forðgesceaft* 'all the angels of the Lord, fair through all time, gazed on it there' (9b–10a). Parallelism of phraseology, stylization of syntax, and accretion to words of unfamiliar connotations strongly emphasize the steps through which the Dreamer passes in his spiritual transformation.

Nor is this all. Toward the end of the historical explanation that passes into the hortatory address to future action (and as a matter of fact suddenly transcends the battle metaphor), the Cross suddenly refers to 'Mother Mary' without any apparent preparation for the simile:

> Hwæt, me þa geweorðode wuldres ealdor
> ofer holmwudu, heofonrices weard!
> Swylce swa he his modor eac, Marian sylfe,
> ælmihtig god for ealle menn
> geweorðode ofer eall wifa cynn. (90–94)

> Lo! Then the Prince of Glory, the Lord of Heaven,
> Honored me above the other trees of the forest
> Just as God Almighty for the sake of mankind
> Also honored his Mother Mary above
> All the race of women.

The various elements of the poem cohere so faithfully that we unconsciously expect and immediately understand the relationship of a Cross that opens the true way of life to the people and the Virgin Mary whom God honored *ofer eall wifa cynn*. We have seen that the *Rood* poet manipulated Adam's fall in such a manner as to fuse it with Christ's crucifixion, the tree with the Cross, the instrument of death with the vessel of salvation. Now, relying on the same technique, the poet apparently assumes that we will think of Eva, the mother of death and type of Mary. In *The Dream of the Rood* this identification and contrast of the two women is strengthened by the earlier evocation of the Adam-Christ contrast. The churchman, the poet, and the playwright had no difficulty in entertaining and enjoying such manipulations of names. They saw the saiutation "Ave" made to the Mother Mary, who brought new life to man, as a reversal of Eva (*e vae* 'from woe'). Certainly something very much like this appears in the Breviary hymn *Ave, maris stella*, but perhaps its appearance in the drama will indicate its common currency. In the Hegge *Salutation and Conception* Gabriel descends to Mary and says:

> *Ave, Maria, gratia plena, Dominus tecum!*
> Heyl, fful of grace, God is with the!
> Amonge alle women blyssyd art thu!
> Here this name Eva is turnyd Ave;
> That is to say, with-owte sorwe ar ȝe now.
>
> Thow sorwe in ȝow hath no place,
> Ȝett of ioy, lady, ȝe nede more;
> Therefore I adde and sey "ful of grace,"
> ffor so ful of grace was nevyr non bore. (220–28)

And something very much like this appears in the Wakefield *Annunciation.*

The transformative, spirit-bearing Cross becomes the sign of rebirth for the Dreamer; the intercessive Mother Mary becomes the vessel of birth for Christ, the warrior-hero, and through him for all mankind. Mary, the Mother who reopened the gates of heaven, is linked with the Cross that performs the same function in *The Dream of the Rood* for the transformed Dreamer. The antiphon for the purification of the Blessed Virgin Mary begins, "Embrace Mary, for she is the very gate of heaven who brings to you the glorious king of the new light." In the Litany of the Virgin, the Mother of Christ is variously symbolized as "Vessel of Honor," "Ark of the Covenant," "Gate of Heaven," and "Morning Star." Gate and Cross, Virgin and tree are even more closely linked through the "root" image in the Compline, final antiphon to the Blessed Virgin Mary:

> Hail, Queen of Heaven!
> Hail, Lady of the Angels!
> Salutation to thee, root and portal,
> When the Light of the world has arisen.

Symbolized by the sky at daybreak, Mary, the Queen of Heaven, the Morning Star, in turn symbolizes the root from which the Son grows to become that tree of life whose fruit all men shall share in paradise—the eschatological banquet at the end of the poem.

Both Cross and Virgin "opened the true way for all people," and the Dreamer learns from their metamorphic experiences. When he rises transformed from his slumber of death, he will do as the Cross commands:

> þæt ðu þas gesyhðe   secge mannum,
> onwreoh wordum   þæt hit is wuldres beam,
> se ðe ælmihtig god   on þrowode
> for mancynnes   manegum synnum
> ond Adomes   ealdgewyrhtum.   (96–100)

that thou tellest this sight to men, make clear by words that this is the tree on which God Almighty suffered for the many sins of mankind and for Adam's deed of old.

The poet validates to some extent this conjecture by linking the Dreamer to the sinful Adam, for as Adam stained all mankind and closed the gates, the Dreamer, who has been transformed by his vision, will rise from his sleep (symbolic of indolence, ignorance, and at its worst, death from the woundings of sin) and like Christ and Cross bear the glad tidings of lustration to other men.

THE DREAMER

"For what else is Christ but the word, the sound of God? So the word is this upright beam on which I am crucified; and the sound is the beam which crosses it, the nature of man; but the nail which holds the center of the cross-beam to the upright is man's conversion and repentance."[5]

All transformations and identifications have been for the benefit of the Dreamer, who must be provoked into the metamorphic experience, into a radical change from stained and fallen man into a spiritualized being. Not surprisingly, his transformation imitates and profoundly participates in the dramatic metaphor of war traced with the Cross and Christ. The metaphor of the Christian warrior is common property of the New Testament, Old English poetic tradition, and religious thought through the ages. It is found, for instance, in the secret prayer for the Mass celebrating the finding of the Holy Cross: "May the sacrifice we offer be pleasing to you, O Lord. Let it free us from all the evils of war and destroy the pitfalls prepared by our powerful enemy, so that we may be safely protected under the banner of your son's cross. Through the same Jesus Christ, our Lord." The post-Communion prayer reads: "We have been nourished by the food of heaven and refreshed by spiritual drink. Shield us from our evil enemies, O Almighty God, for you have commanded us to fight through to victory under the cross of your Son, the weapon of justice that will save the world. Through the same Jesus Christ, our Lord." Perhaps even more important for this poem is the appearance of the warrior-hero in the final victory of Christ as described in Revelation: "And I saw heaven opened, and behold a white horse; and he that sat upon him was called Faithful and True, and in righteousness he doth judge and make war. . . . And the armies which were in heaven followed him upon white horses, clothed in fine linens, white and clean" (19:11–14).

The dramatic portrayal of this metaphor of the warrior-Cross and the warrior-God no longer stained but "clothed in fine linens, white and clean" is duplicated with the Dreamer, now a warrior-hero, as the protagonist. His battle has already been waged when the poem opens, and he apparently has been defeated. Cut down by the enemy, he lies bleeding from his wounds in a death-sleep, *ic synnum fah* 'I stained with sins [or injuries]' (13b). He is grievously wounded, *forwunded mid wommum* 'sorely wounded with evil deeds' (14a), and suffers, *Eall ic wæs mid sorgum gedrefed* 'I was completely troubled with sorrows' (20b); *ic þær licgende lange hwile / beheold hreowcearig hælendes treow* 'lying there for a long time, I looked sorrowfully at the Cross' (24–25). Then follows a lacuna in the logical, dramatic development of the battle metaphor, but it is that gap that is of most importance for the dynamic transformation of the warrior-Dreamer.

The warrior, we should observe, frames the poem with his visionary experience and his joyous future life after that vision ends. Within this frame, as within his mind, there occur the dramas of Christ and the Cross. Thus the experience of the Dreamer frames that of the Cross, and that of the Cross frames that of Christ, as though one had to pass through the agency of the Cross to reach the Lord. Precisely symbolic, the structures of the three frames—really three almost identical dramatic battle metaphors—point to Christ and his archetypal experience, the redemptive drama as the magnetic center, the spiritualizing and transformative power of the source of life. The second frame, the story of the Cross, points towards the nucleus that is Christ and outward towards the Dreamer, thus symbolizing something very much like an agent of grace.

Moving inward from the outer frame, we meet, first, the defeated Dreamer, then the defeated tree, and at the heart of the poem, the defeated Christ, followed by references to Adam (who seems to represent all that is gross, weighty, base, and stained in the Dreamer) and Mary (who represents all that releases, gives life, and fructifies in the Dreamer). Moving outward, then, from that transcendent center, we experience, first, the victory of Christ, then the victory of the Cross, and finally the victory of the Dreamer, who has been spiritualized by having lived through, while vicariously participating in, the vivid drama of that numinous center and its immediate frame. Within the frame of the Dreamer's experiences they—Cross and Christ—suffer battles, captures, executions mockeries, burials; yet they suffer not so much for themselves but precisely for the transformation of the defeated warrior-Dreamer. Another way of stating this would be to say that the outer frame contains earthy, Adamic man, sunk in sin and evil deeds, asleep or dead, and in need of radical transformation. This objective outer frame is united with the subjective center —Cross and Christ as redemptive forces—through a dramatic participation of the Dreamer in the Eucharistic vision that takes place in his own sleeping mind as a kind of internal illumination. Personal, subjective, psychic, but sacramental, this process transforms the spirit of the Dreamer because the cohesive battle metaphors consistently reveal his identity with the fallen Adam, the paradoxical destructive-creative Cross, and the resurrected Christ.

Some seventy lines after the battle metaphor is apparently suspended, it is resumed. Reinforcements come to the wounded warrior-Dreamer with orders for salvation: *Nu ic þe hate, hæleð min se leofa,* | *þæt ðu þas gesyhðe secge mannum* 'now, my dear man, I order you to tell this vision to men' (95–96). Upon hearing this, the Dreamer is revived:

> Gebæd ic me þa to þan beame   bliðe mode,
> elne mycle,   þær ic ana wæs
> mæte werede.   (122–24a)

There I prayed to the Cross with great zeal, happy in mind, there where I was alone with little company.

Like his Lord, he is exiled and must *rice gesecan* | *of eorðwege* 'seek the kingdom away from earth' (119b–20a) and return to his homeland: *Wæs modsefa* | *afysed on forðwege* 'the heart was ready for departure' (124b–25a). In anticipation of his return the Dreamer looks, as he says:

> daga gehwylce   hwænne me dryhtnes rod,
> þe ic her on eorðan   ær sceawode,
> on þysson lænan   life gefetige . . .   (136–38)

for the time when the Cross of the Lord, which I formerly saw here on earth, will fetch me from this transitory life . . .

Finally, the battle completed and victory won, the Dreamer will join in celebrating the feast of victory in his true homeland:

> ond me þonne gebringe   þær is blis mycel,
> dream on heofonum,   þær is dryhtnes folc
> geseted to symle,   þær is singal blis,
> ond me þonne asette   þær ic siþþan mot
> wunian on wuldre . . .   (139–43a)

and then bring me where there is great joy, happiness in heaven, where the Lord's people are placed at the feast, where [there] is perpetual happiness, and will set me where I can afterwards live in glory . . .

The Dreamer now transformed in spirit and ransomed from the enemy, the price having been the suffering of Christ, the suffering of the Cross, and his own suffering and awakening, returns successfully to his native land and is given *heofonlicne ham* 'a heavenly home' (148a).

Formerly the poet emphasized the suffering and death of the protagonists, Christ and Cross. Now, in the case of the Dreamer, he places the emphasis on "cleansing" and "lifting," because Christ and Cross, by means of their dramas, have in a large measure carried the burden of agony for the Dreamer, though that is not to imply that he has not shared their pain. He may even have suffered it three times over if we judge the dramas to be purely mental. Strongly emerging imagery of resurrection thrusts itself prominently into the foreground, especially after the Dreamer has participated in the double dramas of Cross and Christ, until ultimately that imagery becomes apocalyptic vision. In describing the act of crucifixion, the poet's images are such that they evoke overtones of resurrection or ascension: *Gestah he on gealgan heanne* 'he ascended on the high gallows' (40b), says the Cross of Christ. *Ahof ic ricne cyning* 'I lifted up the powerful king' (44b); and by implication the Cross will lift up the fallen warrior-Dreamer. *Rod wæs ic arǽred* 'I was set up a cross' (44a). *Ahofon hine of ðam hefian wite* 'they raised him from that heavy torture' (61a). Prefiguring the voice of the penitent Dreamer, who because of the ritualistic purification will not only go up but, obeying the commands of the Cross, will go out to all men, *stefn up gewat / hilderinca* 'the cry of warriors went up' (71b–72a). Because of the former agony the Cross will now *hlifige under heofenum* 'tower under heaven' (85a), moved *on lyft* 'on high' (5a). The *dryhten aras* 'Lord arose' (101b), and *He ða on heofenas astag* 'he then ascended into heaven' (103a). The imagery of resurrection (ascended, lifted, set up, raised, went up, towers on high, arose, and ascended) is then applied to the Dreamer when the Cross enjoins him to *rice gesecan / of eorðwege* 'seek the kingdom away from earth' (119b–20a). Displaying an emotional state consonant with resurrection, the Dreamer is *bliðe mode* 'happy in mind' (122b); the Cross will *gebringe þær is blis mycel, dream on heofonum* 'bring me where there is great gladness, joy in heaven' (139–40a). Likewise, his friends *lifiaþ nu on heofenum mid heahfædere* 'live now with God the Father in heaven' (134). And finally, Christ *mid manigeo com* 'came with a multitude' (151b). 'Seek,' 'happy,' 'bring,' 'arrive,' and 'live in heaven' are words and phrases that approximate emotionally the resurrection imagery and shadow forth the Dreamer's hopes for future life.

Christ offered himself in a voluntary act of love, but in the actual sacrifice he suffered an agonizing and bloody death. The division of God into divine being and human being and his return to himself in the sacrificial act (symbolized in his stripping off his earthly garments and embracing the Cross) hold out the comforting doctrine that in the center of the Dreamer's own darkness there lies a hidden light (symbolized by the structural frames, the movement from Dreamer to Cross to Christ, the evoked memories of Mary and Adam, and then by a reversal from Christ to Cross to Dreamer) which will once again be ignited by its source. The poet makes us see that this light (variously ·symbolized in the bright, shining Cross, but specifically in the body of Christ, 'that bright splendor,' whose tomb is of 'shining stone') actually wished to descend into darkness in order to deliver the 'stained' one who languished there, hidden in the gloomy underworld of his manifold sins and mortal enemies, and lead him to the source of light: *Hiht wæs geniwad | mid bledum ond mid blisse þampe þær bryne þolodan* 'hope was renewed with blessedness and with joy to those who had earlier suffered from fire' (148b–49).

The Christ of Revelation cautions mankind to "Repent; or else I will come unto thee quickly, and will fight against them with the sword of my mouth. He that hath an ear, let him hear what the Spirit saith unto the churches; To him that over-cometh will I give to eat of the hidden manna, and will give him a white stone, and in the stone a new name written, which no man knoweth saving he that receiveth it" (Rev. 2:16–17). Because the poet previously evoked Adam and his misdeeds, the stumbling block for all mankind is the old Adam in the flesh; but specifically for the Dreamer who lies 'stained with sins, . . . wounded with evil deeds,' is this true. Though the poet evokes this stumbling block only through implication —by linking the fallen Adam with the stained and recumbent Dreamer—the evocation of the 'shining stone' of the tomb of Christ might help us understand the accomplishment of the poet. Stone, earth, matter, and indeed, flesh pull man down and drag him into the underworld. Only when Christ as Spirit enters that base matter, that stained and sleeping flesh, only then does that rock tomb of man's body become spiritualized, become 'shining stone.' After all, the entire drama is one man's spiritual crisis. Thus the significantly charged symbol, the 'shining stone' that the Spirit enters, serves as the vehicle for the apocalyptic vision at the end of the poem, the great feast expected to usher in the messianic kingdom, where the Cross will:

> . . . gebringe　　þær is blis mycel,
> dream on heofonum,　þær is dryhtnes folc
> geseted to symle . . .　　　　(139–41a)

And Christ says in Rev. 2:17, "To him that overcometh will I give to eat of the hidden manna." The victorious spiritualized Dreamer will join the chosen at the eschatological feast and partake of the hidden bread, Jesus Christ. The white stone signed with the name of the Lord will, like the Cross signed with the body of Jesus and adorned with shining stones, gold, and silver, assure his passage to the land of glory, where he, the Dreamer, will enjoy pleasure fully with the saints.

If the splendor of Christ's sacrifice reveals the way out of darkness, if the Virgin Mother opened that way, if the shining Cross becomes that way, now the Dreamer will also show the way by rehearsing the grand vision and singing the glory of the Son to other men:

> onwreoh wordum   þæt hit is wuldres beam,
> se ðe ælmihtig god   on þrowode
> for mancynnes   ... synnum ...   (97–99)

make clear with words that this is the tree [wood, ship] on which God Almighty suffered for the sins of mankind ...

His transformation accomplished, the Dreamer fuses with the Cross and Christ. Through his new devotion and willingness to sacrifice his stained ego, the Dreamer, transfigured into a ministering instrument of glory, becomes one with Christ in the mysterious metamorphic process of the poem.

In *The Dream of the Rood* the three dramatic battle metaphors become symbolic means of redemption; they help delineate the purification, consecration, and exaltation of the Dreamer; they serve as centers of organization, cohesion, and wholeness. By emotionally participating in the two dramatic experiences during a dream in the depths of the night, the Dreamer unites himself with the Cross and Christ, is purified and strengthened. He then reveals to us that the thrice-repeated metaphor is essentially one profound drama of self-transcendence.

The poet found the precise means for expressing transformation in this dramatic metaphor of battle, defeat, capture, death, and sudden and climactic *metanoia*, a turning of the dry bones of death into glorious rebirth. This vivid metaphor reproduces the Passion of Christ and dramatizes those means by which a man saves his life: the poet's rehearsal and amplification of the metaphor to include the lowly tree-Cross serves as an example to the benighted Dreamer that not only the good but also the despised, the evil, the fallen and stained may find salvation through an imitation of Christ. The third rehearsal of the transformative metaphor dramatizes the process of redemption on the human level, the miraculous purification, elevation, and spiritualization of the Dreamer.

The *Rood* poet supports, broadens, and strengthens his consistent and cohesive metaphors of battle with a multitude of other images to describe both poles of the transformative process, the initial condition of man suffering from the fires of hell and the final goal of man dwelling in glory. Variously figured, these incidental metaphors appear as fall/ascend, bow down/rise up, tremble/strengthen, transitory/permanent, dark of clouds/bright splendor, troubled with sorrows/renewed in hope, afraid/brave, sorrowful/joyful, spectacle/ritual, criminals' gallows/glorified Cross, enemies that mock/angels that gaze and adore, tree/Cross, blood and wounds/gold and silver, stained/cleansed, no friends on earth/company of saints in heaven, wounding/healing, ignored ritual/celebrated ritual, sing a dirge/tell a vision, and sinners carrying the Cross on their shoulders/Cross carrying the redeemed sinners to the kingdom of heaven. All these incidental metaphors, amplifications of the thrice-repeated cohesive one, dramatize a permanent truth, the living, dramatic, transformational paradox that a man must first lose his life to save it. This is to say that the incidental images fall into dialectical opposites that mirror the larger thematic concerns of the poem's central battle metaphors.

But in the strange metabolism of the language of *The Dream of the Rood* the poet has created other ways of expressing this truth. When speaking in the voice of the Cross, just before the spiritualized Dreamer awakens, the poet creates a syntactical pattern related to sin and death: *Adomes ealdgewyrhtum* (100), *Deað he þær byrigde* (101a), *deaðes wolde | biteres onbyrigan*

(113b–14a). However, radically contrasted with that imagery of death, when the transformed and spiritualized Dreamer begins to speak once again, all is life: *Is me nu lifes hyht* (126b); *lifiaþ nu on heofenum* (134a), *on þysson lænan life gefetige* (138), *ond us lif forgeaf* (147b), etc. The poet's genius lies precisely in his ability to force his syntactical arrangements, as well as metaphors, similes, and the like, to support, emphasize, and dramatize his themes.

In the same manner he may also create a strong thematic dialectic among various syntactical elements, for instance, those beginning with an initial *on*. The first of these, *on lyft lædan* (5a), and the final, *on godes rice* (152b), are symbolic formulas for the reanimation of the spirit. Moreover, within the frame of these syntactical elements at the beginning and end of the poem the thematic conflict shifts, with emphasis first on one, then on the other, pole of the theme, only to be resolved in the final lines of the poetry. Schematized, the pattern looks like this: *on lyft lædan* (5a); *On me syndon þa dolg gesiene* (46b); *On me bearn godes* (83); *on þrowode | for mancynnes manegum synnum* (98b–99); *on þysne middangeard* (104a); *on domdæge* (105a); *on þyssum lænum life geearnaþ* (109); *on þysson lænan life gefetige* (138); *on þam gealgetreowe* (146a); *on þam siðfate* (150b); *on godes rice* (152b). The repetition of the same unit lifts it to a kind of symbolic structure expressive of the vicissitudes of the regenerative process.

Transformation animates the heart and spirit of the poem and the Dreamer. Christ, the second Adam, is transformed into man, into criminal, and then once again into spiritual being. The Rood, transformed from tree to gallows, to torture instrument, to dead and buried object, and finally to adorned Cross and enlightened messenger, towers above the fallen Adam in everyman, as a sign, a way, a vehicle of salvation. The Dreamer, identified with a stained and sinning Adam, changes into a cleansed and spiritualized human being, from grief-stricken man to joyous man, into an announcer of the good news and glad tidings of salvation to other men; and finally he assumes the form of a man hopeful of joining his

Lord at the messianic victory banquet and in the company of all the saints.

NOTES

1. *The Vercelli Book*, ed. G. P. Krapp ("Anglo-Saxon Poetic Records," Vol. II [New York, 1932]), pp. 61–65. Citations of *The Dream of the Rood* in this essay are from this edition. Translations, unless otherwise identified, are from *The Dream of the Rood*, ed. and trans. A. S. Cook (Oxford, 1905). In a number of places I have taken the liberty of changing Cook's translation.

2. The poet must have inherited a knowledge of the language of warfare in a large measure from traditional poetry.

3. *The Exeter Book*, ed. G. P. Krapp and E. van K. Dobbie ("Anglo-Saxon Poetic Records," Vol. III [New York, 1936]), pp. 94–113. *Poems from the Old English*, trans. and introduction Burton Raffel, foreword Robert P. Creed (Lincoln, Neb., 1960). I have used Raffel's translations of *The Phoenix* throughout this essay.

4. There has been some disagreement among scholars concerning the significance of the five gems. William O. Stevens, *The Cross in the Life and Literature of the Anglo-Saxons* ("Yale Studies in English," Vol. XXIII [New York, 1904]), p. 43; J. R. Allen, "Early Christian Symbolism," *Journal of the British Archeological Association*, XXXIV (1878), 357; and Howard R. Patch, "Liturgical Influence in *The Dream of the Rood*," *PMLA*, XXXIV (1919), 233–57, interpret the five as pertaining to wounds. A. S. Cook in his edition of the poem, p. 15, quotes an interpretation from the *Legenda Aurea*: "And in sign of these four virtues the four corners of the cross be adorned with precious gems and stones. And in the most apparent place is charity, and on the right side is obedience, and on the left side is patience, and beneath is humility, the root of all virtues." Harold Bayley, *The Lost Language of Symbolism* (London, 1912), II, 129, denies that "five" refers to wounds: "*five* knobs or bosses, erroneously supposed to represent the 'five wounds of Christ' are of frequent occurrence." In the pattern of transformation I have been discussing, it is of course essential to see the five as wounds.

5. *The Apocryphal New Testament*, trans. M. R. James (Oxford, 1924), p. 334.

THE CONCEPTION OF THE

OLD ENGLISH *PHOENIX*

❧❦❧

J. E. Cross

On occasions, though these are fortunately rare, knowledge can be an obstacle to understanding. So, in a manner, an obstacle was raised to the understanding of the Old English *Phoenix* when J. J. Conybeare noted in 1814[1] that the first and larger part of the poem was based on Lactantius' *De Ave Phoenice*.[2] From that time critical opinion appears to have regarded the description of the bird's life in the Old English poem as a situation that, in the remaining section, is interpreted in terms of Christian life and faith, and thus the whole poem has been seen as a kind of *Lactance moralisé*.[3]

A reading of the poem on this assumption, however, poses two disconcerting questions, both of which are indicated by the results of O. F. Emerson's study some forty years ago.[4] The first question is suggested by his statement that the Old English poet omitted references to pagan classical mythology and to sun worship in Egypt and also by his conclusion that the Latin description has been Christianized in its transfer to Old English verse. If the statement and conclusion are justified, however, it appears that the Old English poet was not bent on explaining the Latin poem, since a Christian writer of the Dark Ages would have no need to withhold pagan names and detail when interpreting a classical story with Christian application.[5] The second question is presented by Emerson's passing comments that parts of the paraphrased Latin poem were not "allegorized." Not all of Emerson's cases are valid, in my opinion, but there are enough, if taken together with other difficulties, to cause concern that a "moralizer" should have so neglected opportunities.

Emerson, however, overplayed his hand when he implied that the omission of "nearly a score" of classical allusions was caused solely by the poet's desire to Christianize a pagan poem.[6] For the classical names appear in phrases that show that they are the poetic idiom of even Christian Latin poets of the time.[7] The Old English poet cannot do other than omit the names in transferring the ideas to a different poetic idiom, especially in such a clearly didactic poem, which assumes an audience less knowledgeable than the author. As most of the examples cited by Emerson show, the Old English poet is quite willing to express the ideas of the Latin.[8] For instance, when he reads in Latin that the Phoenix *Ambrosios libat cælesti nectare rores,* / *Stellifero tenues qui cecidere polo* 'sips the delicate ambrosial dews of heavenly nectar which have fallen from the star-bearing pole' (111–12), he accepts the idea of supernatural food but rejects the allusion to classical mythology in his folkloristic, but not distinctively Christian, phrases:

> No he foddor þigeð,
> mete on moldan,   nemne meledeawes
> dæl gebyrge,   se dreoseð oft
> æt middre nihte . . .   (259b–62a)

He does not take food, meat on earth, unless he tastes a bit of the honey dew which falls at midnight often . . .

The English poet does, however, avoid Latin references to the part that the Phoenix plays in the rites of the sun cult,[9] and his method of dealing with these passages suggests that this is an emphatic rejection. On three occasions he closely follows the Latin text right up to the offensive statement but stops short; in the most notable of these passages there appear to be loose ends in the Old English because of the omission. I refer, of course, to the time after the rebirth when, as in both Latin and Old English, the reincarnated bird gathers the remains of its old body, covers them with herbs,[10] and carries them with its feet.[11] In Lactantius the bird goes *Solis ad urbem / Inque ara residens promit in aede sacra* 'to the city [or rising][12] of the sun and, remaining at the altar, produces it [the body] in the sacred temple' (121–22); in contrast, in Old English *sunbeorht gesetu, seceð on wynnum, / eadig eþellond* 'it happily seeks the sun-bright seats, its blessed native land' (278–79a). Only presumably from the Latin poem[13] but obviously from other versions of the Phoenix story, the temple is in Egypt where Lactantius has an Egyptian host salute the arrival of the bird, which is recorded *sacrato in marmore* 'on consecrated marble' (153). The Old English poet has men from all over the world assemble (323–24) to see the bird and to record its coming simply *on marmstane* 'on marble' (333b),[14] but where? In Old English the bird's journey has been from the Earthly Paradise in the far east (2a) westwards (162a) to an un-inhabited part of the world in Syria (166b), there to die and be reborn, thence to return to its native land (279a, 320b–21a). The lack of logical continuity in the Old English poem at this point emphasizes the precise omission of references to the sun cult.[15]

Even when the bird is living in the Earthly Paradise, its relationship with the sun is presented in a general way, but any indication of veneration or adoration is avoided. Both in Latin (53) and Old English (144b), the bird shakes its wings in salute to the sun, but in Latin alone it *Igniferumque caput ter venerata* 'adores the fire-bearing head three times' (54). Again, in *De Ave Phoenice* the bird is described as *Antistes luci nemorumque verenda sacerdos / Et sola arcanis conscia, Phoebe, tuis* 'the overseer of the grove, a venerable priestess of the woods, and alone knowing your secrets, O Phoebus' (57–58). These lines are not "wholly passed over"[16] since *wudubearwes weard* 'guardian of the wood grove' (152a) is as close as one could get in Old English alliterative verse to Latin *antistes luci* (57), although the specific sense of *antistes* as 'overseer of a temple, chief priestess'[17] is evaded; so too are the indications of a cult in the remainder of the Latin sentence. Finally, the

Old English poet omits the Latin phrase *Paret et obsequitur Phoebo memoranda satelles* 'it obeys and submits to Phoebus, a memorable attendant' (33), although A. S. Cook regarded the disputed Old English MS reading *þegn* (288a) as a verbal echo of Latin *satelles* within this phrase.[18] This appears to me unlikely, since the Old English poet carefully follows the order of the Latin poem, admittedly with omissions and additions but with no juxtapositioning.[19] MS *þegn* is a term for the bird at its rebirth, Latin *satelles* a name for it when it still lives in the Earthly Paradise.[20]

Emerson's second point, that certain ideas in *De Ave Phoenice* were not "allegorized," perhaps makes a stronger argument against the view of the Old English poem as a *Lactance moralisé* than his first statement. This second premise needs further discussion, however, partly in order to disagree with some of Emerson's examples but also to strengthen his general case.

One of Emerson's major points is that there was no "allegorizing" of the relationship of the Phoenix to the sun in its original home.[21] N. F. Blake has satisfactorily opposed this view in a perceptive paper under a deceptively modest title.[22] Many of the bird's actions are dependent on the sun's progress, and this relationship between bird and sun is reflected in the connection between the good man and Christ *seo soþfæste sunne* 'the true sun' (587), who *scineð* 'shines' (589b) on the blessed and who is praised in song by them as the Phoenix sings to the sun in the Earthly Paradise.

There is also a hint, I believe, of an interpretation for the description of the bird, despite Emerson's opinion to the contrary,[23] since the *beaga beorhtast* 'brightest of rings' (306a) around the neck of the Phoenix *swylce sunnan hring,* / ... *brogden feðrum* 'like the circle of the sun, woven of feathers' (305b–6) is surely echoed in *se beorhta beag, brogden wundrum* 'the bright ring, wondrously woven' (602), which adorns the head of each good man in heaven, although this *beag* is more appropriately formed of *eorcnanstan[as]* 'precious stones' (603a). This, however, is a small detail, and the beauty of the spectrum seen in the clashing colors of the bird is certainly not used in the description of the good man.

On another occasion the Old English poet seems to set up a situation for interpretation when, in extension of the Latin text, the Phoenix lives for a while in the wilderness with the company of birds before driving them away in preparation for its solitary cremation (158b–68). But neither is this dispersal of the attendants "allegorized," nor, as Emerson said, is the later return of the sad followers when the Phoenix flies home (347–54a).[24] Emerson speculated on the second return that the poet "perhaps means to imply that the Phoenix, type of the soul in its flight to heavenly bliss, must go its way unaccompanied," but this "reading," I fear, is unfounded fancy.[25] These features of the bird's journeys were not interpreted.

Other Old English additions in the descriptive section indeed would not have been easy to explain in terms of Christian interpretation. There appears to be a second thousand-year cycle for the reborn Phoenix if *eft* 'again' (366b) has real meaning, as it seems to in the context.[26] The bird has returned to the Earthly Paradise, its attendants have gone sadly home on earth, and the Phoenix, says the poet, may live in its native land *oþþæt wintra bið | þusend urnen* 'until a thousand years have run' (363b–64a), when it will die, *Hwæþre eft cymeð | aweaht wrætlice wundrum to life* 'yet again it will come wonderfully to life' (366b–67). Lactantius makes no mention of a second cycle of life, and indeed, if interpreted, this idea would savor more of the Stoic belief in cyclic conflagrations than of Christian teaching about the life of the world. But the Old English poet has already presented the Christian view of world history in adapting Lactantius' statement that the Earthly Paradise was not injured by the fires of Phaeton or the waters of Deucalion (11–14). In his own poetic idiom and Christian faith, the English poet accepts a past Flood but recognizes no historic Great Fire and changes the Latin past tense to a present-future: *bideð swa geblowen oð bæles cyme, | dryhtnes domes* 'it shall remain flourishing thus until the coming of fire, the judgment of the Lord' (47–48a; compare *ne him lig sceþeð |*

æfre to ealdre, ærþon edwenden / worulde geweorðe 'nor will
flame injure them, for ever and ever, until the end come
to the world' [39b–41a]). Relevantly, this seemingly slight
change would also raise an awkward difficulty for Christian interpretation. As we realize both from the general
interpretation and the sequence of negative clauses used in *The
Phoenix* to describe both the Earthly Paradise and the good
Christian's heaven (14b–18, 50–61, 611–14a), these two places
are meant to be equated in the poem. But now, by the change
of tense, the Old English poet has posited an end to the
Earthly Paradise (and, if interpreted, to the Christian heaven),
an idea that Lactantius had avoided.

A final change recalls the discussion above of the Latin
description of the bird's journey to the sacred temple in Egypt
when its remains were covered in herbs and carried with its
feet. The last detail is accepted in Old English, *fotum ymbfehð*
(276a), and repeated much later, although admittedly in
alliterative phrase: *fugel on fotum* (578a). But the only mention
of the bird's carrying herbs in the explanatory section expressly
states that this is done with the wings, *swa se fugel swetum his
fiþru tu / ond wynsumum wyrtum gefylleð* 'thus the bird fills his
two wings with sweet and pleasant herbs' (652–53), apparently
to fit an interpretation found in the *Physiologus* literature:[27]

> Þæt sindon þa word,   swa us gewritu secgað,
> hleoþor haligra,   þe him to heofonum bið,
> to þam mildan gode,   mod afysed . . .   (655–57)

As the writings tell us, these are the words, the speech of
the holy whose minds are prepared [to go] to heaven to
the benignant God . . .

Summing up at this point, we realize that the Old English
poet has noticeably adapted *De Ave Phoenice*, although
clearly paraphrasing the Latin poem at many points in the
same order. The adaptations indicate a desire to Christianize,
although the omission of classical names and detail is no
evidence of this desire. Hints or mention of a sun cult are

positively rejected. The adaptations do not always anticipate a possible Christian interpretation; some ideas are neglected in explanation, some are inserted that cause difficulties for interpretation, and in one case (wings, feet) even the correspondence is lost. If the Old English *Phoenix* is *Lactance moralisé*, we may feel that the explicator has not been very diligent. Fortunately, the detail of the poem fits quite a different conception of its genesis and structure.

As has always been quite clear to see in the explanatory section of the poem, the Phoenix represents, first, the good Christian who by his deeds gains admittance to his heavenly home after the Fire in the last days and the general resurrection, and second, Christ in his resurrection.[28] Within the interpretation, however, there is a third dimension that has not so far been noticed, possibly because man's journey from Eden to earth and back again to heaven is parallel to the Phoenix' departure and return. The extra meaning is indicated by a double interpretation of the Phoenix' nest (described only once in Lactantius and in the first section of the Old English poem)[29] as a shelter for the good Christian on earth and as a place to live in heaven. On earth *þær him nest wyrceð . . . / dædum domlicum dryhtnes cempa* 'the warrior of the Lord makes a nest for himself by glorious deeds' (451–52) in the lofty tree of the favor of God in this world (446–47), *in þam halge nu / wic weardiað* 'in which the holy now have their dwelling' (447b–48a); but also *Beoð him of þam wyrtum wic gestaþelad / in wuldres byrig* 'a dwelling shall be built for them [*meotudes cempan* 'the warriors of the Lord' (471b)] from the plants in the city of glory' (474–75a). The indication of a dividing line here in the good man's journey home is, of course, strengthened by a general observation that death for a Christian ends the continuous present but begins the everlasting future.

When the different interpretations are distinguished and enumerated in this way, every medievalist will recognize that these are the three *spiritual* senses of Scripture, familiar in patristic exegesis and transmitted in Old English homily. At the risk of boring, it may be said that the representation of the

Phoenix as the good Christian in his earthly nest is a *moral* or *tropological* interpretation, the bird as Christian in his heavenly dwelling is an *anagogical*[30] interpretation, and the bird as Christ is a *typical* or *allegorical* interpretation.

These distinctions became obvious to me some years ago when I first considered this poem in detail. But understanding of the whole poem was still blocked by the knowledge that the first part was based on *De Ave Phoenice* and by the consequent assumption that the remainder was an attempt to "allegorize" it. Unfortunately, as I then thought, I knew of no evidence that full scriptural exegesis was applied to secular poetry. Even if there were such a tradition or if the Old English poet had the unique idea of using exegetical methods in this way, why did he do the job so haphazardly?

The old assumption began to be shaken when I considered the vocabulary of the poem, especially the oral poetic feature, the dead epithet. *Haswigfeðra* (153b) was a clear example, since it is quite incongruous to apply this epithet, whose precise meaning is 'gray-feathered,' to a bird that is later portrayed in bright and startling color.[31] So, too, older scholars regarded *beaducræftig* (286a), for, if given full meaning of 'strong in battle,' the adjective seems to add an incongruous element to the bird's nature. But the poet had already named the bird's nest as *heaþorofes hof* 'the court of [one] brave in battle' (228a) and later called the Phoenix a *guðfreca* 'battle-warrior' (353a), words used of warriors elsewhere in Old English poetry. Yet his persistence was explained when, in the interpretation, the good Christian was obviously a *miles Christi* as *dryhtnes cempa* 'warrior of the Lord' (452b), *beald in breostum* 'bold in [his] breast' (458a), and *meotudes cempa* 'warrior of God' (471b). In such a situation the incongruity of a warrior Phoenix must be accepted as a striking poetic effect, and *beaducræftig* deleted from lists of cliché epithets in Old English.

But, relevantly for our thesis, it is a hint that the Old English poet conceived his poem *The Phoenix* as a whole, since at this point he anticipated his interpretation by the introduction of an idea not present in Lactantius. Blake has presented this idea much more fully in his recent discussion of aspects of the Old English poem. As he points out, there is a "distinct tendency to anthropomorphize the phoenix, ... to give the bird characteristics which are more appropriate to men and heroes."[32] This statement is illustrated by a discussion of *beaducræftig, heaþorof,* and the names for the bird's nest in the descriptive section, where it is "commonly referred to as a *hus,* otherwise as a *solere,* a *willsele,* a *hof* and twice as a *nest,*"[33] while the Christian men later build themselves a *nest* in heaven. Blake's illuminating study considers other adaptations of the Latin poem, all the examples to show that "the poet rewrote the phoenix story in the light of the allegory which he wished to attach to it."[34] The facts he presents do warrant such a conclusion but, to my mind, do not explain other difficulties: why, for example, the poet did not reject out of hand any reference to a Fire, why the retinue of birds on the way to Syria is inserted and not explained, and so on.

Yet Blake has made it clear that the Old English poet fitted *De Ave Phoenice* into his own plan and did not first paraphrase the Latin and then explain it with the three spiritual explanations of patristic exegesis. To a medieval reader, these three beg the fourth, the historical description or explanation, and this demand instigates a proposal that is modest but, I think, fitting. The English poet wished to write a poetic homily on the significance of the Phoenix and took *De Ave Phoenice* as the fullest and most suitable historical description of the bird.[35]

For him, as for Pseudo-Epiphanius, Tertullian, Philip the Presbyter, Pseudo-Ambrose, and probably Ambrose,[36] the Phoenix was a scriptural bird (and thus a suitable object for exegesis). This is both stated in the paraphrase of Job 29:18 (548–69), where the poet has read *phoenix* for Vulgate *palma,* and implied by the equation of the Phoenix with the good Christian, since this equation is based on such readings of scriptural phrase as Tertullian's *Deus etiam scripturis suis: Et florebit enim, inquit, velut phoenix* 'So God in His Scriptures:

And he shall indeed flourish, he says, as the phoenix' (Psalm 91:13) or Pseudo-Ambrose's *Spiritus sanctus, qui Deus est, in Scripturis posuit sanctis dicens: "Et florebunt velut phoenix"* 'Holy Spirit, which is God, speaking in the holy Scriptures, asserts: "And they shall flourish as the phoenix"' (Isa. 35:1),[37] where in both cases the reference is to the general resurrection.

It is, I think, significant that when Lactantius names the tree in which the bird is to die as the palm *Quae Graium phoenix ex ave nomen habet* 'which has the Greek name of phoenix from the bird' (70), the Old English poet omits the alternative name (173b–74), probably because, if Greek φοῖνιξ could be an equivalent of Latin *palma* here, this might admit doubt of the scriptural testimony from Job given later, a testimony on which he firmly relies: *Ne wene þæs ænig ælda cynnes | þæt ic lygewordum leoð somnige* 'Let no man think this, that I compose my song in lying words' (546–47).

The Phoenix is also a real bird to the poet, as it was to those Fathers who told its story as an "analogy from nature" for the Resurrection and coupled this analogy with less remote comparisons such as to the seed, trees in winter and spring, the moon, day and night, even flies and bees that survive after apparent drowning, and the hibernating dormice.[38] Its reality is used in a different way by Rufinus in his *Commentary on the Apostle's Creed*,[39] where the bird appears in company with other natural phenomena as a testimony for the Virgin Birth, and such a tradition would give our poet authority to speak of the Virgin Birth (637b–40a) as a parallel to the mystery of the bird's birth (355b–60).

Strong patristic tradition also accepted the physical reality of the Earthly Paradise, as Howard R. Patch points out, citing some well-known names: "The Garden of Eden was universally believed to exist, and . . . was supposed still to be waiting for the saints[40] before their ascent to Heaven."[41] This attitude is obviously reflected in the Old English poem and explains the change of tense in the reference to the Fire, for now the Earthly Paradise is subject to the same control as the physical world and is fitted into the Christian concept of world-history. The poetic sequence of events is the Christian sequence as stated in II Pet. 3:6-7: "Whereby the world that then was, being overflowed with water, perished: But the heavens and the earth, which are now, by the same word are kept in store, reserved unto fire against the day of judgment ..."[42]

As the Old English poet implies on different occasions, God controls the Earthly Paradise in exactly the same way as he holds the physical world. The home of the Phoenix was made by God (9b–10), removed from evildoers by his might (5b–6), and protected from the Flood through his grace (43b–46); its trees remain green through his command (36–39a), and the streams gush forth at his behest (68b–70). But, like the things of the world, it has an end when the Flames of Judgment destroy it and its delights (83–84) at the same time that God removes his protection from the earthly Phoenix tree in Syria, which *gescylded a | wunað ungewyrded, þenden woruld stondeð* 'shall remain unharmed, always protected, while the world stands' (180b–81), and presumably destroys the Phoenix bird, which will not die *þenden woruld stondeþ* 'while the world stands' (89b).

These additions or changes are among "more than a score of direct allusions to the Creator" by Emerson's count[43] and were made not merely to "Christianize ... the source before him," in my view. In these ways he adapted the Latin poem to fit Christian reality and to place the Phoenix story within a Christian historical context.

Now it is of no account that the Old English poet omits Latin ideas such as the fountain of life,[44] which could have easy Christian application, or that additions are made such as the second thousand-year cycle of life for the Phoenix—after all, the bird could have had at least six such cycles within the Christian conception of the physical world's age, since the last of the six ages had at least a scriptural thousand years. Within his own Christian terms the Old English poet is free to write a historical description as he wishes; to extend, change, or omit material from Lactantius; even to anticipate his own interpretation. But there is no need for him to interpret every detail that he has presented in that historical description. In Cassian's classic case, to illustrate the fourfold method of interpretation, Jerusalem "historically" is a city of the Jews,[45] but in the "allegorical" interpretation, when Jerusalem represents the Church of Christ on earth, no one would ask openly whether the Jews should not be Christians.

It is now necessary to return to analysis of the spiritual explanations, where the Old English poet has been served, at times, rather unkindly by translators and somewhat loosely by commentators, so that the distinction between the three interpretations has appeared confused in places and needs disengagement from the overlying comment.

The poet begins his "moral or tropological" interpretation at line 381 with a general comparison of the good man with the Phoenix, which serves as a heading for the details that follow. The first of these details, the story of Adam and Eve, is not a "digression"[46] but a necessary chronological reversion in order to present the bird's likeness to man. The bird lived in the Earthly Paradise as the first man lived in Eden, but both bird and man have to go to our world, *in þas deaðdene* 'into the valley of death' (416a) for Adam and into the wilderness for the bird (153–58a).[47] *Se halga wong* 'the holy plain' (418b)[48] was opened again, however, through the advent of Christ many years later (420–21) for the holy, the sons of Adam, who have suffered because of his guilt (409–10). The story of Adam is clearly introduced to give the reason why man has to work for heaven and to indicate the parallel situation of a return after resurrection.

Adam has served his dogmatic purpose, and the Old English poet now speaks of his chosen subject, the select sons of Adam who obey their Maker (444) *þæt him dryhten wearð | . . . hold on mode* 'so that the Lord became gracious in mind towards them' (445–46). As the bird found in Syria *holtes hleo heah* 'high protection of the wood' (429), the *heah beam* 'high tree' called the Phoenix (171–74), so the good man finds his *hea beam* (447a) defined as the favor of the Lord on earth; and as the bird built its nest in its tree *tanum ond wyrtum* 'of twigs and plants' (430b), so the good man *him nest wyrceð* 'makes a nest for himself' (451a) *dædum domlicum* 'with glorious deeds' (452a) illustrated as almsgiving, prayer, and the avoidance of sin. Within this section R. K. Gordon and Sir Israel Gollancz have confused the symbolism by inaccurate translation of lines 455b–56, *forð onetteð, | lænan lifes leahtras dwæsceþ*, as 'hasteneth forth from this frail life, blotteth out transgressions.'[49] There is, however, no evidence in Old English of a genitive (*lænan lifes*) expressing 'motion from,' and the phrase should clearly be read 'strives always, quenches[50] sins of this transitory life.'[51] By their translation Gordon and Gollancz imply that the good man is dying, but he is simply trying hard to do God's will while still in this world, as the poet says later:

> Swa nu in þam wicum   willan fremmað
> mode ond mægne   meotudes cempan,
> mærða tilgað . . .   (470–72a)

So *now* do the warriors of the Lord fulfill his will with mind and strength, practice virtue in their homes . . .

This is a conclusion to a restatement of his equation: namely, that the materials for the nest are the good deeds of the Christian (465–69).

But the eternal reward for these works on earth now allows the poet to introduce the anagogical interpretation in a clear statement that the materials for the earthly dwelling in God will also, in the future, form a habitation in heaven (474–75a). Following Chaucer's teaching maxim, "sothly me semith better to writen unto a child twyes a god sentence, than he forgete it onys,"[52] we may state again that death for the individual divides things temporal, the material for moral interpretation, from things of the eternal future, the stuff of anagoge. So the poet describes the Christian future in orthodox dogma by his elaboration on the Last Things and on the eternal joy for those who have chosen right. At the death of man the body, separated from the soul (488b), goes into the earth to await the Fire at the end of the world. All men will then be resurrected (495) at the sound of the trumpet (497b) and be brought to judgment (491–94). Everyone will be afraid as the Fire destroys the transitory wealth of the world (503b–5a), but death will end for the blessed (499–503a) when the sinful world burns. Then, says the poet, the meaning of the bird will become clear (508b–12). All will be well for those who please God at that time (516b–17). Their bodies *leahtra clæne* 'purified of sins' (518b), as the bird's flesh was *synnum asundrad* 'separated from sins' (242a), will be united with their souls and go forward happily because they are *weorcum bifongen* 'encircled with their deeds' (527b),[53] which are *wyrta wynsume* 'the pleasant plants' (529a) of the bird's nest at the time of its destruction by flame. These elect shall be beautiful and young again and praise God in song (536–43).

In the anagogical interpretation Christ is to the elect as the sun is to the Phoenix in the historical section. At the Judgment he *halgum scineð* 'shall shine upon the holy' (515b) from his throne as a *wlitig wuldres gim* 'radiant gem of glory' (516a), repeating *wuldres gim* (117b), a metaphor for the sun, and echoing four other occasions (92a, 183a, 208b, 289a) when the sun is called a 'gem.' This identification is repeated after the testimony from Job (546–82) when the righteous journey to the *wuldres byrig* 'city of glory' (588b) *þær seo soþfæste sunne lihteð / wlitig ofer weoredum* 'where the true and beautiful sun shines over the hosts' (587–88a), varied in the immediately succeeding lines as *soðfæstum sawlum scineð / ... hælende Crist* 'the Savior Christ shines for the righteous souls' (589–90). At this point critics and editors have been perturbed by the plural *fuglas scyne* 'beautiful birds' (591b) that follow Christ. Emerson thought that these were the flock of birds that follow the Phoenix;[54] Krapp and Dobbie assumed that they were angels but felt that "the poet may simply have become confused by his Phoenix-symbolism,"[55] and E. M. L. Ettmüller emended the text.[56] But there may be a simpler explanation that credits the poet with better control. Throughout the anagogical interpretation Christ is clearly the sun and the Phoenix is each good Christian and all good Christians. As the poet says, *þær lifgað a leohte werede,* / *swa se fugel fenix* 'they [*gæstas gecorene* 'chosen spirits' (593b)] live there [in heaven], always clothed in light, like the Phoenix bird' (596–97a) and, as I have suggested above, the righteous appear to simulate one feature of the Phoenix' beauty in *se beorhta beag* 'the bright ring' (602a), which adorns each of them in heaven. Since the *fuglas scyne* are *beorhte gebredade* 'brightly restored' (592a), a verb used of the Phoenix (372b) to describe its resurrection, *fuglas* must refer to the Phoenix. If the text is not corrupt, it seems to me that the plural *fuglas* may well have been written under the grammatical influence of plural *sawlum* 'souls' within the preceding lines.

Heaven is now described in a sequence of negative clauses (611–14a) to echo two similar descriptions of the Earthly Paradise (14b–18, 50–61), and the hosts of heaven sing praises to the Lord, a passage that repeats and extends the description of the praise of the righteous in heaven (539–43). There is no need to equate this anthem with the song of the birds attending the Phoenix (337–40) on its return home, since the Phoenix itself *singeð swegle togeanes* 'sings toward heaven' (124) in the Earthly Paradise in song more beautiful than any other sound. The poet, however, does not point either of these two equations by verbal echo or direct statement. Perhaps we should follow him and leave such equations aside here. It is not necessary to ponder over neglected equations if the poet conceived his work as I suggest he did.

The anthem to the Father/Son ends the anagogical interpretation, but praise of him offers an introduction to the poetic description of Christ in New Testament and dogmatic idea. Here, of course, the Old Testament Phoenix prefigures the New Testament Christ in a brief but clear typological or allegorical interpretation. The power of the Son of God to rise again from the death of his body is identified in direct statement with that peculiar property of the Phoenix,[57] and the identification of Christ and Phoenix is strengthened in the few phrases on the Virgin Birth (637b–40a), which recall the mystery of the bird's birth (355b–60, 374b–76) as in the patristic tradition mentioned above.

If we accept Kennedy's opinion[58] and Cook's suggestion of the influence of the Greek *Physiologus*[59] and translate, using the philological comments of Schaar,[60] the interpretation appears to continue into the next passage:

swa se fugel swetum his fiþru tu
ond wynsumum wyrtum gefylleð,
fægrum foldwæstmum, þonne afysed bið.
Þæt sindon þa word, swa us gewritu secgað,
hleoþor haligra, þe him to heofonum bið,
to þam mildan gode, mod afysed
in dreama dream, þær hi dryhtne to giefe
worda ond weorca wynsumne stenc
in þa mæran gesceaft meotude bringað,
in þæt leohte lif. (652–61a)

in like manner[61] the bird fills its two wings with sweet and pleasant plants, the fair fruits of the earth, when it is ready [to die];[62] as the writings tell us, these are the words, the speech of the holy, whose minds are prepared[63] [to go] to heaven, to the merciful God, into the joy of joys, where they bring the pleasant fragrance of their words and deeds as a gift to the Lord, the Creator, in that glorious creation, that radiant life.

Although the bird appears to be Christ, the good men are not forgotten as the poet prepares to end his homily, since their words and deeds are carried in the wings of Christ to heaven. The words instigate the song of praise to God (661b–66), but the necessity for deeds is stressed in the promise that concludes the poem in macaronic verse:

Hafað us alyfed lucis auctor
þæt we motun her merueri,
goddædum begietan gaudia in celo,

  .   .   .   .

agan eardinga   almæ letitiæ,

. . . . .   blandem et mitem

geseon sigora frean   sine fine,

ond him lof singan   laude perenne . . . (667–76)

The Author of Light has allowed us to merit, to obtain joys in heaven with good deeds here . . . to possess dwellings of heavenly joy,[64] . . . to see the Lord of victories, merciful and mild,[65] to sing His glory in everlasting praise . . .

The simplicity with which the ideas of the poem are fitted without (at least conscious) manipulation or pressure into this theory of the poem's conception and execution is, I believe, strong evidence for the probability of the theory. I therefore restate that this poem is an effective medieval homily on the Phoenix, in which Lactantius' *De Ave Phoenice*, the fullest description of the bird, was adapted as a Christian historical explanation, and ideas taken from patristic exegesis and polemic, as well as the *Physiologus* literature, were elaborated to provide distinguishable tropological, anagogical, and typological explanations, so to present a fourfold interpretation of a real and scriptural bird.[66]

NOTES

1. *Archiv*, XVII (1814), 193, cited by A. S. Cook in his edition of *The Old English Elene, Phoenix, and Physiologus* (New Haven, 1919), p. xxviii, n. 5.

2. Now regarded as an authentic work of Lactantius by Eligius Dekkers, *Clavis Patrum Latinorum* ("Sacris Erudiri," Vol. III.2 [rev. ed.; Brugge, 1961]), 19, but still recorded as "peut-être Lactance" in P. Glorieux, "Pour Revaloriser Migne," *Mélanges de Science Réligieuse*, IX (1952), 10. The edition of the poem cited in this paper is that in Lactantius *Opera Omnia*, ed. Samuel Brandt and Georg Laubmann ("Corpus Scriptorum Ecclesiasticorum Latinorum," Vol. XXVII.1 [Leipzig, 1897]), II.1.

3. Expressly stated in *The Poems of Cynewulf*, trans. Charles W. Kennedy (London, 1910), p. 60: "The latter half of the poem is simply an interpretation of the fable of the first half in terms of the Christian faith." Compare also Charles W. Kennedy, *The Earliest English Poetry*

(London, 1943), p. 298: "The second half . . . is devoted to an elaborate interpretation of the Christian allegory implied in the narrative of . . . the Phoenix," and *Early English Christian Poetry*, ed. and trans. Charles W. Kennedy (London, 1952), p. 224. Others who agree in different wording to this view are W. L. Renwick and Harold Orton, *The Beginnings of English Literature to Skelton* (rev. ed.; London, 1952), p. 182: "Part II is a homiletic interpretation . . . of the theme of Part I"; G. P. Krapp and E. van K. Dobbie in their edition of *The Exeter Book* ("The Anglo-Saxon Poetic Records," Vol. III [New York, 1936]), p. xxv: "The remainder of the poem, ll. 381–677, is devoted to a homiletic amplification of the earlier part of the poem"; E. G. Stanley, in his article "Old English Poetic Diction and the Interpretation of *The Wanderer, The Seafarer*, and *The Penitent's Prayer*," *Anglia*, LXXIII (1956), 416: "there is the allegory of *The Phoenix* culminating in the long simile towards the end of the poem. In it the allegory of the Phoenix is explained." Others are not so unambiguous, such as Hermann Gaebler, "Ueber die Autorschaft des Angelsaechsischen Gedichtes vom Phoenix," *Anglia*, III (1880), 516; Kemp Malone, "Religious Poetry: Cynewulf and His School," in *A Literary History of England*, ed. Albert C. Baugh, *et al.* (New York, 1948), p. 76; and P. H. Blair, *An Introduction to Anglo-Saxon England* (Cambridge, Eng., 1956), p. 344, since they speak, respectively, of an interpretation of the "*mythus*," "fable," "fiery death and rebirth," of the Phoenix, but one assumes that they mean the information presented about this in the first part of the poem.

4. "Originality in Old English Poetry," *Review of English Studies*, II (1926), 18–31.

5. J. R. Allen, *Early Christian Symbolism in Great Britain and Ireland* (London, 1887), p. 367, refers to the story of Ulysses and the Sirens being adapted to Christian purposes as early as the third century and noted by Clement of Alexandria. See also J. Seznec, *The Survival of the Pagan Gods* (New York, 1961), especially chap. iii, "The Moral Tradition," on the *Mythologiae* of the sixth-century Fulgentius and the poem of Theodulf, bishop of Orleans.

6. Emerson, "Originality in Old English Poetry," p. 22, says "as might be expected," but since the paragraph on classical allusions follows that on sun worship, we may assume that he implies the same motive for the Old English poet's rejection of both classical allusion and references to sun worship.

7. I phrase the statement in this way in case there is still doubt that the Christian Lactantius wrote *De Ave Phoenice*. But for an excellent and accessible example see the translation of part of Aldhelm's *De virgine* in Bernard F. Huppé, *Doctrine and Poetry: Augustine's Influence on Old English Poetry* (Albany, N.Y., 1959), p. 70. Many other cases could be given.

8. Emerson, "Originality in Old English Poetry," p. 22, has listed the examples, and I am forced to consider all of these in order to justify my comment. Line references for *De Ave Phoenice* in this paper are to the edition of Brandt and Laubmann, and those for the Old English *Phoenix* are to the Krapp and Dobbie edition of *The Exeter Book*. The following examples are equivalent in idea:

(a) *Solis nemus* (9); *sunbearo* (33b)

(b) The deluge or waters of Deucalion (13–14); *wætres þrym | ... mereflod* (41b–42)

(c) Nascent Phoebus (41) repeated as *Atque ubi Sol pepulit fulgentis limina portae*, Sol's opening of the doors of the shining gate (43); *on eastwegum | ... swegles tapur* (113b–14) and *siþþan wuldres gim | ofer geofones gong grund gescineþ* (117b–18)

(d) Æolus shutting in the winds (73); *Đonne wind ligeð, weder bið fæger* (182)

(e) The *corona* on the Phoenix' head resembling the glory of the head of Phoebus (139–40); *beaga beorhtast* (306a), *swylce sunnan hring* (305b) around the neck of the Old English Phoenix, but compare *se beorhta beag* which *hlifað ofer heafde* for the blessed in heaven (602a, 604a).

The following examples reveal adaptation that, however, does not obscure the Latin idea:

(a) Stars being put to flight when Aurora comes (35–36); *Tungol beoþ ahyded* (96b), *bideglad on dægred* (98a)

(b) The fires of Phaeton (11); *ne him lig sceþeð* (39b)

(c) Cyrrhæan strains (48); *eallum songcræftun* (132a)

(d) Cyllenean lyre (50); *ne hearpan hlyn* (135a)

(e) Phoebus bringing back the horses of the sun into the open heaven (51); in Old English the time sequence is changed, and the Phoenix sings *oþþæt seo sunne on suðrodor | sæged weorþeð* (141–42a), but the Old English poem has two references to the sun (120–24, 141–42a), as does the Latin (41, 51), to mark the time and object of the Phoenix' song.

The following classical references are omitted from the Old English: Flora (128), Iris (133), the bird of Phasis (144). All are found in the physical description of the bird, and the Old English poet's omission of these from his own description can scarcely be caused by a desire to Christianize. The references to Venus (as love, desire, pleasure) at the end of the Latin poem and, I think, the ideas implied in the references are omitted, although possibly the idea of *Mors illi Venus est, sola est in morte voluptas* 'Venus is death to it, the only pleasure is in death' (165) may be expressed in *dead ne bisorgað* 'it does not fear death' (368b). The above analysis, however, gives evidence for my comment.

9. As emphasized by Emerson, "Originality in Old English Poetry,"

pp. 20, 21, and in *Early English Christian Poetry*, ed. and trans. Kennedy, p. 224.

10. Named in the Latin: *Unguine balsameo myrraque et ture soluto* 'balsam ointment, and myrrh, and soft incense' (119).

11. *Pedibus gestans* (121); *fotum ymbfehð* (276a).

12. MSS *Solis ad ortus*, edited to *Solis ad urbem* (121). Emerson, "Originality in Old English Poetry," p. 21, has a long (and perhaps irrelevant) discussion on the possibility of the English poet's seeing *solis ad urbem* in his Latin text and concludes that the Old English poet would have rejected the implication of the reading even if he had seen it.

13. If *Solis ad ortus* is read.

14. Note also that in the Latin the bird sings a *sacred* song (45) to Phoebus, leaves the *holy* places (63) of its home, and the birds attending the Phoenix exult in their *pious* duty (158). None of these adjectives is echoed in Old English.

15. See also the review by J. E. Cross of *The Phoenix*, ed. N. F. Blake (Manchester, Eng., 1964), in *Journal of English and Germanic Philology*, LXIV (1965), 158, on the bird's journey.

16. Emerson, "Originality in Old English Poetry," p. 20.

17. Ethan Allen Andrews, *A Latin Dictionary*, ed. Charlton T. Lewis and Charles Short (Oxford, 1955), s.v. *antistes* 1, b, c.

18. *The Old English Elene, Phoenix, and Physiologus*, ed. Cook, p. 117, followed by Claes Schaar, *Critical Studies in the Cynewulf Group* ("Lund Studies in English," Vol. XVII [Lund, 1949]), p. 86.

19. As printed in Lactantius *Opera Omnia*, ed. Brandt and Laubmann, following the MSS, but not as rearranged by Jean Hubaux and Maxime Leroy, *Le Mythe du Phénix dans les littératures grecque et latine* ("Bibliothèque de la Faculté de Philosophie et Lettres de l'Université de Liège," Vol. LXXXII [Liège, 1939]), pp. xi–xv.

20. Nevertheless, I prefer the MS reading, since no objections can be raised against it on grounds of alliteration, grammar, contextual meaning, or general meaning of the poem. On grammar and contextual meaning see Schaar, *Critical Studies in the Cynewulf Group*, p. 86; on general relevance of the word in the poem see N. F. Blake, "Some Problems of Interpretation and Translation in the OE *Phoenix*," *Anglia*, LXXX (1962), 60–61.

21. "Originality in Old English Poetry," p. 28.

22. "Some Problems of Interpretation and Translation in the OE *Phoenix*," pp. 60–61.

23. "Originality in Old English Poetry," p. 23.

24. *Ibid.*, p. 24.

25. *Ibid.*; Emerson continues: "Indeed, there seems a first hint of the Phoenix as the soul in lines 348b–49, * þonne duguða wyn | of þisse eorþan tyrf eþel seceð* 'when the pride of men from the soil of this earth seeks his

native land.'" There is no ambiguity of this kind, however, in *duguða wyn*, which means either 'delight of the men' (who are watching) or 'best of warriors,' referring to the Phoenix who is called a *guðfreca* 'battle warrior' (353a), and *beaducræftig* 'powerful in battle' (286a), *heaporof* 'brave in battle' (228a).

26. Critics, of course, should be wary of basing an interpretation on such words as *eft* or *oft* when they are the only alliterating words of an off-verse, since they are obviously so easily useful for vowel alliteration. See the comment by J. E. Cross in a review of Huppé, *Doctrine and Poetry*, in *Journal of English and Germanic Philology*, LIX (1960), 563.

27. *The Old English Elene, Phoenix, and Physiologus*, ed. Cook, p. 123; Schaar, *Critical Studies in the Cynewulf Group*, p. 90.

28. These identifications are a cliché of Phoenix criticism.

29. There appears to be no nest for the Phoenix in the Earthly Paradise, only one in Syria in which it dies and is reborn.

30. Of course, all the references to the Last Things and the heavenly city are part of the anagogical interpretation.

31. See also *se haswa fugel* 'the grey bird' (121b), where the other adjective is *beorht* 'bright' (122a).

32. "Some Problems of Interpretation and Translation in the OE *Phoenix*," p. 53. I had come to this conclusion before reading Blake's essay, but he considers the general problems much more fully than I had done.

33. *Ibid.*

34. *Ibid.*, p. 50.

35. Lactantius' *De Ave Phoenice* already adapts the Phoenix story into poetic form; it is a longer poem than that of Claudian (see the two texts in Hubaux and Leroy, *Le Mythe du Phénix*, pp. xi–xv, xxi–xxiii), and it may well have been the most easily available description, since we know that Lactantius was one of the authors whose works were in the York Library, according to Alcuin, and that he was quoted and named by Aldhelm, despite scanty records of the availability of Latin authors to English writers. On Alcuin's and Aldhelm's references to Lactantius see M. L. W. Laistner, "The Library of the Venerable Bede," in *Bede: His Life, Times, and Writings*, ed. A. H. Thompson (Oxford, 1935), p. 261.

36. Pseudo-Epiphanius *Physiologus* quotes Psalm 91:13 in its application of the Phoenix story to the resurrection in *Patrologiae Cursus Completus, Series Graeca*, ed. J.-P. Migne (Paris, 1857–66; hereafter abbreviated to *Pat. Graec.*), XLIII, 525–27. Tertullian *De Resurrectione Carnis* xiii, in *Patrologiae Cursus Completus, Series Latina*, ed. J.-P. Migne (Paris, 1844–64; hereafter abbreviated to *Pat. Lat.*), II, 857, reads *phoenix* in his quotation of the same verse. Philip the Presbyter knows that the name *phoenix* could have been seen in Latin translations of Job 29:18 (see the quotation in *The Old English Elene, Phoenix, and*

Physiologus, ed. Cook, pp. 121–22). Pseudo-Ambrose *De Trinitate* xxiv, in *Pat. Lat.*, XVII, 575, translates Isaiah 35:1 as *phoenix*. Ambrose *De Excessu fratris sui Satyri* II.59, in *Pat. Lat.*, XVI, 1389, refers to the authority of the Scriptures, which probably recognizes that the name *phoenix* could appear in a Latin translation of the Bible.

37. My attention was drawn to this text by Hubaux and Leroy, *Le Mythe du Phénix*, p. 110, n. 1.

38. See Tertullian *De Resurrectione Carnis* xii; Cyril of Jerusalem *Catecheses Illuminandorum* XVIII.vi, vii, in *Pat. Graec.*, XXXIII, 1021–24, for these other analogies from nature. Other well-known patristic writers who accepted the existence of the Phoenix include Clement of Rome *Epistola I ad Corinthios* xxv, in *Pat. Graec.*, I, 261–65; Gregory Nazianzen *Praecepta ad virgines*, in *Pat. Graec.*, XXXVII, 620; Origen *Contra Celsum* IV.98, in *Pat. Graec.*, XI, 1177; Epiphanius *Ancoratus* lxxiv, in *Pat. Graec.*, XLIII, 173; Ambrose *Hexaemeron* V.xxiii. 79, 80, in *Pat. Lat.*, XIV, 252–53; and Isidore *Etymologiarum* XII.vii. 22, in *Pat. Lat.*, LXXXII, 462.

39. In *Pat. Lat.*, XXI, 350 A–B.

40. This tradition is recorded in the Old English homily printed in *The Old English Elene, Phoenix, and Physiologus*, ed. Cook, pp. 128–31: *Ðær wunaþ on Godes ængles unrim, mid þām hālgum sāulum, oþ Dōmæsdæg* 'therein dwell a host of God's angels, with the holy souls, until Judgment Day.' The poet of the Old English *Phoenix* may well be indicating his belief in this tradition when he adapts the Lactantian *Qua patet aeterni maxima porta poli* 'where the great gate of heaven stands open' (2) to *Ðær bið oft open eadgum togeanes / onhliden hleoþra wyn, heofonrices duru* 'there the door of the kingdom of heaven is often open towards the blessed, the best of melodies revealed' (11–12), for the blessed seem to be able to hear the best of sounds when heaven's door is open towards this Earthly Paradise. See also Cross, in *Journal of English and Germanic Philology*, LXIV (1965), 157.

41. See *The Other World According to Descriptions in Medieval Literature* (Cambridge, Mass., 1950), p. 134, for the quotation; see chap. v, *passim*, for names including Augustine's.

42. Noted in *Early English Christian Poetry*, ed. and trans. Kennedy, p. 221, and quoted here in the Douai translation.

43. "Originality in Old English Poetry," p. 26. The references are presented in the note on p. 27.

44. *De Ave Phoenice* names the fountain that irrigates the Earthly Paradise *quem vivum nomine dicunt* 'which they call living by name' (25) and later says of the Phoenix *Ter quater e vivo gurgite libat aquam* 'thrice four times it sips water from the living flood' (38), but the Old English poem refers to the waters in general terms without connotation: *lagustreamas* 'waters' (62a), *wæter wynsumu* 'pleasant waters' (65a),

lagufloda wynn 'best of waters' (70b), *æspring* 'spring' (104b), *wylle-streamas* 'running streams' (105b), *burna* 'brooks' (107a), and *wyll-gespryng* 'spring' (109b).

45. Cassian *Conlationes* xiv.8, noted by Beryl Smalley, *The Study of the Bible in the Middle Ages* (Oxford, 1941), p. 15.

46. Malone, "Religious Poetry: Cynewulf and His School," p. 76.

47. Interestingly and explicably, I think, by my theory of the poem's conception the Old English poet omits a Lactantian phrase, *mors ubi regna tenet* 'where death holds sway' (64), in his description of the bird's journey, which would have pointed the parallel with Adam's world.

48. Echoing the occasions when the same noun is used to describe the Phoenix' home (7a, 13a, 19b, 43b).

49. *Anglo-Saxon Poetry*, comp. and trans. R. K. Gordon (London, 1954), p. 247: 'he hastens forth from this fleeting life, quenches sins'; in *The Exeter Book*, ed. and trans. Sir Israel Gollancz ("Early English Text Society," O.S. Vol. CIV [Oxford, 1895; reprint 1958]), Part I, p. 229, the translation appearing in this paper is given.

50. The verb *dwæscan* used here in connection with the reference to almsgiving recalls *adwæscan* in the same collocation within the short poem *Alms-giving* (*The Exeter Book*, ed. Krapp and Dobbie, p. 223) in a comparison deriving from Ecclus. 3:33.

51. With the punctuation of *The Exeter Book*, ed. Krapp and Dobbie, pp. 106–7, placing a comma after *onetteð*. For the translation of *onetteð* see T. Northcote Toller's *Supplement* (Oxford, 1921) to Joseph Bosworth's *An Anglo-Saxon Dictionary*, ed. T. Northcote Toller (Oxford, 1882–98), s.v. *onettan* III.

52. *A Treatise on the Astrolabe*, Preface, in *Complete Works*, ed. F. N. Robinson (2d ed.; Boston, 1957).

53. *The Exeter Book*, ed. and trans. Sir Israel Gollancz, p. 233, translates ll. 526–27, '*shall* the blessed with their works ... *be* encircled, after their wretched time on earth' (italics mine). The tense of *beoð* is ambiguous here, but the poet is describing men in the Flame of Judgment in comparison with the bird in its destroying fire. It seems better to take *beoð* as present tense in order to hold the comparison, since the men *are* encircled by their deeds at that time as the bird *is* surrounded by the plants when the flame burns.

54. Emerson, "Originality in Old English Poetry," p. 30.

55. P. 279. Compare also p. xxxv: "In ll. 589 ff. the symbolism is varied, and the Phoenix with its attendant birds becomes the allegorical representation of Christ surrounded by the spirits of the blessed"; and *Early English Christian Poetry*, ed. and trans. Kennedy, pp. 224–25 and p. 225, n. 2.

56. To *fiðrum scyne* as noted in *The Exeter Book*, ed. Krapp and Dobbie, p. 279.

57. See Schaar, *Critical Studies in the Cynewulf Group*, p. 89.

58. *The Earliest English Poetry*, p. 298.

59. *The Old English Elene, Phoenix, and Physiologus*, ed. Cook, p. 123. The idea of Christ as the phoenix bearing spices in its wings appears later in *Physiologus* literature; e.g., the eleventh-century Peter Damian's *Opusculum*, LII.xi, *De phoenice*, in *Pat. Lat.*, CXLV, 773–74.

60. *Critical Studies in the Cynewulf Group*, pp. 89–90.

61. *Swa*, i.e., 'just as the Phoenix signified God's power, so do the herbs signify': *ibid.*, p. 90.

62. C. W. M. Grein, *Sprachschatz der angelsächsischen Dichter*, ed. F. Holthausen and J. J. Köhler (Heidelberg, 1912), s.v. *Afysed* 2, and Schaar, *Critical Studies in the Cynewulf Group*, p. 90.

63. *Afysed* repeated.

64. *Alma*, see *Mittellateinisches Wörterbuch* (Munich, 1959), I, s.v. *Almus* II, A, 2, and regarding *alma* as an error or scribal variation for *alme* (*-almae*).

65. *Blandem et mitem* (674b) qualify *frean* (675a) not *blæddaga* (674a) as in the translation by Gollancz in his edition of *The Exeter Book*, p. 241.

66. The new edition of *The Phoenix*, ed. Blake, appeared after this essay was written. Blake's general views about the poem are still those expressed in his paper "Some Problems of Interpretation and Translation in the OE *Phoenix*," which are considered in this paper (see n. 20). I have taken up the differences in points of detail in my review of his edition in *Journal of English and Germanic Philology*, LXIV (1965), 153–58.

IMAGE AND MEANING
IN THE ELEGIES

Edward B. Irving, Jr.

In recent years we have made substantial progress toward understanding the Old English elegies, particularly in two main areas: first, in that systematic study of poetic formulas, verbal and thematic, which had its origin in the oral-formulaic theory; and secondly, in the exploration of the nature of early medieval Christian thought and symbol—which indeed we may regard as the exploration of a different set of formulas.[1] Understanding the full meaning of the elegies in the context of both these traditions is difficult—far more difficult than some have suggested—but surely now we can no longer go back to any of our older and simpler views of these poems.

As most readers are doubtless aware, however, there is a certain danger inherent in the method of some of these recent studies. Piling up formulas, themes, and *topoi* in the abundant quantities apparently needed to persuade our colleagues can smother the poems under the guise of explaining them, especially in cases where our attention is constantly being forced outward to what a given poem has in common with other works, often much inferior poems or second-rate homilies. It is true that the meaning of a poem can be partly illuminated by such information, but we are still treating the poem as one document in a bundle of documents. Insofar as it is successful as a poem, it must be because of its unique qualities.

Furthermore, the Old English poetry that has survived was formed by the collision of two cultures and is always, for better or worse, a mixed kind of poetry. Even in the most "Christian"

153

poems the collision is apparent in the very style itself, that language of formulas never perfectly modified or adapted to their new uses. An idea expressed in the Latin prose of a homily is never the same as the idea expressed in Old English verse, unless one ignores style altogether, which has unhappily been the convenient practice of many scholars for many generations.

What may prove of some use in the study of this peculiar blend of heroic poetry and medieval Christianity in the elegies is an examination of some of the recurrent images in hopes of discovering a little more about the kind of meaning generated by the particular combination of commonplaces in a given poem. Perhaps it would be useful, by way of admitting a little oxygen into the field, to suggest a few similarities between these poems and others in quite different traditions.

Let us look first at the image of the ruined wall or building or city—a man-made structure seen as in a state of decay. This image, probably borrowed from Latin writings by the Anglo-Saxons, is, of course, most fully developed in the fragmentary poem called *The Ruin*:[2]

> Wrætlic is þes wealstan,   wyrde gebræcon;
> burgstede burston,   brosnað enta geweorc.
> Hrofas sind gehrorene,   hreorge torras,
> hrungeat berofen,   hrim on lime,
> scearde scurbeorge   scorene, gedrorene,
> ældo undereotone.   (1–6a)

Wonderful is this wall stone, the fates have broken it; city buildings have collapsed, the work of giants crumbles. Roofs are fallen, towers are in ruins, the barred gate has been broken into[?], frost is on the mortar, the gaping roofs are torn open, collapsed, eaten through by age.

Wrætlic is þes wealstan 'wonderful is this wall stone' the poem begins; the first word, *wrætlic* 'wonderful, marvelous,' invites our admiration of the building. This initial verse is followed by ten successive verses that are like the blows of a wrecking hammer, each one describing some form of the process of ruin;

but at the end of this verbal battering we are told that the wall survives, has not fallen, still demands admiration:

> Oft þæs wag gebad
> ræghar ond readfah   rice æfter oþrum,
> ofstonden under stormum ...   (9b–11a)

Often this wall, lichen gray and red stained, endured through kingdom after kingdom, stood against storms ...

A badly damaged passage follows in the MS[3] at the end of which we are told that the structure was well made by the hand of a determined (*hwætred, hygerof*) man, who bound it together by *wirum* 'wires' or metal reinforcements and bound it into *hringas* 'rings' or circles of some kind:

> Mod mo[nade]   [m]yne swiftne gebrægd
> hwætred in hringas,   hygerof gebond
> weallwalan wirum   wundrum togædre.   (18–20)

The mind suggested, set in motion a swift purpose; the resolute brave man bound the wall foundation together by wires into rings in a marvelous way.

The next three lines call up a sudden picture of the city of the past—bright, lofty, resounding with noisy hilarity (*dream*) —a varied assembly of well-bound buildings, bound into a community of human joy. To the Germanic mind, what binds such a community together is the exchange of material wealth, the gold and silver and jewels mentioned later in the poem. It seems worth suggesting as a possibility that some connection may have been hinted at between the wires and rings that are part of the building's structure and wires and rings in the more usual sense (in poetic formulas, at least) of valuable artifacts and hence binders in the social structure. I think I am persuaded of the existence of such a connection, but I can hardly hope to persuade others in a case where the connection, if it had indeed existed, might have been subliminal even to the original audience.

Man, then, erects and binds together walls and civilizations. The universe unbinds and levels them. The protecting roofs collapse; the mortar that has held together the stones of the wall is covered with frost. The *betend*, the repairmen who might have maintained these structures, have themselves fallen. *Brosnade burgsteall. Betend crungon* 'the city crumbled. The menders lay dead' (28)—such a collocation in itself implies the close identification of men and buildings. And, in the phrase a few lines further on, *Hryre wong gecrong / gebrocen to beorgum* (*lit.*: 'falling has fallen to earth, [been] broken to mounds,' [31b–32a]), *beorgum* may be taken to refer both to the piles of broken stone and roof tile and to the burial mounds of men that they suggest. So consistently is this pattern of association carried out in the poem that it seems not impossible that the *hate streamas* 'hot streams' (43b) mentioned in the mutilated conclusion of the poem might find their explanation as much in rhetoric of this kind as in archeology. The dying men too once poured out the 'hot streams' of their blood (*hat on hreþre* 'hot in the breast,' [41a]) from the *beorhtan bosme* 'bright bosom' (40a).

There are probably many analogues to *The Ruin* in the general tradition of laments over mutability in early medieval literature, but the attitude that this poem seems to invite has its own complexities. It is not simply an attitude of mockery of the vain labors of men or of *contemptus mundi*.[4] The very language itself seems to me to carry its inevitable associations over from the world of heroic poetry. The wall—and whatever it may suggest about man's heroic and doomed effort to hold things together, to hold self together, to resist change and death—is crumbling and battered by storm, but it endures, somewhat in the way that the hero's fame endures. We come back to the first word, *wrætlic*, which takes on the meaning of 'to be admired and respected for fine workmanship.'

The traumatic vision of a falling city seems to have originated among writers of the late Roman Empire from Augustine on, but the Anglo-Saxons who inherited it could hardly have felt their own identities in danger of obliteration in the same immediate way as the Romans. Roman ruins were other people's houses, *enta geweorc* 'the work of giants,' perhaps even the creation of another race of beings. Such structures were beyond their power to build and hence to the Anglo-Saxons may often have served simply as material evidence for the heroic will of the past.[5]

Assuming that a wall represents in part a complex of social relationships in a poem like *The Ruin*, it is natural then to see the individual who has been stripped of these relationships, who no longer has a social role, as something like a single stone fallen from a wall. Not that this particular image occurs in the elegies, to my knowledge;[6] this kind of isolation is typically expressed in Old English poetry by the images that cluster around the figure of the exile.[7] No longer locked into a meaningful place in the intricate pattern of relationships, the exile wanders halfway between life and death, surrounded by cold and darkness, in lonely places like ships and fens and caves and islands. Yet, as these exiles pass out beyond the safety of the walled society and into the cold emptiness of their own desert places, they often seem to gain a new depth of understanding. So Widsith travels: 'So I traversed many a foreign land, all over the wide ground. There—deprived of family, far from noble kinsmen—I made trial of good and evil, traveled very far.'[8] Such traveling in exile is often more than merely geographical; explored here are the existential spaces of moral reorientation. This kind of insight through lonely suffering is usually given meaning within a Christian context. Perhaps Christian poets saw an advantage in representing individuals as separated from a society that was still overwhelmingly pagan in its basic nature and in confronting the isolated individual with simultaneous visions both of his own death and of the death of the society itself. But there seem to be secular forms of this insight, too.[9]

The one thing that is beyond dispute about the situation of the heroine of *The Wife's Lament*, for example, is that her situation is expressed by the formulas of exile. The gravelike earth cave or barrow she lives in offers few chances for vision, surrounded as it is by dim dales and towering hills and thorny stockades.[10] Only the imagination can move out of this prison, and in the puzzling final lines of the poem her imagination seems to move out beyond her own dismal situation to a sharply visualized picture of her lover as another exile, alone, cut off, beaten by storms. Thus the poem seems to end with the fusion of an acutely felt personal experience and the imaginative intuition of another's suffering into a small but "earned" general observation on the pain of human isolation: *Wa bið þam þe sceal | of langoþe leofes abidan* 'it is misery to have to wait in longing for someone you love' (52b–53). In a different way the exiled speaker in *Deor*, reflecting on other instances of misery, seems to gain some comfort in the mere fact that he is not completely alone in his suffering.

The first sixty-four and one-half lines of *The Seafarer* (quite distinct in style if not wholly in theme from the rest of the poem) offer a complex attitude toward extreme physical danger and suffering. The opening lines link certain things together: truth is experience, and experience is suffering. The sailor who here represents the exile type is contrasted throughout with the man who stays at home *in burgum* 'in towns' (28a) and thus never gains this suffering and knowledge.[11] While the sailor's ship is described (ironically) as a kind of 'care hall' where the squawking of gulls and sea birds is a mockery of human song and conversation, the main emphasis is on his exposure—alone, naked, hungry, cold—to the violence and danger of actuality. Because he is not merely meditating in an idle literary way but has the real function of standing watch on a ship, he stares with particular intentness as the storms pound the sea cliffs while the eagle, the death bird, screams overhead. The image of storm against wall we have seen before; here it seems to occupy the center of his vision, perhaps his vision of life, which he pictures as a precarious clinging to the edge of the abyss of extinction. The well-known "dialogue" rhythm of alternate attraction and repulsion in this poem may suggest that such a vision is both desired because it is true and feared because it is unbearable.

Such an attitude toward danger and death has its parallels in heroic poetry. As Hrothgar points out in the not exclusively Christian sermon that he preaches to Beowulf, true heroism is to face squarely the fact of one's own mortality; it is arrogance and false pride to avoid this vision.[12]

The Mesopotamian epic of Gilgamesh deals explicitly with this theme of mortality. Here Gilgamesh is celebrated as a wise man who has gained insight through ordeal by making a long journey to the other world, where he comes to realize his own mortal condition. At one point his comrade Enkidu has an *ubi sunt* vision of the house of the dead: "I entered the house of dust and I saw the kings of the earth, their crowns put away for ever; rulers and princes, all those who once wore kingly crowns and ruled the world in the days of old."[13] Gilgamesh's response to this vision seems to state clearly the same kind of ambiguous heroic attitude that we see in *The Seafarer*. Note especially the sentence here italicized: "Who is there in strong-walled Uruk who has wisdom like this? Strange things have been spoken, why does your heart speak strangely? The dream was marvellous but the terror was great; *we must treasure the dream whatever the terror*; for the dream has shown that misery comes at last to the healthy man, the end of life is sorrow."[14]

Of all the elegies *The Wanderer* contains the greatest number of the themes and images I have been discussing and may be the most successful in fusing secular and Christian sentiments.[15] As in the other poems the speaker first grasps the full implications of his own situation and then is able to move out into a broader view of man's life in the universe. There are other interesting similarities to the other poems in the way these themes are organized. *The Wanderer* is characterized by a rhythmical pattern of emotions so marked as to be fairly called structural. The pattern lies in the violent surging of the speaker's emotions against or beyond various kinds of restraints:

> Oft him anhaga   are gebideð,
> metudes miltse,   þeah þe he modcearig

> geond lagulade longe sceolde
> hreran mid hondum hrimcealde sæ ... (1–4)

Often the solitary man lives to see favor, the Lord's mercy, even though, sad in heart, he is compelled for a long time to stir the frost-cold sea with his hands over the ocean-ways ...

In these opening lines, for example, the patient, enduring, disciplined attitude suggested by the word *gebideð* is opposed to the intensity of the *anhaga*'s suffering at sea and on the paths of exile, an intensity conveyed with direct sensuous impact in line 4, where the alliteration virtually places the hand in ice-cold water.

Images of restraining, binding, holding in, chaining, and the like occur often in the Wanderer's speech: for example, the word *anhaga* itself, or the verb *bindan* (used five times), or the compounds with *-loca* 'enclosure' and *-cofa* 'coffer, room' as second element. These are contrasted with images of expansion, bursting out, or searching longingly outside oneself; notable among these is the word *geond* as preposition and as verbal prefix.[16] The phrase *se hreo hyge* 'the rough (troubled) spirit' (16a) suggests that these violent emotions are conceived as being like a storm or stormy sea (an image found elsewhere in Old English poetry).[17]

The images of binding are particularly associated in the early part of the poem with the aristocratic decorum of self-restraint and stoical silence under adversity; and they are there juxtaposed to and contrasted with descriptions of the restless desperate search for the security of a new lord. Such searching is not only spatial but temporal; the speaker ranges back over his memories of the past. The opposition between the roaming spirit and its imprisonment in a situation of suffering reaches its moment of greatest tension when the longing for past joy becomes so acute that the dreams of lost affection and loyalty gain hallucinatory reality in the vision of old comrades; the world of dream and the world of reality blur and mingle in those haunting, whirling forms of sea birds and remembered faces, those known and unknown voices just at the threshold of understanding. Here the images are of expansion and the impelling forward of the imagination to traverse great space: *geondhweorfeð* 'roves through' (51b); *georne geondsceawað* 'eagerly surveys' (52b); *þam þe sendan sceal swiþe geneahhe / ofer waþema gebind werigne sefan* 'for the one who must over and over send his weary spirit out over the binding [*lit.*] of the waves' (56–57).

This heroic effort of the imagination in sending out the weary spirit seems to be closely related to the following passage, where the speaker also fights against limits, but here by sending his thought out beyond the bonds of his own situation:

> Forþon ic geþencan ne mæg   geond þas woruld
> for hwan modsefa   min ne gesweorce,
> þonne ic eorla lif   eal geondþence . . .   (58–60)

Indeed I cannot think through all this world why my heart should not grow dark, when I contemplate all the life of warriors . . .

Such a sending out is followed by a binding in, for so I would interpret the series of precepts of temperance, self-control, and nothing too much that follows. It is almost as if the speaker, appalled by his brief glimpse of annihilation, had fallen back on these memorized rules of conduct, these attempts to impose a kind of order on experience. These examples of gnomic wisdom end with the recommendation that a man wait cautiously to see just what direction his spirit will take when it goes out:

> Beorn sceal gebidan,   þonne he beot spriceð,
> oþþæt collenferð   cunne gearwe
> hwider hreþra gehygd   hweorfan wille.   (70–72)

A warrior ought to wait, when he utters a boast, until, stout-hearted, he is sure in what direction the thoughts of his heart will move.

Then again, in the same rhythmical pattern the restless

spirit moves out to see the vision that makes up most of the concluding lines of the poem—moves out, as before, in phrases of expansiveness (*ealre . . . worulde wela* 'the wealth of all the world' [74a]; *missenlice geond þisne middengeard* 'variously all over the earth' [75])—and focuses on a familiar pair of images: the wall and the storm. The compact antitheses formed by alliteration and juxtaposition stress the opposition of these two images; they seem also as in *The Ruin* to stress the close symbolic relationship of man and wall. The word *worian*, for example, here applied to the crumbling of the wine-halls, is elsewhere almost always used of human beings, in the sense 'wander' or 'go off the path.' The line in which it appears, *Woriað þa winsalo, waldend licgað* (78), seems almost to suggest one progressive action with the shift in subject of minor importance: 'the wine-halls totter, [and then] the rulers lie still.'[18] Similarly the phrase *dreame bidrorene* 'bereft of joy' (79a), used of the men, echoes *hrime bihrorene* 'covered with frost,' used of the walls just two lines before.

Hence it is not surprising that the twin objects of *geond-penceð* 'think over, consider' (89b) are *þisne wealsteal* 'this wall foundation' and *þis deorce lif* 'this dark life,' for much of the mystery of this dark life clings around the symbol of the wall. As if beginning from the word *deorce*, the poem moves into a passage of falling darkness, an image that gives special poignancy to the traditional *ubi sunt* passage. Horse, man, giver of treasure become objects groped for, lost in the night, vanished from the view of man like the warriors in the preceding section, who were taken off in various ways or hidden in a grave. Time itself darkens under night as if it had never been. Yet a marvelous wall remains standing in this dark storm of annihilating violence: *Stondeð nu on laste leofre duguþe / weal wundrum heah, wyrmlicum fah* 'the wondrously high wall, decorated with images of serpents, stands now after [the departure of] the beloved band of retainers' (97–98). It is clearly somehow the center of the necessary vision, what man is compelled to see when he sends his spirit out to its farthest reach.

Let me suggest a connection, one of those strange connections that poetry is likely to make, between the two sets of images in the two parts of the poem. Man lives his life as part of a wall or perhaps behind a wall of restraints—social compacts, aristocratic codes, ethical rules; but he lives perpetually racked by storm, both from within himself in the form of emotion and from outside himself in the form of change and death. We first see the Wanderer torn by terror and insecurity, by his *hreo hyge*, his storm of emotions. It is perhaps his experience of this storm that leads him to the vision of that other storm of death and annihilation that concludes his meditation.

But a wall stands in that storm, for which we feel the same kind of admiration as for the wall in *The Ruin*. The wall in both poems is so closely associated with man himself that it seems to represent some aspect of his strength. The great bonds that hold society together and the self-discipline of the isolated individual are both associated with protective walls and enclosures and are both representative of what—at least in the context of heroic poetry—are the fundamental human virtues: courage and open-eyed resistance to the irresistible forces of the world. In the world of epic this is man's ultimate greatness and all that can survive of him, even though it will not last forever. In the Christian world we can turn to that wall that cannot fall into ruin, the *fæstnung* 'firmness, stability; fortress [?]' of God the Father: *Wel bið þam þe him are seceð, / frofre to fæder on heofonum, þær us eal seo fæstnung stondeð* 'it is well for the man who seeks mercy and comfort from the Father in heaven, where all that *fæstnung* stands for us' (114b–15). The profound differences between the two world views need not be explored here, but we may note that the heroic tradition and medieval Christianity are both preoccupied with the facing of death with full knowledge of all its implications.

Let me make an end of these hints and guesses by quoting a poem by William Butler Yeats entitled *Meru* that seems to bear a remarkable resemblance to the poems we have been discussing, for it uses the same combination of themes and images: binding and leveling, the simultaneous craving for and fear of the truth of reality, the fallen city and the winter-cold exile:

> Civilisation is hooped together, brought
> Under a rule, under the semblance of peace
> By manifold illusion; but man's life is thought,
> And he, despite his terror, cannot cease
> Ravening through century after century,
> Ravening, raging, and uprooting that he may come
> Into the desolation of reality:
> Egypt and Greece, good-bye, and good-bye, Rome!
> Hermits upon Mount Meru or Everest,
> Caverned in night under the drifted snow,
> Or where that snow and winter's dreadful blast
> Beat down upon their naked bodies, know
> That day brings round the night, that before dawn
> His glory and his monuments are gone.[19]

NOTES

1. In briefer form this paper was read at a meeting of the Old English Group of the Modern Language Association in December, 1963. Oral presentation partly accounts for its sketchy documentation, but I have made some attempt to indicate indebtedness to other critics where I have been conscious of it.

2. The text of *The Ruin* quoted here and the text of the other elegies are those of *The Exeter Book*, ed. G. P. Krapp and E. van K. Dobbie ("The Anglo-Saxon Poetic Records," Vol. III [New York, 1936]), pp. 227–29. See also the full annotation of the poem in its most recent edition: R. F. Leslie, *Three Old English Elegies* (Manchester, Eng., 1961).

3. The text of ll. 12–17 is more than half gone. Leslie's reading of l. 18 as *Mod mo[nade m]yne swiftne gebrægd* 'the mind suggested, stimulated a swift purpose' seems as likely as any.

4. I would agree with I. L. Gordon's statement that "there is an essential difference between the old poetic view of transience, which sees it as a tragic fact, a part of the woes of men, and the Christian view which sees it as a proof of the vanity of worldly things" ("Traditional Themes in *The Wanderer* and *The Seafarer*," *Review of English Studies*, N.S. V [1954], 8).

5. Such a native tradition, implying that men were mightier in ancient times, might have been reinforced somewhat by the classical and post-classical belief in the deterioration of mankind since the Golden Age. See J. E. Cross, "Aspects of Microcosm and Macrocosm in Old English Literature," *Comparative Literature*, XIV (1962), 1–22.

6. But it might be noted here that the opening lines of *Christ I* (i.e., what would now be called the fragmentary first poem of the *Advent Lyrics*) deal with the scriptural image of the stone rejected by the builders. Christ as the *weallstan* 'wall stone,' exiled, returns to reconstruct and repair the house that *nu gebrosnad is* 'is now crumbled.' Even though the liturgical origin of the image is certain here, it seems possible that the verse itself makes use of some secular connotations.

7. See Stanley B. Greenfield, "The Formulaic Expression of the Theme of 'Exile' in Anglo-Saxon Poetry," *Speculum*, XXX (1955), 200–206.

8. *Widsith*, ll. 50–53:

> Swa ic geondferde fela   fremdra londa
> geond ginne grund.   Godes ond yfles
> þær ic cunnade   cnosle bedæled,
> freomægum feor,   folgade wide.

9. See the discussion of this point by I. L. Gordon, "Traditional Themes in *The Wanderer* and *The Seafarer*," pp. 6–7.

10. See the comments on this poem by Ralph W. V. Elliott, "Form and Image in the Old English Lyrics," *Essays in Criticism*, XI (1961), 1–9.

11. Perhaps the kind of man referred to contemptuously as *seldguma* in *Beowulf*. See Cecil Wood, "*Nis þæt Seldguma: Beowulf* 249," *PMLA*, LXXV (1960), 481–1784.

12. *Beowulf*, ll. 1700–1784, especially ll. 1761b–68.

13. *The Epic of Gilgamesh*, trans. N. K. Sandars (Baltimore, 1960), p. 89.

14. *Ibid.*, p. 90.

15. Since writing this, I have seen John Collins Pope's remarkably persuasive argument for two speakers in *The Wanderer* ("Dramatic Voices in *The Wanderer* and *The Seafarer*," in *Franciplegius: Medieval and Linguistic Studies in Honor of Francis P. Magoun, Jr.*, ed. Jess B. Bessinger, Jr., and Robert P. Creed [New York, 1965], 164–93). Pope's second speaker, the *snottor on mode* or meditative man, begins his speech at l. 58 after the *eardstapa*, the lordless wanderer, has concluded his plaint. This hypothesis undeniably clarifies the poem in many ways and (if I had known it earlier) would have modified what I say here, but some of the connections that I think I see between the two parts may still have validity, even if the poem is seen as a "double elegy" of two speakers.

16. The memorable and much-discussed image of the roaming bird/soul in *The Seafarer* (58–64a) seems to be an even more concrete way of representing this feeling.

17. For example, in the Exeter Book *Maxims*, ll. 50–58a, where the sequence of associations seems to be, first, the necessity to control violent passion (the verb *styran* 'steer, control' is used, then a description of a storm at sea, then the comparison of a calm sea to peace among peoples and to social harmony). See also E. G. Stanley, "Old English Poetic Diction and the Interpretation of *The Wanderer, The Seafarer,* and *The Penitent's Prayer*," *Anglia*, LXXIII (1956), 429–30; Elliott, "Form and Image in the Old English Lyrics," and Randolph Quirk, "Poetic Language and Old English Metre," in *Early English and Norse Studies*, ed. Arthur Brown and Peter Foote (London, 1963), especially p. 161. Something of an analogy to the image pattern in *The Wanderer* may be found in a passage like *Beowulf*, ll. 2111–14:

> hwilum eft ongan   eldo gebunden,
> gomel guðwiga   gioguðe cwiðan,
> hildestrengo;   hreðer inne weoll,
> þonne he wintrum frod   worn gemunde . . .

sometimes the old warrior, bound by age, would lament his youth and strength in battle; his breath surged up inside him when, ancient in years, he recalled many things . . .

Here the "surging" of nostalgia for youth is opposed to the "binding" limitations of old age.

18. Such free-floating formulas establish semantic relationships with each other in more than one way, of course; another meaning suggested here is that the halls totter because the rulers are dead and unable to maintain them.

19. Number XII in a series called "Supernatural Songs," in *The Collected Poems of W. B. Yeats* (New York, 1955), p. 287.

ALDHELM AND THE *LEIDEN RIDDLE*

❧❀❧

George K. Anderson

Aldhelm innocently supplies the beginning to my discussion with his riddle *De Lorica*, among his *Ænigmata*:[1]

> Roscida me genuit gelido de viscere tellus;
> Non sum setigero lanarum vellere facta,
> Licia nulla trahdunt, nec garrula fila resultant
> Nec crocea Seres[2] texunt lanugine vermes
> Nec radiis carpor duro, nec pectine pulsor;
> Et tamen en vestis vulgi sermone vocabor,
> Spicula non vereor longis exempta pharetris.

> Dewy earth engendered me in its cold vitals;
> I am not made with the bristly fleece of wool;
> No looms stretched me, nor prattling threads leaped back,
> Nor with saffron floss have Eastern worms becovered me,
> Nor was I pulled with wheels nor pushed by carding-
>   combs.
> Yet, lo! I am called a coat in the language of the people.
> I fear not stings drawn forth from the long quivers.

The solution has always been, by common consent, "coat of mail."

In MS Leiden University Cod. Voss 106 there is a version of Aldhelm's *Ænigmata* (folios 10b–25b), followed by an epilogue (*Expliciunt ænigmata*, etc.) and then an Old English poem, that is a reasonably close translation of *De Lorica*. This is in Old Northumbrian and has been known since its first printing as the *Leiden Riddle*:[3]

> Mec se ueta uonȝ   uundrum freoriȝ
> ob his innaðae   aerest cændæ.

167

Ni uaat ic mec biuorhtæ uullan fliusum,
herum ðerh hehcraeft hyȝiðoncum min.[4]
Uundnae me ni biað ueflæ, ni ic uarp hafæ, 5
ni ðerih ðreatum ȝiðraec ðret me hlimmith.
Ne me hrutendu hrisil scelfath,
ni mec ouana aam sceal cnyssa.
Uyrmas mec ni auefun uyrdi craeftum,
ða ði ȝeolu ȝodueb ȝeatum fraetuath. 10
Uil mec huethrae suaeðeh uidæ ofaer eorðu
hatan mith heliðum hyhtlic ȝiuæde;
Ni anoeȝum ic me aeriȝfaerae eȝsan brogum
ðeh ði numen siæ niudlicae ob cocrum.

Me the wet plain, wondrous cold
From its womb first brought forth.
I know I am not wrought from the fleece of wool,
From hairs with high skill (I know in my mind).
The woof is not wound about me, nor have I the warp, 5
Nor through the thrust of many strokes does a thread of
 mine resound.
Nor does the whirring shuttle move or shake me,
Nor in any place shall the weaver's rod smite me.
Silkworms did not weave me through the skill of Fate,
That the yellow precious cloth deck with adornments. 10
Nevertheless one will, far and wide over the earth,
Among the heroes call me a delightful garment.
Nor (need) I fear the showers of arrows terribly frighten-
 ing
Though they be taken in times of need from the quivers.

Even with the use of reagents and lights, the *Leiden Riddle* is
difficult to read. In fact, the last line is imperfect and has had
to be reconstructed. The poem can be dated on the basis of
palaeographical evidence only, and this points to the ninth
century. A. H. Smith, a more recent editor whose text I have
followed, suggests the possibility that Aldhelm himself might
have been the original translator.[5] The noted Bishop of Sher-
borne is always associated with Wessex, but he still could have

made a translation, which would have been made around 700. Then, perhaps a century later, came a rendering of the riddle into Northumbrian, either the riddle we know as the *Leiden Riddle* or a predecessor. The point must remain a matter of speculation, but I shall return to it in a moment.

There is, of course, a West Saxon version of the translation in Riddle 35 of the *Riddles of the Exeter Book*:[6]

Mec se wæta wonȝ wundrum freoriȝ
of his innaþe ærist cende.
Ne wat ic mec beworhtne wulle flysum,
hærum þurh heahcræft hyȝeþoncum min.
Wundene me ne beoð wefle, ne ic wearp hafu, 5
ne þurh þreata ȝeþræcu þræd me ne hlimmeð,
ne æt me hrutende hrisil scriþeð,
ne mec ohwonan sceal amas cnyssan.
Wyrmas mec ne awæfan wyrda cræftum,
þa þe ȝeolo ȝodwebb ȝeatwum frætwað. 10
Wile mec non hwæþre se þeah wide ofer eorþan
hatan for hæleþum hyhtlic gewæde.
Saȝa soðcwidum, searoþoncum gleaw,
wordum wisfæst, hwæt þis ȝewædu sy.

The last two lines may be translated 'Tell in true speech, [you] sagacious in knowing, / Wise in your words, what this garment may be.'

It is customary to take the position that the Exeter Book riddle was written later than the *Leiden Riddle*. At least this particular version of the translation appears to have been. First of all, there is the rather careless argument that all surviving Northumbrian pieces are older than their West Saxon counterparts, as is illustrated by Cædmon's *Hymn*, Bede's *Death Song*, and the Lindisfarne Glosses (as compared to the West Saxon Gospels). More cogent is the fact that the Exeter Book riddle does not complete the translation. For the last two lines of the *Leiden Riddle*, which are a fair rendering of the last line of *De Lorica*, it substitutes the not-unusual "tell-what-I-am" formula. Perhaps the West Saxon translator tired of his task of handling a difficult line (which is unlikely); or perhaps, being only a transcriber or copyist, he crowded into the bottom of the folio—he had barely room to complete the riddle in the space available—the formula that he wanted to be sure to include. Most telling of all is the fact that while both the *Leiden Riddle* and the Exeter Book riddle are rather loose as to grammar,[7] the latter is more so, and some of its variations bespeak a later date. Finally, it may be that the *-æ* endings of the Old Northumbrian indicate a period of composition some time before 850.[8]

The method of translating here is the same as that found in Exeter Book Riddle 40, which is a rendering of Aldhelm's last riddle, *De Creatura*: each hexameter of the Latin riddle requires two full lines of Old English verse. The Old English version is therefore of necessity an elaboration of the Latin original. The traditions of the two systems of prosody cause the Old English translations to be wordier, more repetitious. Some of the additional words are merely formulas, particularly in the second half-line (as, for example, in lines 1b, 4b, 6a, 9b, 11b, 13a, and 13b), or of formulaic potential (3a, 6a, 12a). In one instance, however, the Old English translator improves slightly upon the Latin, if only in the interest of a tighter coherence. By transposing, he binds together in better consecutiveness the references to the actual tools of the weaver. Thus Aldhelm's lines 4–5 are not translated as Old English lines 7–8, 9–10, but as 9–10, 7–8. A pioneer scholar in the field, Dietrich (the first to point out the parallels between the *Leiden Riddle* and the Exeter Book riddle), was of the opinion that the Old English riddle was made from another and perhaps better version of *De Lorica* than the one now extant. Since there are no other surviving versions of *De Lorica*, this is therefore mere speculation and perhaps fails to give proper credit to the artistic sense of the Old English translator.

This particular device of letting two lines of Old English verse take care of a single hexameter should be studied some time in considering the translation of *De Creatura*, but such a

study lies outside the boundaries of the present article. Moreover, there will be difficulties, because in the Exeter Book
Riddle 40 the method is used for only a part of the poem.
Much of the remainder is a paraphrase rather than a translation, and the poem as a whole gives every sign of being the
product of more than one translator. The first eighty-four lines
of Exeter Book Riddle 40, however, correspond to the first
forty-two lines of Aldhelm's poem. The translator of these
first forty-two lines, whom I may designate as Translator A,
uses the same system as the translator of *De Lorica*, who may
be the same A, or Aldhelm himself, or someone else committed to the same method of translation. One tenable theory
is that the system is peculiar to A, a kind of translator's signature. One can only raise questions that cannot be answered:
Does A, with his method of translation, represent an individual
with a particular prosodic idiosyncrasy? Or is he representing
a traditional way of translating a hexameter, a tradition without surviving material sufficient either to confirm or disprove
the theory?[9]

For, save the *Leiden Riddle* and Exeter Book Riddle 35 and
Riddle 40, no further examples of this method survive. If we
look into the most extensive Old English translation of Latin
verse—the *metra* of Boethius' *De Consolatione Philosophiae*[10]
—no trace of this particular system is discernible. But here the
problem is quite different. The Latin *metra* of Boethius are of
varying verse-forms to begin with; moreover, the Old English
versions are based primarily upon the Alfredian prose translations of the *metra* and hence are once removed from the
original. They are on the whole in orthodox Old English
alliterative verse, although they contain a rather large number
of hypermetric lines, specifically *sechstakters*.

It was never intended as a joke, though it was certainly a
tour de force, but Otto B. Schlutter's re-rendering of the
Leiden Riddle into Latin is a curious episode in the history of
Old English scholarship.[11] His transcription of the riddle was
for a time the authoritative one, although he was working
without the benefit of ultraviolet light. At any rate, I include

here his contribution to the tradition of Anglo-Latin(?) poetry.

> Me humida tellus mire gelida
> ex visceribus suis principio genuit.
> Ignoro me coopertam lanae velleribus,
> villis per artificium, laborem mentis.
> Volutae non mihi sunt panuculae, non ego licium habeo, 5
> non per tortile opus filum mihi garrulat (garrulavit),
> Non stridens mihi radius vibrat (vibravit),
> non me ulla parte pecten pulsabit.
> Bombyces me non texuerunt plumaria arte
> qui quidem flavum sericum vestibus fabricant. 10
> Verumtamen homines me vocabunt late per orbem
> desiderabile vestimentum apud heroas.
> Non expavesco iaculationis terrorem timorose,
> quamvis promant sagittas hostiliter ex pharetris longis.

> Me the wet earth wonderfully ice cold
> In the beginning brought forth from its vitals.
> I do not know myself to be wrapped around with the
>   fleece of wool,
> With hairs through skill, a labor of the mind.
> Nor are clews of yarn wound about me; I have no warp. 5
> Nor does the twisted necessary thread chatter at me,
> Nor does the noisy shuttle shake me,
> Nor does the weaver's rod strike me in any part.
> Silkworms have not covered me in feathery wise,
> That make indeed yellow silk for garments. 10
> Truly men will call me, far and wide through the world,
> A desirable garment among heroes.
> I do not grow afraid of the hurling of missiles, cowering
>   in terror,
> However much men may bring forth, in hostile fashion,
>   their arrows from their long quivers.

The contrast between this and *De Lorica* is, of course, striking. Aldhelm's hexameters are usually acceptable; Schlutter's prosody is neither fish nor fowl and belongs to the school of the midnight lamp. One is reminded of the trick perpetrated by Mark Twain in *The Jumping Frog of Calaveras County*: he gives a French translation of the story and then literally translates French back into English with humorous though not exactly lucid results. In less facetious tone I should observe that the contrast is not altogether due to Schlutter's inept Latin verse. The whole business is a kind of off-beat commentary on the differences between Latin and Old English verse and of the difficulties of translation when literary traditions are so different.

The actual implements in the Anglo-Saxon's art of weaving are well represented in the *Leiden Riddle*. We have named here the woof (*uefl* 5a), the warp (*uarp* 5b), the thread (*ðret* 6b), the shuttle (*hrisil* 7b), and—of special interest—the slay-rod (*aam* 8b), whose appearance here is unique in surviving Old English literature. I suppose that the phrase ʒeolu ʒodueb (10a) might be considered a kenning for 'silk,' but the worms are not, as in *De Lorica*, vaguely Chinese. The other words, of course, are all in Aldhelm. As a matter of fact, although we hear much of the Anglo-Saxon's mastery of achievement in the art of weaving, we are not overburdened with information concerning the actual mechanics and technique of the art as he practiced it. One tends to believe that he did well with not too highly developed means, for only a few more technical terms have survived from the period than we have in this riddle.[12]

Leaving such matters of *Kulturgeschichte* aside, I think we are justified in considering the *Leiden Riddle* a poem of interest above the average, like many other riddles. Its uncommon vocabulary of the weaver's profession lends freshness to the style, and the relative paucity of trite formulas is a further help. The preponderance of type A verses is striking. Of the twenty-eight hemistichs I should say that twenty are of this type, and the resulting trochaic push is most appropriate to a subject as martial as a coat of mail. It echoes in this respect the approach of the Geats to Heorot:

> Stræt wæs stanfah,   stig wisode
> gumum ætgædere.   Guðbyrne scan

heard hondlocen,   hringiren scir
song in searwum,   þa hie to sele furðum
in hyra gryregeatwum   gangan cwomon.[13]

The street was paved with bright stones; the path showed the way to the warriors together. The war byrnie shone, hard and hand locked; the bright iron rings sang out in the armor, as they came walking to the hall in their terrible trappings.

NOTES

1. IV. 3 in the authoritative edition, that of Rudolf Ehwald, *Aldhelmi Opera*, in *Monumenta Germaniae Historica, Auctorum Antiquissimorum* (Berlin, 1919), XV. A most convenient edition, however, with English verse translation printed synoptically, is James H. Pitman, *The Riddles of Aldhelm* (New Haven, 1925). An indispensable reference work is Erika von Erhardt-Siebold, *Die lateinischen Rätsel der Angelsachsen* ("Anglistische Forschungen," Vol. LXI [Heidelberg, 1925]).

2. Latin *Ser* (from Greek *Ser*), plural *Seres*, defined in *A New and Copious Lexicon of the Latin Language*, ed. Frederick P. Leverett (Boston, 1845), as "people who dwelt in the eastern part of Asia, and are generally supposed to be . . . Chinese. From them the Roman ladies, according to Pliny, received the *vestes Sericae*."

3. A facsimile by Franz Dietrich, *Kynewulfi Poetae Aetas Aenigmatum fragmento* (Marburg, 1860), p. 27. An earlier defective transcription by Ludwig C. Bethmann in 1845 should be dismissed.

4. We should have expected *minum*, but both the *Leiden Riddle* and the Exeter Book riddle give *min*. This is a good example of the grammatical eccentricity of both riddles; but see n. 7.

5. The most recent printing, of course, is in the most attractive essay by R. W. Zandvoort, "The Leiden Riddle," *English and Germanic Studies*, III (1949–50), 42–56, which discusses the Old English riddle in general and the *Leiden Riddle* in particular, giving by far the best facsimiles of this poem yet to be found. Yet I do not think of it as an "edition" in the same sense that *Three Northumbrian Poems*, ed. A. H. Smith (London, 1933), in the Methuen Old English Library (see in particular pp. 7–10, 17–19, and 23–25) is one. There have been various other discussions of the readings, notably in *The Oldest English Texts*, ed. Henry Sweet (London, 1885), pp. 150–51; Otto B. Schlutter, "Das Leidener Rätsel," *Anglia*, XXXII (1909), 384–88, and "Zum Leidener Rätsel," *Anglia*, XXXIII (1910), 457–66; and J. H. Kern, "Das Leidener

Rätsel," *Anglia*, XXXIII (1910), 452–56, and "Noch einmal zum Leidener Rätsel," *Anglia*, XXXVIII (1914), 261–65. Schlutter's reading of the manuscript was accepted by Sweet and by Frederick Tupper for his edition of *The Riddles of the Exeter Book* (Boston, 1910), but Kern disagreed on many points. Smith calls attention to the disagreements: "The mere fact that there is disagreement amongst editors proves how inadequate the evidence of the manuscript might be, and the fact that Dr. Schlutter's second text varies from his first [as given in the two articles cited above] shows how personal the interpretation can be." The chief problem is the relative illegibility of the manuscript. Here the modern tests that Zandvoort was able to give the manuscript are revealing: he differs very little from Smith's reading.

6. See *The Riddles of the Exeter Book*, ed. Tupper, Riddle 36 and notes, pp. 26–27 and 150–54. Tupper follows the older numbering based upon the fact that *Wulf and Eadwacer* was for a long time considered Riddle 1. I follow here the present numbering as found in *The Exeter Book*, ed. G. P. Krapp and E. van K. Dobbie ("The Anglo-Saxon Poetic Records," Vol. III [New York, 1936]). The riddle is also in *Die altenglische Rätsel*, ed. Moritz Trautmann (Heidelberg, 1915), and *Old English Riddles*, ed. A. J. Wyatt (London, 1912). There have been various translations; the most recent is Paull F. Baum's (Durham, N.C., 1963).

7. See also n. 4. Obvious incongruities are the plural *hrutende* in the Exeter Book riddle (7a) with a singular noun and verb. The *Leiden Riddle* gives a singular participle-adjective and noun but a plural verb, but if *hrisil* is a neuter a-stem, there is no incongruity in the Northumbrian version. *Wyrda* (9b) represents a change of number in the Exeter Book riddle, which also changes *aam* (8b) to the plural *amas* with a singular verb, etc.

8. Uno L. Lindelof, *Die südnorthhumbrische Mundart* (Bonn, 1901), paragraphs 115 and 116.

9. The point, which I do not wish to labor, is that there is a gap of more than a century between the composition of *De Lorica* and the manuscripts of the two riddles we have in Old English, and much could have intervened. We know when Aldhelm wrote the *Ænigmata* (*ca.* 690–700), but there is no knowing when the translations were made—by Aldhelm himself before his death in 709, by another translator in the same period, or perhaps not until the ninth century. It is the same old unanswerable problem—to reconcile the date of the writing of a given Anglo-Saxon poem with the date of its surviving manuscript and form. If Translator A is only a tradition, all that has been suggested will merely complicate the unanswerable question. It is as one likes it.

10. "Die altenglischen Metra des Boetius," ed. Ernst Krämer, *Bonner Beiträge zur Anglistik*, VIII (Bonn, 1902); the best text is that in *The Paris Psalter and the Meters of Boethius*, ed. G. P. Krapp ("The

Anglo-Saxon Poetic Records," Vol. V [New York, 1932]). See also Carl
H. Schmidt, *König Alfreds Boethius-Bearbeitung* (Göttingen, 1934).

11. Schlutter, "Das Leidener Rätsel," printed in *The Riddles of the
Exeter Book*, ed. Tupper, p. 153.

12. Charles McLean Andrews, *The Old English Manor* (Baltimore,
1892), pp. 275–76; there is here a direct reference to the *Leiden Riddle*
or the Exeter Book Riddle 35.

13. *Beowulf*, ll. 320–24.

PART THREE

BEOWULF

JOTTINGS ON *BEOWULF* AND THE AESTHETIC APPROACH

❧❧❧

Adrien Bonjour

The controversy that arose in the wake of the spectacular launching of the singer theory in Anglo-Saxon poetry shows no sign of abating. Indeed the gap between the supporters of unity of authorship in *Beowulf* and the neodisintegrators of the text of the poem is wider than ever. It therefore looks as if any attempt to span the gap by ever so tenuous a flying bridge is doomed from the outset to utter failure or at best bound to turn into a *dialogue de sourds*. Despite such gloomy prospects, I suggest that one more or less tacit point of agreement by itself provides a meeting ground susceptible of a fair and not entirely idle exchange of arguments.

The position of the two schools of *Beowulf* criticism are diametrically opposed mainly when it comes to over-all generalizations. As soon as they leave the vast field of large theorizing and ample extrapolations to come to grips with precise and particular points, there occurs an inevitable *rapprochement* owing to the fact that both parties are ultimately bound to use a roughly similar criterion. This does not mean, of course, that their conclusions should suddenly come close to one another. Far from it. But the very fact that both contending parties actually resort, whether they want it or not, to the same type of criterion renders a confrontation interesting and useful. This I shall try to prove by examining some of the arguments that Francis P. Magoun, Jr., has recently propounded in favor of a multiple authorship of the *Beowulf* poem.

Until recently, the father of the oral-formulaic theory in Anglo-Saxon poetry had not explicitly drawn some of the bolder conclusions to which the theory could be expected to lead and had not ventured on a closely argued vindication of the composite origin of the poem. We must therefore be grateful that he should have decided to cross the Rubicon and argue, with full provision of proof, that the *Beowulf* material in Cotton Vitellius A.xv is made up of originally independent songs by different singers, so that it is suitable to speak of a *Beowulf A* and a *Beowulf B*, soldered together by means of a *Beowulf A¹*. His arguments in favor of this supposed trinity are certainly worth discussing—not only because of the important issue involved but also because he presents them in a rather moderate and far from overmilitant way. Though he seems to invite controversy, his very restraint calls for as balanced as possible an attempt to put things into focus.

Let us begin with Hrothgar's prophecy of Beowulf's future kingship. Magoun writes:

> In view of what is told about Béowulf's gradual advance in the Gautish line of royal succession and his final accession to the throne, . . . these passages in *Béowulf A* take on the air of a prophecy, as indeed they are, but again they can point in no special way to a single poet anticipating an event which he plans to deal with a bit later. To me it only points to the fact that almost any singer who knew any part of the *Béowulf* material was likely, though not perhaps inevitably, to know all parts. Hence, given a situation such as Hróthgár's in the present context, namely, the need of making an appreciative and flattering farewell speech, the singer could look into the future in a general way without in the least committing himself to sing about it in the immediate future or perhaps ever.[1]

On the face of it nothing prevents us from supposing that this prophecy, as such, may have been introduced by a poet who knew that Beowulf finally ascended the Geatish throne, even if he had no intention of carrying his story thus far, and was bent on celebrating his hero's exploits in Denmark only. On the other hand, to answer the mere requirements of a flattering farewell speech, the reference to Beowulf's future kingship would have been amply sufficient. The allusion to Beowulf's earlier refusal of the throne in favor of young Heardred—a very veiled one at that, which, to be fully grasped, required that even an attentive member of the audience have a nimble mind—makes it likely, implicit as it is, that the poet meant to refer to the fact in a more explicit way in its appropriate context. Thus Magoun's statement that this prophecy has no bearing one way or another on the question of unity of authorship is perhaps a little too categorical. Probability ever so slightly tips the balance one way rather than the other.

But even if we should agree with Magoun's conclusions on this particular point, there is yet a group of anticipations that do have a bearing on the question and much more eloquently speak in favor of unity of authorship than the prophecy about Beowulf's future kingship. Take what I have called "allusive anticipations," forecasting events beyond the scene of action of the poem. It is quite significant that, however numerous these anticipatory hints and whatever the circumstances in which they are introduced, scattered as they are throughout the poem from the foreshadowings of the burning of Heorot to the Messenger's epic prophecy, they always imply a tragic event. There is no single exception: in every individual instance of an allusive anticipation there looms the destruction either of something most beautiful, like the splendid royal palace of the Danes; or of present peace between two nations, like the Scyldings and the Heathobards; or of the actual independence of a glorious people, like the Geats. Present beauty, peace, harmony, stability, national glory—these are the things most precious that are doomed to be destroyed (so the allusive anticipations clearly imply) within a very near future. Thus it is really fit to speak of a common function that may be said to characterize these anticipations as a group. Their total effect is to stress the transience of everything in this world, above all the things most valued and valuable. Surely the motive has something to do with the prevailing mood of the poem and its tragic atmosphere.[2] How strange that the *A* singer (to use Magoun's terminology), whose only object was to celebrate the triumph of the young hero in Denmark, should have resorted to exactly the same subtle use of allusive anticipations as the *B* singer, who was composing a poem on the old hero's death. I am no expert in matters statistical, but from an aesthetic point of view the chances that we have to deal here with pure felicitous coincidence are decidedly remote. On the other hand, the common function that must be attributed to these anticipatory hints makes it much more likely that they have been used—to good purpose and with relevant artistry— by one and the same poet. In other words, their presence in *Beowulf A* can best be explained and justified by the assumption that they strike the first notes of a leitmotiv that finds its full scope and climax towards the end of *Beowulf B*.

Let us now pass to the well-known discrepancy between Beowulf's promising and unpromising childhood. According to Magoun, "it is only natural to feel that this small but telling difference in the knowledge in the *Béowulf* tradition points to two different singers. Were all this body of material a play by T. S. Eliot or the American poet-dramatist Archibald MacLeish with their studied subtleties one might well imagine that the unpromising child was the reality and that the highly regarded child represented wishful thinking on the part of the aging king. But we do not have to do with T. S. Eliot nor apparently with a lettered work at all and accordingly should probably not indulge in such psychologizing."[3] No doubt a psychological interpretation on the lines that are humorously suggested here would hardly convince anybody. But while keeping in mind what we know of the poet's psychology—such as his use of indirect characterization—we do not have to go far to seek a much more likely explanation for the discrepancy.

As a recent critic puts it, "the poem is not intended to have the consistency of James Joyce's *Ulysses*: if we are troubled by the conflicting accounts of Beowulf's youth, we must take comfort in the fact that the poet draws on different traditions to suit his particular purpose in different parts of the poem."[4] The poet's purpose in employing the sluggish-youth motif is clear and perfectly justified in its immediate context: its deliberate effect of surprise, far from being detrimental to our opinion of the hero, makes his ascent the more extraordinary and skillfully serves to enhance his present glory.[5] His purpose when using the opposite tradition is more difficult to assess.

But what must be remembered—and this does not seem to have been noticed or at least duly stressed—is that in the former passage it is the narrator who speaks, whereas in the second it is the hero himself. And this makes all the difference. For the poet more than once deftly uses this shift in the angle of vision to make us grasp a characteristic point. He thus gives his own narration of Beowulf's fight against the dragon in such a way that Wiglaf's part can be discerned with a fair amount of objectivity. But when he has Wiglaf tell of his own version of the fight, it is clear that a conspicuous difference takes place as against the poet's account: the young hero underestimates the actual part he played in the whole business in order to enhance the old king's heroism. Wiglaf's modesty could not have been better conveyed than by this brilliant piece of indirect characterization. It is quite possible that in the present instance we have to deal with a similar process. Old Beowulf only remembers his former sovereign's liberalities and the favor he enjoyed at court and magnanimously forgets a period when gifts were withheld from him at the mead bench. He pays his dead lord and protector unrestricted homage. His generosity is thus strongly emphasized and confirmed, and such delicacy of feeling is only what might have been expected from Beowulf as the gentlest of men.[6] There is no need to conjure up a piece of psychologizing in the manner of MacLeish in order to explain the possible meaning of the discrepancy.

On the other hand, even if this suggested interpretation should be waved aside, the discrepancy does not necessarily imply that two different singers were at work. Hrothgar tells us that he has no idea whither Grendel's mother has escaped and then, after some twelve lines only, passes to his famous evocation of the haunted mere. Surely Magoun would hardly conclude that this discrepancy is the result of multiple authorship. As everybody knows, "even Shakespeare is not without sins of this kind!"[7]

Magoun finds another argument against unity of authorship in the various accounts of Hygelac's death in the Rhineland.

He first observes that "the *A*-singer refers to this event, and in a sense casually, only once," whereas "for the *B*-singer it seems to be of far greater interest, for he refers to the event five times . . ." As the critic himself is aware, this difference may be accounted for by the fact that in the first part of the poem the Frisian raid had not yet taken place. According to his usual technique, the poet therefore only referred to it in the form of an allusive anticipation: there was no question of anticipating the part played by Beowulf in the expedition any more than the part he played in the dragon fight. A single and casual (though by no means trifling) allusion is therefore perfectly normal. But what strikes Magoun as particularly significant is not so much this difference as such as the fact that "the *B*-singer is obviously far more interested in the Rhineland episode than in the Heorot adventure to which he refers only twice. . . . When, for instance, Béowulf reminisces about the former strength of his grip, he thinks of the time he crushed the Frank Dæʒhræfn to death (2501–8a), not of Grendel. So marked a difference in interest in Béowulf's own past does not strike me as compatible with the attitude of a single person composing a continuous song."[8] This argumentation calls for the following remarks.

The reasons for the poet's interest in the Frisian expedition lie close at hand, and his references to the event are justified both from a structural and a technical point of view. Furthermore, there is a feature common to each of the different accounts, whether belonging to the first or the second part of the poem. This common feature confers upon them a particular significance in relation to the hero's exceptional stature and therefore unites them into a coherent pattern.

As a matter of fact, Beowulf's reminiscences about the former strength of his grip include both his victory over Grendel and his killing of Daeghrefn in the Frisian raid. After mentioning his duel with the Frankish champion, whom he crushed with the sheer strength of his arm, the hero says that he is going to use a sword to fight for the hoard: *Nū sceall billes ecg, | hond ond heard sweord ymb hord wīgan* 'now must the edge of the sword, the hand and the brave sword, do battle over the hoard' (2508b–9).[9] He actually would not want to use one (he stresses a few lines further) if only he knew how to come to grips with the monster as he did with Grendel; but he fears the dragon's fire and poison and therefore also takes a buckler and a coat of mail:

> Nolde ic sweord beran,
> wǣpen tō wyrme,   gif ic wiste hū
> wið ðām āglǣcean   elles meahte
> gylpe wiðgrīpan,   swā ic giō wið Grendle dyde;
> ac ic ðǣr heaðu-fȳres   hātes wēne,
> oreðes ond attres;   forðon ic mē on hafu
> bord ond byrnan.   (2518b–24a)

I would not carry a sword, a weapon against the serpent, if I knew how else I could grapple boldly with the monster, as I did before with Grendel; but I expect hot battle fire [from] poisonous breath: therefore I have on my shield and byrnie.

The two references to his exceptional handgrip, which made these victories possible, are therefore quite parallel and complete each other. How can it be said that Beowulf does not think of Grendel? Moreover, these two different references pointing to the same conclusion are introduced in perfect accordance with the poet's technique of variation.

To these correspond two other parallel mentions of Beowulf's exploits at Heorot and on the Frisian coast, introduced this time by the poet himself; normally enough they are as closely linked as the former, though in a different way:

> nō hē him þā sæcce ondrēd,
> nē him þæs wyrmes wīg   for wiht dyde,
> eafoð ond ellen,   forðon hē ǣr fela
> nearo nēðende   nīða gedīgde,
> hilde-hlemma,   syððan hē Hrōðgāres,
> sigor-ēadig secg,   sele fǣlsode
> ond æt gūðe forgrāp   Grendeles mǣgum
> lāðan cynnes.

> Nō þæt læsest wæs
> hond-gemōta, þær mon Hygelāc slōh,
> syððan Gēata cyning gūðe ræsum,
> frēa-wine folca Frēs-londum on,
> Hrēðles eafora hiora-dryncum swealt,
> bille gebēaten. Þonan Bīowulf cōm
> sylfes cræfte, sund-nytte drēah;
> hæfde him on earme āna þrītig
> hilde-geatwa, þā hē tō holme stāg. (2347b–62)

he did not dread the fight at all, nor did he care much for the war craft, the might and the courage of the serpent; indeed, he had earlier survived terrors, strokes of battle, daring difficulties, after he, a man blessed with victories, cleansed Hrothgar's hall and in battle crushed Grendel's kin, the hated race, to death. That was not the least of hand-to-hand encounters when one slew Hygelac, after the king of the Geatas, the lord of the people, Hrethel's heir, died in Frisia in the surges of battle of the drinks of the sword, beaten by the sword. Beowulf came from there by his own strength, he survived through swimming; he had by himself on his arm thirty suits of armor, when he went into the sea.

This repeated close association is significant enough and proves that the poet has used both striking events on the same level and with excellent purpose. I can hardly see there a marked difference in interest in Beowulf's own past. The poet, to be sure, makes another two or three mentions of the Frisian expedition; but what really counts is that he had very good reasons to do so. In the last of these references, which occurs in the Messenger's great speech, the political aspect of Hygelac's expedition and death in Frisia is clearly stressed and acquires ominous significance:

> Nū ys lēodum wēn
> orleg-hwīle, syððan underne
> Froncum ond Frȳsum fyll cyninges
> wīde weorðeð. Wæs sīo wrōht scepen

heard wið Hūgas,   syððan Higelāc cwōm
faran flot-herge   on Frēsna land,
þǣr hyne Hetware   hilde genǣgdon,
elne geēodon   mid ofer-mǣgene,
þæt se byrn-wiga   būgan sceolde,
fēoll on fēðan;   nalles frætwe geaf
ealdor dugoðe.   (2910b–20a)

Now I expect a time of battle for people, after the death of the king becomes widely known to the Franks and Frisians. Harsh hostility has been shaped against the Hugas, after Hygelac came moving with a sea-borne army against Frisia, where the Hetwara attacked him in battle, advanced boldly with their superior strength, so that the corseleted warrior had to bow down, to fall in the troop; the prince did not give an ornament to his comitatus.

It is obvious, therefore, that the recurrence of references to Hygelac's fall can be explained mainly by the poet's wish to keep before the audience's eyes the image of that fateful raid that not only carried in its train, as Arthur G. Brodeur has convincingly demonstrated,[10] a decisive weakening of Geatish might but bore in itself the seed of future disaster. Once the power of the Geatish nation has suffered a further blow with the fall of its old heroic king, the Franks and Frisians are likely to remember the feud, and renewed hostility is bound to break out. Just as the repeated mentions of the Swedish-Geatish wars provide an impressive basis on which a renewal of the strife could be prophesied and presented as ineluctable,[11] so the frequent references to the Frisian raid also pave the way for the full effect of the somber forebodings that lend the Messenger's speech its haunting reverberations. Structurally the two outstanding feuds in Geatish history, which had so far been glanced at separately, are now closely linked together and complete each other as so many intimations of the fire of future war smoldering under the ashes. Mentions of Hygelac's death in the Rhineland thus deftly achieve what a host of further reminiscences of the Grendel fight would have been utterly unable to do. No wonder that the poet is far more interested in the Rhineland episode than in the Heorot adventure, which he had already told twice at some length and out of which he still managed to squeeze additional dividends by means of two retrospective references.

Finally, whatever the particular emphasis and function of each separate mention of the Frisian expedition in its own immediate context, there is one constant element that binds the various accounts into a closely knit and meaningful unit within the larger framework of the poem. The first reference to the raid is introduced in connection with the great and famous neck ring presented to Beowulf after his victory over Grendel:

> Þone hring hæfde   Higelāc Gēata,
> nefa Swertinges,   nȳhstan sīðe,
> sīðþan hē under segne   sinc ealgode,
> wæl-rēaf werede;   hyne wyrd fornam,
> syþðan hē for wlenco   wēan āhsode,
> fæhðe tō Frȳsum.   Hē þā frætwe wæg,
> eorclan-stānas   ofer yða ful,
> rīce þēoden;   hē under rande gecranc.
> Gehwearf þā in Francna fæþm   feorh cyninges,
> brēost-gewædu   ond se bēah somod;
> wyrsan wīg-frecan   wæl rēafodon
> æfter gūð-sceare . . .   (1202–13a)

Hygelac of the Geatas, the nephew of Swerting, had that ring on the last occasion, when he protected the treasure under the standard, defended the spoil of battle; fate took him off, after he asked for trouble, a feud with the Frisians, out of pride. He, powerful prince, carried the treasure, the precious stones, over the cup of the waves; he fell beneath his shield. The king's body, his coat of mail, and the ring with it, came then into the possession of the Franks; worse warriors despoiled the corpse after the fall in battle . . .

The political consequences of the raid are left implicit and the whole emphasis is laid on the loss or gain of arms and jewels as war spoils. Thus the reference looks casual only on the surface. The remarkable point is that this emphasis strikes the actual leitmotiv common to each of the different accounts of the raid with *frætwe* as the key word.

In the next account, indeed, war spoil is again heavily stressed. The poet, as we have seen, tells us how Beowulf escaped with an armful of spoils. The *Hætt-ware*, he says, got no booty from him (implying a contrast with Hygelac, who left not only his body but his valuable arms and splendid necklace in enemy hands).

In the Daeghrefn episode, in its turn, strong emphasis again lies on the loss or gain of armor and jewels. It is stressed that the Frankish champion was by no means allowed to bring to his king the precious necklace that Beowulf had on, but fell at his hands in the fight:

> Nalles hē ðā frætwe   Frēs-cyninge,
> brēost-weorðunge   bringan mōste,
> ac in campe gecrong   cumbles hyrde,
> æþeling on elne . . .   (2503–6a)

He could not bring the treasure, the ornament of the breast, for the Frisian king at all, but, guardian of the standard, the prince in his boldness fell in battle . . .

In the last account, as we have just seen, the political aspect of the Frisian raid is finally singled out and given a significant share. But for that matter the theme of the battle spoils is neither forgotten nor left in the background: 'no treasures indeed did the leader [i.e., Hygelac] give to his duguth.' The irony implicit behind the understatement is eloquent: instead of bringing back precious war spoils—which would have been his duty towards his faithful retainers—the king abandoned in enemy hands all the treasures he had brought from across the sea. The disastrous consequences of the king's defeat and death are now clearly intimated by the Messenger.

The evidence is conclusive: the *frætwa* 'treasure' worn on his *brēost-gewǣdu* 'coat of mail' by Hygelac in the Frisian raid (1207), which is the same *frætwe* mentioned in the Messenger's speech (2919), is closely linked with the *frætwe*, or *brēost-weorðunge* 'heart ornament,' the hero had on in the same expedition. "But whereas Hygelac's most precious neck-ring (ironically the very one which had been received by Beowulf at the Danish court and handed over to Hygelac's Queen by the hero, mindful of his duty as a retainer, on his return from Denmark) fell into enemy hands together with the king's protective armour when he died on the battle-field, Beowulf's own 'breast-adornment' escaped a similar fate and was brought back unscathed together with enemy spoil."[12] In other words, Beowulf managed to perform as a retainer what his own sovereign should have done but failed to achieve. From an aesthetic point of view the masterly use of such a leitmotiv as the theme of battle spoils to evince once more the hero's exceptional stature cannot possibly be fortuitous—unless mere coincidence be subtly and methodically creative.

It could likewise be shown why the handling of genealogical data in the dragon part by means of several flashbacks[13] so strongly differs, technically speaking, from the smooth way the genealogical question is approached at the very opening of the poem. As to Magoun's contention that "the consistency of Béowulf's character throughout the preserved material is in itself no argument for unity of authorship, no more, in fact, than is the high degree of consistency in the style, diction, and syntax of the poetic corpus in general,"[14] we may well endorse it as far as it goes. But again what is of much greater importance for the question of unity of authorship is the poetic power displayed in the first as well as in the second part of the poem. The quality of the poetry and its reverberations both within a restricted and in a larger context (think of the ship burial on the one hand, of the Messenger's prophetic speech on the other) is such that it would by itself distinguish *Beowulf* and set it apart from anything else in the corpus. Furthermore, only the aesthetic approach allows us to realize how both parts of the poem mutually (and considerably) gain in significance and appeal when they are viewed as two contrasting, but complementary, panels of a great diptych.

Such arguments, I am aware, can best be applied when the pre-eminence of the poetic perception is fully recognized. Now I am afraid it is precisely on this point that the gap between the upholders of unity of authorship and the neodisintegrators will be most difficult to bridge. For, in the last resort, it is the poetry that counts. And it so happens that we might read on end most of the numerous interesting and valuable *Beowulf* articles written by Magoun and his followers without being aware that what they deal with is poetry. I mean great poetry, as contradistinguished from mere metrical matter—whether a legion of alliterative lines, a crowd of competent cadences, or a stack of staves.

In a recent review I have been wittily reproached with training my heaviest cannon on a couple of sparrows.[15] In the present instance, at least, the game is much weightier and the gun, I hope, of normally decent caliber.

NOTES

1. "*Béowulf B:* A Folk-Poem on Béowulf's Death," in *Early English and Norse Studies*, ed. Arthur Brown and Peter Foote (London, 1963), p. 139.

2. See Adrien Bonjour, *Twelve "Beowulf" Papers 1940–1960, with Additional Comments* (Geneva, 1962), pp. 27–28.

3. "*Béowulf B*," pp. 136–37.

4. Bruce Mitchell, "*Until the Dragon Comes* ... Some Thoughts on Beowulf," *Neophilologus*, XLVII (1963), 127.

5. See Bonjour, *Twelve "Beowulf" Papers*, p. 95.

6. *Ibid.*, pp. 95–96.

7. Mitchell, "*Until the Dragon Comes.*"

8. "*Béowulf B*," p. 134.

9. Quotations are from the text of C. L. Wrenn's edition of *Beowulf* (Boston, 1953).

10. *The Art of Beowulf* (Berkeley, Calif., 1959), pp. 81–86.

11. See Adrien Bonjour, *The Digressions in Beowulf* (Oxford, 1950), pp. 42–43.

12. Bonjour, *Twelve "Beowulf" Papers*, p. 88.

13. See Magoun, "*Béowulf B*," pp. 132–33.

14. *Ibid.*, p. 138.

15. See *Modern Language Review*, LVIII (1963), 550. One of the "sparrows" in question, by the way, happens to be Father Maurice B. McNamee, whose theory of *Beowulf* as an allegory of salvation I countered with some serious objections. In a recent article by an Oxford scholar his plea is considered as "by no means impossible" (Mitchell, "*Until the Dragon Comes*," p. 135), which proves after all that his identity as a feathered denizen in the groves of *Beowulf* criticism is far from definitely settled.

THE PAGAN COLORING OF *BEOWULF*

❧

Larry D. Benson

The old theory that *Beowulf* is an essentially pagan work only slightly colored with the Christianity of a later scribe has now been dead for many years, and critics today generally agree that the poem is the unified work of a Christian author.[1] Indeed, most of the elements in *Beowulf* that once supplied arguments for its essential paganism—the function of Wyrd, the emphasis on the comitatus, the duty of revenge—are now recognized not as pagan but as secular values that were easily incorporated into the framework of Anglo-Saxon Christianity.[2] Likewise, though the stories of Beowulf and the monsters probably originated in pagan times, it is now generally acknowledged that they have been assimilated into a Christian world view with the monsters allied with the devil and Beowulf (or so Friedrich Klaeber and others have held) fitted to the pattern of Christ himself.[3] Yet the ghost of the old pagan-versus-Christian dispute still lingers, for along with the Christian and Christianized secular elements the poem does contain some indisputably pagan features that have remained intractable to modern criticism. Moreover, the knockings of that spirit have become steadily more insistent, for the more deeply Christian the meanings of *Beowulf* are discovered to be, the more difficult become the still-unanswered questions raised by H. M. Chadwick in 1912: "If the poem preserves its original form and is the work of a Christian, it is difficult to see why the poet should go out of his way in v. 175 ff. to represent the Danes as offering heathen sacrifices. . . . Again why should he lay Beowulf himself to rest with heathen obsequies, described in all possible detail . . .?"[4] Why, one must ask, should the poet's whole representation of

193

the Danes and Geats include all the other details that Chadwick notes—the funeral ship (27 ff.), the observation of omens
(204), and the use of cremation (1108 ff., 2124 ff., 3137 ff.)?[5]

The intrusion of these pagan elements into an otherwise
completely Christian work presents more difficult problems
than the simple matter of factual inconsistency. Certainly the
poet is inconsistent in first showing us the Danes listening to
the Christian account of the Creation and then, a few lines
later, telling us that they knew nothing of God and sacrificed
to idols. That is only the sort of historical inaccuracy that one
expects in medieval poetry; Chaucer and Shakespeare confused pagan and Christian elements in much the same way.[6]
Poets (especially medieval poets) are responsible for total
aesthetic effect rather than documentary accuracy. The difficulty in *Beowulf* is that the pagan elements seem to confound
the aesthetic effect, to destroy the consistency of tone. Instead
of casually mixing pagan and Christian, as so many medieval
poets do, the *Beowulf* poet goes out of his way to draw our
attention to the Danes' heathen sacrifices. Furthermore, the
paganism that he describes is not simply literary or historical;
it was a still strong and threatening force in his own day. For
him to present his characters as heathens is, so we assume, to
show them in the worst of possible lights. Alcuin, in his famous
letter to the monks at Lindisfarne, defines for us the Christian
Englishman's attitude toward the pagans: *Quid Hinieldus cum
Christo? Angusta est domus: utrosque tenere non poterit. Non
vult rex cęlestis cum paganis et perditis nominetenus regibus
communionem habere* 'what has Ingeld to do with Christ?
Narrow is the house; it cannot hold both. The King of Heaven
wants no fellowship at all with pagan and damned kings.'[7]
Given this attitude toward the heathens, our poet's insistence
that his characters are both emphatically pagan and exception-
ally good seems self-contradictory, and that apparent contradiction has seemed to many critics a touch of feebleness at the very
heart of the poem, so feeble that even his warmest admirers have
been forced either to fall back on the old theory of scribal
tampering or to conclude that the poet simply blundered.[8]

The blunder may be our own, for the apparent contradiction arises, not from the poem itself, but from our assumptions about the meaning of paganism to the poet and his audience. These assumptions have been based on our knowledge of one letter by Alcuin, written in a spirit of reforming zeal at the end of the eighth century, and scattered comments by Bede, who is not quite so inflexible in his attitude toward pagans as his doctrinal pronouncements make him seem.[9] The extreme distaste for everything pagan that these comments exhibit is not typical of the age to which the composition of *Beowulf* is usually assigned; beginning in the last years of the seventh century and extending throughout the eighth, the dominant attitude of Christian Englishmen toward the Germanic pagans was one of interest, sympathy, and occasionally even admiration. This was the period during which the English church was engaged in an intense missionary activity on the Continent, sending missionaries in significant numbers first to the Frisians and Danes and then to the Old Saxons and the tribes in central Germany. This major undertaking, the great interest that it aroused in England, and the attitude it fostered toward pagandom has received relatively little attention from students of *Beowulf*; yet it can shed considerable light on the problems raised by the pagan elements in the poem, revealing artistry where we thought we detected blunders.

I

The missionary activity of the English church began by accident when Wilfred, on his way to Rome to protest his deposition as Bishop of York, landed in Frisia to avoid falling into the hands of his political enemies and spent the winter of 678–79 as guest of the pagan king Aldgisl.[10] He preached the gospel to the heathens, apparently with some success, and then traveled on to Rome. He returned to England, where he occupied a number of sees during his contentious career, but evidently he always maintained an interest in the missionary work in Frisia. In 697 he consecrated a bishop, Suidbert, for the Frisian mission, and the founder of the most successful mission there was Willibrord, who had been Wilfred's student at Ripon and whom Wilfred visited when he again passed through Frisia in 703.

The next missionary effort came from English monks living in Ireland. As Bede tells it, the mission began with the plan of Egbert, who *proposuit animo pluribus prodesse; id est, initio opere apostolico, verbum Dei aliquibus earum quae nondum audierant gentibus evangelizando committere: quarum in Germania plurimas noverat esse nationes, a quibus Angli vel Saxones qui nunc Brittaniam incolunt, genus et originem duxisse noscuntur; unde hactenus a vicina gente Brettonum corrupte Garmani nuncupantur. Sunt autem Fresones, Rugini, Danai, Hunni, Antiqui Saxones, Boructuari: sunt alii perplures eisdem in partibus populi paganis adhuc ritibus servientes . . .* 'set his mind on doing good to many; that is, by undertaking the apostolic work, to preach to some of those peoples that had not yet heard the word of God; he knew that there were several such nations in Germany, from which the Angles or Saxons who now inhabit Britain are known to have taken their stock and origin; hence, by the neighboring race of the Britons they are to this day corruptly called "Garmani." These are the Frisians, the *Rugini*, the Danes, the Huns, the Old Saxons, the *Boructuari*; there are many other peoples in these same parts still in servitude to pagan rites . . .' [11] Egbert was deterred from this undertaking by a series of visions and a shipwreck. Yet he had established the plan, basing it on the idea of the kinship between the insular and Continental "Garmani" that was to remain a basic motivation of this missionary work. One of his disciples, Wictbert, took up the task next and preached for two years, though without success, to the Frisians and to their king Rathbod.[12]

The next year, 690, Willibrord, who had spent several years in Ireland as a pupil of Egbert after his studies at Ripon, set out for Frisia with a company of twelve English missionaries.[13] Shortly thereafter, two more English priests, both named Hewald (known as "White" and "Black" Hewald, from the colors of their hair), journeyed to the Continent and met martyrdom among the Old Saxons (whose alderman, though a pagan, was incensed at this murder and avenged their deaths).[14] But despite this setback the mission flourished. Suidbert, one of Willibrord's twelve helpers, was consecrated bishop by Wilfred and carried the mission to the *Boructuari*, and Willibrord received the pallium at Rome and extended his work in Frisia. He carried the gospel even to the Danes, whose king, Ongendus, received him with "every mark of honor" but was unimpressed by his preaching.[15] Nevertheless, Willibrord brought back with him from Denmark thirty Danish youths whom he instructed in the Christian faith, and on his return journey he visited and desecrated the famous pagan shrine at Heligoland. At the time Bede was writing, Willibrord still lived among his converted flock in Frisia, one of the heroes of the English church.

The next and greatest stage in the movement was the mission of Boniface.[16] With two companions he sailed with a trader from London to Frisia in 716. He spent the winter among the Frisians and, meeting with no success, returned to England. After a trip to Rome he went again to Frisia, preaching in places as yet untouched by missionaries. He succeeded Willibrord as leader of the movement and turned his attention to the Old Saxons. From Britain an "exceedingly large number of holy men came to his aid, among them readers, writers, and learned men trained in the other arts."[17] In his last years he went back to Frisia and, pushing farther into heathendom, was martyred near the border of Denmark in 754. He was succeeded by Lull, another Englishman, and the missionary effort of the English church continued unabated throughout the eighth century; the later intellectual expeditions of scholars such as Alcuin were only extensions of the movement that Wilfred and Willibrord began.

One of the most remarkable features of these missions was the close relation that they all maintained with the homeland. We have already noted Wilfred's continuing interest in Frisia and the fact that Suidbert returned to England to be consecrated a bishop at Wilfred's hands. We also know that another of Willibrord's helpers visited Lindisfarne, and in general, even though Willibrord's correspondence does not survive, there is evidence of frequent intercourse between his mission and England.[18] Likewise, it is probable that a good many other Englishmen joined him, for the missionary expeditions were fairly large, involving not one or two wandering preachers but the mission *suorum tantum stipatus clientum numero* 'accompanied by a great number of servants,' including even armed soldiers.[19] Boniface's letters do survive, as do those of his successor, Lull, and beginning with the first quarter of the eighth century, we have ample evidence for Levison's assertion that "the continental mission was regarded as a national undertaking of the whole English people ..."[20] It was to England that Boniface looked for advice, books, and the help of prayer, and his correspondents included clergy and laymen alike from Thanet to Lindisfarne. On one occasion he addressed a letter, which we shall shortly examine, to the entire English nation. The nation responded by turning its eyes to the pagan Continent—hoping for the conversion of the heathen, for the prayers of the missionaries, or like King Ethelbert of Kent, for a pair of falcons of the sort that Boniface had sent along with shields and spears as a gift to the king of Mercia.[21]

II

The extent and intensity of this traffic with the Continent has long been known, but this knowledge has had little effect on the study of *Beowulf*. This is largely because the English missions have been considered only in relation to the history of the plot. As early as 1816 Outzen proposed that the missions in Frisia supplied the route by which the story of Beowulf reached the poet.[22] The more recent discovery of the possible English origin of the *Liber Monstrorum* with its account of Hygelac, which probably came to England by way of Frisia, has led critics to reflect anew that a good many Englishmen of the late seventh and eighth centuries must have seen or heard of

Hygelac's grave on that island in the mouth of the Frisian Rhine.[23] It does seem likely that English travelers would have brought home some tales of Hygelac and Hrothgar, of Finn, and perhaps even of Beowulf—if not the tales our poet used, at least some related tales that helped kindle new interest in the old materials. Likewise, the Frisians, that "great trading people of the North" who dealt with Christian London on the west and pagan Scandinavia on the east,[24] are the most likely means by which tales of the Swedes and stories of Sigmund would have reached England. We know that the Frisians had a recognized class of minstrels,[25] and it would be surprising if their store of songs did not include at least some of the tales used in *Beowulf*. Yet this is only conjecture, and critics have rightly set aside the impossible task of tracing the exact sources of the plot and have turned their attention elsewhere.

Unfortunately, in turning away from the Continent as a contemporary source for the poet's plot, they have also turned away from it as a source of the poet's knowledge of heathen customs, such as the burials in *Beowulf*. The study of *Beowulf* has been needlessly complicated by a search of the English past for the possible hints and memories upon which the poet could have based his accounts of pagan funerals. Even the Sutton Hoo discovery has been of little help; but on the Continent, where the English missionaries were working, pagan burials both by cremation and by interment in mounds continued throughout the eighth century, as we know from laws directed against anyone who *corpus defuncti homini secundum ritum paganorum flamma consumi fecerit et ossa eius ad cinerem redierit* 'has had the body of a deceased man consumed by flame and returned his bones to ashes according to the rite of the pagans' or who buried the dead *ad tumulus paganorum* 'at a grave-mound of the pagans.'[26] Likewise, such practices as augury and sacrificing to idols might reflect a memory of England's own past but are more likely based on some knowledge of the Germanic pagans themselves, for throughout the Continent divination and idol-worship were widely and persistently practiced.[27] That Christians of this period were

199

interested in learning about such practices is shown by the contemporary references to pagan beliefs that have survived,[28] and certainly some information of this sort must have been a common subject of conversation whenever a cleric or trader returned to England with news of the missions. We cannot be sure that any of the poet's plot reached him by this route, but we can be positive that he had at his disposal a good deal of information about the pagans that he chose to celebrate.

More important to the student confronted with the problem of the poet's characterization of his pagans is the attitude toward the Germanic heathen which the missionaries maintained and encouraged among their supporters in England. They had none of Alcuin's disdain, and from Egbert to Lull one of the prime motives for the missions was the sympathy fostered by the kinship between the English and *noster gens*, the Germanic tribes on the Continent.[29] This sympathy appears in Bede's account of Egbert's decision to become a missionary, quoted above, and it is stated even more emphatically in the celebrated letter that Boniface wrote in 738 to the whole English nation, from the bishops to the laymen, *immo generaliter omnibus catholicis* 'indeed, to all Catholics in general': *Fraternitatis vestrae clementiam intimis obsecramus precibus . . . ut deus et dominus noster Iesus Christus, "qui vult omnes homines salvos fieri et ad agnitionem Dei venire," convertat ad catholicam fidem corda paganorum Saxonum, et resipiscant a diabuli laqueis, a quibus capti tenetur, et adgregentur filiis matris ecclesiae. Miseremini illorum, quia et ipsi solent dicere: " De uno sanguine et de uno osse sumus"* 'We implore the mercy of your brotherhood with deepest prayers [that you pray] . . . that God and Our Lord Jesus Christ, "who wants all men to be saved and to come to the knowledge of God," may turn the hearts of the pagan Saxons to the Catholic faith, and that they may repent of the devilish snares by which they are held captive, and be joined to the sons of Mother Church. Have mercy upon them, for they themselves are accustomed to say, "We are of one blood and one bone." '[30] The tone of this letter, its certainty that the pagan Saxons are damned if they

are not converted, and its intense sympathy with their plight
is almost the same as that which we find in one of the most
difficult passages in *Beowulf*, the poet's overt comment on the
Danes' idol worship:

Swylc wæs þēaw hyra,
hǣþenra hyht;   helle gemundon
in mōdsefan,   Metod hīe ne cūþon,
dǣda Dēmend,   ne wiston hīe Drihten God,
nē hīe hūru heofena Helm   herian ne cūþon,
wuldres Waldend.   Wā bið þǣm ðe sceal
þurh slīðne nīð   sāwle bescūfan
in fȳres fæþm,   frōfre ne wēnan,
wihte gewendan!   Wēl bið þǣm þe mōt
æfter dēaðdæge   Drihten sēcean
ond tō Fæder fæþmum   freoðo wilnian![31]

(178–88)

Such was their custom, the hope of the heathens; they
remembered hell in their minds, they did not know the
Ruler, the Judge of Deeds, nor did they know the Lord
God, nor indeed did they know how to praise the Protector of Heaven, the Ruler of Glory. Woe be to him who
must, in terrible affliction, thrust his soul into the embrace of fire, expect no consolation, no change at all!
Well is it for him who, after the day of death, can seek the
Lord and ask for peace in the embrace of the Father!

Critics have often suggested that these lines must refer to some
relapse into idolatry, but the remarkable quality of this
passage is its tone of compassion, and a return to idolatry
is a sin for which compassion is not the appropriate emotion.[32]
To describe such relapses even the gentle Bede employs the
conventional image of the "dog returning to his own vomit."[33]
It is to those who have not had a chance to know of God, *ne
wiston hīe Drihten God*, that one can be compassionate. Their
sin, as the missionaries repeatedly tell us, is "ignorance." They
are "blundering in the darkness," ensnared in devilish errors
through no fault of their own. The poet's insistence on the

Danes' ignorance of God (*ne wiston, ne cūþon*) places them clearly with those blameless and pitiful heathens of whom Boniface speaks.

The poet's sudden shift from the past tense, which he uses to refer to the Danes, to a more generalized present provides an even more important link between his fictional pagans and those real pagans still living on the Continent in his own time. If there is a "Christian excursus" in *Beowulf*, it is not in the account of the sacrifices themselves but in the lines beginning *Wā biÐ þǣm*, for the changed tense shows that the object of the poet's compassion includes not only those long-dead Danes in his poem but also those heathens who exist at the moment he is speaking and who are compelled—*sceal*—through ignorance to thrust their souls *in fȳres fæþm*. Their plight is made even sadder by the parallel consideration of those—perhaps their kinsmen—whose lot is the happier because they may *Drihten secean*. Marie P. Hamilton has suggested that "by presenting Scandinavian men of good will as looking in the main to the governance of God he [the poet] might bring them within the sympathetic ken of their English cousins." [34] This is true enough, but given the English attitude toward Continental heathens, it may also be that the poet engages his audience's sympathy for his characters by emphasizing their very paganism. Certainly in this "excursive" passage he seems to step aside from the course of his narrative to draw attention to the similarity between the Danes in *Beowulf* and the real Danes whose salvation had become a matter of widespread concern.

The characters in *Beowulf* are men of good will, despite their paganism, and this has seemed to most critics the central contradiction in the poem. In the face of the attitude represented by Alcuin the only way out of this dilemma seems to be that proposed by Charles Donahue: the possibility that the poet was touched by the Pelagian heresy, which taught that pious heathens could be saved for their natural goodness and thus made it possible for a Christian to admire a native heathen hero. [35] Donahue shows that in early medieval Ireland some native heroes were regarded as having lived under the "natural law," virtuous even though heathen and eligible for salvation because they were born outside the Judaic and Christian dispensations. Yet in England and on the Continent, as Donahue also shows, a strict Augustinian orthodoxy prevailed. Bede, writing an attack on the Pelagian heresy, states flatly that even the great philosophers *nullam veram virtutem nec nullam veram sapientiam habere potuerunt. In quantum vero vel gustum aliquem sapientiae cujuslibet, vel virtutis imaginem habebant, totum hoc desuper acceperunt* 'could have no true virtue or knowledge of God. Indeed, insofar as they had any taste of knowledge or image of virtue, they received it from above.'[36] The second sentence seems to grant that the pagans may have some virtue after all, but even so Bede affirms that all those born outside the Judaeo-Christian law are damned, even those born between Adam and Moses, *quia regnavit mors ab Adam usque Moysen, etiam in eos qui non peccaverunt* 'since Death ruled from Adam until Moses, even over those who had not sinned.'[37] This was the attitude the missionaries upheld. In the famous near-baptism of Rathbod a touch of Pelagianism would have saved that "Scourge of Christians" and made the conversion of Frisia much easier, but when Rathbod, with one foot in the water, turned to ask Bishop Wulfram whether he would meet his ancestors in heaven, Wulfram said they were in hell, Rathbod withdrew his foot, and the great chance was lost.[38] Boniface was as orthodox as Wulfram and Bede, and when it came to his attention that a Celtic bishop named Clement was teaching that Christ brought all from hell, "believers and unbelievers, those who praised God and the worshippers of idols," he lost no time in bringing the matter to the attention of Rome, where the "folly" was roundly condemned in 745.[39] The fact that Boniface and Bede paid so much attention to this heresy may indicate that Pelagianism was more widespread than is usually thought. The lives of the early missionaries, who were trained in Ireland, show that relations between the English and Celtic churches were quite close despite their differences, and the works of Pelagius himself were circulating in England (some even under the name of Augustine).[40]

However, we need not hunt for heresy to explain the poet's presentation of his heroes as both virtuous and pagan, for despite the Pelagian dispute (which turns really on the functions of nature and grace) even the most orthodox eighth-century churchmen could regard the pagans as quite virtuous, following the natural law and lacking only the knowledge of God necessary for salvation. The *Translatio Sancti Alexandri* puts this most clearly in its account of the Saxons: *Legibus etiam ad vindictam malefactorum optimis utebantur. Et multa utilia atque secundum legem naturae honesta in morum probitate habere studuerunt, quae eis ad veram beatitudinem promerendum proficere potuissent, si ignorantiam creatoris sui non haberent, et a veritate culturae illius non essent alieni* 'indeed, they made use of excellent laws for the punishment of wrongdoers. And they were diligent to maintain in their conduct a very useful and, according to the law of nature, decent probity, which would have helped them to a truly deserved blessedness, if they had not been ignorant of their Creator and were not alien to true religion.'[41] The praise for Germanic institutions in this work is drawn from Tacitus, and among early Latin writers—Horace, Tacitus, Martianus Capella—there was a slender tradition of idealizing the Germanic pagans for their good morals and institutions.[42] As early as the fifth century one finds Christian writers employing this idealized view. Salvianus writes of the Goths and Vandals who were attacking the Empire: *tantum apud illos profecit studium castimonia, tantum seueritas disciplinae non solum quod ipsi casti sunt, sed, ut rem dicamus nouem, rem incredibilem, rem paene etiam inauditam, castos etiam Romanos esse fecerunt* 'so much did the zeal for chastity prevail among them, so great was the severity of their discipline, that not only were they chaste themselves, but—to say a new thing, a thing incredible, a thing almost unheard of—they made even the Romans chaste.'[43] This view was strong enough to survive even among those who fought against the Germanic pagans, as we see in Einhard's

Vita Karoli Imperatoris: *Saxones, sicut omnes fere Germaniam incolentes nationes, et natura feroces, et cultui daemonum dediti, nostraeque religioni contrarii, neque divina neque humana iura vel polluere vel transgredi inhonestum arbitrabantur* 'the Saxons, though, like almost all the nations inhabiting Germany, by nature fierce and given to the worship of demons and opposed to our religion, are yet said neither to violate nor indecently to transgress divine and human laws.'[44]

In addition to the weight of this minor tradition of the "honest Germanic pagan," some of the missionaries must have been led to accept the idea that virtue can exist among the pagans simply from meeting an occasional good heathen, like this Frisian nobleman of the early eighth century: *qui quamvis fidem sanctae Trinitatis nondum sciret, erat tamen adiutor pauperum, defensor oppressorum, in iuditio quoque iustus* 'though he did not yet know the faith of the Holy Trinity, he was nevertheless a helper of paupers, a defender of the oppressed, and also just in pronouncing judgments.'[45] Such decent men, of the sort that exist in all societies, often performed acts of kindness to the missionaries, even when they refused the chance to be converted, and they must frequently have impressed the English priests with their natural goodness.[46] They thus exemplified the most important source of the idea that pagans observe the natural law, the statements in the Bible itself, which taught that the Gentiles "show the work of the law written in their hearts, their conscience also bearing witness, and their thoughts the mean while accusing or else excusing one another" (Rom. 2:15).

Boniface drew on all three sources—the literary tradition represented by Tacitus, his own knowledge, and the Bible—in what must have been the most famous use of natural law in the eighth century, his letter to King Ethelbald of Mercia. Ethelbald's loose sexual conduct had become an international scandal, and it was a matter of concern to English churchmen (and probably laymen) on both sides of the Channel. Finally (around 745–46), Boniface wrote directly to the king, rebuking him for his sin: *Quod non solum a christianis, sed etiam a paganis in opprobrium et verecundiam deputatur. Quia ipsi pagani verum Deum ignorantes naturaliter quae legis sunt et quod ab initio Deus custodiunt in hac re. . . . Cum ergo gentiles, qui Deum nesciunt et legem non habent iuxta dictum apostoli, naturaliter ea quae legis sunt faciunt et ostendunt opus legis in cordibus suis. . . .* 'which not only by Christians but even by pagans is held in shame and contempt. For these pagans, ignorant of the true God, by nature maintain in this matter those things which are lawful and what God established in the beginning. . . . When thus the gentiles, who do not know God and have no law according to the word of the apostle, do by nature what is lawful and show the work of the law written in their hearts. . . .'[47] Since Boniface himself, the persecutor of the heretical Clement, held this opinion, we need have no lingering doubts about the theological respectability of admiring the virtues of the pagans. Even Bede, despite his doctrinal rigidity, found some admirable pagans in the course of his history, and he held that at least one unbaptized pagan had been saved.[48] Certainly the author of *Beowulf*, even if he was a cleric addressing a clerical audience, would have encountered no difficulty in presenting his characters as both virtuous and pagan.

III

In the light of what we now know of attitudes toward the pagans in the late seventh and eighth centuries, it appears that the paganism of the poet's characters may have been a positive advantage to him rather than the insuperable difficulty that it seemed to early critics. Those critics assumed that *Beowulf* was originally and essentially pagan, and what pagan elements the poem contains were therefore most easily explained as mere undigested lumps of primitive matter. We are still accustomed to think of the pagan elements as part of the original essence of the poem, the Christian elements as additions—beautifully integrated, but additions nevertheless. Yet our reading of the poem does not accord with our theory. Christianity is part of the very fabric of *Beowulf*; the pagan elements are not. When we examine those elements that are actually pagan rather than secular, references to practices that ceased altogether or became criminal with the introduction of Christianity—augury, cremation, the worship of idols—we find that they are few in number and easily isolable. Their removal would harm but not destroy the poem (which may explain why good critics have wanted to take some of them out), for one cannot imagine *Beowulf* in anything like its present state without its Christian basis, but one can easily conceive of it without its few touches of paganism. Without them, it would simply be a more ordinary medieval poem, a narrative in which the past is seen through the eyes of the present, as Chaucer viewed Troy in *Troilus* or Shakespeare ancient Denmark in *Hamlet*. The tales that the poet used must have come to him in that more ordinary state, originally created in pagan times but insensibly altered to fit the requirements of new audiences by each succeeding generation of oral poets.[49] Probably it was the *Beowulf* poet who deepened the Christian meanings when he reshaped the inherited material; but probably it was also he who added the "pagan coloring," drawing on contemporary information about the Germanic pagans and on the prevalent attitude toward them to add both interest and a new dimension of meaning to his materials.

The most obvious advantage that the poet gained by his use of pagan materials is that of "local color." He was able to capitalize on the general interest in pagandom that the missions had aroused, and by providing vivid, even sensational, accounts of rites such as cremation of which his audience had only heard, he was able to engage their attention for his more important purposes. For those more sober members of his audience who, like the later Alcuin, could see no good in stories of pagan kings, the very reminders that the kings in *Beowulf* are pagan serve to build interest and sympathy, for the poem functions as a kind of proof of the missionaries' reports that the heathens are indeed virtuous, while the pagan elements have something of the same function as Boniface's letter to the English nation, emphasizing the perilous condition of these good heroes and thus appealing for a compassionate, serious consideration of their state. Perhaps that is why the "Christian excursus" comes so early in the poem, providing the framework within which the good Christian can ponder the deeds of the good pagans.

There must have been a good many more in the poet's audience who, like the monks at Lindisfarne, simply enjoyed a good secular tale, and for them most of all the touches of paganism are means of building interest and sympathy in the dual purpose of this poem. *Beowulf* is now recognized as a skillful blend of secular and religious values; it is simultaneously a celebration of the ideal Germanic warrior and a statement of Christian morality.[50] These values were not necessarily opposed, as poems like *The Dream of the Rood* show, but they were nevertheless quite different. Aldhelm apparently recognized this, for we are told that he would stand at crossroads, singing the old songs until he had gathered crowds for his more edifying discourses.[51] The *Beowulf* poet seems to employ his secular materials in the same way, using his tales of monster killing as an occasion for a meditation on life and on the meaning of victory and defeat. For those who were drawn to listen primarily to hear again the deeds of heroes, the insistence on the paganism of those heroes provided the larger context of that present day, helping to reinforce the point of Hrothgar's sermon that strength alone is not enough and to state the further requirement that even that "intelligent monotheist" cannot meet, that to strength and natural piety must be added the New Law of Christ. In this way the touches of paganism in *Beowulf* place the fictional ironies and tragedy of the poem within the dimension of the real irony and tragedy of Germanic history as it was viewed by an eighth-century audience newly aware of the sad condition of their Continental kinsmen to whom the gospel had not yet been preached. Thus the poet builds a link between the doomed heroes of his poem and the sad but admirable pagans of his own time, whose way of life seemed likewise fated to disappear before the apparently certain victory of the Church.

PAGAN COLORING

The final irony of *Beowulf* is that which Wyrd visited on the poet himself, when the pagans he celebrated swept down to destroy their Christian kinsmen in England. After the burning of Lindisfarne in 793, it would be another two centuries before English missionaries would again set out for the Continent and the attitude toward pagandom expressed in *Beowulf* would again be appropriate. We can only speculate, but it may be that we owe the survival of the poem to its touches of paganism, for the only manuscript in which it survives was written at that other moment in English history, around the year 1000, when English churchmen were again concerned with the fate of their heathen kinsmen in northern Europe.[52]

NOTES

1. William Whallon, "The Christianity of *Beowulf*," *Modern Philology*, LX (1962), 81–94, argues that the poet is a very naive Christian who knows little except for the tales of the Old Testament, but this is as close as critics today come to assuming a pagan author. For a full discussion see E. G. Stanley, "The Search for Anglo-Saxon Paganism," *Notes and Queries*, N.S. XI (1964), 205–9, 242–50, 282–87, 324–33, 455–63, and XII (1965), 9–17, 203–7, 285–93, 322–27, especially XI, 326–31.

2. On Wyrd see, for example, Alan H. Roper, "Boethius and the Three Fates of *Beowulf*," *Philological Quarterly*, XLI (1962), 386–400; on revenge see Dorothy Whitelock, *The Audience of Beowulf* (Oxford, 1951), pp. 13–17; the comitatus is, of course, found throughout Old English religious poetry (e.g., *Andreas*).

3. *Beowulf and the Fight at Finnsburg*, ed. Friedrich Klaeber (3d ed.; Boston, 1950), p. cxxi: "in recounting the life and portraying the character of the exemplary leader . . . he [the poet] was almost inevitably reminded of the person of the Savior . . ."

4. *The Heroic Age* (Cambridge, Eng., 1912), p. 53.

5. *Ibid.*, pp. 52–53; I have included Scyld's funeral ship, although it seems to represent the departure of a legendary hero, as Klaeber suggests, rather than a real burial like that of Baldr.

6. Marie P. Hamilton, "The Religious Principle in *Beowulf*," *PMLA*, LXI (1946), 309–31; reprinted in *An Anthology of Beowulf Criticism*, ed. L. E. Nicholson (Notre Dame, Ind., 1963), p. 125; in *The Knight's Tale* Chaucer shows his essentially Christian characters worshipping in pagan shrines.

7. Alcuin, *Albini Epistolae*, ed. E. L. Dummler, in *Monumenta Germaniae Historica, Epistolae* (Berlin, 1895), IV, letter 124, p. 183.

8. For example, J. R. R. Tolkien, "*Beowulf:* The Monsters and the Critics," *Proceedings of the British Academy*, XXII (1937), 245–95; reprinted in *An Anthology of Beowulf Criticism*, ed. Nicholson, pp. 101–2. In his edition of *Beowulf and the Fight at Finnsburg*, note to ll. 175–88, Klaeber holds that the poet "failed to live up to his own modernized representation of [the Danes]."

9. Chadwick, *The Heroic Age*, p. 73; his work is still the most recent full discussion of the problem, and it has been accepted without question.

10. Eddius Stephanus, *Vita Wilfridi Episcopi*, cap. xxvii, in *Rerum Britannicarum Medii Aevi Scriptores*, ed. James Raine ("The Historians of the Church of York and Its Archbishops," Vol. I [London, 1879]), LXXI, 38. For a full account of the missions in Frisia see Wilhelm Levison, *England and the Continent in the Eighth Century* (Oxford, 1946), pp. 45–69. Translations of some of the relevant materials are provided in *The Anglo-Saxon Missionaries in Germany*, ed. and trans. C. H. Talbot (New York, 1954).

11. *Historia Ecclesiastica Gentis Anglorum*, V, ix, in *Opera Historica*, trans. J. E. King (New York, 1930), II, 234; the translations of Bede in this essay, however, are mine.

12. *Ibid.*, pp. 238–40.

13. *Ibid.*, v, x–xi, pp. 240–52; Alcuin, *Vita Willibrordi*, ed. Wilhelm Levison, in *Monumenta Germaniae Historica, Scriptores Rerum Merovingicarum* (Hanover, 1919), VII, 81–141.

14. Bede, *Historia Ecclesiastica Gentis Anglorum*, V, x (II, 244).

15. *The Anglo-Saxon Missionaries in Germany*, ed. and trans. Talbot, p. 9, notes that this king has been identified with Ongentheow in *Beowulf*, but I can find no basis for the identification.

16. Levison, *England and the Continent in the Eighth Century*, pp. 70–93. Willibald, *Vita S. Bonifacii*, ed. G. H. Pertz, in *Monumenta Germaniae Historica, Scriptores* (Hanover, 1829), II, 331–53.

17. Willibald, *Vita S. Bonifacii*, cap. vi (pp. 340–42), trans. Talbot, in *The Anglo-Saxon Missionaries in Germany*, p. 47.

18. Levison, *England and the Continent in the Eighth Century*, p. 61.

19. Hermann Lau, *Die angelsächsische Missionweise im Zeitalter des Bonifaz* (Kiel, 1909), p. 39.

20. *England and the Continent in the Eighth Century*, p. 92.

21. *Die Briefe des heiligen Bonifatius und Lullius*, ed. Michael Tangl, in *Monumenta Germaniae Historica, Epistolae Selectae* (Berlin, 1916), I, letter 105; trans. Ephraim Emerton, in *The Letters of St. Boniface* ("Records of Civilization: Sources and Studies," Vol. XXXI [New York, 1940]), pp. 177–79.

22. See *Beowulf and the Fight at Finnsburg*, ed. Klaeber, p. cxvi, n. 1, for a summary of early scholars' views on this question.

23. Antoine Thomas, "Un manuscrit inutilisé du *Liber Monstrorum*,"

PAGAN COLORING

Bulletin du Cange: Archivum Latinitatis Medii Aevi, I (1925), 232–45; Whitelock, *The Audience of Beowulf*, p. 50; Kenneth Sisam, *Studies in the History of Old English Literature* (Oxford, 1953), pp. 288–90.

24. Matts Dreijer, *Häuptlinge, Kaufleute, und Missionare im Norden vor Tausend Jahren* ("Skrifter Utgivna av Ålands Kulturstiftelse," Vol. II [Mariehamn, 1960]), pp. 71–80.

25. Cf. Bernlaf who joined St. Liudger's retinue and was "loved by his neighbors because he was of an open and free nature, and would repeat the actions of the men of old and the contests of kings, singing to his harp," *Vita Liudgeri*, ed. G. H. Pertz, in *Monumenta Germaniae Historica, Scriptores*, II, 403; cited and trans. W. P. Ker, in *The Dark Ages* (New York, 1958), p. 57.

26. On Sutton Hoo in relation to the burials in *Beowulf* see the Supplement by C. L. Wrenn, "Recent Work on *Beowulf* to 1958," especially p. 513, in R. W. Chambers, *Beowulf: An Introduction* (3d ed.; Cambridge, Eng., 1959); for the Continental sources quoted in the text see *Capitulatio de Partibus Saxoniae* in *Texte zur germanischen Bekehrungsgeschichte*, ed. Wolfgang Lange (Tübingen, 1962), pp. 154–55, nos. 7, 22. This text dates from about 789.

27. They are frequently mentioned in the texts collected in *Texte zur germanischen Bekehrungsgeschichte*, ed. Lange; e.g., *Dicta Pirmini* (written between 718 and 724), pp. 90–91.

28. In the ninth century more extended accounts of the pagans were written, such as the *Translatio Sancti Alexandri*, ed. G. H. Pertz, in *Monumenta Germaniae Historica, Scriptores*, II, 673–81, and the *Indiculus Superstitionem et Paganiarum*, ed. G. H. Pertz, in *Monumenta Germaniae Historica, Leges* (Hanover, 1885), I, 19–20.

29. Lau, *Die angelsächsische Missionweise im Zeitalter des Bonifaz*, p. 3, quotes an Englishman, Wigbert, writing to Lull (*Die Briefe des heiligen Bonifatius und Lullius*, letter 137).

30. *Die Briefe des heiligen Bonifatius und Lullius*, letter 46.

31. The text is from *Beowulf and the Fight at Finnsburg*, ed. Klaeber.

32. For example, Whitelock, *The Audience of Beowulf*, pp. 78–79.

33. *Historia Ecclesiastica Gentis Anglorum*, II, v (I, 228): *Quo utroque* [Eadbald and his wife] *scelere occasionem dedit ad priorem vomitum revertendi* 'by both crimes [Eadbald and his wife] he gave occasion for returning to the previous vomit.' Cf. Caesarius of Arles, *Sermones*, in *Texte zur germanischen Bekehrungsgeschichte*, ed. Lange, p. 61; Prov. 26:11.

34. "The Religious Principle in Beowulf," in *An Anthology of Beowulf Criticism*, ed. Nicholson, p. 125.

35. "Beowulf, Ireland, and the Natural Good," *Traditio*, VII (1949–51), 263–77.

36. *In Cantica Canticorum*, in *The Complete Works of the Venerable*

Bede, ed. J. A. Giles (London, 1844), IX, 197. The *desuper* is a reminder that even a pagan like Ongendus (see n. 46) or Beowulf can be touched by grace.

37. *Ibid.*, p. 199.

38. *Annales Xantenses*, in *Monumenta Germaniae Historica, Scriptores*, II, 221.

39. *Die Briefe des heiligen Bonifatius und Lullius*, letter 59.

40. Sister M. Thomas Aquinas Carroll, *The Venerable Bede: His Spiritual Teachings* ("Catholic University of America Studies in Medieval History," N.S. Vol. IX [Washington, D.C., 1946]), p. 95. For a further discussion of this doctrine in relation to *Beowulf* see the suggestive article by Morton Bloomfield, "Patristics and Old English Literature: Notes on Some Poems," *Comparative Literature*, XIV (1962), 36–43; reprinted in *Studies in Old English Literature in Honor of Arthur G. Brodeur*, ed. Stanley B. Greenfield (Eugene, Ore., 1963), pp. 36–43, and in *An Anthology of Beowulf Criticism*, ed. Nicholson, pp. 367–72. In writing the present article, I have had the benefit of Bloomfield's suggestions and criticisms.

41. *Monumenta Germaniae Historica, Scriptores*, II, 675.

42. Horace *Odes* III.xxiv (referring to *Getae*); Tacitus *Germania*; Martianus Capella, *De Nuptis Philologiae et Mercurii*, ed. F. Eyssenhardt (Leipzig, 1866), pp. 227–28, 240. Adam of Bremen takes the references in Horace and Martianus to refer to the Danes and the Geats: see *History of the Archbishops of Hamburg-Bremen*, trans. F. J. Tschan ("Records of Civilization: Sources and Studies," Vol. LIII [New York, 1959]), pp. 195, 199, 204.

43. *De gubernatione Dei*, in *Texte zur germanischen Bekehrungsgeschichte*, ed. Lange, p. 16. Bede takes a somewhat similar view when he (following Gildas) speaks of the Saxon invaders as agents of God's just vengeance for the crimes of the Celtic Christians: *Historia Ecclesiastica Gentis Anglorum*, I, xiv–xv (I, 64–74).

44. Ed. G. H. Pertz, in *Monumenta Germaniae Historica, Scriptores*, II, 446; the same passage appears in the *Translatio Sancti Alexandri* in the same volume, p. 675.

45. *Vita S. Liudgeri*, II, 405.

46. See, for example, the alderman who avenged the two Hewalds (see n. 14), the Danish king Ongendus who, though a pagan, "nevertheless, through divine intervention, received the herald of truth with every mark of honour" (trans. Talbot, in *The Anglo-Saxon Missionaries in Germany*, p. 9), the pagans who spare the lives of St. Lebuini (ed. G. H. Pertz, *Monumenta Germaniae Historica, Scriptores*, II, 363) and of St. Willehad (ed. G. H. Pertz, in *Monumenta Germaniae Historica, Scriptores*, II, 381), those pagans *naturaliter prudentia* 'naturally wise' reported in the *Historia Translationem Sanctae Puissinae*, ed. G. H. Pertz,

in *Monumenta Germaniae Historica, Scriptores*, II, 681, and the pagan Frisians who honorably received Wilfred: *Cujus loci incolae, nondum imbuti fide Christi, solo humanitatis affectu eos obvii benigne suscepere, et relevantes lassitudinem ipsorum quaeque necessitas exigebat gratis obtulere* 'the inhabitants of this place, not yet filled with the faith of Christ, moved by human kindness alone, received them kindly along the way and, relieving their weariness, brought them freely whatever necessity required,' *Breviloquium Vitae S. Wilfridi*, in *Rerum Britannicarum Medii Aevi Scriptores*, LXXI, 231 (cf. *Vita Wilfridi*, cap. xxvi–xxvii, pp. 37–58, in the same volume).

47. *Die Briefe des heiligen Bonifatius und Lullius*, letter 73. In parts of the letter not quoted Boniface draws on Tacitus for his account of the pagans' attitude toward adultery, and he draws on his own experience by extending that account to cover also the Wends; in the passage quoted Boniface cites the Bible.

47. In parts of the letter not quoted Boniface draws on Tacitus for his account of the pagans attitude toward adultery and he draws on his own experience by extending that account to cover also the Wends; in the passage quoted Boniface cites the Bible.

48. *Historia Ecclesiastica Gentis Anglorum*, I, vii: a pagan who refuses to execute St. Alban is himself executed, *de quo nimirum constat, quia etsi fonte baptismatis non est ablutus sui tamen est sanguinis lavacro mundatus* 'of whom it is clearly apparent that though he was not bathed in the baptismal font yet he was cleansed by the washing of his own blood' (I, 43). Likewise, Edwin before his baptism is described as a man of 'extraordinary sagacity' (II, ix).

49. Cf. Albert B. Lord, *The Singer of Tales* (Cambridge, Mass., 1960), p. 100: "I believe that once we know the facts of oral composition we must cease trying to find an original of any traditional song. From one point of view each performance is an original."

50. Arthur G. Brodeur, *The Art of Beowulf* (Berkeley, Calif., 1959), demonstrates that Beowulf and Hrothgar are "exemplars of an ideal and a course of conduct in harmony with both the best traditions of antiquity and the highest ideal of Christian Englishmen" (p. 185).

51. However, William of Malmesbury is our only authority for the story.

52. Cf. Adam of Bremen, *History of the Archbishops*, pp. 80–93; Dreijer, *Häuptlinge, Kaufleute, und Missionare im Norden vor Tausend Jahren*, pp. 199–207.

THE CONVENTION OF
PERSONIFICATION IN *BEOWULF*

ۮۮۮ

Neil D. Isaacs

The development and growing acceptance of the oral-formulaic theory as it applies to the poetry of the Anglo-Saxons has opened up vast areas of exploration and means for analysis of *Beowulf* and Old English poetry in general.[1] Now that we are reasonably sure of the method of composition in the larger sense, it is most important that we re-examine the art of the *Beowulf* poet and other Anglo-Saxon singers within the framework of their poetic conventions, examining the conventional formulas and themes they use in order that we may find the methods of composition in a narrower sense. Variations from one singer to another will indicate what makes up the style of the individual singer, but we must first set about analyzing the style produced by these conventions if we are to recognize individuality when it appears. The present study concerns one aspect of the *Beowulf* poet's style—the use of the convention of personification—which is seen to be both a vital part of his style and one of the principal devices within the Old English poetic convention.[2]

The term "poetic convention" is used here in its true sense—a compact, an agreement, between poet and audience to use and understand certain things in certain ways. Thus, it is probably as much a part of the Old English poetic convention for an audience to expect a certain formula or theme at a certain time as it is for the scop to use that formula or theme. Furthermore, it is a part of the compact that the audience accepts without question, even with appreciation, certain poetic devices and expressions that would seem absurd out of

15

context or to one who was not a party to the convention. In this way ideas obsolete or obsolescent may be accepted within the framework of the poetic convention. This acceptance goes further than a willing suspension of disbelief; it is a positive agreement to actively believe, not only for the sake of maintaining an art form but also for the sake of more perfect communication. In oral-formulaic poetry formulas and themes impart a denotative meaning elicited according to the precision with which they are used in the particular context. Over and above this denotative meaning they supply a whole host of connotative meanings evoked from the common store of suggestions, emotional and intellectual, that the particular formulas and themes hold in the hearts and minds of hearers and singers.

An important part of the Old English poetic convention is what is here called personification because of its similarity to the rhetorical device of that name, the representation of inanimate objects or abstract ideas as endowed with personal attributes. The Old English device goes far beyond the more familiar device, however, for it is one of the terms of the Old English oral-formulaic convention to understand that any person or animal or object or concept (hereafter called "inanimate") may be spoken of in terms of another person or animal or inanimate. This convention is accepted because it seems to have been understood by singer and audience that each thing in nature from man to stone and each thing created by man as well has a living, moving spirit of its own. Somewhere along the line there must have been a personification in the merely rhetorical sense, but this step was a mechanical, almost automatic operation within the framework of an already-established convention, not the framework upon which the convention was built.

It should be noted that the Anglo-Saxon singer would never endow an abstraction with a living spirit or personal characteristics (nor use an abstraction in such a way as to call forth such an endowing) without first figuring forth a concrete representation of the abstract. The Old English convention of personification deals only with concrete, particular images; the figures that do appear to be abstractions are based on a previous concretizing, usually visual, of the abstraction. We should not forget this even though we may find it difficult to recognize the intermediate steps, for we are not party to the convention, have not read the small print in this unwritten contract.

This is not to say, however, that either singer or audience literally believed that a spirit resided in a tree or a tool. In this respect the Anglo-Saxon matches the sophistication of the eighteenth-century Englishman who accepted the convention of capitalized abstraction without literally believing that Caution could creep, Declamation roar, or Passion sleep. Yet the Anglo-Saxon was so unsophisticated as still to form a visual image of something he did not literally believe possible.

The figures used in this convention fall naturally into two major divisions, personifications and what I shall call inversions of personification. Under the first category are animals spoken of in terms of humans, inanimates spoken of in terms of humans, inanimates spoken of in terms of animals, parts of humans spoken of in terms of whole humans, and parts of animals or inanimates spoken of in terms of whole humans (the last two forms are clearly synecdochical). Under inversions of personification are humans spoken of in terms of animals, humans spoken of in terms of inanimates, animals spoken of in terms of inanimates, and finally, figures based on previous personification but without explicit personification or inversion, i.e., inanimates spoken of in terms of other inanimates (often barely distinguishable from ordinary metaphor).

I do not mean to suggest that such a method of classification has any correspondence with the poet's method of composition. In fact, there is every indication from the general way in which the *Beowulf* poet uses the convention that such distinctions are out of place in a discussion of his poetic theory. The singer does not have to concern himself with whether he is calling a man a sword, or a sword a man, or a sword a spade. It is all one to him and to his listeners as well. Let us now examine several passages in *Beowulf* that demonstrate the workings of the convention.

I

For all the variegated uses and forms taken by the convention of personification, the outstanding phase of that convention that remains most vividly in the mind of a reader of *Beowulf* is the personification of weapons.[3] This personification is continually implicit throughout the poem and comes to the surface frequently. Perhaps it is nowhere so explicit as in the lines that relate the failure of Hrunting:

> þæt se beadu-léoma   bítan nolde,
> ealdre scieþþan   ac sío ecg ʒeswác
> þéodne æt þearfe;   þolode ǽr fela
> hand-ʒemóta,   helm oft ʒescær,
> fǽʒes fierd-hræʒl.   Þá wæs forma síþ
> díerum máðme   þæt his dóm alæʒ.[4]

(1523–28)

that the battle-light [sword] would not bite [or] harm life, but the blade failed the chief in need; in the past many hand-to-hand encounters had it endured, had often cut through the helmet, the byrnie of the doomed; that was the first time for the precious treasure that its glory ceased.

Even here all is not so straightforward. The personification of a sword by its ability to endure, cut, and have glory, is not all that is involved. The sword is a light, a treasure, and an animal that will not bite, and its blade is personified by its action of failing. Adding to the figurative content of the passage are the personifications of battle, which is given a sword or light, and hands, whose meetings occasion skirmishes. A parallel passage describes the failure of Beowulf's shield in his fight with the dragon:

> Scield wél ʒebearg
>
> lífe and líċe   lǽssan hwíle
> mǽrum þéodne   þanne his myne sóhte;
> þǽr hé þý friste   forman dógre
> wealdan móste   swá him wyrd ne ʒescráf
> hrǽþ æt hilde.   (2570b–75a)

The shield protected well life and body for his famous prince a shorter time than his desire sought to, if he at that time, the first day, might control, [but] not thus did fate decree for him victory in battle.

I have called attention to the personification of the shield in this passage some time ago, as a resolution of the problems involved.[5] To be sure, the shield's ability to protect and control and its possessing a desire are explicit enough (especially with the clue in *forman dógre* 'the first day'; compare lines 2337 ff., where the new shield is prepared for Beowulf to use); but beyond that, its desire does the wishing for the shield, and finally fate steps in, the personified figuration becoming explicit in its ability to decree.

II

The characterizing of helmets as boars is the most common form of the figure in which inanimates are spoken of in terms of animals. The first time it appears in *Beowulf* is a crucial passage:[6]

> Eofor-líċ scinon
>
> ofer hléor-beorgum: ʒehroden golde,
> fág and fýr-heard,   feorh-wearde héold
> gúþ-mód [gum-mann].   (303b–6a)

The first part of this passage spells out the relationship of boar to helmet. There is actually the image of a boar on the helmet and the symbolism of boar for helmet is explicit: 'The boar-images shone [atop helmets] over the cheek-guards.' In the next part the boar *is* the helmet, and the helmet therefore partakes of the qualities of the boar: 'covered with gold, shining and tempered, the war-like warrior stood guard.' Seeing the various parts of the convention of personification at work together renders unnecessary any emendations that sacrifice syntax to context or vice versa. I have used the emendation *gum-mann* for MS *grummon* as proposed by F. Holthausen[7] and accepted by Carleton Brown[8] and Magoun, but there is no reason why it may not be other than nominative and singular, so that the lines could read 'the war-like one [helmet, boar] stood guard over the warrior(s).' Still, there is no reason to deny the figuration of either boar or helmet as warrior. There seems to be no need at all, then, to emend *feorh-wearde* to *fær-wearde* 'boat-watch,' as suggested by P. J. Cosijn[9] and accepted by Moritz Trautmann,[10] Holthausen,[11] Brown,[12] and now Magoun. One of the reasons for this emendation was that it helped explain the plural number of *grimmon*, the standard emendation of MS *grummon* (by Friedrich Klaeber, E. van K. Dobbie). But this argument loses its validity when it is remembered that the boar image was a decoration on more than one helmet and that the spirit of the boar (*Freyr?*) was therefore protecting several 'grim [ones].' *Grimmon*, then, would also be acceptable as an emendation, in which case the passage could be rendered 'the war-like [one] stood guard over the grim [ones].' Even if we accept with C. L. Wrenn the MS *grummon*, the plural conception would remain in the direct object.

III

The personification of weapons becomes so complete in some cases that the personified weapon, in these cases a sword, is not only given human attributes but is also given a distinct personality all its own and an individualizing name. The most famous of these, of course, is Hrunting, the sword of Unferth, lent to Beowulf for his impending fight with Grendel's dam. Hrunting is introduced in lines 1457–64:

> wæs þǽm hæft-méce   Hrunting nama.
> Þæt wæs án foran   eald ʒestréona:
> ecg wæs íren,   átor-tánum fág,

ahierded heaðu-swáte;   næfre hit æt hilde ne swác
manna ǽnigum   þára-þe hit mid mundum bewand,
se-þe gryre-síðas   ʒegán dorste,
folc-stede fára.   Næs þæt forma síþ
þæt hit ellen-weorc   efnan scolde.

to that hilted sword was Hrunting the name, which was one of the foremost of ancient heirlooms; blade was iron, colored by deadly stripes, hardened by battle-blood; never in battle had it failed any man of those who grasped it with hands, those who dared go [to] grim adventures, battle-place of foes. That was not the first time that it had to do bold work.

Characterized by a proper name and the fact that it 'was one of the foremost of ancient' swords, Hrunting is further personified by the statements that 'never in battle had it failed any man' and that this 'was not the first time that it had to do bold work' (compare line 3, where æðelingas do 'bold work'). Accepting the loan, Beowulf speaks of the sword as of a companion: Ić mé mid Hruntinge / dóm ʒewyrće 'I will, along with Hrunting, gain fame for myself' (1490b–91a). The use of mid, where the instrumental dative would suffice, suggests this meaning. Again, reporting the fight, Beowulf treats the sword as a fellow: Ne meahte ić æt hilde mid Hruntinge / wiht ʒewyrćan þéah þæt wǽpen duge 'nor could I in the battle, along with Hrunting, accomplish anything, although that weapon is good' (1659–60). The personification is intensified by the use of the verb dugan, which is consistently used in Beowulf for persons, except for three other cases in which it is involved in personifications.[13] Finally, before Beowulf's departure he returns Hrunting to Unferth:

Hét þá se hearda   Hrunting beran
suna Ecg-láfes,   hét his sweord niman,
léoflíć íren,   sæʒde him þæs lǽnes þanc,
cwæþ he þone gúþ-wine   gódne tealde,
wíʒ-cræftiʒne,   nealles wordum lóg
méćes ecge.   Þæt wæs módiʒ secg!   (1807–12)

The brave one then ordered Hrunting brought to the son of Ecglaf, bade [him] take his sword, the precious iron [weapon]; said thanks to him for the loan of it, said he considered it a good battle friend, strong in war; not at all in words did he find fault with the sword's edge. That was a fine warrior!

Adding to the personifying force of the proper name and the preceding passages, these lines make perfectly clear the poet's idea that Beowulf considers Hrunting as a companion. He calls him a 'good battle friend' and 'strong [or skillful] in war.' Not only are *-wine* and *-cræfti3ne* humanizing words, but the adjective *gódne* emphasizes the idea and especially the formula of which it is a part, *gódne tealde*.[14] This formula is also found in lines 2184 and 2641, both times concerning men. I take it that *þæt wæs módi3 secg* 'that was a fine warrior' is ambiguous, being both a comment on Beowulf himself and Beowulf's final comment on Hrunting. A similar ambiguity occurs in 1569b—*secg weorce 3efeah* 'warrior rejoiced in his deed'—where the singer is commenting on Beowulf and the sword he has used to kill Grendel's dam.[15]

Beowulf's own sword, which he uses against the dragon, is named and further personified:

> þæt hit on hafolan stód
> níðe 3eníeded.   Næ3ling forbærst,
> 3eswác æt sæcce   sweord Bío-wulfes,
> gamol and gráe3-mǽl.   (2679b–82a)

so that it stood in the head, driven in by the attack; Næ3ling snapped, failed in battle, Beowulf's sword, old and gray-colored.

The humanizing force of the proper name is reinforced by the verbs *3eswác* 'failed' and *stód* 'stood' and also by *gamol* 'old.' Used twenty other times in *Beowulf*, this adjective modifies people eighteen times and is involved in personifications the other two times.[16]

To these swords may be added the sword mentioned in the

Finn episode—*hilde-léoman, | billa sǽlest* (1143b–44a). The sword is personified by the adjective *sǽlest* 'best,' but it has also been suggested that *hilde-léoman* 'battle-light' be capitalized,[17] that it may be the name of the sword. The analogy with *beadu-léoma* (1523a), however, indicates that this may have been a standard figure for sword.

The phrase *brand Healf-Denes* 'sword of Healfdene' (1020b) should also be discussed here. This MS reading was emended to *bearn Healfdene* by N. F. S. Grundtvig[18] and followed by most later editors. Klaeber's edition keeps the emendation, but the second supplement[19] takes note of Hertha Marquardt's argument for the rehabilitation of *brand*.[20] Her idea that 'Healfdene's sword' means "Healfdene's distinguished warrior" is certainly valid, but her argument that the poet never uses the *bearn* formula for Hrothgar does not support her case very well. Far better is her citation of the *helm* formula as a parallel. Dobbie rejects this, however, because of differences in the "semantic development" of the two words *helm* and *brand*, and he retains the emendation *bearn*.[21] Sherman M. Kuhn's argument for *brand* is still different.[22] He rejects *bearn* because the scribe would not have recorded a rare term for a common one and especially because "an expressed subject is optional in Old English poetry whenever the context and the verb itself are such that omission of the subject will result in no ambiguity."[23] This makes perfectly good syntactical and contextual sense, but there seems little reason to suppose that the poet took his weapon-plus-genitive-of-proper-name formula, which in every extant usage is a figure for a person not mentioned—a hero, chief, or leader—and suddenly used it in the literal sense of the weapon of the expressed person. Wrenn simply says that emendation is "probably not necessary . . . *Brand Healfdenes* may well be a kind of kenning—'Healfdene's sword'—i.e., his support in war,"[24] and both he and Magoun restore *brand*. On formulaic grounds *brand Healfdenes* is eminently acceptable and in terms of the convention of personification and inversion of personification is surely the most desirable reading.

IV

The most extended passage governed by the convention of personification describes Beowulf's weapons as he seeks out Grendel's dam.[25] In addition to personifying byrnie, helmet, and sword (Hrunting) these lines, dominated as they are by an extended use of the convention, also personify a hand, treasure, blood, and battle and speak of swords and helmets in terms of animals. Then the poet goes on to compare Hrunting's owner, Unferth, to its present user, Beowulf, whom he calls *sǽlran sweord-frecan* 'a better sword-warrior' (1468a). In this single verse several aspects of the convention are at work at once. A man is called a wolf (*-freca*), and both man and wolf are called a sword. But they are all described as *sǽlran*, which serves to personify sword(-man) and wolf(-man).

V

On one occasion, several personifications are made explicit by the use of a single verb:

> þæt þeć ádl oþþe ecg   eafoðes ʒetwǽfeþ
> oþþe fýres fenġ   oþþe flódes wielm
> oþþe gripe méćes   oþþe gáres flyht
> oþþe atol ieldu   oþþe éaʒna bearhtm
> forsiteþ and forsweorceþ;   semninga biþ
> þæt þeć, dryht-guma,   déaþ oferswíðeþ.
>
> (1763–68)

that illness or blade will cut you off from power, or fire's embrace or water's surging or sword's grip or spear's flight or terrible old age, or brightness of eyes will diminish and grow dark; finally it will be that death will overpower you, noble chief.

The multiple subjects of *ʒetwǽfeþ*, emphasized by the polysyndeton, are all personified because any one of them, Hrothgar tells Beowulf, may 'cut you off from power.' In addition, fire is said to have an embrace and sword a grip. Notice also that it is the blade or edge, standing for the whole sword, that is listed at the beginning. Finally, another personifying verb, *oferswíðeþ*, is used with death as its subject. Death, then, is said to conquer man, and it is shown that he has many henchmen, any one of whom he may employ at any time. But most important for this analysis of the convention is the fact that weapons and natural phenomena and "abstractions" are used together, all subjects of a single verb. This instance represents the best proof in the poem that singer and audience did not distinguish between aspects of the convention, that but a single poetic principle was at work.

VI

Nowhere is there a better demonstration of the personification of weapons than in the passage describing the scene in Heorot after Grendel's death and the great banquet:

Setton him to héafdum hilde-randas,
bord-wudu beorhtan. Þǽr on benće wæs
ofer æðelinge éaþ-ȝesíene
heaðu-stéapa helm, hringed byrne,
þræc-wudu þrymmlíć. Wæs þéaw hira
þæt híe oft wǽron án-wíȝ-ȝearwe
ȝe æt hám ȝe on herȝe ȝe ȝehwæðer þára
efene swelće mǽla swelća hira mann-dryhtne
þearf ȝesǽlde. Wæs sío þéod tilu. (1242–50)

They set at their heads battle-shields, bright shieldwood. There on the bench over each noble was easily seen the battle-towering helmet, linked byrnie, glorious spear-wood. It was their custom that they regularly were ready to be placed in battle both at home and at the front, and, in either case even at such times as need might befall their liege lord. That was a good band.

In the beginning of this passage there appears to be no direct, explicit personification of the weapons. The singer tells us merely that shields, helmets, byrnies, and spears were there.

But then he begins to talk about a custom of "theirs." Can it be that he is referring to the men, the understood subject of *setton* or the *æðelingas*? If this is true, it removes most of the figurative content from the passage, for then it would also be the men who are ready, have a liege lord, and comprise a good band, statements that are neither striking nor necessary (nor entirely accurate). Such a reading is also undesirable because of the aesthetic comments implicit therein. The four-line listing of paraphernalia would seem mere ornamentation, the separation of pronoun from an unexpressed antecedent by nine verses would seem awkward, and the failure of the passage to contribute to the poem in the way of image, action, or dramatic context would seem artistically deficient.

If we follow our belief in the poet's excellence (and also the subtle but clear suggestions of the passage), we may view it as a good one that adds drama to the situation and is rich in imagery of a certain kind. If we remember that personification of weapons was always implicit, we may begin to perceive the wealth of connotations here. When the men set the shields at their heads, the suggestion is that the function of protection is not limited to the battlefield, but that the shields sitting at the heads of the men while they sleep are watching over them. This sense is carried particularly in *ofer æðelinge* and *heaðu-stéapa helm*. Moreover, while the men are lying and the shields sitting, the helmets, byrnies, and spears are easily seen on the bench. That is, they are upright, alert, and ready for action. Now when the singer goes on to say that it was their custom regularly to be ready for battle, there is a strong suggestion that he means the weapons that are standing or sitting up, always ready to fight and protect, rather than the men who are lying asleep. The vivid image of the scene and the rich connotations of the personification are expanded when the relationship of weapons to warrior is made analogous with that of *duguth* to lord. And the scop's final comment on these ever-ready, faithful servants is that they are a good band. (Is there, perhaps, also the implication that they are a better band than the sleeping warriors because of their vigilance and foresight—they sense the approaching attack—and their lack of human weaknesses, even their suprahuman, myth-based relationship to a god?) Adding to the highly figurative nature of the passage are the references to *hilde-randas* 'battle-shields,' i.e., the shields of the concrete figuration of battle, which must always have been evoked by such expressions. Moreover, *bord-wudu* 'shield wood' and *þræc-wudu* 'spear-wood' add to the characterization of these weapons by having them partake also of the spirit of the wood from which they are made.

VII

When Grendel's mother attacks, the personification of weapons is again made very plain in some impressive images:

> þanne heoru bunden,   hamore ʒeþuren,
> sweord swáte fág   swín ofer helme,
> ecgum dyhtiʒ,   andweard scireþ.
> Þá wæs on healle   heard-ecg togen,
> sweord ofer setlum,   síd-rand maniʒ
> hæfen handa fæst;   helm ne ʒemunde,
> byrnan síde   þá hine se bróga onʒeat. (1285–91)

when the bound blade, forged by hammer, sword stained by blood, trusty of edge, shears the opposite [or opposing] boar atop the helmet. Then was the hard edge taken down in the hall, swords over seats, many a broad shield raised firm in hands; helmet [or protector] was not mindful of broad byrnie when the horror seized him.

The first part of the passage is the ordinary conventional personification of weapons, mostly submerged, with incidental personification of hammer and blood that forge and stain. The firmness expressed in *fæst* refers to the shield—it is an adjective describing the way it customarily behaves in battle, rather than an adverb telling how the hand performs. The last three verses, however, constitute a crux because of the ambiguity of *helm* and *bróga*. The former can be read, literally, 'helmet' (inanimate spoken of in terms of human) or, figuratively, 'protector' (human spoken of in terms of—possibly—inanimate). The latter can be read, literally, as 'terror' or 'horror' personified (inanimate as human) or, figuratively, 'Grendel's dam' (human as inanimate). One possible rendering, then, is 'the protector [warrior] didn't think of his byrnie when Grendel's dam seized him'—which makes sense in the broader context of the passage, but which is rather free with the words and does not seem to fit the immediate context. Another possibility is 'the protector [warrior] didn't think of his byrnie when terror seized him'—also reasonable in general, although, aside from the immediate juxtaposition with weapon imagery, the use of *helm* by itself for 'protector,' which would be a unique usage, militates against it. Or it could be read, 'the helmet was not mindful of broad byrnie, when Grendel's dam [*or* terror, personified] seized him'— acceptable in the immediate context of weapon personification, but not quite clear in meaning, unless it is to be inferred that the personification is being carried further and that this warrior (personified helmet) in this situation pays no heed to his companion-at-arms (personified byrnie). This interpretation gains credence when it is remembered that this is a typical situation and reaction, a familiar motif throughout the Old English heroic corpus, the theme of the cowardly retainers.[26] Moreover, in the light of the previous passage (1242–50), this interpretation would indicate the poet's continued interest in comparing the behavior of weapons and warriors in battle. Where the good band of weapons had been regarded as being of better stuff before, they now appear to be only human. In any case it does not seem desirable to emend this passage.[27]

VIII

The figuration of battle that I have earlier alluded to seems to me one of the most striking personifications in the poem. Its depiction is complete, and a figure emerges that rivals in detail many an epic portrait of Mars or Ares. Battle is, naturally, an active figure who frequently takes warriors off (*nime* 452b, 1481b; *fornam* 557b, 1080b, 1123b; *nimeþ* 1846b, 2536b) and can play (*heaðu-lace* 584a, 1974a; *beadu-lace* 1561a), rush (*gúðe ræsum* 2356b), or strike (*heaðu-swenge* 2581a).

He has certain clothes (*gúþ-ʒewædu* 227a, 2617b, 2623b, 2730a, 2851a, 2871b), which include, of course, helmet (*beadu-gríman* 2257a, literally 'battle-mask') and byrnie (*gúþ-byrne* 321b), and he carries the typical weapons (*hilde-wǽpnum* 39a) of the Anglo-Saxon warrior, the spear (*here-scæfta* 335a), the shield (*hilde-bord* 397a; *hilde-randas* 1242b), and the sword (*gúþ-billa* 803a, 2584b; *beadu-mécas* 1454a; *hilde-mécas* 2202b). Other attributes, though expected, are somewhat more colorful: he is grim (*grimmre* 527a; *heoru-grimm* 1564a, 1847a; *heaðu-déorum* 772a); has a hand that is bloody (*blódiʒe beadu-folme* 990a); a grasp (*hilde-gráp* 1446a, 2507a); a light, i.e., a sword (*hilde-léoma* 1143b); a horn (*gúþ-horn* 1432a); a greedy song (*grǽdiʒ gúþ-léoþ* 1522a); and blood (*heoru-dréore* 487a; *heaðu-swát* 1460a, 1606a, 1668a). Some of these compounds, taken individually, have questionable personifying force, but the contexts of poem and poetic convention and the accretion of detail produce an impressively concrete figure.

IX

Perhaps the most interesting thing about the workings of the convention is the way in which a single personification can extend personifying qualities to related images. A good example occurs at the cremation in the Finn episode:

Æt þǽm áde wæs   éaþ-ʒesíene
swát-fág sierće,   swín eall-gylden,
eofor íren-heard,   æðeling maniʒ
wundum awierded.   Sume on wæle crungon! (1110–13)

At the pyre easily seen was the blood-stained corselet, the boar-image all golden, the iron-hard boar, and many a nobleman killed by wounds; many had fallen in slaughter!

In this passage the dominant personification consists of a series of things that were killed and fell in battle, including corselets, helmets, and noblemen. The use of *swín* and *eofor* for 'helmet' implies the previous figuring of helmets as animals (compare II above). Finally, the highly figurative content of the passage imparts secondary personifications to the blood that does the staining and the wounds that do the killing. Shortly thereafter the personification of blood comes to the surface along with several other figures:

þanne blód ætsprang,
láþ-bite líćes. Líe3 ealle forswealg,
gǽsta 3ífrost, þára-þe þǽr gúþ fornam
bǿ3a folces. Wæs hira blǽd scæcen!

(1121b–24)

then blood sprang forth, wounds [*lit.*: enemy bites] of the body. Fire, greediest of spirits, swallowed all of those whom battle had carried off there of either people. Their glory had departed [*or* hastened off].

Blood, fire, battle, and glory are given, respectively, the human actions of springing,[28] swallowing, carrying off, and departing, and the wounds are enemies that bite. But the important clue to the entire convention here is the phrase that calls fire *gǽsta 3ífrost* 'greediest of spirits.' Not only is the personification made quite explicit by the adjective 'greediest,' but the noun 'spirits' indicates the reason for the personification. That is, fire, like other things, is a spirit that can swallow something greedily.

X

The traditional beasts of battle, too, are personified in adjective, noun, and verb:

ac se wanna hræfn
fús ofer fǽ3um fela reordian,
earne secgan hú him æt ǽte spéow
þenden hé wiþ wulfe wæl réafode. (3024b–27)

but the dark raven, ready over fated [ones], shall recount many [things], tell the ern how it sped him at the feast when he, against the wolf, plundered the slain.

The raven is described as being 'ready' or 'eager,' and he can engage in conversation with the ern, to 'recount' things and 'tell' how it 'sped him' at the 'feast.' Moreover, both he and the wolf, in competition with one another (*wiþ*), 'plundered' the slain. Wrenn notes that, "This poetical use of birds of prey over the battlefield, which was almost a convention in O.N. and O.E. literature, is unique in putting speech into the beaks of the birds here with very striking effect."[29] The word "almost" is an unnecessary qualification, as shown by Magoun in "The Theme of the Beasts of Battle in Anglo-Saxon Poetry."[30] The word "unique" is also misleading, because in lines 1801–2a the same bird is personified in the same way: *oþ-þæt hræfn blaca heofenes wynne | bliþ-heort bodode* 'until the black raven with blithe heart announced heaven's delight.' Here the raven 'announced' the coming of day, and the figure is expanded and greatly enforced with the attribution of a 'blithe heart' to the bird.

XI

A graphic illustration of the way one use of the convention suggests and leads to another appears in the following passage:

Þéah-þe se hǽþ-stapa   hundum ȝeswencéd,
heorot hornum trum,   holt-wudu sǿce,
feorran ȝeflíemed,   ǽr hé feorh seleþ,
ealdor on ófre,   ǽr hé inn wile
hafolan [hýdan].   N'is þæt híeru stów!
Þanan ýþ-ȝebland   upp astíȝeþ
wann to wolcnum   þanne wind styreþ
láþ ȝewidru   oþ-þæt lyft þrysmaþ,
rodoras réotaþ.   (1368–76a)

Although the heath-stalker, pressed by hounds, the hart strong in horns, put to flight from afar, may seek the forest, he would rather give up his life, [his] spirit on the bank, before he would hide his head within. That is no pleasant place! From there the surging water rises up dark[ly] to the clouds when the wind stirs up hostile storms, until the air grows oppressive, the heavens weep.

In the first nine verses the hart is personified by actions of being pressed and put to flight, seeking, preferring to give up life (doubly humanizing, in action and choice of action), and not wishing to hide his head (again a doubling). He is called a stalker of the heaths and is given attributes of strength, life, and spirit. Moreover, the humanizing of one pressed and put to flight imparts a personification to the pursuers, the hounds. Again, the personified seeker implies the personification of the one sought, and the forest assumes its conventional personified form. Now, by the last seven verses the audience is completely prepared for the personification of water, wind, storm, and heavens; it probably even expects it from the way the convention has taken over.

XII

Some interesting suggestions may be found in. *wulf-hliðu* 'wolf-slopes' (1358a). Norman E. Eliason has sought to answer the question of why *wulf* should be used in the compound when (1368 ff.) animals are said to shun the place.[31] One explanation he offers is that "there existed a traditional association of wolves and precipices,"[32] because burial mounds were often on top of headlands or cliffs; because of the casting off (perhaps as part of rituals) of bodies of dogs, cats, cattle, and especially horses for the wolves; and because of suicides. He concludes, however, that "it does not seem to be a far-fetched inference to assume that *wulf-hlið* connoted a great deal more than 'wolf-slope.' It may merely represent a traditional association of wolves with cliffs . . . or—in the poet's mind and in the minds of his auditors—it may have conjured up a picture of a cliff where wolves lurked, feeding upon animal and human carcasses."[33] This is a good indication of some of the possible ways in which the convention of personification may work. The oral-formulaic style derives much of its poetic power from this kind of suggestive conventional usage. One should be careful, however, of the pejorative connotations of "merely . . . a traditional association." It is these very associations, traditional and conventional, which enable poet and auditors to conjure up pictures from the suggestions of the word. The traditions of *wulf-hlið* may have been stronger than Eliason supposes. If there were rituals in which animals were sacrificed from cliffs for wolves, it is likely that there was an identification of the wolf with a god to whom wolves were sacred. The spirit residing in the hill, then, would have been identical with the spirit residing in the wolf, i.e., the spirit of the god to whom both wolf and cliff were sacred.

XIII

The conventional personification of a building is made very suggestive in *Beowulf* when Heorot is spoken of in terms of a wounded warrior. This submerged metaphor appears several times:

> Þanne wæs þíos medu-heall   on morgen-tíd,
> dryht-sele dréor-fág   þanne dæ3 líexte,
> eall benć-þelu   blóde bestíemed,
> heall heoru-dréore.   (484–87a)

Then in the morning, when day shone, this mead-hall, noble chamber, was bloodstained, all the benchboards soaked with blood, hall [all] battle-gory.

>   þæt se wín-sele
> wiþhæfde heaðu-déorum,   þæt hé on hrúsan ne féoll,
> fǽ3er fold-bold . . .   (771b–73a)

that the wine-hall, the fair building, held out against the battle-brave [ones], that it didn't fall to earth . . .

233

þanne blóde fág

húsa sǽlest   heoru-dréoriჳ stód . . .   (934b–35)

when stained by blood the best of houses stood battle-gory . . .

In this last instance the personification is explicit in the words *sǽlest* and *stód*[34] but is reinforced when Heorot is given the attributes of a wounded warrior (*blóde fág* and *heoru-dréoriჳ*). All of this may give the further suggestion that it is a personification of *blóde* 'blood' which may cause the staining of a warrior, building, or ground.[35] Heorot is elsewhere personified by humanizing verbs of enduring (*bád* 82b),[36] remaining (*wunaþ* 284b), standing (*stande* 411b), and receiving the noise (*swǽჳe onféng* 1214b). It is also given a *múða* 'mouth' (724a) and is described as *eall-ჳearu* 'all ready' (77b) and *sǽlest* 'best' (146a, 285b, 412a, 658b). Another interesting modifier for Heorot is *ídel* (413a), which might possibly be closer to the modern meaning 'idle' than the 'empty' that is usually given in the glossaries.

XIV

There appears to be personification in the crucial passage *ná hé þone ჳief-stól grǽtan moste, | máðum for Meotode, né His myne wisse* (168–69). Klaeber's "final statement" says, "The general meaning is: (Grendel 'inhabited' Heorot at night, but), in the daytime he let the hall alone. This thought is expressed in a strikingly concrete and ironical way: he did not approach the king's throne (like a retainer) nor did he receive gifts from him, . . ."[37] Far from resolving the difficulties, this explanation raises new problems of syntax. Wrenn's solution, that the lines refer to Cain and belong between lines 110 and 111, is a good one, but it does not erase the possibility of a satisfactory explanation for the lines where they are.[38] The analogy of Grendel to Cain, however, might be kept in mind if we are to make sense out of the passage. Arthur E. DuBois' suggestion that ӡief-stól is equivalent to 'altar' but means, by synecdoche, 'kingdom,' is a fruitful one that also might be kept in mind.[39]

One way in which the convention of personification may operate opens up several possibilities that do not do violence either to syntax or to context. First, the word grǽtan implies a human greeter and a human greeted. The greeted one, the -stól 'seat,' is further personified as one who is capable of bestowing ӡief- 'gifts.' This gift seat is clearly a throne of some kind, and the possible synecdoche is 'throne' for 'king' or 'gift-giving seat' for 'gift-giving lord' (compare line 347 where grǽtan is used by Beowulf when he is expressing a wish to greet Hrothgar by approaching his throne). This would simply be the inversion of personification, speaking of a human in terms of an inanimate, no uncommon figure throughout the poem. But this will not clear up the passage unless it is seen that here the convention of personification is at work along with another significant poetic device, the submerged metaphor comparing a liege lord's distribution of gifts at his throne to God's dispensing of judgment, mercy, and grace at his throne. It is not inconceivable, then, that these lines mean 'but he [Grendel] might not approach the throne of heaven for [heavenly] gifts, because the Lord forbade it, nor did he know the spirit [or will] of God.'

XV

Part of the passage describing the funeral of Scield Sceafing affords an early example of the convention at work in *Beowulf*:

> Ne híerde ić cýmlícor   ćéol ӡeӡierwan
> hilde-wǽpnum   and heaðu-wǽdum,
> billum and byrnum;   him on bearme læӡ
> máðma meniӡu   þá him mid scoldon
> on flódes ǽht   feorr ӡewítan.   (38–42)

I have never heard of a vessel more attractively prepared with battle weapons and battle trappings, swords and byrnies; on his [its] bosom lay a host of treasures, which with him [it] had to go afar into the flood's possession.

Personification of weapons, ships, and ocean is always implied throughout the poem, but here all three seem to be explicitly personified. The weapons are subjects for the possibly humanizing verb *læʒ* 'lay [down],' and the ship is given the human property *bearme* 'bosom.' The weapons along with the ship (*him* 41b)[40] are further personified by the poet when he says they *scoldon . . . feorr ʒewítan* 'had to travel far.'[41] The sea is explicitly personified when given *æht* 'possession.' Moreover, the weapons and the armor are *hilde-wǽpnum* and *heaðu-wǽdum*, i.e., the weapons and clothing of the personified figure of battle.

This would be all one could say about this passage if one were dealing with the individual words in it. But the way in which the context of the five lines is suffused with the ideas of the personification convention lends new meaning to other words. As far as we know, the comparative adjective *cýmlícor* had not yet become specifically applicable to humans ('comely'),[42] but in this case, perhaps, it adds to the personification of *céol*. Furthermore, because the weapons, always implicitly personified, are here explicitly humanized by the actions of lying and having to travel far, it is possible that *ʒeʒierwan* 'prepared,' the only other verb in the passage, also has the personified weapons as subjects. It is, then, the fact that the weapons adorn the ship that makes it 'more attractive.'

The last verse of the description of the funeral says that men do not know *hwá þǽm hlæste onféng* 'who received that load' (52b). The figurative connotations are many in this short clause. The load is comprised of the body of Scield and the personified weapons, so that inversion of personification and submerged inversion are carried in the noun *hlæste*. Besides, the ability to have or carry a load adds somewhat to the personification of the ship. Both the pronoun *hwá* and the verb *onféng* serve to personify the body of land or even part of the sea to which the boat was carried (unless, of course, the poet was suggesting the person in the place who would find the boat cast up). The very fact that the indefinite pronoun is used with a personifying verb indicates that any and every body of land (or part of the seas) was subject to personification. Put another way, *hwá* could mean 'what god' or 'what spirit,' i.e., the god or spirit that gives life to a body of land or water in the first place.[43]

XVI

Ships, of course, are consistently personified, and it is in regard to them, perhaps, that it is easiest for the modern reader to see the convention at work. Our pronominal "she" retains the concept that ships are always to be imagined as living creatures. The personification is often on the surface, as in the fine passage describing Beowulf's return voyage from Denmark:

3ewát him on naca
dróefan déop wæter,   Dena-land of3eaf.
Þá wæs be mæste   mere-hræ3la sum,
se3l sále fæst;   sund-wudu þunode;
ná þǽr wǽ3-flotan   wind ofer ýðum
síðes 3etwǽfde.   Sǽ-genga fór,
fléat fámi3-heals   forþ ofer ýða,
bunden-stefna   ofer brim-stréamas,
þæt híe 3éata clifu   on3ietan meahton,
cúðe næssas;   céol upp 3eþrang
lyft-3eswencéd,   on lande stód.   (1903b–13)

The ship set out to stir up the deep water, left the Danish land when there was to the mast a sea-garment, a sail secured by rope; the ship [sea- *or* swimming-wood] creaked; not at all did the wind over the waves deprive of [its] journey [throw off course] the [ship] floating on waves. The ship [sea-goer *or* -walker] went forth, floated foamy-necked over the waves, the twisted prow over the ocean streams, until they could perceive the Gautish cliffs, well-known nesses; the ship pressed forward driven by the wind, stood on land.

The force of the humanizing verbs ʒewát 'set out,' dráfan 'stir up,' ofʒeaf 'left,' fór 'went forth,' ʒeþrang 'pressed forward,' and stód is supported by the attribution to the ship of a mere-hrǽʒla 'sea-garment' and a heals 'neck' and by the substantival constructions sund-wudu and sǽ-genǵa that refer to the ship as 'swimming-wood' and 'one who goes on the sea.' But there remains more to say about this passage. Wind, for instance, is personified by verbs of throwing and driving, and rope by its ability to secure. These, perhaps, should be expected in lines that deal mainly with the personification of a sailing vessel, and so might the figurative term sund-wudu 'swimming-wood' for ship, but there is a suggestion of a more subtle use of the convention in the line þæt híe ʒéata clifu onʒietan meahton 'until they could perceive the Gautish cliffs.' It is just possible that 'they' does not refer to the men in the ship (the antecedent would in that case be thirty-two verses away, unless Hé at line 1900a serves that function, still twenty-three verses away), but that the ship itself, which has been described in terms of various parts or attributes (mast, wood, prow, neck), is doing the perceiving.[44]

Often in company with ships, the sea is meant continually to be thought of as a living being. It has ǽht 'possession' or 'power' (42a, 516b) and can carry (beran 48b). It also has an expanse (begang 362a, 1497b, 1826b), i.e., an area that it holds or controls because it encircles or goes about it; it has a back (hrycg 471b) and can cast up (ætbær 519b); it can be savage (hréo 548b) and drive apart (todráf 545b); it can carry up (oþbær 579b) or strive with the wind (wann wiþ winde 1132a); and it may strike (ofslóg 1689b), cut off from power (ʒetwǽfeþ 1763b), or embrace (fæðmian 3133a). But over and above all this, the sea is characterized as a gár-secg 'spear-warrior' (49a, 515a, 537b). Caroline Brady accepts Kemp Malone's opinion that gár (as in Genesis 316) is equivalent to 'storm' and says, "gársecg in the sense of 'warrior with a storm = ocean' would be a doubly metaphorical periphrasis, expressing a third notion standing outside the compound itself."[45] She prefers, however, to consider it a "literal descriptive compound," meaning "the open sea characterized by storms." [46] But there is no reason for accepting questionable minority readings for *gár* or *-secg*, once one recognizes just what the "third notion standing outside the compound" is, and "literal" it certainly is not. Klaeber's glossary offers the following cryptic though fruitful clue: "cp. Neptune?" [47] Helen Thérèse McMillan Buckhurst may have picked it up: "This word, not uncommon in OE poetry as a term for 'sea' or 'ocean,' is of doubtful origin. It has been explained as a kenning meaning 'spear-man,' the sea being personified as a spear-armed warrior. If this is so, it is the one instance among OE terms for the sea, of the mythological type of kenning so frequent in ON Skaldic verse; but the explanation is open to doubt." [48] Mrs. Buckhurst's doubts seem to arise from the fact that it is the only term of its kind for the sea. These doubts surely ought to be dispelled, however, when other terms of the kind are used for other things. The idea of a mythological basis for the figure is sound—singer and audience must have accepted the idea of a spirit, a warrior-like, perhaps even Neptune-like god residing in the ocean. But there is no need to equate the *gár* with Neptune's trident, for the element outside the compound to be reckoned with is a previous inversion of personification: warrior spoken of in terms of spear (fellow warrior). The sea is a warrior, and a warrior is a spear—both parts of the figure are conventional.

XVII

Beowulf's version of the swimming contest with Breca owes much of its vividness to the stunning sequence of personifications:

> oþ-þæt unc flód todráf,
> wadu weallendu,   wedera ćealdost,
> nípende niht,   and norðan wind
> heaðu-grimm andhwearf;   hréo wǽron ýða,
> wæs mere-fisca   mód onhrǿred.
> Þǽr mé wiþ láðum   líc-sierće mín

heard, hand-locen,   helpe ȝefremede;
beadu-hræȝl brogden   on bréostum læȝ
golde ȝeȝierwed.   Meć to grunde téah
fáh fíond-scaða,   fæste hæfde
grimm on grápe . . .   (545b–55a)

until the tide drove us apart, the surging waves, very cold
weather, darkening night, and the north wind, battle-
fierce, turned on us; savage were the waves, the spirit[s]
of the sea fish were aroused. There for me against the foes
my hard, hand-linked corselet furnished help; the woven
byrnie lay on [my] breast adorned with gold. The hostile
dire foe dragged me to the bottom, the grim [one] held
[me] fast in his grip . . .

In the first place tide, waves, weather, and night are the subjects of the humanizing verb *todráf* 'drove [us] apart.' Then,
in turn, the wind performs the human action of turning on the
swimmers; the byrnie performs help and lies on Beowulf's
breast; and the fish, already aroused in spirit, drag him and
hold him. It seems as though one personification leads to or
suggests another, for in the entire passage every substantive
mentioned is personified. The personifications by means of
humanizing verbs are supported by several other words.
Thus, the north wind is *heaðu-grimm* 'battle-fierce' when it
turns on the swimmers (with the secondary personification of
battle); the waves are *hréo* 'savage'; the fish are *láðum*
'enemies' or 'hostile ones,' and one of them is *fáh* 'hostile,' a
fíond-scaða 'dire foe,' a *grimm* 'grim [one],' and has a *grápe*
'grasp' with which it can hold *fæste* 'fast.' Most important of
all, these fish have a *mód* 'spirit' that becomes *onhrǽred*
'enraged.' It is possible that the poet intended the collective
"temper" or "spirit" to be enraged. Finally, the reflection of
personification from one thing to another throughout the
passage may extend to *hand-locen* 'hand-linked' and *gold
ȝeȝierwed* 'adorned with gold,' so that the images conveyed
are of a personified hand doing the linking and personified
gold doing the adorning.

XVIII

Again in the Finn episode there is one of the clearest
examples of the personification of natural phenomena:

> holm storme wéoll,
> wann wiþ winde; winter ýða beléac
> ís-ʒebinde oþ-þæt óðer cóm
> ʒéar on ʒeardas swá nú ʒíet dǽþ,
> þá-þe sin-gáles sǽle bewitiaþ,
> wuldor-torhtan weder.
>   Þá wæs winter scæcen,
> fæʒer foldan bearm . . .   (1131b–37a)

the sea surged with storm, strove with the wind; winter
locked the waves in an icy bond, until spring [*lit.*: other
year] came into yards, as it still does, when the gloriously
bright weathers continually observe their proper time.
Then winter had departed, the bosom of the earth was
fair . . .

Sea and wind are personified by striving with each other,
winter by locking the waves in bonds of ice and later departing,
spring by coming (not as strong as the others but unmistakable
in context)[49] as it still does, and weathers by observing their
proper time. Earth is also personified by the attributes of a
bosom and fairness. But perhaps the key word in the passage
is *ʒeardas* 'yards' or 'dwellings.' Since there are no people in
the context, this does not seem to refer to people's homes.
There is instead the implication that the seasons take up
residence at their proper time on earth, but that one season
must vacate the premises before the other can move in. The
very terminology of *sǽle bewitiaþ* connotes an image of a real
estate transaction.

XIX

The close interaction of various aspects of the convention is
again illustrated in the description of Beowulf as an old man,
knowing he is soon to fight his last fight:

Him wæs ʒeómor sefa,
wǽfre and wæl-fús,   wyrd unʒemete néah,
sío þone gamolan   grǽtan scolde,
sǽċan sáwle hord,   sundor ʒedǽlan
líf wiþ líċe;   ná þon lange wæs
feorh æðelinges   flǽsce bewunden.   (2419b–24)

To him was his spirit sad, restless, and ready [or eager] for
slaughter, fate [was] exceedingly near which was to greet
the wise old man, to seek his soul's treasure, to separate
asunder life from body; not [for] long after that was the
spirit of the noble surrounded by flesh.

The personification of fate is closely related to the personification of Beowulf's soul: the soul owns the treasure that fate is
seeking. Then, by extension, other parts of Beowulf's whole
self are personified—his sad, restless, ready spirit; his flesh,
which is a surrounder; and again his spirit, which is the one
surrounded. It may be misleading to call this an "interaction
of aspects" because this may suggest that the poet was consciously relating one aspect of the convention to another. It is
far more likely that the use of the convention in certain formulas and themes suggested to the singer that he employ other
formulas and themes using the same convention.
    This kind of extended use of the convention would seem to
explain some rather startling transitions in the poem in places
where several aspects of the convention are used without the
coherence of lines 2419b–24. A good case in point occurs in
these lines:

Nú sceal glǽd fretan,
—weaxan wanna líeʒ—   wiʒena strenʒel,
þone-þe oft ʒebád   ísern-scúre,
þanne strǽla storm   strenʒum ʒebǽded
scóc ofer scield-weall,   scæft nytte héold,
feðer-ʒearwum fús,   fláne fulléode.   (3114b–19)

Now shall fire consume—dark flames grow—the ruler of
warriors who often endured a shower of iron, when a

storm of arrows impelled by strings passed over the shield wall; the shaft did its duty, hastening by the feather gear, followed the arrowhead.

If the idea in this passage was that Beowulf had lived through the dangers of battle, where he might have been killed by arrows, only to die in a fire, there would be no need to explicate these lines any further. But the fire is the funeral pyre, not the dragon's breath; and Beowulf did die in battle. On the other hand, the poet does wish to make a contrast between the present fate of the hero and his past glories and imperviousness in battle. Therefore, having used a conventional expression personifying the fire, he does not merely go on to describe Beowulf as one who had endured in battle. Instead, he hits happily upon another use of the convention and personifies some weapons, arrows and their parts. Moreover, the contrast he sets up on the figurative level is the striking one between fire and water (the arrows are spoken of in terms of a shower and a storm). The use of the opposing elements in a way that can be called symbolic gives added power to a poignant passage. But the vital points to be observed here are the way the convention operates as a whole and the way the figurative qualities of the conventional expressions maintain their own level of coherence.

XX

The part of the convention that is similar to synecdoche (parts of humans spoken of in terms of whole humans) is quite clearly seen in the three verses, *Nú sío hand liʒeþ, | sío-þe íow wél-hwelćra willna dohte* (1343b–44). These verses also illustrate how the introduction of the convention into a passage colors other parts of the passage. The personification of hand for the retainer, Aeschere, is explicit in the first half-line— 'now the hand lies dead.' Then the relative clause is introduced with *sío-þe*, which must be translated 'which' because its antecedent is the hand no matter how clearly the idea of the whole man is carried over. Therefore, *dohte* 'treated well' continues the personification, for it is the hand that treated well. Now the important point is that *íow wél-hwelćra willna* should not be rendered 'each of your desires.' Rather, it must be 'every desire for you,' because the convention has been extended by implication (and syntax) to the object of the personifying action. The desires are now seen to stand for the whole men who were treated well by Aeschere's hand, probably both as a strong ally in battle and as a dispenser of gifts.

XXI

A fitting final passage for discussion would stress the personification of weapons but would introduce various other aspects of the convention as well. Ideal for this purpose is the following passage:

> Sceal se hearda helm,   hyrsted golde,
> fǽttum befeallen;   feormiend swefaþ,
> þá-þe beadu-gríman   bíewan scoldon;
> ȝe swelće sío here-pád,   sío æt hilde ȝebád
> ofer borda ȝebræc   bite írena,
> brosnaþ æfter beorne;   ne mæȝ byrnam hring
> æfter wíȝ-fruman   wíde fœran
> hæleðum be healfe.   N'is hearpan wynn,
> gamen glíeȝ-béames   né gód hafoc
> ȝeond sæl swinȝeþ   né se swifta mearh
> burg-stede béateþ.   Bealu-cwealm hafaþ
> fela feorh-cynna   forþ onsended!   (2255–66)

The hard helmet, adorned with gold, will be deprived of ornaments; caretakers sleep, those who had to be shining the battle-masks; and the armor likewise, which endured in battle over the crash of shields the bite of swords, decays like the warrior; nor may the ringed byrnie along with the warrior range widely by the side of heroes. There is no joy of harp, [no] mirth of the glee-wood, nor does a good hawk swing through the hall, nor does the swift horse beat the castle court. Baleful death has banished forth many of the race of living beings!

There is no great hierarchical chain of being represented in this convention. Rather, all things are seen as part of one *feorh-cynn* 'race of living beings.' Personified in these lines are helmet, gold, battle, armor, shields, swords, byrnie, harp, wood, hawk, horse, and death. The personification of one naturally leads to that of others, and they are all summed up in a word (*feorh-cynn*) that carries the essence of the entire convention in it. For, as has been seen in this study, singer and audience must have agreed that every kind (*cynn*) of thing had its own living spirit (*feorh*). This passage shows as clearly as any the truth of this statement, while it is also a good example of the effectiveness of the poet's use of the convention.

Most important, the passage demonstrates the way the convention works. First a variety of things is personified in a brilliant sequence of images. Then the meaning of the whole passage is expressed in a statement that also explains the conventional device used to illustrate that meaning. That is, the transience of this world is described in terms of the transitory nature of the things that people this world (helmet, gold, battle, and the rest). Thus the statement 'Baleful death has banished forth many of the race of living beings' is a summing up of the philosophical concept and the poetic concept of the passage.[50]

NOTES

1. The important statements in this development are Francis P. Magoun, Jr., "Oral-Formulaic Character of Anglo-Saxon Narrative Poetry," *Speculum*, XXVIII (1953), 446–67; Albert B. Lord, *The Singer of Tales* (Cambridge, Mass., 1960); and Robert P. Creed, "Studies in the Techniques of Composition of the *Beowulf* Poetry" (Unpublished Ph.D. dissertation, Harvard University, 1955). I am very grateful to Creed for his generous advice and helpful criticism.

2. Most of the material in this study is taken from my findings in "Personification in *Beowulf*" (Unpublished Ph.D. dissertation, Brown University, 1959). Of earlier commentators on *Beowulf*, only Francis B. Gummere recognized the pervasiveness of personification: *The Anglo-Saxon Metaphor* (Halle, 1881).

3. See Knut Stjerna, *Essays on Questions Connected with the Old English Poem of Beowulf*, ed. and trans. John R. Clark Hall (London, 1912), for an enlightening discussion of the weapons, especially the first essay, "Helmets and Swords in *Beowulf.*"

4. Quotations from *Beowulf* are taken from *Béowulf and Judith: Done in a Normalized Orthography*, ed. Francis P. Magoun, Jr. (Cambridge, Mass., 1959).

5. *Notes and Queries*, N.S. IV (1957), 140.

6. My only departure from Magoun's text is *feorh-wearde* for his *fær-wearde* (305b).

7. *Beowulf, nebst dem Finnsburg-Bruchstück*, ed. F. Holthausen ("Alt- und mittelenglische Texte," Vol. III [Heidelberg, 1906]).

8. "*Beowulf* and the *Blickling Homilies* and Some Textual Notes," *PMLA*, LIII (1938), 910–11.

9. *Aanteekeningen op den Beowulf* (Leiden, 1892), p. 7.

10. "Das Beowulflied," *Bonner Beiträge zur Anglistik*, XVI (1904).

11. *Beowulf, nebst dem Finnsburg-Bruchstück*, ed. Holthausen.

12. "*Beowulf* and the *Blickling Homilies* and Some Textual Notes," 910–11.

13. Cf. ll. 573, 589, 1344.

14. The simple adjective *gód* 'good' is used mostly of persons and always retains human connotations of 'able,' 'efficient,' 'excellent,' 'strong,' 'brave.' Of the two comparative forms *betera* is used only twice in *Beowulf*, both times of people, and *sælra* ten times, only four times of people. Three of the other uses, however, refer to humans indirectly, as in 'a better thing to do,' 'a better place to visit,' and 'a better way to act.' The other three are dubious personifications: referring to death (2890); to a jewel of heroes (1197); to treasure in the form of a sword (2193). 'Better' seems less of a personifying word than either 'good' or 'best.' Of the two forms of the latter *betst* appears six times, four times of humans, once of a generalized human quality, and once in a supported personification (453); while *sælest* appears eighteen times, only six times of humans, but four other times referring to human actions. Of the eight remaining occurrences two are of weapons where the personifications are supported (454, 1144), and six of Heorot or other buildings. Four of the latter also have personification supported by other words (146, 285, 412, 935), while the other two use it without other personifying words (658, 2326). The implication seems to be that the word was meant to convey a personification.

15. I am indebted to Paul B. Taylor for this suggestion and others.

16. Cf. ll. 2563, 2610.

17. See *Beowulf and the Fight at Finnsburg*, ed. Friedrich Klaeber (3d ed.; Boston, 1950), p. 176; *Beowulf*, ed. C. L. Wrenn (Boston, 1953), p. 207.

18. *Beowules Beorh eller Bjovulfes-Drapen* (Copenhagen, 1861).
19. *Beowulf and the Fight at Finnsburg*, ed. Klaeber, p. 455.
20. "Fürsten- und Kriegerkenning im *Beowulf*," *Anglia*, LX (1936), 391 ff.
21. *Beowulf and Judith*, ed. E. van K. Dobbie ("The Anglo-Saxon Poetic Records," Vol. IV [New York, 1953]), pp. 167–68.
22. "The Sword of Healfdene," *Journal of English and Germanic Philology*, XLII (1943), 82–95.
23. *Ibid.*, p. 92.
24. *Beowulf*, ed. Wrenn, p. 203.
25. Ll. 1443–64.
26. See, for example, *Maldon*, ll. 185 ff., where the deserters did not ʒemundon their lord's gifts.
27. Cf. *Beowulf and Judith*, ed. Dobbie, p. 190.
28. Personification (weak or supported by other words) with *springan* is found also in ll. 18, 817, 884, 1588, 2582, 2966.
29. *Beowulf*, ed. Wrenn, p. 227.
30. *Neuphilologische Mitteilungen*, LVI (1955), 81–90.
31. "*Wulfhlið (Beowulf*, l. 1358)," *Journal of English and Germanic Philology*, XXXIV (1935), 20–23.
32. *Ibid.*, p. 20.
33. *Ibid.*, pp. 22–23.
34. The verbs *standan*, *cuman*, and *springan* by themselves constitute only weak personifications, but they are generally found, when not actually referring to humans, supported by other personifying words. Personification with *standan*, often supported, appears in ll. 411, 726, 783, 935, 1037, 1362, 1416, 1434, 1570, 1913, 2227, 2271, 2313, 2545, 2679, 2760, 2769.
35. Perhaps this may help explain the crux in *Brunanburh* (12b). See Neil D. Isaacs, "Battlefield Tour: Brunanburg," *Neuphilologische Mitteilungen*, LXIII (1962), 239.
36. *Bídan*, ʒebídan, and *onbídan* are used of people or monstrous creatures thirty-one times, but are used for personifying purposes in ll. 397, 1882, 2258.
37. *Beowulf and the Fight at Finnsburg*, ed. Klaeber, p. 465.
38. *Beowulf*, ed. Wrenn, pp. 188–89.
39. "*Gifstol*," *MLN*, LXIX (1954), 546–49. In an ingenious recent analysis of the passage in "Grendel and the *Gifstol*: A Legal View of Monsters," *PMLA*, LXXVII (1962), 513–20, William A. Chaney has compiled evidence and argument from anthropology; folklore; magic; and history of culture, law, religion, and monarchy in order to justify and explain the passage (or at least most of it: l. 169b remains with "ambiguities [which], . . . finally, cannot, I think, be definitely solved" [p. 520]). One cannot help but be impressed, even overwhelmed, by the weight of

such scholarship, but alas, Chaney has omitted one discipline, literature or criticism. He has forgotten that he is dealing with poetry, not with a socio-historio-cultural curio without form.

40. Although the *Beowulf* poet occasionally uses successive pronouns where he is referring to different people, I take it that both uses of *him* in this passage refer to the ship.

41. Of twenty-seven other uses of *ʒewítan* in *Beowulf*, all but five refer to people or the dragon: ll. 210, 217, 1360, 1903, 2819.

42. The earliest use with persons cited by *The Oxford English Dictionary*, ed. James A. H. Murray, *et al.* (Oxford, 1933), is *Sir Gawain and the Green Knight*, l. 53.

43. Variations of this formula are found in ll. 1563, 2989, and 3090, all having people as subject. Personification with *onfón* also is found in ll. 688, 852, 1214, 1494.

44. But Creed has suggested to me that another convention is at work here, that of the measure of distance by "proceeding until seeing."

45. "The Synonyms for 'Sea,'" in *Studies in Honor of Albert Morey Sturtevant* (Lawrence, Kans., 1952), p. 41.

46. *Ibid.*, p. 42.

47. *Beowulf and the Fight at Finnsburg*, ed. Klaeber, p. 338.

48. "Terms and Phrases for the Sea in Old English Poetry," in *Studies in English Philology: A Miscellany in Honor of Frederick Klaeber* (Minneapolis, 1929), p. 108.

49. The verb *cuman* is used thirty-six times of people or monstrous creatures, fourteen other times in personifications (weak or supported by other words): ll. 569, 650, 731, 1077, 1133, 1235, 1600, 1802, 2058, 2103, 2124, 2303, 2404, 2646. In three other cases it is *bót* 'remedy' (281) or *edwenden* 'change' (1774, 2188) that 'comes.' These may also be weak personifications, but there is no other evidence that 'remedy' or 'change' is meant to be visualized as a concretized, individualized, personified character.

50. Some of this material has appeared in "Six *Beowulf* Cruces," *Journal of English and Germanic Philology*, LXII (1963), 119–28. The present essay is the older, however, and I thought it better not to delete those segments.

THEMES OF DEATH IN *BEOWULF*

❦

Paul Beekman Taylor

A theme in traditional poetry may be defined simply as the formulaic[1] repetition of incidents and descriptive passages.[2] A theme is a verbal unit whose size and elasticity, compared to the limitations of the single word or formula, make possible the transmission of long traditional poems or songs. The oral poet does not have to memorize a once-heard text verbatim in order to repeat the story himself; nor does he even have to know or memorize an order of formulas and themes to construct his tale within the limitations of his alliterative and metrical line. The traditional poet in still-living traditions, as observed by Milman Parry and Albert B. Lord, retains the skeletal outline of a story he has heard and then, according to his individual skill, imagination, and knowledge of the materials of his tradition, fills out this skeleton with a body of narrative, dramatic, and descriptive themes.[3] The oral poet, even though his intention may be to transmit rather than create an art form, does what every artist must do—he fragments what he has observed and then reconstructs it in such a way as to force his own ideas and feelings upon it.

Because the formulaic and thematic method of creating a poem is so elastic and because it relies so much upon the imagination of the poet, we should expect any two versions of a single story to differ in details (except in those easily noted cases where one manuscript is used as a model for copies). In the Volsung group of poems in the Old Norse poetic *Edda*, for example, there are three different versions of Sigurd's death. In *Brot af Sigurðarkviðu* Gudrun is told that Sigurd died in a field "south of the Rhine." In *Sigurðarkviða in Skamma* Gudrun awakens in the middle of the night to discover Sigurd dying beside her; and in *Guðrúnarkviða* Gudrun learns of Sigurd's death when the hero's horse Grani returns riderless to the assembly. In each case the fact of Sigurd's death and its impact upon Gudrun are the same, but in each version the manner of the discovery of death differs. Certainly details are of concern to the traditional poet, but his inherent dramatic sense and his habit of producing a story without the prior opportunity to order carefully the details of his tale overbalance his conscious desire to reproduce a story exactly as he heard it. The details or themes of the oral poem are produced "spontaneously" as the poet's imagination reacts to the needs of the dramatic situation at hand, and no two poets could be expected to react similarly. A comparison of the use of themes in the Old English *Finnsburg*, *The Battle of Maldon*, and *The Battle of Brunanburh* reveals differing levels of skill and greater and lesser imagination in dealing with basically similar situations.

The skill of the oral poet depends not only upon the number of ornamental themes with which he can color a dramatic situation but also upon his ability to maintain at dramatically crucial times a thematic relevance between the repetition of formulas and the contexts of the repetitions. The recurrence of a theme carries with it not only the particular idea that its formulas and formulaic systems explicitly state[4] but also some hint of the contexts in which these formulas had previously appeared. Sometimes a thematic idea associated with a formula or group of formulas appears to develop within a single poem; at other times thematic values depend upon contexts in other tales within the tradition. Nevertheless, each time a theme is repeated its full meaning is generated by both the immediate context and the whole association of ideas that that theme carries with it from previous occurrences.[5] The amount of tension between a theme's immediate meaning in context and its general connotation derived from previous contexts may be significant or insignificant depending upon the demands of the story and the amount of subtlety or irony developed by the poet. For example, in *Beowulf* the theme characterized by the formulaic system (*gúþ-déaþ/heaðu-ræs/wíჳ ealle*) *fornam* 'battle death/battle storm/war all took away' is a theme of death by virtue of explicitly stating the fact of death;[6] its independent and contextual associations are identical. On the other hand, the meaning of the formula *þá þæt onfunde* 'then [he] discovered that' in *Beowulf* has no explicit suggestion of death; yet, in the context of battle scenes the formula forecasts the death of whomsoever it is associated with. It is a metaphor or subtheme of death. The formula, therefore, as it constructs a theme, qualifies it in one or more of three ways: by explicit statement, by special meaning derived from its immediate context, and by the association of ideas that the formula carries with it from its previous contexts. The latter two methods are certainly more typical of the skilled poet in an oral tradition.

The composition of a theme may vary in length from a single formulaic system to many, although rarely does a single system comprise a theme and even more rarely, if ever, does the repetition of a single formula characterize a theme. An example of a theme composed of a single formulaic system is the theme described later as "the sorrowful journey," and a theme composed of several systems is the "song of death."

Although the themes I have chosen to discuss are associated with the idea of death, I find it convenient to deal with them as "subthemes" and to designate them by titles distinguishing the predominant metaphor used by the poet to suggest death. My list of subthemes is not exhaustive but is particularly selected to illustrate the art of the poet in telling and ornamenting his tale. The subthemes I shall discuss are "the discovery of death," "the fatal venture," "the sorrowful journey," and "the song of death" (which still lingers in current imagination in the familiar metaphor "swan song").

THE DISCOVERY OF DEATH

Beowulf in each of his three battles kills his opponent and in the third battle is himself killed. Before each of these four deaths the one about to die is associated with a formula whose literal rendering is 'he immediately discovered that . . .' The first of the two formulas that convey this meaning, *sóna þæt onfunde*, occurs as a type A-3 whole-verse formula in the first verses of lines 750 and 1497. In its first appearance the formula describes Grendel as he breaks into Heorot and unexpectedly finds a strong warrior awaiting him:

> Sóna þæt onfunde   firena hierde,
> þæt hé ne mœtte   middan-ȝeardes,
> eorðan scéata   on ellran menn
> mund-gripe máran.[7]   (750–53a)

The shepherd of crimes at once discovered that he had not met on earth, in the regions of the earth, in another man a greater handgrip.

Grendel's discovery of Beowulf's strength is a forecast of his own doom.

The second occurrence of the formula describes Grendel's mother as she becomes suddenly aware of Beowulf's invasion of her den. Again, this description forecasts her own death, for the invasion of her den is the prelude to her destruction:

> Sóna þæt onfunde   sío-þe flóda begang
> heoru-ȝífre behéold   hund misséra,
> grimm and grǽdiȝ,   þæt þǽr gumena sum
> ell-wihta eard   ufan cunnode.   (1497–1500)

She who, fiercely ravenous, had held for fifty years the region of the waves, grim and fierce, discovered that there a certain man from above tested the land of alien creatures.

In the dragon episode a second formula with the same meaning as the first (differing only in the preterit form of the verb *findan*) appears as a type B verse in the second half of lines 2300 and 2713, where it characterizes the impending deaths of the dragon and Beowulf, respectively. In line 2300 the formula describes the dragon's discovery of the plunder of his treasure hoard:

> hé þæt sóna onfand,
>
> þæt hæfde gumena sum   goldes ȝefandod,
>
> héah-ȝestréona.   (2300b–2302a)

he at once discovered that a certain man had searched out
the gold, the splendid treasures.

The dragon has discovered, as had Grendel's mother earlier,
the invasion of a stranger. This invasion by a thief foreshadows Beowulf's later invasion, which will cause the
dragon's death, just as his invasion of Grendel's mother's den
had caused her death. The repetition of the whole-measure
formula *gumena sum* from its earlier context (1499) further
strengthens the association between the two incidents.

The discovery-of-death theme occurs later, as Beowulf
realizes he is about to die of the mortal wound inflicted by the
dragon:

> hé þæt sóna onfand,
>
> þæt him on bréostum   bealu-níðe wéoll
>
> átor on-innan.   (2713b–15a)

he at once discovered that the poison surged in his breast
with deadly rage.

So, in each of these four occurrences death is characterized
by a particular formula that appears in association with someone about to die. The formula foreshadows death, and no
matter what is explicitly discovered by the subject of the
phrase, the implicit object is his own death.

The poet uses other formulas based upon the verb *onfindan*
to characterize the same subtheme. For example, the [X]
onfunde formulaic system, the same A-3 system as *sóna þæt*
onfunde, describes Grendel as he flees from his fatal fight
against Beowulf:

> Þá þæt onfunde   se-þe fela ǽror
>
> módes myrðe   manna cynne,
>
> firena ȝefremede   —hé [wæs] fáh wiþ God—
>
> þæt him se líc-hama   lǽstan nolde . . .   (809–12)

Then he who earlier had, in the affliction of his spirit,
done many crimes against mankind—he was feuding with
God—discovered that his body would not serve him . . .

Grendel dies shortly after this realization that his body cannot
withstand the might of his adversary, and he knows from his
discovery that he is soon to die:

> wisse þý ʒeornor
> þæt his ealdres wæs ende ʒegangen,
> dógra dæʒ-rím. (821b–23a)

he knew the more certainly that the end of his life, the
number of his days, had come about.

Later, the system appears (according to Magoun's emendation) in line 2226 where it describes the thief of the barrow:
Sóna onfunde | þæt [þǽr] þǽm ʒiest [e gryre] -bróga stód
(2226b–27); the construction is not altogether clear ('he
immediately discovered that a grisly horror rose up in the
guest [himself]'), and the thief, so far as we know, does not
die. Since the formula appears to comprise a subtheme of
death, however, it seems to refer to the deaths of those people
upon whom the dragon soon avenges himself. This analysis
implies the association of the thief with the people of the land,
a not unlikely association considering the symbolic nature of
the crime and its final atonement by the death of Beowulf.
Yet another formulaic system using the preterit form of the
verb *onfindan* is the *þá/þæt se [X] onfand* group. This system
first occurs as a subtheme of death in the description of
Beowulf's discovery of the failure of Hrunting to succeed
against Grendel's mother:

> þá se ʒiest onfand
> þæt se beadu-léoma bítan nolde,
> ealdre scieþþan ac sío ecg ʒeswác . . . (1522b–24)

Then the guest discovered that the light of the battle would
not cut, harm life, but the edge failed . . .

Beowulf survives this struggle. Hrunting fails, and although the sword is a component of the grammatical object of *onfand* rather than the subject of *onfand*, its destruction is forecast.

The system seems to occur again in the dragon episode to describe the discovery by the people of the land of the aroused dragon's anger: *þæt sío þéod [onfand], / bú-folc beorna, þæt hé ʒebolgen wæs* 'that the people [discovered], the neighboring people, that he was angered' (2219b–20).

Later, in a passage contrasting with the description of Hrunting's failure, the theme appears when the dragon discovers the awful might of Wiglaf's sword:

> Ne ʒemealt him se mód-sefa   né his mǽʒes láf
> ʒeswác æt wíʒe.   Þæt se wyrm onfand
> siþþan híe togædere   ʒegán hæfdon.   (2628–30)

His courage did not melt away nor did his kinsman's heirloom fail at battle. That the serpent discovered after they had encountered.

The repetition of the *onfand* system allows the *Beowulf* poet to associate Beowulf and his people and the dragon as common discoverers of a violent fate and to strengthen the suggestion that more misery will fall upon the Geats after their hero has perished.

THE FATAL VENTURE

Another formulaic system that characterizes a subtheme of death by virtue of its consistent appearance in contexts describing death is the type B whole-verse system *[né] wæs [þá/þæt] forma síþ*. The system appears early in the poem to describe the circumstances of Grendel's attack on Heorot the night Beowulf awaits him: *Ne wæs þæt forma síþ / þæt hé Hróþ-gáres ham ʒesóhte* 'that was not the first time that he had sought Hrothgar's home' (716b–17). The statement that this was not the first time that Grendel visited Heorot provides an ironic contrast to the fact that it is indeed his last visit.

Later, at the edge of the pool by the den of Grendel's mother Unferth lends Beowulf the sword Hrunting. The sword is personified as its heroic past is recalled: *Næs þæt forma síþ / þæt hit ellen-weorc efnan scolde* 'that was not the first time that it had to perform a bold deed' (1463b–64). When, consequently, Hrunting fails in Beowulf's fight with Grendel's mother, we are told that this is the first time that it has ever failed. Its first failure, ironically, marks its last venture: *þá wæs forma síþ / díerum máðme þæt his dóm alæʒ* 'that was the first time for the beloved treasure that its glory failed' (1527b–28).

The same ironic implications recur when Wiglaf joins Beowulf in the fight against the dragon. It is the first time that Wiglaf has fought by his lord's side; and because Beowulf is to die in the battle, it is the last time Wiglaf will fight by his side:

> þá wæs forma síþ
> ʒeongan cempan   þæt hé gúðe ræs
> mid his frío-dryhtne   fremman scolde.   (2625b–27)

That was the first time for the young warrior that he had to perform the attack of battle with his noble lord.

The repetition of the *forma síþ* system as well as the [*efnan/ fremman*] *scolde* (1464b, 2627b) formulaic system subtly associates Wiglaf with Hrunting, both as protectors of Beowulf. However, these "first ventures" share another significant, if not ironic, relationship: Grendel's first ventures into Heorot were all successful, but his last venture is a fatal one; Hrunting's earlier exploits, we are told by the poet, were similarly marked by success, but the sword's last venture against Grendel's mother ends in failure; then, Wiglaf's first venture with his lord in the fight against the dragon is successful, but Wiglaf's first and successful venture is Beowulf's last and fatal fight. In each instance "first ventures" foreshadows a "last venture," death.[8]

The *Beowulf* poet uses another, but quite similar, formulaic system to characterize again this subtheme of death. Although lacking the striking ironic implications of the "first-venture" system, it is not without irony altogether. For example, the poet describes Beowulf's battle with the dragon by the litotes "not an easy venture":

> Ne wæs þæt íeðe síþ
> þæt se mǽra   maga Ecg-þéowes
> grund-wang þone   ofȝiefan wolde ...   (2586b–88)

That was not an easy adventure that the renowned son of Edgetheow had to give up the earth ...

The substitution of *íeðe* for *forma* satisfies the demands of alliteration and the special meaning needed in context (for "first venture" makes no sense here).[9]

Grendel's last journey to Heorot is also described by this system, again characterized by litotes: *Þæt wæs ȝéocor síþ / þæt se hearm-scaða to Heorote atéah* 'That was a sad adventure that the pernicious enemy took to Heorot' (765b–66). Again, the context has demanded alliterative substitution and a change of meaning. *Ȝéocor* 'sad' or 'mournful' fits the context without damaging either the B-verse pattern or the association with death that the formulaic system has already acquired through its many recurrences.

The theme reappears when Beowulf refuses to be aided in his battle against the dragon. He insists that it is his venture alone:

> N'is þæt íower síþ
> né ȝemet mannes   nefne mín ánes
> þæt hé wiþ ag-lǽćan   eafoðu dǽle,
> eorlsciepe efne.   (2532b–35a)

That is not your adventure nor the measure of a man except me alone, that he should fight with the monster, perform noble deeds.

Then, just nine lines later, the poet comments on Beowulf's courage with the litotes "not a cowardly journey": *strenȝe ʒetruwode | ánes mannes. Ne biþ swelć earges síþ* '[he] trusted the strength of a single man. Such was not the adventure of a coward' (2540b–41).

The repetition in this passage of *ánes* and *mannes* (see line 2533) further insists that Beowulf alone is to fight the dragon. The implicit thematic suggestion in both passages is that Beowulf alone of all the warriors is to die.

Another formula associated with the theme of the fatal venture is the type A whole-verse formula *forman síðe* 'as a beginning' or '[for] [the] first time,' which occurs in the second verse of lines 740 and 2286. Grendel's attack upon Heorot and his subsequent murder of a sleeping Geat are described 'as a beginning':

> Né þæt se ag-lǽća ieldan þóhte,
> ac hé ʒeféng hræðe forman síðe
> slǽpendne rinc, slát unwearnum ... (739–41)

Nor did the monster think to hesitate, but he quickly, as a beginning, seized a sleeping warrior, tore him greedily...

Ironically, the 'beginning' here, the murder of a Geat warrior, is followed directly by Grendel's ending at the hands of Beowulf.

In the dragon episode the theme is applied to a description of Beowulf as he looks upon the plundered hoard 'for the first time' (or, carrying a hint of the first context in which the formula appeared, 'as a beginning'—in this case, a beginning to the episode that results in Beowulf's death):

>   Fréa scéawode
> fíra fyrn-ʒeweorc forman síðe.
> Þá se wyrm onwóc, wróht wæs ʒeníewod ...
>   (2285b–87)

The lord looked for the first time on the ancient work of men. Then the serpent awoke, strife was renewed ...

Even though this theme appears some time before the description of the battle against the dragon, it may perhaps suggest

Beowulf's impending death. The viewing of the treasure by Beowulf precedes his battle, as Grendel's murder of Handscóh 'as a beginning' preceded Grendel's last fight. As Grendel is killed by a warrior who remains awake while others sleep, so Beowulf is killed by an awakened opponent: *þá se wyrm onwóc, wróht wæs ʒeníewod*. The parallelism suggests that Beowulf's inspection of the treasure incites the dragon, just as Grendel's murder of Handscóh had incited Beowulf. The fact that everyone who views the treasure is subjected to tragedy (a parallel to the curse on the Rhine gold in the Old Norse Volsung poems) further associates Beowulf's view of the treasure with his own doom.

A substitution of the adjective in the *forman síðe* system produces another group of formulas belonging to the theme of the fatal venture. For example, the formula *hindeman síðe* characterizes a last venture quite explicitly and without the ironic implications of *forman síðe*. The death of Ingeld's father is described this way:

> méce . . .
> þone þín fæder   to ʒefeohte bær
> under here-gríman   hindeman síðe,
> díere íren,   þǽr hine Dene slógon . . .
> (2047b–50)

sword . . . precious iron, which your father bore to battle beneath his war helmet on the last occasion when the Danes slew him . . .

Similarly, when Beowulf greets his companions before his fight against the dragon, the formula forecasts the result of the fight:

> ʒegrǿtte þá   gumena ʒehwelćne,
> hwæte helm-berend   hindeman síðe,
> swǽse ʒesíðas . . .   (2516–18a)

Then he greeted each man, the brave helmet bearers, beloved companions, for the last time . . .

Both heroes, Beowulf and Froda, die; and, as if to make the alliterative and semantic association between the two yet more striking, the poet notes in each case that the hero dies 'under his helmet.'

It is interesting to note, in comparing the two occurrences of *hindeman síðe* with the two occurrences of *forman síðe*, that the poet is able to use either formula, despite the opposition in meaning, to characterize the same theme. Whereas one formula is explicit, the other gains its thematic impact through its recurrence in contexts where the implication of death is strong.

In two other places in the poem the poet uses, instead of *hindeman*, *níehstan* (which has approximately the same meaning), in order to fulfill the alliterative needs of his line. This formula is used in the description of Hygelac's last venture—his ill-fated Rhineland raid:

> Þone hring hæfde   Hyʒe-lác Ʒéata,
> nefa Swiertinges   níehstan síðe
> siþþan hé under seʒne   sinc ealgode,
> wæl-réaf werede.   (1202–5a)

Hygelac of the Geatas, the grandson of Swerting, had that ring on the last occasion after he protected the treasure beneath the banner, defended the spoils of battle.

Beowulf is associated with the formula when he formally addresses his retainers for the last time: *Bío-wulf maðelode, bíot-wordum spræc | níehstan síðe* 'Beowulf spoke, he said boasting words for the last time' (2510b–11).

All of the formulas discussed above as components of the theme of the fatal venture can be classified in one of two formulaic systems, the type B whole-verse system *[ne] wæs [þá/þæt] forma síþ* or the type A whole-verse system *[forman/hindeman/níehstan] síðe*,[10] both of which appear typically in the second half of the alliterative line. All of the formulas are founded upon the noun *síþ* ('journey,' 'adventure,' 'occasion'); and yet, within the metrical and semantic limitations of these systems, the poet is able to vary the meanings of the formulas through effective placement in his narrative and through skillful substitution of variable elements in the formulaic systems, while at all times maintaining the thematic association with death.

THE SORROWFUL JOURNEY

The type E whole-verse formula *sorg-fullne síþ* characterizes another subtheme of death. It appears three times in *Beowulf* —as the first verses in lines 512, 1278, and 1429. "Sorrowful journey," like "last venture," in itself suggests death. However, the death with which the formula is associated is not always the death of the journeyer. The sorrowful journey is more often a forecast of the death of the person or persons journeyed to. The formula carries with it the idea of doing harm more often than of receiving harm. For example, it occurs in the passage describing the intention of Grendel's mother to avenge her son's death:

> And his módor þá-ʒíet
> ʒífre and ʒealg-mód   ʒegán wolde
> sorg-fullne síþ,   suna déaþ wrecan.   (1276b–78)

And his mother, greedy and gloomy, would yet pursue a sorrowful venture, to avenge her son's death.

Shortly thereafter she kills Æschere and is, consequently, herself killed.

The sea journeys of the nicors are described as 'sorrowful' in the passage where Beowulf and his band look down into the pool that protects the den of Grendel's mother:

> ʒesáwon þá æfter wætere   wyrm-cynnes fela,
> seldlíće sǽ-dracan   sund cunnian,
> swelće on næss-hliðum   nicoras licgan
> þá on undern-mǽl   oft bewitiaþ
> sorg-fullne síþ   on seʒl-ráde,
> wyrmas and wildor.   (1425–30a)

Then they saw about the water many of the serpent kind,
strange sea dragons exploring the water, [they] also [saw]
water monsters, snakes and wild beasts lying on cliff
slopes, who in the morning often take a sorrowful journey
on the sail road.

The repetition here of the formula suggests an appropriate
identification of the nicors with Grendel's mother, all as doers
of evil.

In an earlier occurrence the formula appears in Unferth's
denunciation of Beowulf. Unferth calls Beowulf's open-sea
swim with Breca a sorrowful journey:

	Ne inc ǽniȝ mann,
né léof né láþ,	beléan meahte
sorgfullne síþ	þá ȝit on sund réowon. (510b–12)

Nor could any man, neither friend nor foe, keep you two
from the sorrowful journey when you both swam in the
sea.

Unferth's version of the swimming match is designed to deni-
grate Beowulf's boyish exploit; yet, 'sorrowful journey'
seems to be an irrelevant expression. It would seem that
Unferth calls the journey sorrowful only because Beowulf's
supposed failure to fulfill his boast brings shame upon his
name; but the inclusion of Breca in the charge (*ȝit*) implies
that the journey was sorrowful because it was a futile, silly, and
vain exploit, characteristic of headstrong but foolish boys.
When Beowulf replies with his own version of the story,
however, he insists that his boast was fulfilled. He suggests,
furthermore, that his journey was indeed sorrowful and that
death did ensue from his *síþ*—the death of the nicors that
attacked him. So the formula, meant as slander, fulfills its
function as a theme of death and becomes, ironically, a statement of heroic accomplishment. Not only this, but Beowulf
destroyed the sea monsters so they would no longer detain
sea voyagers (567–69), not because of the mischievous whim
of a boyish mind. Beowulf's sorrowful journey prevents future

sorrows, and so Beowulf's reply to Unferth twists the latter's terms of abuse into descriptions of his own heroic deeds.

The [*X*] *síþ* E-verse system reappears in the digression about the death of Heremod. Here the compound *swíþ-ferhþes* is substituted for *sorg-fullne* in order to identify the journeyer. Whether the journeyer causes harm or is himself killed is uncertain in the text:[11]

>Swelce oft bemearn ǽrrum mǽlum
>swíþ-ferhþes síþ snotor ćeorl maniʒ,
>se-þe him bealwa tó bóte ʒelíefde,
>þæt þæt þéodnes bearn ʒeþíon scolde,
>fæder-æðelum onfón, folc ʒehealdan,
>hord and hléow-burg, hæleða ríće,
>ćeðel Scieldinga. (907–13a)

So, often in earlier times, many a wise man deplored the adventure of the strong-spirited, he who believed in him [the strong-spirited] as a help for troubles, that that prince's child should prosper, receive the paternal rank, keep the people, the treasure and the castle, the country of heroes, the homeland of the Shieldings.

A hint of the *sorg-fullne síþ* formula appears when Beowulf recounts his adventures before Hygelac in the Geatish court. He mentions how Grendel's mother had journeyed 'full of sorrow' on her way to Heorot:

>Þá wæs eft hræðe
>ʒearu gryn-wræce Grendles módor,
>síðode sorgfull; sunu déaþ fornam,
>wíʒ-hete Weðera. (2117b–20)

Then in turn Grendel's mother was quickly ready for revenge, she journeyed sorrowfully; death, the warfare of the Geatas, had taken her son.

Not only is the sorrowful-journey theme suggested here (in this form probably because the poet found himself without a verb when he came to the point in his narrative where he might have expected to use the formula) but *sunu déaþ* occurs here in conjunction with the theme of the sorrowful journey as it had earlier (1278); it is itself an explicit statement of death.

So far as I know, the *Beowulf* poet is the only Old English poet to use the sorrowful-journey theme. However, death represented as a journey is a common enough metaphor in Old English writing. The *Beowulf* poet exploits the familiarity of the journey metaphor by suggesting that the journey to a battle is a foreshadowing, for those who are fated, of the journey of the soul after death. The suggestion of death is discernible in the meaning of the formula itself; yet the most effective context of the formula is its misuse by Unferth, for Unferth does not realize, in calling Beowulf's exploit a 'sorrowful journey,' in what manner it was sorrowful and for whom the venture toward death is forecast.

The Song of Death

The theme of the song of death is represented by three formulaic systems in *Beowulf*. One is a type E whole-verse system, the second measure of which is the single word *sang*. Another is a type D/A whole-verse system whose second measure is a compound of *léoþ*; and the third is a type A whole-verse system whose first measure consists of a nominal compound, the object of an inflected form of the verb *galan*, which, in turn, comprises the second measure of the verse. These systems very often appear in the same narrative passage, but they also occur independently to foreshadow death.

Grendel sings his own death song, a grisly song of defeat, when he is caught fast in Beowulf's grip:

> Norþ-Denum stód
> atol-líć eȝesa, ánra ȝehwelćum
> þára-þe of wealle wóp ȝehíerdon,
> gryre-léoþ galan Godes andsacan,
> siȝe-léasne sang . . .   (783b–87a)

Deadly terror struck the North-Danes, each of those who from the wall heard weeping, God's enemy singing his terrible lay, his song of defeat . . .

Here two of the formulaic systems representing the song-of-death theme are coupled to intensify the significance of Grendel's horrible song.

Later, as the group of Danes and Geats view the head of Æschere on the edge of the dark pool, the battle horns are sounded, probably to incite the band to avenge the death of their comrade:

> Flód blóde wéoll   —folc tó sáwon—,
> hátan heolfre.   Horn stundum sang
> fúslić fierd-léoþ.[12]   (1422–24a)

The water surged with blood, with hot gore—the people looked at it. From time to time a horn sang an eager battle song.

Here *sang* is a preterit form rather than a noun. Nevertheless, the formulaic system is the same, and the association of the formula with death is clearly indicated. The song is at once a song commemorating Æschere, a battle cry to incite Beowulf to battle against Grendel's mother, and a death song forecasting her doom. The immediate effect of the battle song is to frighten the nicors, who flee from the sound as if they perceive its ominous message:

> Híe on-weʒ hruron
> bitere and ʒebolgne: bearhtm onʒéaton,
> gúþ-horn galan.   (1430b–32a)

Bitter and enraged, they slithered away: they perceived the noise, the battle horn singing.

During the ensuing fight against Grendel's mother, Beowulf's sword Hrunting sings 'a greedy battle song' that ironically forecasts its own failure[13] as well as the death of Grendel's mother:

> > hand swenǵ ne ofteah
> þæt hire on hafolan hring-mǽl agól[14]
> grǽdiʒ gúþ-léoþ.   (1520b–22a)

the hand did not hold off the stroke so that the ring-patterned sword sang a greedy battle song on her head.

The song-of-death theme appears next before the final and fatal battle against the dragon. It occurs in the digression about the man who sings a sorrowful dirge over the loss of his only son:

> > þanne hé ʒeidd wrece,
> sáriʒne sang,   þanne his sunu hangaþ
> hræfne to hróðre . . .

> . . . .
> ʒewíteþ þanne on sealman,   sorg-léoþ gæleþ[15]
> án æfter ánum . . .   (2446b–61a)

Then he sings a lay, a sorrowful song, when his son hangs, a joy to the ravens . . . He goes then to his bed, he sings a sorrowful lay, one man for another . . .

Because the digression appears shortly before the battle against the dragon, the association of the song of death seems appropriate to both Beowulf and the dragon as well as to the episode in the digression. Furthermore, the image of someone singing a sorrowful song after the passing of a loved one foreshadows the grief of Wiglaf and the 'Geatish woman' who mourn Beowulf after his death. Adrien Bonjour has pointed out that the digressions "convey certain impressions . . . creating subtle links of relevance which are mostly suggested by means of delicate hints and very light touches rather than fully expressed and explicit statements."[16] The theme of the song of death is the "delicate hint" of death here that links the action of the digression to the main body of the story and intensifies the dramatic situations in each.

At Beowulf's funeral the lamentations of a Geatish woman before the funeral pyre are described by a formula whose significance links the lamentations to the theme of the song of death. Her lamentation is a sorrowful song:

> swelće ʒeómor-ʒiedd   Ʒéatisc méowle,
> Weder-cwǽn awræc,   wunden-heorde
> sang sorg-cariʒ [17]   swíðe ʒeneahhe
> þæt hío hire héofung-dagas   hearde ondréde,
> wæl-fiella worn,   weorodes eʒesan,
> híenþe and hæft-níed.   (3150–55a)

so the Geatish woman, the queen of the Geatas with wound hair, sang a sorrowful song again and again, [sang] that she dreaded hard days of mourning, much slaughter, the fear of the host, humiliation and captivity.

The song of death here is a dirge mourning the passing of Beowulf and the passing of an era of peace. The lone woman mourning the death of her lord represents the entire land mourning a happy past and bewailing the evil that is to come.

CONCLUSION

The formulas comprising the themes discussed above have been grouped according to the kinds of actions or situations they describe. They could perhaps as well be considered together as representing a general theme of death; yet the variety of ways in which the poet characterizes death and the variety of images with which he does so suggest that he associates many subthemes with the idea of death. These subthemes are not peculiar to *Beowulf* (see note 21), and many other subthemes of death belonging to the Old English tradition are not to be found in *Beowulf.*

The themes of death and the formulas that compose them can be studied and evaluated individually, for some are undoubtedly more effective and important to the text than others. However, the traditional poet rarely uses a theme in isolation to foreshadow death. The strength of a theme, or its formulas, depends upon its contextual relationship with associated themes. The traditional poet "clusters" his themes about the dramatic situation they qualify. For example, several formulas belonging to subthemes of death appear in the description of Beowulf's fight with Grendel's mother in her underwater cavern:

> Onȝeat þá se góda   grund-wierȝenne,
> mere-wíf mihtig;   mæȝen-ræs forȝeaf
> hilde-bille,   hand swenȝ ne ofteah
> þæt hire on hafolan   hring-mǽl agól
> grǽdiȝ gúþ-léoþ.   Þá se ȝiest onfand
> þæt se beadu-léoma   bítan nolde,
> ealdre scieþþan   ac sío ecg ȝeswác
> þéodne æt þearfe;   þolode ǽr fela
> hand-ȝemóta,   helm oft ȝescær,
> fǽȝes fierd-hræȝl.   Þa wæs forma síþ
> díerum máðme   þæt his dóm alæȝ.   (1518–28)

The brave man then saw the cursed she-monster of the deep, the mighty water witch; he gave a mighty rush with his sword, his hand did not hold off the stroke, so that the ring-patterned sword sang a greedy battle song on her head. Then the guest discovered that the light of battle would not cut, harm life, but the edge failed the prince at need; earlier it had endured many close encounters, had often cut through the helmet, the battle garment of a doomed man. That was the first time for the beloved treasure that its glory failed.

Three of the four subthemes of death which were discussed earlier are represented in this short passage: the discovery of death, the fatal venture, and the song of death. There are here other formulas whose meanings explicitly associate them with the idea of death (they are also underlined).[18]

Both Beowulf and Grendel's mother are in danger of losing their lives. The poet, in order to suspend the battle's outcome, which is either known or suspected by his audience from the beginning, avoids direct statement of what is to come in favor of a number of hints designed to heighten anticipation. He personifies Hrunting as the singer of a death song and the subject of a venture that ends in failure.[19] The sound of the song is the clue to Hrunting's failure. It sings because it glances off the head of Grendel's mother; had it cleft through there would not be any resounding vibrations. Hrunting is also the venturer in this passage. Although a theme of death is grammatically connected to Beowulf—'Then the guest discovered that the light of battle would not cut, harm life, but the edge failed'—his discovery is of the sword's failure rather than of his own. We sense Beowulf's peril through Hrunting's failure.

By making Hrunting the object of themes associated with death, the poet establishes a significant and ironic relationship between all three battlers: Beowulf, Hrunting, and Grendel's mother. The sword fails Beowulf, yet Beowulf survives the battle. The sword itself sings a song of death on the head of Grendel's mother as if to pronounce doom there, but the perceiver of doom is Beowulf who realizes his sword's failure. The failure almost costs Beowulf his life, yet, curiously, leads him to the discovery of a more efficacious weapon with which he kills his antagonist.

There are interesting parallels between this battle and Beowulf's earlier fight against Grendel. Hrunting sings his death song just as Grendel had earlier discovered his impending doom after singing a death song (809–12). The striking analogies between Beowulf's fight against Grendel and the struggle against Grendel's mother (with formulaic associations reversed) intensifies the sense of Beowulf's distress and contributes unusual suspense in an otherwise stock situation.

Such skillful weaving of formulas shapes the thematic pattern of the poem. It can not be overemphasized that the skillful traditional poet uses themes not only as "asides" to forewarn his audience of what is to follow but also to further the immediate situation. The use of the song-of-death theme in the passage above is not just an ornamental motif, but a narrative description of what is actually happening.

Summary

The repetition of certain formulas and formulaic systems to compose themes contributes to the poet's over-all effectiveness as a storyteller in many ways. First of all, repetition immediately, if not subtly, establishes a parallelism of ideas and an identification of one element of the text with another. Stanley B. Greenfield has pointed out, for example, that the repetition of *dréame [-um] bedǽled* (*Beowulf* 721, 1275) repeats the theme of exile, and by this repetition the poet "is able to suggest Grendel's kinship with all other exiles, especially with the devils, indicating the monster's deprivation of both human joys and eternal blessedness." [20] In the theme of the sorrowful journey the repetition of *sorg-fullne síþ* in association with Grendel's mother and the nicors about her pool suggests a similar kinship.

Secondly, repetition carries to a particular context the sense of previous contexts in which a theme has appeared. It is the context of impending death that clothes the *[ne] wæs [þá/þæt] forma síþ* formula with its ironic color. Unferth's contemptuous characterization of Beowulf's swimming feat turns to irony as soon as we realize the typical context and associations of *sorg-fullne síþ*.

Thirdly, thematic repetition is a unifying principle. It shapes the structure of traditional poetry into repetitions of traditional ideas and images. The mode of progression tends to be typological. Each formula, each theme, foreshadows the context of its next appearance. When the *Beowulf* poet describes the dragon's discovery of the robbery of his barrow, the formulas conveying the theme of the discovery of death subtly foreshadow the deaths that are forthcoming as a directs result of the discovery. Because the plot of traditional poetry is generally known by the listening audience, suspense is contained in the detailed description of events—in the formulas and themes. What is suspended is not *what* happens, but *how*.

This paper hardly exhausts the discussion of themes of death in *Beowulf*. It concentrates mostly upon those themes whose appearances in particular contexts accumulate a thematic significance associated with death. Most of the formulaic systems cited above appear elsewhere in Old English poetry,[21] as we might expect knowing that the oral poet relies upon the stock of formulas and themes belonging to the entire tradition.

APPENDIX

The discovery of death—
A-3 whole-verse systems: *sóna þæt onfunde* (750a, 1497a), *þá þæt onfunde* (809a), *sóna onfunde* (2226b).

B whole-verse systems: *hé þæt sóna onfand* (2300b, 2713b), *þá se ȝiest onfand* (1522b), *þæt se wyrm onfand* (2629b), *þæt sío þéod [onfand]* (2219b).

The fatal venture—
B whole-verse systems: *ne wæs þæt forma síþ* (716b), *næs þæt forma síþ* (1463b), *þá wæs forma síþ* (2625b), *ne wæs þæt íeðe síþ* (2586b), *þæt wæs ȝéocor síþ* (765b), *N'is þæt íower síþ* (2532b), *Ne biþ swelć earges síþ* (2541b).

A whole-verse systems: *forman síðe* (740b, 2286b), *níehstan síðe* (1203b, 2511a), *hindeman síðe* (2049b, 2517b).

The sorrowful journey—
E whole-verse systems: *sorg-fullne síþ* (512a, 1278a, 1429a), *swíþ-ferhþes síþ* (908a); cf. A verse *síðode sorgfull* (2119a).

The song of death—
A whole-verse systems: *gryre-léoþ galan* (786a), *sorȝ-léoþ gæleþ* (2460b), *gúþ-horn galan* (1432a).

E whole-verse systems: *hring-mǽl agól* (1521b), *siȝe-léasne sang* (787a), *horn stundum sang* (1423b), *sáriȝne sang* (2447a).

D-A whole-verse systems: *sang sorg-cariȝ* (3152a), *fuslíć fierd-léoþ* (1424a), *grǽdiȝ gúþ-léoþ* (1522a).

NOTES

1. Robert P. Creed, "The Making of an Anglo-Saxon Poem," *ELH: A Journal of English Literary History*, XXVI (1959), 447, adapting Milman Parry's now classic definition to Old English poetry, defines a formula as "a word or group of words regularly employed under certain strictly determined metrical conditions to express a given essential idea."

2. For other definitions of "theme" see Francis P. Magoun, Jr., "The Theme of the Beasts of Battle in Anglo-Saxon Poetry," *Neuphilologische Mitteilungen*, LVI (1955), 82–83; and Albert B. Lord, *The Singer of Tales* (Cambridge, Mass., 1960), p. 4.

3. Robert E. Diamond, "Theme as Ornament in Anglo-Saxon Poetry," *PMLA*, LXXVI (1961), 461–68, argues that themes in traditional poetry are essentially ornamental and do nothing to advance the main action. This may be so for descriptive themes, but it seems to me that Diamond fails to consider narrative and dramatic themes.

4. I define a formulaic system (paraphrasing Milman Parry, "Studies in the Epic Technique or Oral Verse-Making, I: Homer and Homeric Style," *Harvard Studies in Classical Philology*, XLI [1930], 80), as a group of formulas with identical metrical value and having in common at least one stressed word in the same position within the verse or measure. For example, *forman síðe* and *hindeman síðe* belong to the same formulaic system because both have the same metrical value, and *síðe* recurs with stress in the same position.

5. "Although the themes lead naturally from one to another to form a song which exists as a whole in the singer's mind with Aristotelian beginning, middle, and end, the units within this whole, the themes, have a semi-independent life of their own. The theme in oral poetry exists at one and the same time in and for itself and for the whole song. . . . the theme is in reality protean; in the singer's mind it has many shapes, . . . It is not a static entity, but a living, changing, adaptable artistic creation. . . . In a traditional poem, therefore, there is a pull in two directions: one is toward the song being sung and the other is toward the previous uses of the same theme" (Lord, *The Singer of Tales*, p. 94).

6. Direct statements of death or statements whose reference to death is quite obvious comprise a large group of formulas in *Beowulf*. [*X*] *fornam* is a common example, the (X) element of which never appears twice the same. [*X*] *ʒenam* and [*X*] *nimeþ* are others with approximately the same value. *Ealdre* [*X*] appears three times in *Beowulf* (1447, 2825, 2924) and its (X) element is never the same. [*X*] *swefeþ* and [*X*] *ʒecrang* are yet two others that denote death. Following accepted practice, I have marked formulas with solid underlining, while variable elements in formulaic systems are marked with broken underlining.

7. Quotations from *Beowulf* are from *Béowulf and Judith: Done in a*

Normalized Orthography, ed. Francis P. Magoun, Jr. (Cambridge, Mass., 1959).

8. The relationship between first success and final failure is reasserted at the end of the poem without any subtle implications when the poet, after telling of Wiglaf's victory, forecasts the difficulties that are to follow:

> Nú is léodum wœn
> orle3-hwíle   siþþan undierne
> Francum and Frísum   fiell cyninges
> wíde weorðeþ.   (2910b–13a)

Now the people expect a time of battle as soon as the death of the king becomes widely known, revealed to the Franks and the Frisians.

9. Margaret E. Goldsmith, "The Christian Perspective in *Beowulf*," *Comparative Literature*, XIV (1962), 86, takes exception to the view that l. 2586b is a figure of litotes: "If these lines are taken as a litotes for "Beowulf did not wish to die," they are intolerably verbose and clumsy. Who, one asks, would find the journey from this world to a home elsewhere an easy one to take? Once posed in this context, the question is answered. The man who leaves the world willingly is the man who puts his hope in 'ece raedas,' not in earthly possessions."

10. There are other formulas (*forman dógre*, *óðra síðe*, and *þridda síðe*) metrically and semantically associated with the *forman síðe* system; but they have no necessary connection to the idea of death.

11. *Beowulf*, ed. C. L. Wrenn (Boston, 1953), pp. 201–2, notes that, "It is not clear whether the *sið* of 908 refers to his journey into exile, his death . . . or to a civil war he began against his own brother."

12. Gustaf Stern, "Old English *Fuslic* and *Fus*," *Englische Studien*, LXVIII (1933), 169, cites many places in Old English poetry where a *fúsléoþ* is a death song. In commenting on *Beowulf* 1422–24, Stern says, "if a *leoð* that is *fus* is a 'death-song,' a *leoð* that is *fuslic* may be the same thing" (p. 172).

13. An analogue to this particular song of death can be noted in *The Battle of Maldon* (284b–85a) where a byrnie sings the appropriate song: *and sío byrne sang | gryre-léoða sum* 'and the byrnie sang a terrible song.'

14. This formulaic system does not appear elsewhere in *Beowulf*, but it is fairly common in Old English poetry. See, for example, *fyrd-léoþ agól* (*Elene* 27b), *dryht-léoþ agól* (*Elene* 342b), *fus-léoþ agól* (*Guthlac* 1346b), *hearm-léoþ agól* (*Juliana* 615b).

15. Friedrich Klaeber in his notes to the third edition of *Beowulf and the Fight at Finnsburg* (Boston, 1950), 214, comments on *sorg-léoþ gæleþ* by saying "we cannot be quite sure that this is not merely a

high-flown expression implying 'lamentation.'" The expression seems to me a very accurate description of what is actually happening.

16. *The Digressions in Beowulf* (Oxford, 1950), p. 43.

17. At first sight this formula appears to be a D-verse formula formed by reversing the two measures of a typical E-verse song-of-death system; yet, the formula belongs to a [*X*] *sorg-cariʒ* system. See, for example, *ʒesiehþ sorg-cariʒ* 'sad he sees' (*Beowulf* 2455a), *aswebban sorg-cariʒ* 'to sleep sad' (*Juliana* 603a), *siomaþ sorg-cariʒ* 'depart sad' (*Juliana* 709a), *sitteþ sorg-cariʒ* 'sits sad' (*Deor* 28a), *settan sorg-cariʒ* 'to sit sad' (*Christ and Satan* 188a).

18. *Ealdre scieþþan* 'to harm life' is underlined because it is found elsewhere as a formulaic statement of death (see n. 6). The [*X*] *ʒeswác* system also appears elsewhere to suggest death, and it always refers to the failure of a sword and Beowulf's subsequent peril (*Beowulf* 2584, 2681).

19. For a fuller study of the personification in *Beowulf* see Neil D. Isaac's paper in the present volume, "The Convention of Personification in *Beowulf*."

20. "The Formulaic Expression of the Theme of 'Exile' in Anglo-Saxon Poetry," *Speculum*, XXX (1955), 205.

21. *Þa þæt éadiʒ onfand* 'then the blessed [one] discovered' (*Solomon and Saturn* 462a); in Old Norse there is a comparable formula with the same foreshadowing suggestion, *þá þat finnr* 'then he discovers that' (*Hávamál* 25.4, *Fáfnismál* 17.3). [*Ne*] *wæs* [*þá/þæt*] [*X*] *síþ* (*Elene* 910b, *Exodus* 22b); *forman síðe* (*Finnsburg* 19b, *Genesis* 319a, *Widsith* 6b). According to Grein-Köhler-Holthausen, *sorg-fullne síþ* does not appear outside of *Beowulf*. *Fyrd-léoþ galan* (*Exodus* 578b), *fús-léoþ galan* (*Christ* 623b, *Andreas* 1549b), *hearm-léoþ galan* (*Andreas* 1128b, 1342b), *ongunnon him þá sorg-léoþ galan* (*Dream of the Rood* 67b), *siʒe-léoþ galen* (*Elene* 124b). An Old Norse analogous formula is *angrlíoþ kveþa* 'to speak a sorrowful lay' (*Helgi Hundingsbana* II, 46.6).

GRENDEL'S APPROACH TO HEOROT:
SYNTAX AND POETRY

❦

Stanley B. Greenfield

Grendel's approach to Heorot is one of the famous passages in *Beowulf*, but although it is often referred to approvingly by commentators, it has been little analyzed by critics. The extent of the analytical comment may be briefly summarized. The repetitive device of the three *cōm* verses (702b, 710a, 720a) is more than a simple return to the subject after digressions and more even than the "threefold bell-like announcement of Grendel's approach" that Friedrich Klaeber attributes to "some enthusiasts."[1] It represents several distinct stages of the action, stating, first, the time when Grendel came (*on wanre niht*); then, the place from which he descended (*of mōre*); and finally, after suggesting the difficulty of his journey in the verb *wōd* (714a), the goal arrived at (*tō recede*). The effect is incremental rather than repetitious; other word echoes within the passage further help to bind the whole into an effective unity, rounded off by the phrase *ofer þā niht* in line 736a, which reflects the *on wanre niht* of the opening half-line.[2] Further, the passage is essentially an extended form of the technique of variation, building suspense in its "hair-raising depiction of death on the march" despite the poet's several assurances of the outcome of the prospective engagement.[3] Finally, the poet has made excellent use of visual details in something like a cinematographic technique, alternating point of view between the outside and inside of the hall in creating a design for terror.[4]

Unless I have overlooked some relevant criticism, the above is in essence the published insight into this passage; and although they are suggestive of the over-all mood and of the most prominent features evocative of that mood, these critical *aperçus* only begin to indicate the wealth of poetic power packed into these lines. More can be suggested, I believe, by following analytical methods set forth in Randolph Quirk's essay "Poetic Language and Old English Metre" and in my article "Syntactic Analysis and Old English Poetry."⁵ To facilitate matters, it will be best to place the lines before us:

Cōm on wanre niht
scrīðan sceadugenga.   Scēotend swæfon,
þā þæt hornreced   healdan scoldon,
ealle būton ānum.   Þæt wæs yldum cūþ,   705
þæt hīe ne mōste,   þā Metod nolde,
se s[c]ynscaþa   under sceadu bregdan;—
ac hē wæccende   wrāþum on andan
bād bolgenmōd   beadwa geþinges.
  Ðā cōm of mōre   under misthleoþum   710
Grendel gongan,   Godes yrre bær;
mynte se mānscaða   manna cynnes
sumne besyrwan   in sele þām hēan.
Wōd under wolcnum   tō þæs þe hē wīnreced,
goldsele gumena   gearwost wisse   715
fǣttum fāhne.   Ne wæs þæt forma sīð,
þæt hē Hrōþgāres   hām gesōhte;
nǣfre hē on aldordagum   ǣr nē siþðan
heardran hǣle,   healðegnas fand!
Cōm þā tō recede   rinc sīðian   720
drēamum bedǣled.   Duru sōna onarn
fȳrbendum fæst,   syþðan hē hire folmum (æthr)ān;
onbrǣd þā bealohȳdig,   ðā (hē ge)bolgen wæs,
recedes mūþan.   Raþe æfter þon
on fāgne flōr   fēond treddode,   725
ēode yrremōd;   him of ēagum stōd
ligge gelīcost   lēoht unfǣger.
Geseah hē in recede   rinca manige,
swefan sibbegedriht   samod ætgædere,

magorinca hēap.   Þā his mōd āhlōg;   730
mynte Þæt hē gedælde,   ǣr Þon dæg cwōme,
atol āglǣca   ānra gehwylces
līf wið līce,   Þā him ālumpen wæs
wistfylle wēn.   Ne wæs Þæt wyrd Þā gēn,
Þæt hē mā mōste   manna cynnes   735
ðicgean ofer Þā niht.   (702b–36a)

In the lines preceding this passage we have seen Beowulf and his band of warriors take possession of Heorot for the night and have been assured that although the warriors felt they would never see their homeland again, God, through the strength of the hero alone, enabled them to overcome their enemy. The passage under consideration seems to me to fall into four distinct sections: the first three are marked by the varied *cōm* verses, the last by *geseah* (728a). The first part arranges the prospective antagonists: Grendel, Beowulf, and Beowulf's men; the second focuses exclusively on Grendel's movements and motivations; the third brings Grendel to the door of Heorot and thence onto the floor of the hall itself; and the fourth emphasizes what Grendel sees and his great expectations therefrom. Each phase has its own particular character and special poetic emphasis.

The disposition scene at the beginning is a brilliant tableau. The three forces that are soon to be brought into collision in combat are presented here as separated, each with its own attitude and behavior toward the impending event. The walker-in-darkness is on the march, his murderous intention implicit in the association with night and darkness; the warriors are sleeping, believing that the monster will, if God so wills, have no power to harm them; Beowulf is watching, enraged and anticipating the outcome of battle. These differences are rendered poetically effective by the syntactical, metrical, and rhetorical patterns in which they are rooted.

The first contrast is conceptually between the striding Grendel and the sleeping shooters, a contrast reinforced by the complete syntactic break in the middle of line 703; by the

chiastic arrangement of the whole line; and by the complementary infinitive *scrīðan*, suggesting durative action, as
opposed to the preterite plural *swǣfon*, depicting the warriors'
*in*action. At the same time, the metrical-alliterative pattern and
the chiasmus associate the *sceadugenga* and the *scēotend*,
satisfying the lexical expectation of the line, intimating that the
scēotend are indeed the objective of Grendel's movement. The
second contrast is between the sleeping band and Beowulf,
conveyed at first by the dangling appositional phrase *ealle
būton ānum*, separated from *scēotend* by line 704, in which in
a subordinate clause the duty of the men to guard the hall is
mentioned. But even more striking are the syntactic differences
in lines 705b–9, which portray the states of mind of the men
and their chieftain. The comitatus' reliance on God's will is
expressed in a periphrastic manner, via a proleptic *þæt* in a
pseudo-passive principal clause *Þæt wæs yldum cūþ*, plus the
specifying *þæt* clause in the following two lines in which there
is further subordination in the divisive *þā Metod nolde* clause.
It may also be noted that the presentation of the warriors as a
grammatical object, *hīe*, underlines their passivity, following
up *swǣfon* and the initial prolepsis. Against all this (*ac*)
Beowulf's watchfulness and rage are set forth vigorously in
subject–modifier–adverb–modifier–verb–subject–modifier–object
word order. Notable is the modifier *wæccende*, the only present
participle in this whole passage, which in contrast to the
swǣfon describing the warriors' "action" suggests duration,
implies that Beowulf is wide awake and watching through all
the following description even though he does not reappear
until line 736b at the beginning of the next long passage.[6] We
might suggest further that the noun *scēotend* applied to
Beowulf's warriors, being a participle *manqué* as it were, in its
transformed grammatical nature itself reinforces the inactive
state of those who should be "shooting." The lexical collocation in line 708 is reinforced by the metrical and syntactical
patterns: unlike line 703 where *sceadugenga* and *scēotend* were
completely separated syntactically, *wæccende* and *wrāþum* [*on
andan*] here are grammatically related. The whole introductory

part comes to a fitting climax in the phrase *beadwa geþinges*, which lexically, grammatically, and metrically satisfies the expectations aroused by the *bād bolgenmōd* of the a-verse of that line and ideationally fulfills the whole drift of lines 702b–9, that is, the positioning of the three separate forces—striding, sleeping, watching—for conflict.

Grendel as subject occupied only two half-lines of the initial section; in the next part all attention is focused upon him by the poet as he moves from the moor toward the hall. Interestingly enough, there is but one mention of the hall (*hornreced*) in lines 702b–9; now the hall is referred to four times (713b, 714b, 715a, 717b), as Grendel's movements and intentions (*cōm, wōd, gesōhte, mynte*) culminate in his ironic findings (*fand*) in the striking zeugma of the last line (719): *heardran hǽle, healðegnas fand*, which even includes a fifth reference to the hall in the compound *healðegnas* '[Grendel never before] found harder luck, braver hall thanes.'[7] Quirk has pointed out how in line 179 *hæþenra hyht; helle gemundon*, presenting the plight of the pagan Danes, their hope is metrically collocated with, and thus made equal to, hell, despite the syntactic division;[8] with even greater force here the 'harder luck' that Grendel encounters is grammatically connected in the rhetorical pattern with the hall guardians he finds as well as being made equivalent to them metrically.

There is further syntactical significance in this section in lines 712–13, but it will best be discussed in connection with an analysis of the last segment of the whole passage. First, the third *cōm* clause deserves attention in its relation to what has preceded and as introductory to its own division of the over-all structural pattern.

It is at this point where Grendel is depicted as arriving at Heorot that the poet brings monster and building into lexical, grammatical, and metrical union at the center of the poetic line *Cōm þā tō recede rinc sīðian*[9] and applies to the *rinc* the epithetic formula *drēamum bedǽled*. In the first presentation of the stalking monster *cōm* and the stressed syllable of its complementary infinitive *scrīðan* occupy the initial dip and lift of sequent b- and a-verses respectively; in the second presentation *cōm* and the stressed syllable of *gongan* occupy the initial and second lifts of successive a-verses respectively; but in this third "repetition" *cōm* and the stressed syllable of *sīðian* occupy the first and second lifts of sequent verses in the same line and, in fact, are part of a chiastic pattern of the whole line that contrasts, in its syntactic suggestion of the swiftness with which Grendel reaches the hall, with the similar rhetorical pattern of line 703, which in its entirely different syntactic structure and lexical polarity opposes the striding *sceadugenga* and the sleeping *scēotend*.

If we look further at the description of the subject on each of these occasions, we find, in another way, poetic emphasis. At first Grendel is presented simply as *sceadugenga*; this *hapax legomenon*, as has been observed above, in its association with darkness implies the murderous intention in the monster's heart.[10] But at the same time it also implies Grendel's outcast state, as one deprived of God's light. In the second representation, although Grendel's ruthlessness is made explicit in the following lines 712–13, the actual description of him in line 711 lies in the paratactic semiformulaic clause *Godes yrre bær*,[11] which emphasizes the *reason* for his outcast state. Finally, in lines 720–21a the common participial-phrase formula *drēamum bedǣled*[12] describes the *rinc*, explicitly characterizing the effect of God's anger upon this descendant of Cain, his deprivation of joys. The progression from noun *hapax* to semiformulaic clause to formulaic phrase thus presents a semantic pattern moving from implicit representation of Grendel's exiled condition to explicit reason therefor and explicit effect thereon. More than this, the poet has saved the most common associative formula for last, immediately after he has, through negative clauses in lines 716b following and in the zeugma of line 719, stated that Grendel has this time met his match. The impact of *drēamum bedǣled* is thus twofold, suggesting not only, as a permanent epithet, the transgressor's habitual deprivation of joys but the additional and final separation he is about to suffer this time. Surely there is no need to stress the effectiveness with which the *Beowulf* poet has here handled diction, syntax, and formula within his larger structural patterning.

Turning now to the rest of the section introduced by the line and one-half just discussed, we may glance at the actual passage of Grendel from outside to inside the hall. This movement is beautifully suggested in lines 721b–24a, three lines in a rough chiastic pattern, beginning and ending with a reference to the door of the hall itself. But the first one and one-half lines give us the scene objectively, *duru* being the grammatical subject of the main clause and Grendel's action, being presented in the subordinate *sypðan* clause.[13] In the remaining one and one-half lines we are shifted to Grendel's point of view, as he becomes the grammatical subject of the main clause (his anger mentioned subordinately in the *þā* clause); and the door, now presented in a highly appropriate metaphor (considering Grendel's eating habits) as *recedes mūþan*, is the grammatical object of Grendel's action, *onbrǣd*, as the monster passes through it. These lines are a striking demonstration, it seems to me, of the contribution of syntax to poetic meaning. In the remaining lines of this section we are shown Grendel stepping onto the floor of the hall, and with attention focused on his eyes through the simile *ligge gelīcost*, we are prepared for the description of what he sees in the following section.

The monster and his true objective, victim(s) in the hall, syntactically as well as referentially separated at the very beginning of this whole passage, are finally, in all ways, brought together here in lines 728 following: *Geseah hē in recede rinca manige . . .* Although *recede* and *rinca* provide a verbal and pattern echo of line 720, the syntax is different: the *rinca* here are Beowulf's warriors, and they are the object, not the subject, of the action being described. There is a further verbal echo of line 712 in line 731, *mynte þæt hē gedǣlde*, but again there is a difference. The full import of lines 728–34, however, necessitates our returning at this point to examine lines 712–13, previously passed over.

As Grendel comes from the moor bearing God's anger,

mynte se mānscaða manna cynnes / *sumne besyrwan in sele þām hēan* (712–13). The intention, the evildoer, and the race of men are metrically, grammatically, and lexically linked, but more important is the directness of the verbal expression of Grendel's intention, reflecting the directness and single-mindedness of the monster in his desire to trap someone in the high hall. There is no variation, no interrupting phrases or clauses: finite verb-subject-objective phrase–complementary infinitive-adverbial phrase. Grendel presumably has not found game plentiful in Heorot since his initial ravages twelve years ago, as witness his modest hope of ensnaring *one* (*sumne*) man. To his surprise and delight, upon entering the hall he sees *many* warriors and has now the expectation of a full-course dinner. Brodeur denies that there is any significant variation in the approach and fight until lines 750 following,[14] but lines 728–30a *do* provide one, and lines 731–33, echoing but differing from lines 712–13, lend extra significance in their syntactic complexity:

> Geseah hē in recede   rinca manige,
> swefan sibbegedriht   samod ætgædere,
> magorinca hēap.   Þā his mōd āhlōg;
> mynte þæt hē gedælde,   ær þon dæg cwōme,
> atol āglǣca   ānre gehwylces
> līf wið līce . . .   (728–33a)

For Grendel's exultation at this unexpected human cornucopia is neatly captured by the triple variation of *rinca*, *swefan sibbegedriht*, and *magorinca hēap*. We can almost feel his glare lingering on the bounty of warriors fate has so generously bestowed upon him, as the variations pile up, slowing the pace of the verse. 'Then his heart laughed'—and in the following expression of his intention, the syntax and word order themselves suggest the slow savoring by the monster of his windfall. For now the directness and simplicity of lines 712–13 are missing, and instead we find the verb *mynte* followed by a subordinate clause that is interrupted in its grammatical progress by *ær þon dæg cwōme* and includes a variation of *hē* in *atol āglǣca*; and beyond all this the object of the verb *gedǣlde*, *līf wið līce*, is held up for one and one-half lines. Only when the implications of the syntactic structure have made themselves felt is an explicit statement made in a concluding subordinate clause, 'since to him had befallen expectation of a feast.' With the last sentence of this section and of the whole passage, the poet's negative assertion about the future feasting of Grendel, we are ready for the bold beginning of the next passage: *Þrȳðswȳð behēold.*

To assert, as I have done, that the poet's manipulation of diction and syntax achieves subtle poetic effects in bringing Grendel, Beowulf, and the warriors from a polarity of position, action, and attitude to confrontation in Grendel's vision of the band within the hall is not to deny, of course, that verse formulas or even syntactic formulas abound in the passage. But formulas of whatever sort, as Quirk and I and others have been trying to show, were but counters for the Old English poet to use either conventionally, in the worst sense of that word, or brilliantly and strikingly, as the *Beowulf* poet has used them in presenting Grendel's approach to Heorot.

NOTES

1. *Beowulf and the Fight at Finnsburg*, ed. Friedrich Klaeber (3d ed.; Boston, 1950), p. 154. All citations from *Beowulf* are from this edition. This paper was read in substantially the same form at the meeting of the Modern Language Association in New York, December, 1964.

2. See A. C. Bartlett, *The Larger Rhetorical Patterns in Anglo-Saxon Poetry* (New York, 1935), pp. 49–51, and Arthur G. Brodeur, *The Art of Beowulf* (Berkeley, Calif., 1959), pp. 90–92.

3. Brodeur, *The Art of Beowulf*, pp. 90–91.

4. Alain Renoir, "Point of View and Design for Terror in *Beowulf*," *Neuphilologische Mitteilungen*, LXIII (1962), 154–67. Renoir's is the most elaborate analysis of the passage and a very good one. Its methodology, however, is quite different from the one adopted in this article.

5. See Quirk's essay in *Early English and Norse Studies*, ed. Arthur Brown and Peter Foote (London, 1963), pp. 150–71; my article appeared in *Neuphilologische Mitteilungen*, LXIV (1963), 373–78. Quirk's final paragraph is worth quoting: "It should . . . be emphasized that, while formulaic utterances and habitual collocations are the necessary starting

point in the study of the early alliterative poetry, they are *only* the starting point. The very fact that he could depend on his audience having a firm expectation of certain dependences and determined sequences involving metre, vocabulary, and grammar gave the poet his opportunity to stretch linguistic expression beyond the ordinary potentialities of prose, and to achieve a disturbing and richly suggestive poetry."

6. "It would seem desirable to have a paragraph break at 736a. At that point the poet turns from Grendel to Beowulf for a few lines" (Bartlett, *The Larger Rhetorical Patterns in Anglo-Saxon Poetry*, p. 50).

7. MS *hæle* has been something of a crux. I accept the reading *hæle* as preferable on metrical grounds, taking it with Klaeber as accusative singular. See *Beowulf and the Fight at Finnsburg*, ed. Klaeber, pp. 154–55.

8. Quirk, "Poetic Language and Old English Metre," p. 159.

9. It might be argued that a similar collocation occurs in ll. 713 and 717, but to me *sumne besyrwan in sele* and *hē Hrōþgāres hām* lack the forceful simplicity of the *recede-rinc* juxtaposition. In l. 714, although *hē* and *winreced* are cheek by jowl at the end of the line, the metrical pattern in the *wōd . . . winreced* at the beginning and end of the line stresses the distance Grendel has yet to cover, but here in l. 720 the distance between subject and objective has been completely closed, positionally, metrically, grammatically, and grammatically.

10. Cf. Brodeur, *The Art of Beowulf*, p. 90.

11. The verse seems to combine two formulas: formulas with *bær* taking a direct object usually have an ale cup or a battle sark as the object (cf. *Beowulf* 1982, 2021, 2539). The two occasions on which *Godes yrre* is used apart from the present one refer to Adam and Eve and use the verb *habban*: *þæt hie Godes yrre / habban sceoldon* (*Genesis* 695b–96a) and *hæfdon Godes yrre* (408b).

12. See Stanley B. Greenfield, "The Formulaic Expression of the Theme of 'Exile' in Anglo-Saxon Poetry," *Speculum*, XXX (1955), 202, 205.

13. *Duru* is of course linked metrically with *drēamum bedǣled*, suggesting the misery that is to befall the hall itself (as well as one of Beowulf's warriors).

14. Brodeur, *The Art of Beowulf*, p. 56.

THE *EOTENAS* IN *BEOWULF*

❧❀❧

R. E. Kaske

Of the ten possible occurrences of *eoten* 'giant' and its declensional forms in *Beowulf*, the first five are universally assumed to carry that meaning. Attached to the poet's introduction of Grendel is an account of the descendants of Cain:

> Þanon untydras ealle onwocon,
> eotenas ond ylfe ond orcneas,
> swylce gi[ga]ntas, þa wið gode wunnon
> lange þrage ... [1] (111–14a)

Thence arose all the evil brood, giants and elves and wicked spirits—also [those] giants who for a long time fought against God [*or* such giants, who for a long time fought against God] ...

Beowulf, in his first speech to Hroðgar, recalls how he *yðde eotena cyn ond on yðum slog | niceras nihtes* 'destroyed the race of giants and struck down water monsters on the waves at night' (421–22a). His watch against Grendel is referred to by the compound *eotonweard* (668b), and Grendel himself by the epithet *eoten* (761a). Finally, in a lay recited by one of Hroðgar's thanes, Sigemund and Fitela *hæfdon ealfela eotena cynnes | sweordum gesæged* 'had with their swords felled a very great number of the race of giants' (883–84a).

Besides these undisputed examples, there are two instances of the form *eotenum*—which, though properly corresponding only to the dative plural of *eoten*, have been taken by most modern scholars as somehow equivalent to *Eotum*, the dative of a plural *Eotan* 'Jutes.' [2] In the latter part of the lay concerning Sigemund, the singer alludes to the fall of Heremod:

285

> He mid eotenum wearð
> on feonda geweald   forð forlacen,
> snude forsended.   (902b–4a)

Amidst the *eotenum*, into the power of enemies, he was led forth treacherously, quickly dispatched.

And near the end of the Finn episode the scop pauses briefly over the sword of vengeance: *þæs wæron mid eotenum ecge cuðe* 'its edges were known [i.e., felt?] among the *eotenum*' (1145).

Our three remaining instances—also from the Finn episode —present the genuinely ambiguous form *eotena*, which can be construed as the genitive plural of either *eoten* or *Eotan*. At the beginning of the episode is the comment *Ne huru Hildeburh herian þorfte | eotena treowe* 'certainly Hildeburh had no need to praise the good faith [of the] *eotena*' (1071–72a). The treaty between Finn and Hengest includes a stipulation that *hie*, presumably the Danes, *healfre geweald | wið eotena bearn agan moston* 'should have possession of half [of the hall], along with the sons [of the] *eotena*' (1087b–88). And later in the episode we are told that Hengest

> to gyrnwræce
> swiðor þohte   þonne to sælade,
> gif he torngemot   þurhteon mihte
> þæt he eotena bearn   inne gemunde. (1138b–41)

thought rather of vengeance than of a sea voyage, [thought of] whether he might manage a hostile encounter—so that he had the sons [of the] *eotena* in his mind.

In all three passages modern scholarship seems generally agreed that *eotena* can refer only to the Jutes.[3]

Though the prevailing opinions may well be correct, I think it more likely that the Jutes (*Eotan*) are never mentioned in *Beowulf*;[4] that in all the passages quoted above the words in question are in fact declensional forms of *eoten* and should be rendered 'giant' or 'giants'; and that throughout the Finn episode (and perhaps also in line 902) the term is to be understood as a hostile epithet for the Frisians. Let us begin by noticing that among our ten pertinent nouns the eight plural forms offer no grammatically unambiguous examples of the proposed *Eotan*. Instead, they include five examples that are grammatically ambiguous (421, 883, 1072, 1088, 1141), the first two in contexts that clearly identify them as forms of *eotenas*, the plural of *eoten*; and three grammatically unambiguous examples of *eotenas* (112, 902, 1145), the last two of which are generally not accepted at their grammatical face value. Now as the manuscript stands, these two instances of the dative plural *eotenum* in lines 902 and 1145 bear unequivocally the meaning 'giants,' and can be made to refer to the Jutes only by way of some more conjectural explanation—like, for example, R. W. Chambers' suggestion that a West Saxon scribe, confronted by an Anglian form *eotum* or *eotnum* meaning 'Jutes,' understood it as a word for 'giants' and so copied it in both places as *eotenum*.[5] On exclusively textual grounds even this rather plausible hypothesis is surely much less probable than its obvious alternative: that in each place the reading *eotenum* in our manuscript may reproduce accurately an original reading *eotenum*, along with its meaning 'giants.' It happens, moreover, that these two readings fall within two of the most sharply defined "digressive" passages in *Beowulf*—the Sigemund-Heremod passage and the Finn episode—which between them contain six of our eight plural forms (883, 902, 1072, 1088, 1141, 1145), including all five disputed ones. This concentration of apparently identical and otherwise rather infrequent words, occurring within two self-contained and relatively brief passages, is remarkable enough if the repeated words are declensional forms of the same noun; that in both passages the repetitions should include a pair of plural nouns similar in form but different in meaning, and in each passage the same pair (*eotenas* and *Eotan*), is difficult to believe without further evidence of a kind that has never been presented.[6] If this principle is sound, the a priori probability of the meaning 'giants' in the *eotenum* of the Sigemund-Heremod passage (902) is strengthened by the already recognized meaning of *eotena* earlier in the passage (883); while in the Finn episode the a priori probability of the meaning 'giants' in the form *eotenum* (1145) can itself be extended in some degree to the occurrences of the ambiguous *eotena* within the episode (1072, 1088, 1141).[7]

Such probabilities are of course far from decisive, and might be nullified almost completely by some positive evidence for an appearance of the Jutes in *Beowulf*. Their presence in the poem, however, though historically plausible once it has been assumed, seems in no way to be required (or, in fact, to be made any more credible than their absence) by either the action or the thematic development of the episodes in which they are supposed to appear; their introduction brings with it none of that further enlightenment by which hypotheses are in large part confirmed, and indeed seems able to justify itself only with the help of further theorizing about their precise role, both at Finnsburg and in the decline of Heremod.[8] If so, our long-standing recognition of the Jutes in these two passages may be essentially a remnant of the earlier shift from mythological to historical interpretation of the poem, kept alive by the belief that "how 'giant' can be applied to the Frisians, or to either of the contending parties in the Finnsburg fight, remains inexplicable."[9] The past thirty years have seen an increased emphasis not only on the interpretation of *Beowulf* as a coherent literary work but also on the role of the monsters, the relation of Grendel to the giants of the Old Testament, and his significance as an inclusive symbol of external violence,[10] thus providing at least a more promising general context for an appearance of some sort of 'giants' within the two episodes. What remains, I take it, is to find a plausible connection between 'giants' or 'giants' sons' and the specific contexts of *eotena* and *eotenum* in lines 902, 1072, 1088, 1141, and 1145. Though independently compelling evidence is hardly to be looked for, there are a number of belated hints, which—considered along with the grammatical probabilities outlined above and the lack of a really convincing alternative—seem to me to provide this connection.[11]

I suppose it will be generally agreed that the Finn episode, for all its omissions, is presented throughout from the point of view of Hengest and the Danes rather than that of Finn and the Frisians. That the Frisians are to be recognized as enemies of the Danes, at least within the world of *Beowulf*, seems obvious from the episode itself and the further testimony of the Finnsburg fragment—an impression supported implicitly by the evident expansion of the Frisian nation between the third and seventh centuries and the known hostility between Danes and Frisians in the ninth century and after.[12] A resulting possibility is that *eotena* and *eotenum* may be used in the Finn episode as an insulting figurative epithet for 'enemies.' In all four instances the immediate contexts of the word would be not merely compatible with the use of such an epithet but positively appropriate to it through their emphasis on various more intense aspects of the general hostility: in lines 1071–72 a memory of the initial treachery; in lines 1087–88 the ironic prospect of a hall to be shared with recent foes; and in lines 1138–41 and 1145 the mention of vengeance. I begin with the two occurrences of *eotena bearn* (1088, 1141), the first referring evidently to the Frisians, the second to either the Frisians or Finn himself.

In the *Skáldskaparmál* an enumeration of traditional *heiti* for man includes the term 'giants,' which is further designated as a vehicle of insult: *Mann er ok rétt at kenna til allra ásaheita. Kennt er ok við jǫtnaheiti, ok er þat flest háð eða lastmæli* 'it is also proper to paraphrase man by all the names of the *Æsir* [the gods]. He is paraphrased also by giant terms, and that is mostly for purposes of mocking or slander.'[13] A fourteenth-century redaction of the *Skáldskaparmál* quotes an example of the term *miðjúngr* applied to an opponent, interpreting the word as a synonym for *jǫtunn* 'giant': *Kenna skal mann heítvm Oðins ǫllvm ok allra ása heitvm. Vel þikkir kent til aulfa. Kent er ok til iǫtna ęða dverga. Sva qvað Gestr:*

> *Gestr hefvir Geitis* || *rastar*
> *galdrs miðjúngi skjaldar*
> *dundi djúpra benja*
> *dǫgg rǫskligast hǫggvit.*

Hér er maðr kenndr við jǫtun 'Man is to be paraphrased by all the names of Óðinn and by the names of all the gods. He is thought to be suitably paraphrased by [terms for] elves. He is paraphrased also by [terms for] giants or dwarves. Thus Gestr said: "Most bravely has Gestr struck the shaker-of-Geitir's-witchcraft [i.e., scatterer-of-gold, i.e., man]; the dew-of-deep-wounds [i.e., blood] streamed from the *miðjúngr*-of-the-shield." Here man is paraphrased with [a term for] giant.'[14] The poems of the *Edda*, though they offer no example of 'giants' used as figurative epithet, give great prominence to the literal role of the *jǫtnar* as enemies of gods and men. In addition, the *eotena bearn* of the Finn episode is paralleled almost precisely in the *Edda* by literal references to *iǫtna sonom* 'giants' sons'; and the possible significance of this correspondence seems favored by a further parallel between the Eddic commonplace *iǫtna ætt* 'giants' race' and the expressions *eotena cyn* and *eotena cynnes* in *Beowulf* (421, 883), where *eotena* clearly does mean 'giants.'[15] In the ninth-century *Haustlǫng* by Þjóðólfr of Hvin, *dólgr ... manna* 'enemy of men' appears as a kenning for 'giant.'[16] Somewhat more impressive is a part of the probably ninth-century inscription on the stone of Rök (Östergötland–East Götland), transcribed by Otto von Friesen as *knuąknat / [i]atun uilinisþat* 'he knew how to smite a giant; this is [my] will.'[17] Von Friesen interprets these statements as a conjuration by the bereaved inscriber, expressing his wish for vengeance on the slayers of his son Uamoþ by associating them with the 'giant-born' slayer of Baldr (i.e., Loki); the slayers themselves are identified by Von Friesen—with dramatic if tentative relevance for our problem—as Frisians.[18] Whatever one may think of this solution, the generalized or noncommittal reference to an obviously hostile 'giant' or 'giants,' surrounded by an apparently historical context, may at least be suspected of more than literal intent.

These possible bases for a figurative association of 'giants' with enemies, and so with the Frisians of the Finn episode, can be enriched from early Christian interpretation of the Old

Testament *gigantes*, who are also notorious enemies of God and man.[19] They are pertinently characterized in the Old English *Genesis*, along with an approximation of *eotena bearn* in the compound *gigantmæcgas*:

> frea wolde
> on wærlogan   wite settan
> and on deað slean   dædum scyldige
> gigantmæcgas,   gode unleofe,
> micle mansceaðan,   metode laðe. (1265b–69)

the Lord wished to fix his punishment on the oath-breakers and to smite to death the giant race guilty of deed, displeasing to God—great criminal foes, hateful to the Creator.

We may notice incidentally the later free application of 'giants' to the Saracens in the *chansons de geste* (for example, the *Jaianz* of the *Chanson de Roland*, 3253, 3285, and 3518), presumably depending to some extent on the same tradition.[20] In the Finn episode an insulting designation of hostile tribes as 'giants' might be favored also by the common explanation of the biblical giants as descendants of Cain, Cham, or Nemrod, with its obvious latent antithesis to the Christianized derivation of Germanic tribes from Noe or Sem, or to the original pagan one from Óðinn (Woden).[21] And finally, if the giants of the Old Testament do somehow contribute to the meaning of *eotena bearn* as a name for the Frisians and Finn, this connection may in turn give special point to the designation of the Frisian king by the epithet *eorðcyninges* (1155)—a compound unique in *Beowulf*, although it is employed elsewhere in Old English poetry with evident echoes of the *rex terræ* 'king of earth' or *reges terræ* 'kings of earth' which appears more than thirty times in Scripture.[22] Within our present context *eorðcyning* might reflect figuratively the traditional relationship between the giants and earth itself, explained for example by Isidore: *Gigantes dictos iuxta Graeci sermonis etymologiam, qui eos γηγενεῖς existimant, id est terrigenas, eo quod eos fabulose parens terra inmensa mole et*

similes sibi genuerit. Γῆ enim terra appellatur: γένος, genus;
licet et terrae filios vulgus vocat: quorum genus incertum est
'those who think [the giants] to be *gegeneĩs* (that is, born of
the earth, because the earth which, according to fable, brought
them forth [is] of immense size and produced beings resembling itself) believe them to be called *gigantes* according to the
etymology of the Greek word. For *gẽ* is explained as "earth,"
génos as "race"—though the people at large also call those
whose origin is uncertain "sons of earth."'[23] More specifically,
it might carry an echo of the biblical description of Og, the
giant king of Basan: *Solus quippe Og rex Basan, restiterat de*
stirpe gigantum. . . . cunctaque Basan vocatur terra gigantum. . . .
[*Filii Israel*] *possiderunt . . . terram Og regis Basan* 'for only
Og, king of Basan, remained of the race of giants. . . . and all
Basan is called the land of giants. . . . [The children of Israel]
possessed . . . the land of Og, king of Basan' (Deut. 3:11, 13;
4:47). And one interpretation offered by Gregory for the giants
of Job 26:5, *Ecce gigantes gemunt sub aquis* 'behold, the giants
groan beneath the waters,' is that *gigantum nomine potentes*
hujus sæculi designantur 'the rulers of this world are designated
by the name of "giants."'[24]

As a supplementary or alternative conjecture there are a few
slight indications—all, unfortunately, after the fact—that the
Frisians or Finn may themselves have had some reputation as
giants in the early Middle Ages. Von Friesen's proposed
interpretation of the stone of Rök, with its emphatic parallel
between a hostile giant and hostile Frisians, has been mentioned above. Saxo, recounting the battle of Brávellir
(variously dated between 550 and 750), tells of one *Ubbo*
Fresicus, promptissimus Haraldi miles ac præ aliis habitu cor-
poris insignis 'Ubbo the Frisian, the readiest soldier of Harald,
and distinguished beyond others in size of body.'[25] The
gigantic stature of the Frisians is also alluded to, surprisingly
enough, in the ninth circle of Dante's *Inferno*, where the upper
part of Nemrod's body is described as so huge that *di giungere*
a la chioma | tre Frison s'averien dato mal vanto 'three Frisians
[standing one on top of the other] would have boasted vainly

to reach [from his middle] to his hair (XXXI, 63–64). More interesting still are the sober confirmations by fourteenth-century commentators on the *Commedia*. Benvenuto da Imola, for example, explains that *quamvis . . . Alemanni naturaliter et comuniter sint magni, tamen illi de regione Frisie sunt maximi* 'although . . . the Germans naturally and in common are large, those from the region of Frisia are nevertheless the largest'; and Guido da Pisa knows of other giant-like traits among the Frisians: *Frisia vero provinciola est in finibus inferioribus Germanie super littus Occeani constituta, cuius incole "Frisones" a Germanicis nuncupantur. . . . Est autem gens viribus fortis, magni corporis, severi animi et ferocis, corpore agilis, lanceis utens ferreis pro saggittis* 'Frisia is a small province situated in the lower parts of Germany upon the shore of the ocean; its inhabitants are called by the Germans "Frisians." . . . The race is strong in martial force, of large physique, of stern and fierce spirit, active of body, using iron lances for arrows.'[26] With all allowances for the tendency of commentators to create the "fact" that seems implied by a particular allusion, these descriptions leave little doubt that in fourteenth-century Italy, at any rate, the unusual size of the Frisians was an established belief; and a number of widely scattered approximations of Guido's further remarks suggest a possible tradition concerning the heedless violence and ferocity of the Frisians, resembling that of the Eddic and biblical giants as well as of Grendel[27]—though the characterization, to be sure, is by no means a monopoly of the Frisians. The oral saga of King Finn from the North Frisian isle of Sylt, recorded by C. P. Hansen in 1858 but evidently much older, presents the early inhabitants of Sylt as *Käämpers* 'giants.'[28] And the name "Finn," here and elsewhere attached to dwarves or the king of the dwarves, can in Scandinavia be the name of a giant or troll; as early as the ninth century, for example, the *Haustlǫng* by Þjóðólfr of Hvin employs *Finnr* as a *heiti* for 'giant.'[29]

My rather tentative suggestion, then, is that *eotena bearn* in lines 1088 and 1141 is a kenning meaning 'giants' sons' (or, in line 1141, 'giants' son') and applied to the Frisians (or, in line

1141, to Finn) as a paraphrase either for 'enemies,' for the Frisians themselves, or conceivably for both. The miscellaneous hints assembled above—separated as they are from the poem in time and place and offering no ideal example of 'giants' used figuratively for enemies or Frisians—can, of course, constitute no direct proof for this thesis; what they do indicate, I think, is that the appearance of such an epithet would in itself be no less possible than would the presence of the Jutes in the Finn episode, so that our pattern of grammatical evidence favoring it need not be explained away as somehow erratic. The remaining *eotena* and *eotenum* in the episode (1072, 1145) can be dealt with more briefly.

If we understand *eotena bearn* as a specific kenning for the Frisians, the *eotena* of *eotena treowe* in line 1072 will be almost necessarily a *heiti* for the Frisians, with lines 1071–72a meaning simply that Hildeburh had no reason to praise their good faith (i.e., had reason to dispraise it). If we understand *eotena bearn* as a kenning here applied to the Frisians but actually meaning no more than 'enemies,' *eotena* in line 1072 may still be a *heiti* for the Frisians; or the whole expression *eotena treowe* 'giants' faith' may just possibly be a kenning for 'lack of good faith,' 'treachery,' or the like, with the term 'giants' serving also to attach it allusively to the hostile Frisians. Though I know of no parallels to such a kenning, its substance at least would be supported by the epithet *wærlogan* applied to the giants in the Old English *Genesis* (1266, quoted above); and in Scandinavian tradition by the notorious duplicity of Loki and possibly by the slender evidence of a fragmentary quotation in the *Sturlungasaga*: "*Trautt mun ek trúa þér, troll!*" *kvað Hǫskollr* '"scarcely can I trust thee, troll!" said Hǫskollr.'[30] The attitude toward *treow* in Frisian heroic society and the resulting depth of insult in lines 1071–72 are probably illustrated accurately enough by Tacitus' story of the Frisian leaders "Verritus" and "Malorix," who, on a visit to the theater of Pompey in Rome, declared *nullos mortalium armis aut fide ante Germanos esse* 'that no mortals are ahead of the Germans in either arms or good faith';[31] it may also be worth noticing, however, that a modern study of the late classical commonplace of "Germanic perfidy" names the Frisians as among the tribes responsible for its origin.[32]

In line 1145 the sword's being *mid eotenum . . . cuðe* 'known [felt?] among the *eotenum*' might, I suppose, mean simply that it is an *eald sweord eotenisc* like those mentioned elsewhere in *Beowulf*, though the emphasis on its *ecge* seems to imply a grimmer meaning. Again, the line might be an allusion establishing the worth of the sword by identifying it with some famous weapon of myth or legend—most appropriately, perhaps, with the sword of Freyr, which appears later in the *For Scírnis*, and *siálft vegiz / við iǫtna ætt* 'fights of itself against the giants' race.'[33] If the three preceding occurrences of *eotena* in the Finn episode have indeed referred to the Frisians, however, it seems reasonable to expect some further reference to them in the present *eotenum*. I would begin, therefore, by suggesting that lines 1144b–47a should be punctuated as follows:

> . . . on bearm dyde.
> Þæs wæron mid eotenum ecge cuðe;
> swylce ferhðfrecan Fin eft begeat
> sweordbealo sliðen . . .

Line 1145 can then be understood as beginning the account of the vengeance on Finn: 'Its edges were felt among the "giants" (i.e., Frisians); so also did a cruel sword-death come in turn to Finn, the mortal foe, etc.' If so, an allusion to the sword of Freyr might still be possible in the line—whether as a literal reminder of the present sword's mythical encounters with past giants or simply as a metaphoric association of the two weapons by way of their common efficacy against 'giants.'

Our last disputed form occurs in the Sigemund-Heremod passage in a description of Heremod's downfall:

>   He mid eotenum wearð
> on feonda geweald forð forlacen,
> snude forsended.   (902b–4a)

Amidst the *eotenum*, into the power of enemies, he was led forth treacherously, quickly dispatched.

Let us recall at this point that the dative plural *eotenum* can, grammatically considered, mean only 'giants'; and that in the absence of contrary evidence this meaning seems supported also by the clear meaning 'giants' in the *eotena* of line 883. Any conviction produced by my discussion of the forms in the Finn episode will, of course, increase this probability still further. In addition to such factors, the evidence for a rendering of *eotenum* as 'Jutes' here seems generally admitted to be less substantial than in the Finn episode—consisting as it does, besides the usual doubt about the meaning 'giants,' of a passage in the seventeenth-century *Scondia illustrata* of Johannes Messenius, which relates that the Danish king Lotherus (conjecturally identified with Heremod on the basis of a passage in Saxo) fled into temporary exile *in Jutiam* after a defeat that by no means ended his career.[34] As Chambers concedes, "the identification of Lotherus and Heremod is too hypothetical to carry the weight of much argument."[35]

On the other hand, the meaning 'giants' itself seems less unintelligible in line 902 and its context than has usually been assumed. In the *Atlamál in grœnlenzco* a speech of Vingi assigns the *jǫtnar* a role which, proverbial though it is, sounds generally like that filled by the *eotenum* in Heremod's fall: *Eigi hann iǫtnar, ef hann at yðr lygi, | gálgi gorvallan, ef hann á grið hygði* 'let the giants have him if he lies to you; [let] the gallows [have] all of him if he breaks his faith.'[36] Perhaps a more likely lead is offered by Prov. 21:16: *Vir qui erraverit a via doctrinæ, in coetu gigantum commorabitur* 'the man who wanders from the way of doctrine shall abide in the company of giants'—followed by a survey of defects in wisdom (17–31) somewhat resembling those in Hroðgar's later account of Heremod (1709–22) and the psychology of his degeneration (1724–57) and including at least one verse of striking appropriateness (24): *Superbus et arrogans vocatur indoctus, qui in ira operatur superbiam* 'the proud and arrogant is called

296

ignorant, who in anger works pride' (compare *Beowulf* 1713, 1740–41, 1749).[37] Equally promising is Job 26:5: *Ecce gigantes gemunt sub aquis, et qui habitant cum eis* 'behold, the giants groan beneath the waters, and those who dwell with them.' Gregory's extended comment, including also an interpretation of Prov. 21:16, again seems close to the thought of Hroðgar's analysis:

Gigantes . . . superbos quosque homines, nil obstat intelligi. Hinc enim per prophetam dicitur: *Mortui non vivent, gigantes non resurgent* [Isa. 26:14]. Quos namque mortuos nisi peccatores nominat? Et quos gigantes nisi eos qui de peccato etiam superbiunt appellat? Illi autem non vivunt, quia peccando vitam justitiæ perdiderunt. Isti etiam resurgere post mortem nequeunt, quia post culpam suam inflati per superbiam, ad poenitentiæ remedia non recurrunt. Hinc rursum scriptum est: *Vir qui erraverit a via doctrinæ, in coetu gigantum commorabitur* . . .; quia quisquis iter rectitudinis deserit, quorum se numero nisi superborum spirituum jungit? Bene autem contra elatos dicitur: *Ecce gigantes gemunt sub aquis* . . . Si autem gigantum nomine potentes hujus sæculi designantur, in aquis possunt populi figurari. . . .[38]

Nothing prevents "giants" . . . from being understood as any proud men. For hence it is said through the prophet: *Let not the dead live, let not the giants rise again* [Isa. 26:14]. For whom does he name "the dead" unless it be sinners? And whom does he call "giants" unless it be those who in addition take pride in sin? The former "do not live" because by sinning they have lost the life of righteousness; and the latter cannot "rise again" after death because, being swollen with pride following their guilt, they do not return to the remedy of penitence. Hence again it is written: *The man who wanders from the way of doctrine shall abide in the company of giants*— because whoever forsakes the way of righteousness, to whose band does he join himself unless it be to the band of proud spirits? Against those of lofty spirit, moreover, it is well said, *Behold the giants groan beneath the waters*

... If, however, the rulers of this world are designated by the name of "giants," the people can be figuratively represented by the "waters." ...

A successful interpretation of *eotenum* in line 902 must, I take it, relate the word credibly to the following phrase *on feonda geweald* (903), to Heremod's ultimate disaster or death as described in lines 903–4, and more generally to the rest of the Heremod passage (904–15) as well as to Hroðgar's account of Heremod (1709–57). Almost inevitably, however, such an interpretation must also relate the meaning of *eotenum* to that of *eotena* in the Sigemund passage (883)—whether by parallel or by some sort of meaningful contrast—and must define whatever relationship is assumed to exist between *eotena/ eotenum* here and in the Finn episode. Finally, if *eotenum* in line 902 is to be rendered as 'giants,' some account must be taken of its potential relationship to Grendel and the other *eotenas* in the early part of the poem and to any thematic significance they may be thought to carry. With these requirements in mind and with some guidance from the possible parallels quoted above, I suggest that *mid eotenum* is a figurative description of warlike enemies, probably to be conceived of also as *superbi homines* 'proud men' of the kind identified by Gregory with *gigantes*. In the light of the rather strong similarity between this interpretation by Gregory and Hroðgar's analysis of Heremod, one is tempted to the further conjecture that *mid* may here carry some characterizing force along with its more obvious situational meaning—that Heremod, himself a 'giant' through fatal pride and treacherous enmity toward his people (1740–41, 1711–15), finds himself fallen 'among' other proud and cruel 'giants' not only in being at their mercy but by being spiritually their fellow. However that may be, the words *on feonda geweald* (903) seem most satisfactorily explained as a rhetorical variation, expressing in more literal terms the central idea of the figurative *mid eotenum*. Such an explanation of *eotenum* is in obvious accord with my interpretation of the giants and other monsters in the early part of *Beowulf* as embodiments of universalized violence.[39] Its connection with the *ealfela eotena cynnes* 'a very great number of the race of giants' of the Sigemund passage (883) would depend at least partly on this larger significance: whereas Sigemund overcame the *eotenas* by which he was confronted, Heremod was overcome by his. The relation of Heremod's *eotenas* to those of Hengest and the Danes in the Finn episode may, I suppose, be simply the parallelism between two similar bands of violent enemies; or (particularly if the term in the Finn episode should be understood also as a specific kenning for 'Frisians') both passages may actually recall Danish struggles against the Frisians, the first disastrous, the second ultimately triumphant.

A good bit of the evidence presented above is, admittedly, a grabbing at straws; to a great extent straws are what the present problem offers. My total argument, while it by no means eliminates the possibility of the rendering 'Jutes' in these five instances, does seem to me to speak rather for the probability of the rendering 'giants.' A word remains to be said about the "further enlightenment by which hypotheses are in large part confirmed," which I earlier found lacking in the proposed introduction of the Jutes—that is, about the contribution of this suggested pattern to the poem in which it appears. It is certainly a remarkable fact that in ten possible uses of the word *eoten*, the meanings of the first five are so clear that they have hardly been questioned, while those of the last five are notoriously difficult. Equally remarkable is the concentration of the last six instances, including the five difficult ones, within two brief and distinctly marked "digressive" passages. But most remarkable and significant of all is the fact that the entire series, occurring as it does between lines 112 and 1145, occupies precisely that part of the poem containing Beowulf's defeat of the giant Grendel along with its prelude and denouement.[40] Unless we are willing to return to the theory of composite authorship in a comparatively primitive form, this whole arrangement seems to point toward a deliberate manipulation of the word *eoten* by the poet.

His plan, it seems to me, is the familiar but effective one of first establishing the connotations to be carried by a particular image and then utilizing these connotations in unforeseen ways by applying the image itself with greater imaginative freedom. In the first four appearances of the word *eoten*, the creatures it designates are real giants, whom, as I have said, I would explain as embodiments of a universalized external violence. An introductory description of the giants (112) emphasizes their descent from the violent Cain (106–11) and their prolonged strife against God (113–14). Beowulf's account of a past victory over the race of giants (421; accompanied by his reference to Grendel as *þyrs*, 426) and the poet's designation of his present office as *eotonweard* 'watch against a giant' (668) establish him as a champion against violence and anticipate his central struggle with the giant Grendel. Finally, the word *eoten* is applied to Grendel himself (761) within the climactic passage that first reveals Beowulf's mastery over him (750–66). So far, the development of the pattern seems clear enough. Now ever since J. R. R. Tolkien's eloquent declaration of thematic coherence in *Beowulf*,[41] there has been something like a core of general agreement that the monsters are at the center of the action precisely because their universality of meaning transcends what could be expressed through specific human antagonists; and that their roles (like that of Beowulf himself) are somehow complemented by the more limited human figures who appear in the "digressive" passages. If this is so, one might expect the predominantly human perpetrators of violence in these passages to be given some touch of the larger meaning embodied more fully in the monsters, possibly by way of a recognizable figurative connection with the monsters themselves. It is this purpose that seems to be served by the concentration of the epithet *eotenas* within the more difficult contexts of the Sigemund-Heremod passage and the Finn episode. The giants of the Sigemund passage, to be sure, are again real giants—presumably because they were accepted as specific literal foes of Sigemund, though one should not overlook their incidental value of furnishing a transition from the *eoten* Grendel to the *eotenas* who follow in both passages. These *eotenas*, literally tribal enemies of the Danes, gain in terror through their figurative and by now universalizing title—not only in their role as hostile powers but in their affinity to that body unpolitic whose most inclusive image is Grendel.

After the Finn episode the word *eoten* does not occur. Its virtual equivalent, *gigant*, makes one more significant appearance in a passage following the defeat of Grendel's mother (1688–92), paralleling closely the poet's introductory description of the *eotenas* (111–14) and so providing a conclusion of sorts to the motif as a whole. Considered in themselves, however, our series of references to *eotenas* seem to follow a fairly regular progression from monsters to men—beginning with 'giants' who from their description seem less human than monstrous (112, 421) and proceeding in turn to the anthropomorphic giant Grendel (668, 761), the unidentified giants of Sigemund (883), the 'giants' of Heremod who represent unidentified human foes (902), and finally those of the Finn episode who represent human foes identified also as Frisians. A similar transformation is carried out more generally in the poem at large, where the literal and figurative *eotenas* of the earlier part are replaced as embodiments of violence by literally named tribal foes, prominent among whom are the Frisians as enemies of the Geats (1207, 2357, 2503, 2912, 2915). If this observation is accurate, it appears that the poet has contrived a kind of evolution from 'giants' to 'Frisians'—or more accurately and inclusively, from monsters to men—as representatives of external violence. One reason for such a shift of form, I suppose, might be to make room for a dragon of *malitia*, or internal evil, who does in fact seem to me to dominate the second part of the poem;[42] an inevitable effect of the device, however, is to produce a gradual disappearance of the figurative garb from these forces of brute savagery, which are thus revealed with growing inexorability as proceeding from man himself. There is, finally, one curious detail that may be at least partly explained by a design of this kind.

Before his fight with the giant Grendel, Beowulf has boasted that he will use no sword but will rely on his *grap* alone (435–40); this boast he subsequently fulfills. The latter part of the poem includes a strange reminiscence of his similar tactics against the human warrior Dæghrefn, who, though apparently a Frank, is clearly in the service of the Frisian king:

> Syððan ic for dugeðum   Dæghrefne wearð
> to handbonan,   Huga cempan;
> nalles he ða frætwe   Frescyninge,
> breostweorðunge,   bringan moste,
> ac in compe gecrong   cumbles hyrde,
> æþeling on elne;   ne wæs ecg bona,
> ac him hildegrap   heortan wylmas,
> banhus gebræc.   (2501–8a)

Afterwards, before the hosts [*or* by prowess], I was the slayer, by hand, of Dæghrefn, champion of the Franks. By no means was he able to bring those treasures, that breast adornment, to the Frisian king; but in battle he fell, the standard-bearer, the hero in valor. Nor was the sword-edge his death, but my battle grip crushed his body, the surgings of his heart.

Can it be that in this Dæghrefn, possibly the slayer of Hygelac, we are to detect a lingering echo of the figure identifying 'giant' with 'Frisian'?

NOTES

1. All quotations from Old English poetry are from *The Anglo-Saxon Poetic Records*, ed. G. P. Krapp and E. van K. Dobbie (New York, 1931–53); in accord with the interpretation that follows, however, I have removed the capitals from *Eotena/Eotenum* throughout.

2. One or both are explained as 'giants' in the editions of *Beowulf* by A. J. Wyatt, rev. R. W. Chambers (new ed.; Cambridge, 1914), p. 46 (l. 902, very tentatively), and C. L. Wrenn (London, 1953), pp. 201, 207–8 (both); in the translation of John R. Clark Hall, rev. C. L. Wrenn, with prefatory remarks by J. R. R. Tolkien (new ed.; London, 1950), p. 78 (l. 1145); and by R. E. Kaske, "The Sigemund-Heremod and Hama-Hygelac Passages in *Beowulf*," *PMLA*, LXXIV (1959), 493 (l. 902), and N. F. Blake, "The Heremod Digressions in *Beowulf*," *Journal of*

THE *EOTENAS*

English and Germanic Philology, LXI (1962), 282–84 (l. 902). For similar interpretations by earlier scholars see *Beowulf and Judith*, ed. E. van K. Dobbie ("The Anglo-Saxon Poetic Records," Vol. IV [New York, 1953]), p. 160 (for l. 902); and the following note (for l. 1145).

3. A notable exception is R. A. Williams, *The Finn Episode in Beowulf* (Cambridge, Eng., 1924), pp. 139–43. Earlier interpretations of *eotena/ eotenum* as 'giants' throughout the Finn episode (including l. 1145) are summarized by Hermann Möller, *Das altenglische Volksepos in der ursprünglichen strophischen Form* (Kiel, 1883), I, 94–99, including that of Möller himself; and more briefly by R. W. Chambers, *Beowulf: An Introduction*, ed. C. L. Wrenn (3d ed.; Cambridge, Eng., 1959), p. 261, n. 1.

4. The unique reading *Geotena* (l. 443), clearly representing a genitive of *Geatas*, has no bearing on the present problem that I can see.

5. *Beowulf: An Introduction*, pp. 261, 286. Note also Gustav Neckel, "Die Verwandtschaften der germanischen Sprachen untereinander," *Beiträge zur Geschichte der deutschen Sprache und Literatur*, LI (1927), 11.

6. The correspondences might, that is, be the result either of meaningful wordplay or of a fascination with the sounds themselves, conscious or otherwise. I can find no plausible pattern that would support the first of these possibilities; and the very nature of argument compels us (in cases like the present one, at any rate) to table the second as a last resort, along with textual emendation and the like.

7. Essentially the same argument is presented by Williams, *The Finn Episode in Beowulf*, pp. 139–41.

8. An admittedly plausible theory is that of Chambers, *Beowulf: An Introduction*, pp. 268–87. The only further clarification that the Jutes might be thought to bring with them, so far as I can see, concerns the suddenness with which the attack supposedly came upon the men of Finn (l. 1068)—which Chambers (pp. 263, 284) accounts for by citing ll. 1071–72 as evidence that the battle was started by the Jutes rather than the Frisians. The crucial *ða hie se fær begeat* 'when the terror [i.e., the sudden attack] befell them' (1068b), however, seems open to other equally credible explanations. It may refer, "by a characteristic anticipation, to the final triumph of the Danes over their enemies" (Friedrich Klaeber, *Beowulf and the Fight at Finnsburg* [3d ed.; Boston, 1941], p. 171); or the passage may be construed in various ways with *hie* in l. 1068b referring to the Danes (see the survey of opinions by Dobbie in his edition of *Beowulf and Judith*, pp. 170–71).

9. Chambers, *Beowulf: An Introduction*, p. 261. Sophus Bugge, "Studien über das Beowulfepos," *Beiträge zur Geschichte der deutschen Sprache und Literatur*, XII (1887), 37, while arguing that the forms *eotena* and *eotenum* mean 'giants' and refer to the Frisians, also admits "Wie aber *eotenas* 'Riesen' die Friesen bezeichnen kann, weiss ich nicht."

10. For the last two points see my "*Sapientia et Fortitudo* as the Controlling Theme of *Beowulf*," *Studies in Philology*, LV (1958), 423–56, especially pp. 438–40. Many more specific correspondences can be found between Grendel and the giants of early Christian tradition, some derived ultimately from the giants of classical myth. As a single example note Hroðgar's description of Grendel—

<blockquote>

on weres wæstmum   oðer earmsceapen
næfne he wæs mara   wræclastas træd,
           þonne ænig man oðer.

. . . .
           No hie fæder cunnon,
hwæþer him ænig wæs   ær acenned
dyrnra gasta.   (1351–57)

</blockquote>

the other wretched being trod paths of exile in a man's form, except that he was larger than any other man. . . . They [the local inhabitants] know nothing about a father—about whether any of the race of evil spirits was born previous to them [Grendel and his mother].

—and a passage in Avitus IV.88–93 ("*De diluvio mundi*"), ed. Rudolf Peiper in *Monumenta Germaniae Historica, Auctores Antiquissimi* (Berlin, 1883), VI.2, 238, concerning the *saevos . . . gigantes* 'ferocious giants' born of earth,

<blockquote>

Nec tamen effari licitum, quo semine cretos.
Communem cunctis ortum de matre ferebant.
Qui genus, unde patres, prohibent arcana fateri.
Si speciem quaeras, humani corporis illis
Plus vultus quam forma fuit: sic linea membris
Conveniens hominem monstrabat, dissona molem.

</blockquote>

nor is it lawful to utter from what seed they were sprung. As to their mother [the earth], men spoke of an origin common to all [of the giants]; why this offspring, whence the fathers, mystery shrouds from disclosing. If you ask their appearance, the face of mankind was theirs more than the figure. Thus an accurate outline of their limbs represented [the shape of] a man; an inaccurate one, his size.

11. So far as I know, the following interpretation is approximated most closely by that of Max Rieger, "Zum *Beowulf*," *Zeitschrift für deutsche Philologie*, III (1871), 398–400—which, however, makes the 'giants' in ll. 1072 and 1145 the Danes rather than the Frisians and includes none of the documentation offered below.

12. Theodor Siebs, "Friesische Literatur," in *Grundriss der germanischen Philologie*, ed. Hermann Paul (2d ed.; Strasbourg, 1901–9), II.1, 524: "während des Mittelalters, bis zum Ende des 11. Jahrhs., sind ja die Dänen die schlimmsten Feinde der Friesen und sind durch ihre

THE *EOTENAS*

Raubzüge an den Küsten mit ihnen in stetigen Kampfe"; there is, however, no direct evidence that I know of for the eighth century and earlier. For Dano-Frisian hostilities in the ninth century see, for example, Victor Langhans, *Über den Ursprung der Nordfriesen* (Vienna, 1879), pp. 36–38; and for the expansion of the Frisians between the third and seventh centuries, H. Gosses, "Friesische Geschichte," in *Die Friesen*, ed. C. Borchling and R. Muuss (Breslau, 1931), pp. 77–78, and Chambers, "Frisia in the Heroic Age," in *Beowulf: An Introduction*, pp. 288–89. Saxo, *Gesta Danorum*, II, iii, 1, ed. J. Olrik and H. Ræder (Copenhagen, 1931), I, 43, briefly describes a campaign of the legendary Danish king Fróði (son of Hadding) against the Frisians. Note also the role of the Frisians in *Beowulf* (1207, 2357, 2503, 2912–15) as powerful enemies of the Geats.

13. Chap. xxxix, ed. Guðni Jónsson, *Edda Snorra Sturlusonar* (Reykjavík, 1949), p. 146.

14. From the fragmentary *Ormsedda* (bound with the Arnamagnæan Codex Wormianus 242 Fol.), printed in the Arnamagnæan edition, *Edda Snorra Sturlusonar* (Copenhagen, 1848–87), II, 498; completed here from the *Laufássedda* (Arnamagnæan Codex 743), *ibid.*, 628 (both slightly repunctuated and separated by //). The quoted verse is a *lausavísa* composed in 1007 by Gestr Þórhallason, ed. Finnur Jónsson, *Den norsk-islandske Skjaldedigtning* (Copenhagen, 1912), B–I, 190; my translation assumes Jónsson's emendation *hristi* for the apparently untenable *rastar* in the opening line. In the MS the word *iǫtun* appears also as a gloss written above *miðjúngi* (*Den norsk-islandske Skjaldedigtning*, A–I, 199, n. 2); that *miðjúngr* actually carried the meaning 'giant' has, of course, been doubted, e.g., by Rudolf Meissner, *Die Kenningar der Skalden: Ein Beitrag zur skaldischen Poetik* ("Rheinische Beiträge und Hülfsbücher zur germanischen Philologie und Volkskunde," Vol. I [Bonn, 1921]), pp. 349–50. I am indebted to my colleague Vilhjálmur Bjarnar of Cornell University for checking my translation of Gestr's verses here, as well as of the quotation in n. 18.

15. *Edda: Die Lieder des Codex Regius nebst verwandten Denkmälern*, ed. Gustav Neckel, rev. Hans Kuhn (Heidelberg, 1962), I: *iǫtna sonom* 'giants' sons,' *Hávamál* 164:4 (p. 44), *Vafþrúðnismál* 15:5, 16:2, 30:5 (pp. 47, 50); *iǫtna ætt* 'giants' race,' *For Scírnis* 8:6 (p. 71), *ætt iǫtna*, *Hárbarðzlióð* 23:5 (p. 82), etc.

16. 16:2, 4, in *Den norsk-islandske Skjaldedigtning*, B–I, 17.

17. *Rökstenen: Runstenen vid Röks Kyrka Lysings härad Östergötland* (Stockholm, 1920), p. 28; see also pp. 59–61, 87–88.

18. *Ibid.*, pp. 63, 106: *Vämod är i förtid död. Han har stupat i strid mot segersälla fiender. Hans sörjande fader har att ombesörja hämnden i enlighet med hjärtats och hedens kraf. . . . Han tar sin tillflykt till trolldom och söker genom mäktiga trollformler komma de skyldige till lifs. . . . Så*

305

fortsätter trollmannen: "*Brodern slog Balders jätteborne baneman.* (*Så må nu en hämnare slå Vämods baneman hur mäktig genom fränder han än må vara.*) *Detta är min vilja.*" . . . *Vämods banemän voro åtminstone delvis af frisisk börd, sannolikt köpmän från Hedeby eller kanske rent utaf från Dorestad* 'Uamoþ is dead before his time. He has fallen in battle against victorious enemies. His sorrowing father has to make plans for vengeance, in accord with the claims of courage and honor. . . . He has recourse to sorcery and seeks to get at the life of the guilty ones through powerful incantations. . . . The incantator continues thus: "A brother slew Baldr's giant-born murderer [Loki]. (So must now an avenger slay Uamoþ's murderer, however mighty he may be through kinsmen.) This is my will." . . . Uamoþ's murderers were at least partly of Frisian birth, probably merchants from Hedeby or perhaps directly from Dorestad.' See also pp. 75 ff. and 102. The interpretation is, of course, far from being generally accepted; see, for example, the more recent study by Elias Wessén, *Runstenen vid Röks Kyrka* (Stockholm, 1958), pp. 54–55, 60–62.

19. Besides the Old Saxon *Genesis,* ll. 119–28 (in *Heliand und Genesis,* ed. Otto Behaghel [6th ed.; Halle, 1948], p. 239), the Old English *Genesis* (quoted below), and *Beowulf* (113–14, 1691–92), see generally Augustin Calmet, *De gigantibus,* in *Scripturæ Sacræ Cursus Completus,* ed. J.-P. Migne (Paris, 1839–57), VII, 764–77; and Oliver F. Emerson, "Legends of Cain," *PMLA,* XXI (1906), 888–929. Gregory's spiritual interpretation of Job 16:15 (in *Patrologiae Cursus Completus, Series Latina,* ed. J.-P. Migne [Paris, 1844–64; hereafter abbreviated to *Pat. Lat.*], LXXV, 1027) makes clear use of the concept 'giant' as 'enemy.'

20. This feature in the corresponding German epics is surveyed by Ernst Herwig Ahrendt, *Der Riese in der mittelhochdeutschen Epik* (Diss., Rostock; Güstrow, 1923), pp. 14 ff.

21. See, for example, Chambers, *Beowulf: An Introduction,* pp. 72–74, 202–3, 319–22; and Prol. 4, *Gylfaginning* 9, in *Edda Snorra Sturlusonar,* ed. Guðni Jónsson, pp. 5–6, 20–21. For the giants as descendants of Cain or Cham see *Beowulf* (104–14, 1260–67), and Emerson, "Legends of Cain," pp. 888–929. For Nemrod see Ambrose *De Noe et arca* XXXIV, in *Pat. Lat.,* XIV, 416; Augustine *Quaestiones in Heptateuchum* I.18, in *Pat. Lat.,* XXXIV, 551, and *Civitate Dei* XVI.xi.3, in *Pat. Lat.,* XLI, 491; Isidore *Quaestiones in Genesin* IX, in *Pat. Lat.,* LXXXIII, 237–38; and Emerson, "Legends of Cain," pp. 906–14.

22. Besides its use as a translation in the Psalter, it occurs in the Old English *Exodus* 392, *Daniel* 305, *Azarias* 26 (same), *Elene* 1173, and *Meters of Boethius* 9:47.

23. *Etymologiæ,* XI, iii, 13, ed. W. M. Lindsay (Oxford, 1911). See also Avitus in n. 10; Ambrose in n. 21; and Jerome *In Michaeam* II (5:6) in *Pat. Lat.,* XXV, 1201. The idea is, of course, a patristic commonplace.

24. See n. 38, accompanying a fuller quotation. For what survives of

an evidently colorful legend concerning Og the giant see J. A. Fabricius, *Codex Pseudepigraphus Veteris Testamenti* (Hamburg, 1713), pp. 799–800. I am indebted to Thomas D. Hill of Cornell University for pointing out to me that my last two paragraphs above provide support also for the frequently proposed reading *burg enta* in *Elene* 31 (MS *burgenta*), which can be meaningfully rendered 'cities of the giants,' i.e., of the hostile Huns and their allies.

25. VIII, iv, 7, in *Gesta Danorum*, ed. Olrik and Ræder, I, 219. For Saxo's use of *habitus* in connection with size see the glossary by Franz Blatt (Copenhagen, 1957), II, 367.

26. Both in the edition of Guido Biagi, *et al.*, *La Divina Commedia nella figurazione artistica e nel secolare commento* (Turin, 1924–39), "Inferno," p. 734. Note also in the same edition Graziolo de' Bambaglioli: *Frixones sunt qui in Frixia, versus septentrionem posita, oriuntur; homines sunt maximi corpore* '"Frisians" are those who come from Frisia, situated toward the north; the men are exceedingly large of body'; *Chiose anonime: Fresoni sono gente di Frigia ne la Magna; uomini molto grandi* '"Frisians" are people from Frisia, in Germany; very large men'; Jacopo della Lana: *Frixia è una provincia in la quale nasse gl'omini più lunghi che in tutte le parti del mundo* 'Frisia is a province in which are born men taller than in all parts of the world'; l'Ottimo: *Frisia, . . . posta verso tramontana, produce uomini molto grandi del corpo* 'Frisia, . . . situated toward the north, produces men exceedingly large of body'; the "anonimo Fiorentino," *ibid.*, p. 735: "*Tre Frison,*" *tre uomini di Frisia, chè in quel paese àe grandi uomini* '"Three Frisians," three men of Frisia, because in that region there are large men'; Giovanni da Serravalle (early fifteenth century): *Frisia est provincia in Alamania, in qua sunt maximi homines* 'Frisia is a province in Germany, in which there are exceedingly large men.' Francesco da Buti, *ibid.*, p. 734, seems to confuse the Frisians with the Phrygians but also mentions their size. The relative tallness of the Frisians as a race can, of course, be observed even today.

27. See, for example, Eumenius' late third-century panegyric of Constantius Chlorus IX.3 (*Panegyrici veteres*, Delphin edition [London, 1828], III, 1286–87): *Arat ergo nunc mihi Chamavus, et Frisius, et ille vagus, ille prædator exercitio squalidus operatur* 'now, therefore, plows for me the Chamavus and the Frisian; and that rover, that plunderer, grimy with exertion, performs hard labor'; the eighth-century *Vita S. Bonifacii* by a "presbyter S. Martini Ultrajecti," I, 9, in *Acta Sanctorum*, ed. J. van Bolland and G. Henschen, *et al.* (Antwerp, 1643–1867), XXI, 471 (June Vol. I, 5th day): *Hos* [i.e., *Frisones*] *remotos a ceteris nationibus, ideoque brutos ac barbaros* 'these [i.e., the Frisians], remote from other nations, and therefore brutelike and barbarous' (followed shortly by allusions to *gigas ille, qui totum Israel demoliri cœpit* 'that giant, who began to lay waste all Israel' [in *Vita S. Bonifacii*, I, 10], and *Goliath Philisthæus*

'Goliath the Philistine' [in *Vita S. Bonifacii*, II, 12; p. 472 in *Acta Sanctorum*], apparently referring to the spirit of idolatry among the northern German tribes); the continuation of the chronicle of Fredegarius for the year 734 (ed. Bruno Krusch, in *Monumenta Germaniae Historica, Scriptores Rerum Merovingicarum* [Hanover, 1888], II, 176): *gentem dirissimam maritimam Frigionum nimis crudeliter rebellantem* 'the most fearful sea-dwelling race of Frisians, rebelling with great cruelty'; the ninth-century *Vita Hludowici*, XXIV (ed. G. H. Pertz, in *Monumenta Germaniae Historica, Scriptores* [Hanover, 1829], II, 619), characterizing the Saxons and Frisians as *gentes naturali adsuefactae feritati* 'peoples accustomed to a natural savagery'; Saxo, *Gesta Danorum*, XIV, vii, 1, ed. Olrik and Ræder, I, 384, concerning *Frisia minor: Incolæ eius natura feroces, corporibus agiles, anxiam et gravem armaturam contemnunt; ancilibus utuntur, missilibus dimicant* 'its inhabitants are fierce by nature, active of body; they are contemptuous of troublesome heavy armor, carry shields, and fight with javelins'; and a versified chronicle—dating from the fifteenth century, though evidently containing older material—quoted in the sixteenth-century *Chronica regum Danorum* by the Franciscan Peter Olaf, ed. Jakob Langebek, in *Scriptores Rerum Danicarum Medii Ævi* (Copenhagen, 1772–1834), I, 70–71: *Audax incipiens est Frisia vasta rebellis. . . . Multum Friso furit, Saxo super omne superbit* 'a bold beginner is Frisia, rude and rebellious. . . . Much does the Frisian rage, the Saxon domineer over all.' The aquatic existence of the Frisians, as often described, bears some resemblance—perhaps quite accidental—to that of the Grendel family and of most of the other monsters in the early part of *Beowulf*; in the *Vita S. Bonifacii*, for example, the Frisians *fere, quemadmodum et pisces, morantur in aquis, quibus ita undique concluduntur* 'almost after the manner of fish, dwell in the water—by which they, in similar fashion, are inclosed on all sides' (I, 9; in *Acta Sanctorum*, p. 471). Tacitus (*Annales* II.xxiv.2–4) reports that when a trireme of Germanicus ran aground on the coast of the Chauci (the near neighbors of the Frisians), his men were scattered through the surrounding territories and *ut quis ex longinquo revenerat, miracula narrabant . . . ambiguas hominum et beluarum formas, visa sive ex metu credita* 'as each one returned from afar, they related marvels . . . uncertain forms of men and beasts, beheld or believed out of fright.' Finally, though our present concern is with tradition or popular repute rather than actual fact, it may be worth adding that exhumed Frisian skulls are famous for their peculiar shape, which—whether natural or the result of deliberate deformation—might conceivably have contributed to a popular use of 'giants' as an epithet for them; see for example Otto Reche, "Zur Herkunft und Rassenkunde der Friesen," in *Die Friesen*, ed. Borchling and Muuss, pp. 43–45.

28. C. P. Hansen, *Uald Söldring Tialen* (2d ed.; Tondern, n.d.), pp. 17–36, "De Öndereersken en de Söldring Käämpers" ("The Dwarves

and the Giants of Sylt"). See also pp. 36–41, "De Söldring Käämpers en de Däänsken" ("The Giants of Sylt and the Danes"). In the first tale "Finn" is the name not of a giant but of the king of the dwarves, who fight against the Frisian *Käämpers*; Langhans, *Ursprung der Nordfriesen*, p. 48, remarks on the frequent interchange of names between giants and dwarves. The rather credulous early Frisian antiquary Suffridus Petrus in his *Apologia pro antiquitate et origine Frisiorum* (Franeker, 1603), pp. 45–46, mentions and defends a popular tradition that the giants driven out of Britain by Brutus came to Batavia, the territory immediately adjoining that of the Frisians.

29. 13:5, in *Den norsk-islandske Skjaldedigtning*, B–I, 17. Note also the Scandinavian folk legends of a giant or troll named "Fin(n)," cited by Jakob Grimm, *Deutsche Mythologie*, ed. Elard Hugo Meyer (4th ed.; Berlin, 1875–78), I, 455; II, 856. W. W. Lawrence, "*Beowulf* and the Tragedy of Finnsburg," *PMLA*, XXX (1915), 394, admits the possibility of some influence from this giant name "Finn," in suggesting that "Finn, King of the *Eotas*, might easily be confused with a Finn of the *eotenas*."

30. VII, ed. Gudbrand Vigfusson (Oxford, 1878), I, 309; in *Den norsk-islandske Skjaldedigtning*, B–II, 152. More popular, however, is the idea of an unusual trustworthiness or credulity among giants and trolls; for terms like *trǫlla-trygð* 'trolls' trust' see Richard Cleasby and Gudbrand Vigfusson, *An Icelandic-English Dictionary* (2d ed.; Oxford, 1957), p. 641.

31. *Annales* XIII, liv. iii; *fides* would be the obvious Latin equivalent of *treow*.

32. Albert Leiprecht, *Der Vorwurf der germanischen Treulosigkeit in der antiken Literatur* (Diss., Würzburg, 1932), p. 67: "Von diesen Völkern [Batavern, Friesen, Chauken, Cheruskern] nahm der Vorwurf der germanischen Treulosigkeit im 1. Jahrhundert n. Chr. seinen Ausgang." Tacitus *Annales* XI.xix.1 refers to *natio Frisiorum . . . infensa aut male fida* 'the nation of the Frisians . . . either enraged or imperfectly trust-worthy,' though not as a permanent characterization.

33. 8:5–6, in *Edda: Die Lieder des Codex Regius nebst verwandten Denkmälern*, ed. Neckel, p. 71; see also 25:4–6, p. 74 in the edition of Neckel. A similar kind of allusion exists in the description of Beowulf's corselet as *Welandes geweorc* 'Weland's work' (455). I pass over the relevant but apparently unsolved problem of *Hunlafing* (1143).

34. G. Sarrazin, "Der Balder-Kultus in Lethra," *Anglia*, XIX (1897), 392–97. Saxo, *Gesta Danorum*, I, ii, ed. Olrik and Ræder, I, 10–11, as interpreted by Eduard Sievers, "*Beowulf* und Saxo," *Berichte über die Verhandlungen der königlich sächsischen Gesellschaft der Wissenschaften zu Leipzig* ("Phil.-hist. Classe," Vol. XLVII [Leipzig, 1895]), pp. 175–88.

35. *Beowulf: An Introduction*, p. 262; see also p. 97.

36. 33:3–6, in *Edda: Die Lieder des Codex Regius nebst verwandten Denkmälern*, ed. Neckel p. 252; for the corresponding commonplace employing *troll*, see Sveinbjǫrn Egilsson, *Lexicon poeticum antiquae linguae septentrionalis*, rev. Finnur Jónsson (Copenhagen, 1913–16), p. 571, and Johan Fritzner, *Ordbog over det gamle norske Sprog* (2d ed.; Oslo, 1886–96), III, 722. The *Hyndlolióð*, which abounds in references to giants (4, 30, 32, 33, 35, 40; in *Edda: Die Lieder des Codex Regius nebst verwandten Denkmälern*, ed. Neckel, pp. 288, 293–94, 296), contains also a significant pairing of Hermóðr and Sigmundr (2:5–8; in *ibid.*, p. 288).

37. Concerning Hroðgar's sermon and its implications for Heremod see my "*Sapientia et Fortitudo* as the Controlling Theme of *Beowulf*," pp. 432–35, and "The Sigemund-Heremod and Hama-Hygelac Passages in *Beowulf*," pp. 492–93. The parallel with Prov. 21:16 was first pointed out by Blake, "Heremod Digressions," pp. 282–84, who, on the evidence of an early medieval interpretation differing from that quoted below, interprets the 'giants' of l. 902 as devils.

38. *Morialia in Iob* XVII.xxi.30–31, in *Pat. Lat.*, LXXVI, 25. See also a pseudo-Hieronymian commentary on Job 26:5, in *Pat. Lat.*, XXVI, 688; Augustine on Psalms 32:16, in *Pat. Lat.* XXXVI, 297; and Rabanus Maurus on Ecclus. 16:8, in *Pat. Lat.*, CIX, 867.

39. See n. 10.

40. The three occurrences of *eald sweord eotenisc* 'old giant-sword' (1558, 2616, 2979), along with *giganta geweorc* 'work of giants' (1562), *enta ærgeweorc* 'ancient work of giants' (1679), *enta geweorc* 'work of giants' (2717, 2774), and *entiscne helm* 'giant helmet' (2979), though not necessarily irrelevant to our present pattern, are obviously references of a quite different kind—echoing extremely conventional formulas and limited to the static description of objects rather than bearing either directly or indirectly on the action of the poem. *Fifelcynnes eard* 'land of a monster race' (104) and *gi[ga]ntas* 'giants' (113) are both closely attached to our first appearance of *eotenas*. The *giganta cyn* 'race of giants' of l. 1690 is discussed below.

41. "*Beowulf:* The Monsters and the Critics," *Proceedings of the British Academy*, XXII (1936), 245–95.

42. "*Sapientia et Fortitudo* as the Controlling Theme of *Beowulf*," pp. 450–55.

ON TRANSLATING *BEOWULF*

❧❧❧

Burton Raffel

The superb introduction to Edwin Morgan's version of *Beowulf* is a perfect illustration, I think, of the differing approaches taken by scholars and poets. Morgan begins with a brilliant discussion of "The Translator's Task in *Beowulf*," dissecting prior verse translations and examining possible bases for that "notable presentation . . . of a great original" which, writing in 1952, he found did not yet exist. His conclusion, "that a translation of *Beowulf* for the present period may and perhaps should employ a stress metre and not a syllabic one," comes only after an acute examination of work by Christopher Fry, T. S. Eliot, W. H. Auden, Richard Eberhart, and C. Day Lewis. I think Morgan arrives at a sensitively correct conclusion; I have taken a very similar position in my own translation. But it never occurred to me (I had not then seen Morgan's book) to tackle the problem by an examination of anything except the verse produced by the *Beowulf* poet and that produced by me, as I struggled to find the tone I wanted in modern-day English. Indeed, I did not consciously think about metrics at all, until, some hundreds of lines into the translation, I realized that I was finding myself obliged to use more consistent patterns of alliteration than, some years earlier, I had employed in the shorter poems of *Poems from the Old English*. Nor when I'd finished my version did I feel it could be justified either in theory or in practice by anything but itself. That is, at no point was I able (or inclined) to remove myself from the immediacy of direct and largely exclusive contact with the poem. I don't mean that my involvement, as a poet, was greater or more intense than that of Morgan, a scholar-critic, but it was—I think inevitably—a much more subjective involvement with all the advantages and disadvantages that accompany such lack of broader perspective. In general, objectivity, the appeal to external sources and canons, is a necessary aspect of the scholar-critic's approach: that which is external serves both to define and to test that which is primarily under consideration. But the poet, as T. S. Eliot nicely puts it, "is not so much a judge as an advocate" (*On Poetry and Poets*, p. 17). Worse still, "his knowledge even is likely to be partial: for his studies will have led him to concentrate on certain authors to the neglect of others." It remains true that anyone who attempts a translation of *Beowulf* has something of the scholar about him, but neither in making my translation nor in writing the introduction to it was I capable of the kind of analytical distance so vividly attained by Morgan.

There are, of course, many other differences between the approaches likely to be taken by a scholar and the kind of approach I simply fell into. Both parties are able to read the original text, but while the scholar tends to keep the Old English forever in mind, the poet must—*must*—first dive into the Old English, immerse himself in it until it has become a part of his own thinking, until he seems to have it at his finger tips; then he must emerge, leave the Old English behind, and make his way, carrying his immersement with him, into modern English poetry. It may seem paradoxical, but in fact it is not, that the poet needs to master the original in order to leave it and that he needs to leave it in order to produce lines that reflect the original and yet are successful poetry in the modern tongue. To be trapped by the original is far worse than not to have understood it properly. It is a great deal worse to translate the first three lines of *Beowulf*, as R. K. Gordon has done, 'Lo! we have heard the glory of the kings of the Spear-Danes in days gone by, how the chieftains wrought mighty deeds'—far worse than, as Ezra Pound did, to only technically mistreat the Old English text of *The Seafarer*. It is worse, it seems to me, because by definition no poem in translation is the original from which it takes its life; there must be distortion, to a greater or lesser degree, simply by definition. The greatest sin a translator can commit, accordingly, is to fail to breathe life into his re-creation. He can never breathe life into it if he is unable to force himself away from the original and far enough away so that he can be close in spirit and yet be free to actually *create* in the new linguistic medium.

The poet not only brings differentness to *Beowulf* but he also finds different things in it. I was able to translate this 3,182-line epic in what was, effectively, a single sitting lasting six months. It was possible (in addition to being almost necessary, as a practical matter: how else but by single-minded immersion can one sustain oneself through a difficult text of more than three thousand lines?), simply enough, because I found *Beowulf* continuously exciting. The structure may sag in places; when I read the lines dealing with Grendel's mother I realize their comparative weakness, the rather pale repetition involved. But as I was translating them they glowed, line by line, and with a far subtler excitement than is usually credited to their author. Critics usually cite, and casual readers usually remember, the action in *Beowulf*, the great combats, the utterly magnificent sea scenes. When one takes the plunge, however, it is to find that the sustaining element in the poem is in fact the ripe, mature wisdom and insight of the poet, expressed in an unending flow of deft, compact, and extremely forceful language. For me it is Hrothgar, not Beowulf, who is the poem's most notable figure. One knows what Beowulf will do and what he will say; his defeat of everyone in youth and his own defeat by the dragon in old age are alike predictable. It does not lessen the noble hero to be thus categorized: he becomes no less noble, his exploits and his end no less remarkable or interesting. But, like the slightly less than purely noble Adam of *Paradise Lost*, he does become a little less human or at least a bit less warmly attractive to other helplessly fallible humans.

The scholar tends to view Hrothgar rather differently. Even to Friedrich Klaeber, *Beowulf*'s greatest editor, the "much discussed harangue of Hrothgar" (1700–1784), is a bit of a bore. It "shows the moralizing, didactic turn of the poem at its very height" and is "conspicuous for the blending of heroic and theological motives." While "there can be no doubt that this address of the king's forms an organic element in the structural plan of the epic," Klaeber feels obliged to conclude that, "of course, its excessive length and strong homiletic flavor have laid the third division, and even other parts [of the harangue], open to the charge of having been interpolated . . . and it is, indeed, possible that the 'sermon' represents a later addition to the text" (*Beowulf and the Fight at Finnsburg* [3d ed.; Boston, 1950], p. 190). Additions to a text are very rarely made—even today, when forgers and adapters have previously unknown skills at their disposal—without there being some jarring of tone, some failure to adjust the overlayer to what was there to start with. It is, as I have said, a totally subjective poet's judgment, but I feel no such jarring, no such failure of adjustment in Hrothgar's "harangue." On the contrary, not only do I find it a beautiful passage, intensely moving and completely fascinating in its portrayal of the old king, but for me it is completely in harmony with the poem as a whole:

> Our eternal Lord
> Grants some men wisdom, some wealth, makes others
> Great. The world is God's, He allows
> A man to grow famous, and his family rich,
> Gives him land and towns to rule
> And delight in, lets his kingdom reach
> As far as the world runs—and who
> In human unwisdom, in the middle of such power,
> Remembers that it all will end, and too soon?
>
> (1726–34)

Is this, again in Klaeber's words, an interpolation "by a man versed and interested in theology"? The theme is a totally common one, in *Beowulf* as in much of Old English poetry. Indeed, that which Hrothgar "preaches" to the young Beowulf, the old Beowulf comes to know in himself:

Then they came to Beowulf, their king, and announced
That his hall, his throne, the best of buildings,
Had melted away in the dragon's burning
Breath. Their words brought misery, Beowulf's
Sorrow beat at his heart: he accused
Himself of breaking God's law . . .   (2324–29)

Is there anything very complicated, theologically, in such
passages—sufficiently complex, that is, to require that we postulate an ecclesiastical interpolator? I cannot see it. Beowulf's
very last words, gasped out to Wiglaf, make it clear that God
(*Dryhten*) is inclusive of fate (*Wyrd*), which is exactly what one
would expect and exactly the stance taken throughout the
poem by the *Beowulf* poet:

You're the last of all our far-flung family.
Fate has swept our race away,
Taken warriors in their strength and led them
To the death that was waiting. And now I follow them.
                                        (2813–16)

Beowulf is most human in adversity and death and most
appealing: this warmth prepares us beautifully for the long
funeral preparations that conclude the poem. ('And now I
follow them' is not nearly so starkly lovely as *ic him æfter
sceal*, but neither is modern English the same as Old English.)
What these last-quoted lines also help to demonstrate, I think,
is the intense consistency of the poem, a consistency born of
the highest art and founded not on plot or action but on a
series of deeply held inner truths about the proper behavior of
men and about their position in the universal scheme of things.
The *Beowulf* poet is no Handy-Andy of a Jacobean dramatist,
turning a character inside out from act to act in order to
accommodate the demands of his story (see, most notably, the
plays of Beaumont and Fletcher). Everything in *Beowulf* is
inevitable. Everything in *Beowulf* from the hero warrior to the
vicious monsters is natural in the sense that it fits into its world
and plays its role to the hilt.

315

From this realization one can proceed to another fundamental difference between the scholar and the poet. Even a
scholar as devoted to *Beowulf* as was Klaeber, a man who
made it truly his life's work, delivers this "final judgment" on
the poem: "Though lacking in lucidity, proportion, and
finish of form as required by modern taste or by Homeric and
Vergilian standards, the poem exhibits admirable technical
skill in the adaptation of the available means to the desired
ends. It contains passages which in their way are nearly perfect, and strong, noble lines which thrill the reader and linger
in the memory. The patient, loving student of the original no
longer feels called upon to apologize for *Beowulf* as a piece of
literature" (*Beowulf and the Fight at Finnsburg*, p. lxviii). The
poet cannot and will not condescend so, if he is to translate
the poem. How can he, with his subjective approach, take such
a tone of aloof superiority and still immerse himself as totally
as he does, as he must? A poem that arouses in the "loving
student of the original" such feelings as Klaeber here expresses
is not a poem to be translated, but a poem to be picked apart
by philologists, historians, archaeologists, and other essentially nonliterary persons. J. R. R. Tolkien said it from a
different context in his famous 1936 lecture, "Beowulf: The
Monsters and the Critics": "It is of their nature that the
jabberwocks of historical and antiquarian research burble in
the tulgy wood of conjecture, flitting from one tum-tum tree
to another. Noble animals, whose burbling is on occasion good
to hear; but though their eyes of flame may sometimes prove
searchlights, their range is short." I wish I had said that. (I also
wish, but never mind, that I had written Tolkien's magnificent
Lord of the Rings trilogy.) The poet's approach to *Beowulf*,
unlike Klaeber's, is rather more like this affirmation from
Appendix B of the same Tolkien lecture: "More sense can be
made of the poem, if we start rather with the hypothesis, not
in itself unlikely, that the poet tried to do something definite
and difficult, which had some reason and thought behind
it . . ." I classify this hypothesized state as respect. To get into
the heart and soul of what a man dead a thousand years or

more was trying to say—*did* say in his tongue to his contemporary listeners—one must respect both his achievement
and the mind that produced it. This has nothing to do with
sustaining one through long and dreary labors: I'm not
talking of that sort of thing at all. (There were, after all, people
who made concordances long before there were computers to
make concordances for people. Drudges have we always with
us.) I mean that one must admire the poet's mind, his ability
to think through and then to express beautifully what he meant
to express. At each and every point one must start with the
assumption that the poet was too intelligent a man, let alone
too good a poet, to write nonsense. If a line, if a passage
defeats us, then the fault, we must postulate, is ours (or time's),
not the poet's. This assumption will keep us from turning out
quite so much nonsensical translation, in part because we will
try harder, in part because we will be reluctant to admit defeat
by a superior mind, given all the tools for understanding which
scholars, thank God, have now put at our disposal. It will also
keep us from the ho-hum sort of translation, asleep on its feet
with boredom. I have cited R. K. Gordon's turgid version of
the first lines of *Beowulf*. Here is the somnolent version, again
in prose, of a very competent young scholar, capable—as his
striking translation of an Alcuin poem in the introduction to
his *Beowulf* conclusively proves—of infinitely better things:
'Listen. We have learned the song of the glory of the great
kings of the Danes, how those princes did what was daring.'
After this flabby beginning the translation gets rapidly worse.
Here is the next prose sentence: 'More than once, Scyld of the
Sheaf pulled seats in the mead-hall out from beneath troops of
his foes, tribe after tribe, struck fear into the Heruli themselves, after that time in the very beginning he was found in a
bad plight' (*Beowulf*, trans. William Alfred [1963]). Can one
have *respect* for a poet and be capable of fine poetry oneself
and still turn out such flat drivel? But this is, after all, a prose
rendering, even though prepared by an able poet; in this case,
the decision not to make a verse translation may well be significant in itself.

I do not mean, I should perhaps say quite explicitly, that the poet operates entirely subjectively, any more than the scholar is a great block of stolid impartiality and scientific method. The act of affinity which, to my mind, is required of the poet-translator hardly requires the suspension of all judgment. Indeed, I would contend that this identification with and immersion in the language and spirit and thought processes of the original's author actually sharpens one's judgment. Not, to be sure, the kind of judgment that is concerned with such scholarly affairs as sources, or grammatical diversions, or even the assigning of literary grades ("important," "minor," "interesting," "utterly without merit"). I mean, rather, the kind of judgment one would expect from sympathetic understanding: insight into what lies on the page, how it moves, how it is interconnected, what it means, even what it actually says —not at all an insignificant advantage with a text as mangled and well-fought-over as *Beowulf*.

For example, to choose at random a supporting illustration, lines 3074–75 are regarded by scholars as a *locus desperatus*: *næfne goldhwæte gearwor hæfde | Agendes est ær gesceawod*. Klaeber's notes on these two lines run to almost a full page of fine print; E. van K. Dobbie's invaluable "collective" edition of the poem (*The Anglo-Saxon Poetic Records*, IV [New York, 1953]) summarizes scholarly debate on the lines in more than two pages still more closely printed. The lines come near the start of section 42, the next-to-last section of the poem, which begins at line 3058. Lines 3058–75 form a verse paragraph and are so printed in modern editions of the Old English text; it is a tightly woven paragraph, though scholars and translators have tended to undo the webbing. It begins: 'Hiding that treasure deep in its tower, / As the dragon had done, broke God's law ...' After a few lines about the dragon's fate, the poet asks:

> Who knows when princes
> And their soldiers, the bravest and strongest of men,
> Are destined to die ...

Beowulf did not know God's will, the poet points out. Neither did those greedy souls who came seeking the dragon's stolen treasure: their fate, "cursed with the flames of hell," is set forth—and then comes the *locus desperatus*. I suspect that neither a literal translation nor still another summary of scholarly opinion will make my point as well as a selection from various translations. Here is R. K. Gordon: 'He would rather not have beheld the gold-treasure, the owner's might.' That is, the person who robs the dragon's hoard—who as we know is 'cursed with the flames of hell,' if greed motivates him—will regret such dearly bought loot. Gordon's prose reads badly; worse, what might out of context seem to be a plausible rendering actually makes very little sense—and treats the *Beowulf* poet, to boot, as a clumsy tautologist. (Litotes, the Anglo-Saxons' typical irony, is all very well in its place; desperate scholars tend to see it under every linguistic crux.) The curse has been set forth, it is a dreadful thing, the poet takes it terribly seriously: why assume that he is likely to stop in his tracks and vaguely snicker? Why not assume that he has a serious message, and is capable of developing it in an organically sensible way?

David Wright, who inserts a footnote explaining that these are uncertainly understood lines, translates as follows: 'Yet up till then Beowulf had never looked greedily upon their treasure of cursed gold.' But what has Beowulf to do with the curse? He is mentioned, eight lines earlier, as an illustration of the mysteriousness of God's ways: '[He] could never know what God / Had decreed, or that death would come to him, or why.' The poet then proceeds, as I've said, to set forth the curse: the passage neatly parallels the reference to Beowulf, the latter beginning *Swa wæs* and the explanation of the curse beginning *Swa hit*. Why the parallelism, if both Beowulf and the curse do not illustrate the same uncertainty of life on earth, life salvable only by faith and its works? And why the parallelism, if the subject has not changed from one *swa* to the next *swa*, if we are still discussing Beowulf when both grammar and sense indicate that we are discussing, instead, a sequence of things—

Beowulf's death *and* cursed treasure *and* the generalization (3074–75)—which effectively sums up these (and other) examples of God's laws and ways? Alfred has yet another rendering: 'Not that he who was greedy for gold would have any more readily first consulted the owner's good will.' Litotes again, and I will not repeat myself: this is bad prose and bad translation.

Morgan's verse rendering goes like this: 'Unless the gaze of his Master's grace / Had had prior power on the gold-keen man.' This is bewildering; it is also, I think, the right sense of the lines. Morgan is not, I think, a good poet, but his is on the whole a dignified version, written quite plainly out of deep and intelligent respect for the *Beowulf* poet. Here, despite a failure to create good poetry, Morgan seems to me to have had the poetic success of comprehension. Finally, my own translation: let me cite lines 3058–75, the entire verse paragraph, to show how lines 3074–75 (in italics) cannot be taken in isolation:

> Hiding that treasure deep in its tower,
> As the dragon had done, broke God's law
> And brought it no good. Guarding its stolen
> Wealth it killed Wiglaf's king,
> But was punished with death. Who knows when princes
> And their soldiers, the bravest and strongest of men,
> Are destined to die, their time ended,
> Their homes, their halls empty and still?
> So Beowulf sought out the dragon, dared it
> Into battle, but could never know what God
> Had decreed, or that death would come to him, or why.
> So the spell was solemnly laid, by men
> Long dead; it was meant to last till the day
> Of judgment. Whoever stole their jewels,
> Their gold, would be cursed with the flames of hell,
> Heaped high with sin and guilt, if greed
> Was what brought him: *God alone could break*
> *Their magic, open His grace to man.*

I will not argue the grammatical basis of this interpretation, since it is confessedly not grammar upon which it basically rests. To tackle grammar, indeed, to hunt for possible emendations rather than for good sense and to work line by line, each isolated from the ones two above and two below it, the whole search separated from the poem as it is—what is this but the "short range" that Tolkien deplored? This, then, is the scholars' error, and the kind of heightened good judgment I think poets can achieve.

Further, since the poet's kind of judgment is founded on literary taste there is no suspension, either, of that broader judgment that determines whether a work of art is good, bad, or indifferent. (One translates what one likes and cannot translate what one does not like, cannot translate it well or even decently.) In my *Poems from the Old English*, for example, there is a version of *The Phoenix*, a work of 677 lines. The translation I print there, however, is only of lines 1–423. For the sake of the beauty of these lines I, in fact, translated some twenty or thirty lines more, but with increasing dubiousness and difficulty. One cannot make a purse of a sow's ear; one cannot make poetry of sheer doggerel—which is, in my judgment, what *The Phoenix* rapidly descends to after line 423. I could not translate the latter portion of the poem—more accurately, I could not translate it into the kind of poetry I felt I had been able to re-create on the basis of the earlier lines. In the bare literal sense I could (and for twenty or so lines did) translate; but once I had lost respect for what I was working with there was for me no point at all to going on.

Which leads to one last and least readily explained difference in the approaches of scholar and of poet. Helen Waddell observes in her *Mediaeval Latin Lyrics* that "a man cannot say 'I will translate,' any more than he can say 'I will compose poetry.' In this minor art also, the wind blows where it lists." The process of affection, in other words, is not regulated by gaps in knowledge or by the need for such-and-such to be done. "The greatest things in mediaeval Latin, its 'living and victorious splendours,' are not here," reads a note to the fourth edition of Miss Waddell's book, "because I cannot translate them." The scholar noted and conceded the omissions of which critics had complained; the poet could not remedy them. I mean to say neither that the scholar exudes discipline nor that the poet is devoid of it. Desire, however, is a different motivation in each: for me, at least, translation always needs to be discovery. Again, not a discovery like finding the missing Boswell papers, nor solving a Riddle, nor a working out of new ways for interpreting or categorizing existing material: the deciphering of Linear B might be a closer analogy, in scholarly terms, to the kind of discovery I am trying to describe. It is for me the same kind of discovery I find in writing poetry on my own, creating rather than re-creating. Of course, many more people than one single poet are necessarily involved in any translation; a whole host of intervening hands come between the original author and the poet-translator. Yet the most basic and, I think, important act remains the final stage of re-creation in the translator's tongue—and *that* is the discovery I mean, the sense of unearthing, as if from nowhere, a path that expresses what the old poet might very likely have said if he had been a new poet instead—had been me, when I am the translator. That kind of discovery, it seems to me, is patently different from scholarly motivation, in part because the poet is working from the inside out (from *his* inside out), and the scholar tries to work from the outside in; but in part, also, because the poet attempts to withdraw into communion with his task, while the scholar seeks to shed as much light on his work as he can, from any reasonable source, the more the better. There is thus a quality of inherent darkness in the translator's job, of inherent light in the scholar's. It makes for a very different turn of mind.

Let me go back to the first three lines of *Beowulf*, to show something of what I mean. In Old English lines 1–3 read:

> HWÆT, WE GARDEna   in geardagum,
> þeodcyninga   þrym gefrunon,
> hu ða æþelingas   ellen fremedon!

David Wright's prose rendering will do as a starter: 'Hear! We know of the bygone glory of the Danish kings, and the heroic exploits of those princes.' This has none of the fustian of the R. K. Gordon version cited earlier, nor does it fall into the dull flatness of Alfred's recent rendering. Wright is not and is not pretending to be a poet, but he feels the swing of these lines and has caught most of what plain prose has the power to catch. For a thoroughly contrasting example we could not do better than the stupifying jollity of William Ellery Leonard's verse: 'What ho! We've heard the glory of Spear-Danes, clansmen-kings, / Their deeds of olden story—how fought the aethelings!'

I spent several entire days on only the first three lines of *Beowulf*: they were the key, the opening to the secret cave. Once I had them—that is, once I had managed to permit them to have me, to use me, to express themselves in and through me—I knew I would not be fazed by the 3,179 lines still to be done. But to kindle the lines I had simultaneously to kindle myself. I have preserved on foolscap sheets eleven complete attempts, plus additional partial attempts; how many other versions I formulated and did not set onto paper I can no longer say. By long and devious roads I finally arrived at this free translation:

> Hear me! We've heard of Danish heroes,
> Ancient kings and the glory they cut
> For themselves, swinging mighty swords!

This seemed to me faithful enough to the letter, while very faithful indeed to the spirit. It alliterated almost as Old English does: *h* for the first, second, and fourth stress words of line 1; *k* for the second and fourth stress words and *g* (*k* plus voicing) for the third stress word of line 2; and *s* at the first, second, and fourth stresses of line 3. There was a certain swing to the passage, in part because of the enjambement; it set a tone of history and courage and excitement which would permit me to go on. I knew this was not the *Beowulf* poet at his supreme best; I was not concerned that my version would leave Milton, Donne, and Shakespeare sleeping peacefully in their graves. But I was sharply aware of how little room the three-line verse paragraph left me, coming at the very beginning of the poem, and how it was my job to get the reader in and past this "topic sentence" that was in fact no topic sentence at all: this first verse paragraph no more keys the deepest tones of *Beowulf* than does Leonard's hiccoughing wassail-song treatment.

I have been a long time coming to my final dichotomy; I have finally arrived. I was subsequently informed by a knowing and gracious scholar that these first three lines were, to paraphrase him, "sacred." One *could not* handle them freely. The scholarly ranks would rise as one to extirpate the wrong done to their beloved poem. I had by then gone several hundreds of lines past this point, my confidence could permit of revision (it went on to permit of a great deal of revision, much of it scholar-instigated). I therefore tinkered my way to an alternative rendering:

> Hear me! Once there were Danish princes
> So proud of their courage, kings so strong,
> So glorious that their names still live, and are sung.

I was not happy. I went on tinkering, and arrived at this— almost the final resting place:

> Hear me! We've heard how the Danes were ruled
> By heroes, by glorious kings: we know
> How those noble princes fought for their fame!

I was almost happy. This is not inept, I still think; it satisfied the objecting scholar, and it obviously did not irk me. But in time it began to irk badly. The free version I cited, three versions back, had much more life, much more drive. Instead of the history-evoking 'ancient kings' I had descended to the stale-sounding 'glorious kings.' Instead of the free precision of glory cut with swords, I had settled for the tame generality of nobles fighting for fame. These first three lines were, I knew, of great moment to scholars. Yet the necessity of self-expression (even in translation, yes) proved stronger: I had to restore the swinging swords, and (I trust) the swinging version. I had to, please understand, with the full knowledge that this was scholarly heresy and therefore dangerous, in spite of having reached a compromise rendering that would not disgrace what followed. I had to, really, because I had to: I am very conscious of how much rationalization went into this decision and is going into this commentary on it. But I firmly believe I decided correctly.

The scholar must try to shun this sort of decision. If he knows that A is more accurate than B, it does not matter that he prefers B. If he is assured by all the scholarly evidence that King Oscar rather than King Oswald conducted that raid on the French coast, then he must discard his own feeling that King Oswald would be a more appropriate choice. He must certainly discard any consideration of affection for King Oswald, if he has progressed (or digressed) to that point.

The poet-translator, let me emphasize for the last time, deals basically in just the affective irrationalities that the scholar cannot permit himself. For the poet to heed the outer voice rather than the inner is to risk everything and probably to lose everything. It is one thing, of course, to have straightforwardly misconstrued a passage. *Beowulf* makes that extremely easy, and scholarly demonstration of such matters must produce revised translation—but translation that is revised because the original poet has been misunderstood, not because anything or anyone external to the poem has spoken! Translation *is* art, as that rare scholar-poet Helen Waddell knew. It can be aided and corrected and sometimes judged by scholarship, but it can never be accomplished by scholarship. The poets, I think, have always known that. The scholars, to their credit, are at last beginning to find it out.

NOTES ON THE CONTRIBUTORS

NOTES ON THE CONTRIBUTORS

JESS B. BESSINGER, JR.: PROFESSOR OF ENGLISH, NEW YORK UNIVERSITY

Major publications: *A Short Dictionary of Anglo-Saxon Poetry* (Toronto, 1960); *A Concordance to Beowulf* (Ithaca, N.Y., 1967); general editor, *The Harvard Old English Series* (Cambridge, Mass., 1966—); editor (with Fred C. Robinson) *Old English Newsletter* (New York, 1967 —); edited (with A. D. Van Nostrand) *A Prospect of Literature: Eight Films for Television Broadcasting* (Ann Arbor, Mich., 1955); edited (with S. M. Parrish and Harry F. Araden) *Proceedings, Literary Data-Processing Conference, Yorktown Heights, 1964* (White Plains, N.Y., 1964); edited (with Robert P. Creed) *Franciplegius: Medieval and Linguistic Studies in Honor of Francis P. Magoun, Jr.* (New York, 1965); recorded *Chaucer, The Canterbury Tales: General Prologue* (Caedmon: New York, 1962); recorded *Beowulf and Other Old English Poems* (Caedmon: New York, 1962); recorded (with Marie Borroff) *Dialogues from Sir Gawain and the Green Knight and Pearl* (Caedmon: New York, 1965); recorded *Chaucer, Two Canterbury Tales: The Miller's Tale and the Reeve's Tale* (Caedmon: New York, 1967); recorded *Chaucer, The Parliament of Fowls and Selected Short Poems* (Caedmon: New York, 1967); articles and reviews on lexicography, Old and Middle English literature, and folklore.

Work in progress: computer-aided concordance to *The Anglo-Saxon Poetic Records*; (with S. J. Kahrl) *Essential Articles for the Study of Old English Poetry; Beowulf:* a normalized edition with facing translation; a revised *Frequency Word-List for Old English Poetry.*

JOHN NIST: PROFESSOR OF ENGLISH, AUBURN UNIVERSITY

Major publications: *Dulce et Decorum* (Beloit, Wis., 1958–60); *The Structure and Texture of Beowulf* (São Paulo, Brazil, 1959); *Fui Crucificado* (1960); edited and translated (with Yolanda Leite) *Modern Brazilian Poetry: An Anthology* (Bloomington, Ind., 1962); edited *In the Middle of the Road* by Carlos De Andrade Drummond (Tucson, Ariz., 1964); *A Structural History of English* (New York, 1966); numerous articles, essays, and reviews in the fields of Old English linguistics, Brazilian poetry, and comparative literature.

Work in progress: *The Modernist Movement in Brazil; The Performance of Beowulf;* linguistic and aesthetic research into a theory of literary creativity.

ALAIN RENOIR: ASSOCIATE PROFESSOR OF ENGLISH AND COMPARATIVE LITERATURE AND CHAIRMAN, DEPARTMENT OF COMPARATIVE LITERATURE,

CONTRIBUTORS

UNIVERSITY OF CALIFORNIA (BERKELEY); EDITOR OF *ACLAN*, EDITORIAL BOARD OF *SPECULUM*

Major publications: Articles on Old English, Middle English, Middle High German, Old French, and classical and medieval Latin; edited *The Poetry of John Lydgate* (Cambridge, Mass., 1967).

Work in progress: A book-length study of *Beowulf*.

ROBERT P. CREED: ASSOCIATE PROFESSOR OF ENGLISH, THE STATE UNIVERSITY OF NEW YORK AT STONY BROOK

Major publications: Edited (with Jess B. Bessinger, Jr.) *Franciplegius: Medieval and Linguistic Studies in Honor of Francis P. Magoun, Jr.* (New York, 1965); recorded (with Burton Raffel) *Lyrics from the Old English* (Folkways: New York, 1964); numerous articles on and reviews of Old English poetry.

Work in progress: A study of the traditional style of *Beowulf;* a study (with William Hamrick) of the rhythm and the performance of Old English poetry.

LOUIS H. LEITER: ASSOCIATE PROFESSOR OF ENGLISH, UNIVERSITY OF THE PACIFIC

Major publications: Articles on Herbert, Herrick, Kafka, Twain, Stevens, Conrad, Babel.

Work in progress: A critical study of the medieval miracle and mystery plays.

J. E. CROSS: BAINES PROFESSOR OF ENGLISH LANGUAGE, THE UNIVERSITY OF LIVERPOOL

Major publications: *Latin Themes in Old English Poetry* (Bristol, Eng., 1962); papers on Old English, Middle English, and Old Swedish.

Work in progress: Studies in Old English literature and literary thought.

EDWARD B. IRVING, JR.: ASSOCIATE PROFESSOR OF ENGLISH, UNIVERSITY OF PENNSYLVANIA

Major publications: edited *The Old English Exodus* ("Yale Studies in English," Vol. CXXII [New Haven, 1953]); articles on Old English poetry.

Work in progress: A book-length critical study of *Beowulf*; a critique of translations of *Beowulf;* a study of the style of Old English Christian poetry.

CONTRIBUTORS

GEORGE K. ANDERSON: PROFESSOR OF ENGLISH, BROWN UNIVERSITY

Major publications: *The Literature of the Anglo-Saxons* (Princeton, N.J., 1949); *Old and Middle English Literature from the Beginnings to 1485*, in *A History of English Literature*, ed. Hardin Craig, I (New York, 1950; rev. ed., 1963); *The Legend of the Wandering Jew* (Providence, 1965); numerous articles on Old English language and on folklore; editor, with others, of four anthologies of literature.

Work in progress: A review of scholarly work in the field of Old English literature from 1925 to 1960; a study of Chaucer and his works.

ADRIEN BONJOUR: PROFESSOR OF ENGLISH, THE UNIVERSITY OF NEUCHATEL (SWITZERLAND)

Major publications: *Coleridge's "Hymn before Sunrise"* (New York, 1942); edited *Dialogue de St. Julien et son Disciple* ("Anglo-Norman Text Society," Vol. VIII [Oxford, 1949]); *The Structure of Julius Caesar* (Liverpool, 1958); *Twelve Beowulf Papers, 1940–1960, with Additional Comments* (Geneva, 1962); various articles mainly on *Beowulf* and Shakespeare.

LARRY D. BENSON: ASSOCIATE PROFESSOR OF ENGLISH, HARVARD UNIVERSITY

Major publications: *Art and Tradition in Sir Gawain and the Green Knight* (New Brunswick, N. J., 1965); articles and reviews on Old and Middle English literature.

Work in progress: A study of the aesthetics of Old English narrative poetry.

NEIL D. ISAACS: ASSOCIATE PROFESSOR OF ENGLISH, THE UNIVERSITY OF TENNESSEE

Major publications: Edited (with Eric W. Stockton) a special medieval issue of *Tennessee Studies in Literature* (1966); edited (with Louis H. Leiter) *Approaches to the Short Story* (San Francisco, 1963); author of several articles on Old and Middle English poetry, the novel, contemporary literature.

Work in progress: A study of structural principles in Old English poetry; a study of ritual elements in primitive literature.

PAUL BEEKMAN TAYLOR: PROFESSOR OF MEDIEVAL ENGLISH AND AMERICAN LITERATURE, UNIVERSITY OF GENEVA (SWITZERLAND)

Major publications: Numerous articles on Old English and Old Icelandic poetry and linguistics.

Work in progress: A study of the heroic tradition in Old English poetry; a critical edition (with Peter H. Salus) of Middle English prose.

CONTRIBUTORS

STANLEY B. GREENFIELD: PROFESSOR OF ENGLISH, UNIVERSITY OF OREGON

Major publications: *A Critical History of Old English Literature* (New York, 1965); edited *Studies in Old English Literature in Honor of Arthur G. Brodeur* (Eugene, Ore., 1963); bibliographer for *Guide to English Literature from Beowulf through Chaucer and Medieval Drama* by David M. Zesmer (New York, 1961); numerous articles on Old English and later literatures; reviews.

Work in progress: A study of the contribution of syntax to meaning and aesthetic effect in Old English poetry (Guggenheim Fellow, 1965–66).

R. E. KASKE: PROFESSOR OF ENGLISH, CORNELL UNIVERSITY

Major publications: "*Sapientia et Fortitudo* as the Controlling Theme of *Beowulf*," *Studies in Philology*, LV (1958); "Patristic Exegesis in the Criticism of Medieval Literature: The Defense," in *Critical Approaches to Medieval Literature: Selected Papers from the English Institute, 1958–1959*, ed. Dorothy Bethurum (New York, 1960); "Dante's 'DXV' and 'Veltro,'" *Traditio*, XVII (1961); many articles on medieval literature.

Work in progress: A book on the heroic ideal in Old English poetry; several shorter studies.

BURTON RAFFEL: ASSOCIATE PROFESSOR OF ENGLISH, THE STATE UNIVERSITY OF NEW YORK AT BUFFALO.

Major publications: *Poems from the Old English* (2d ed.; Lincoln, Neb., 1964); translated (with Nurdin Salam) *Chairil Anwar: Selected Poems* (New York, 1963); translated *Beowulf* (New York, 1963); *An Anthology of Modern Indonesian Poetry* (Berkeley, Calif., 1964): *The Development of Modern Indonesian Poetry* (New York, 1967).

Work in progress: A study of the translation process, tentatively titled *The Forked Tongue*.